Performance Characterization in Computer Vision

T0122607

Computational Imaging and Vision

Volume 17

Performance Characterization in Computer Vision

Edited by

Reinhard Klette

Department of Computer Science,
Tamaki Campus,
The University of Auckland,
Auckland, New Zealand

H. Siegfried Stiehl

Cognitive Systems Research Group,
Department of Computer Science,
University of Hamburg,
Hamburg, Germany

Max A. Viergever

and

Koen L. Vincken

Image Sciences Institute,
University Medical Care,
Utrecht, The Netherlands

KLUWER ACADEMIC PUBLISHERS
DORDRECHT / BOSTON / LONDON

A C.I.P. Catalogue record for this book is available from the Library of Congress.

ISBN 978-90-481-5487-6

Published by Kluwer Academic Publishers,
P.O. Box 17, 3300 AA Dordrecht, The Netherlands.

Sold and distributed in North, Central and South America
by Kluwer Academic Publishers,
101 Philip Drive, Norwell, MA 02061, U.S.A.

In all other countries, sold and distributed
by Kluwer Academic Publishers,
P.O. Box 322, 3300 AH Dordrecht, The Netherlands.

Printed on acid-free paper

Contents

Contributors

Ruzena Bajcsy
   GRASP Laboratory
   Dept. of Computer and Information Science
   University of Pennsylvania
   200 South 33rd Street
   Philadelphia, PA 19104-6389, USA
   bajcsy@central.cis.upenn.edu

John L. Barron
   The University of Western Ontario
   Dept. of Computer Science
   London, Ontario, Canada, N6A 5B7
   barron@csd.uwo.ca

Steven S. Beauchemin
   School of Computer Science
   Carleton University
   1125 Colonel By Drive
   Ottawa, Ontario, Canada K1S 5B6
   beau@scs.carleton.ca

Carolien J. Bouma
   University Medical Center Utrecht
   room D01.343
   Heidelberglaan 100
   3584 CX Utrecht, The Netherlands
   C.J.Bouma@med.uu.nl

Kevin W. Bowyer
   Computer Science & Engineering
   University of South Florida
   Tampa, Florida 33620-5399, USA
   kwb@csee.usf.edu

Joachim M. Buhmann
   Institut für Informatik III
   Rheinische Friedrich-Wilhelms-Universität
   D-53117 Bonn, Germany
   jb@cs.uni-bonn.de

Dmitry Chetverikov
Computer and Automation Research Institute
Kende u.13-17
Budapest, H-1111 Hungary
mitya@leader.ipan.sztaki.hu

Kyujin Cho
Software Business Team
Samsung SDS Co.
707-19 YokSam, KangNam
Seoul, Korea
kyucho@sdsosc.co.kr

Adrian F. Clark
VASE Laboratory
University of Essex
Colchester CO4 3SQ, UK
alien@essex.ac.uk

Patrick Courtney
Visual Automation Ltd.
Stopford Building, Oxford Road
Manchester M13 9PT, UK
patrick.courtney@acm.org

Dov Dori
Faculty of Industrial Engineering and Management
Technion—Israel Institute of Technology
Haifa 32000, Israel
dori@ie.technion.ac.il

Luc Florack
Dept. of Computer Science
Utrecht University
PO Box 80089
3508 TB Utrecht, The Netherlands
Luc.Florack@cs.uu.nl

Sönke Frantz
Universität Hamburg
FB Informatik
AB Kognitive Systeme
Vogt-Kölln-Str. 30
D-22527 Hamburg, Germany
frantz@informatik.uni-hamburg.de

Nikolaos Georgis
School of Electronic Engineering
Information Technology and Mathematics
University of Surrey
Guildford GU2 5XH, UK
N.Georgis@ee.surrey.ac.uk

Georgy Gimel'farb
Dept. of Computer Science
The University of Auckland
Tamaki Campus, Private Bag 92019
Auckland, New Zealand
georgy@cs.auckland.ac.nz

Cornelis N. de Graaf
Dept. of Networks & Systems
University Medical Center Utrecht, FAC-313
PO Box 85500
3508 GA Utrecht, The Netherlands
C.N.deGraaf@dit.azu.nl

Robert M. Haralick
Intelligent Systems Laboratory
Dept. of Electrical Engineering
University of Washington
Seattle, WA 98195, USA
haralick@ptah.ee.washington.edu

Thomas Hartkens
Division of Radiological Sciences and Medical Engineering
Guy's, King's and St. Thomas' School of Medicine
Guy's Hospital
London Bridge
London SE1 9RT
th04@boris.umds.ac.uk

Horst Haussecker
Research Group Image Processing
Interdisciplinary Center for Scientific Computing
University of Heidelberg
Im Neuenheimer Feld 368
D-69120 Heidelberg, Germany
Horst.Haussecker@iwr.uni-heidelberg.de

Atsushi Imiya
Dept. of Information and Image Sciences
Chiba University
1-33, Yayoi-cho, Inage-ku, 263-8522
Chiba, Japan
imiya@ics.tj.chiba-u.ac.jp

Bernd Jähne
Research Group Image Processing
Interdisciplinary Center for Scientific Computing
University of Heidelberg
Im Neuenheimer Feld 368
69120 Heidelberg, Germany
Bernd.Jaehne@iwr.uni-heidelberg.de

Kazuhiko Kawamoto
Dept. of Information and Image Sciences
Chiba University
1-33, Yayoi-cho, Inage-ku, 263-8522
Chiba, Japan
kazu@icsd7.tj.chiba-u.ac.jp

Josef Kittler
School of Electronic Engineering
Information Technology and Mathematics
University of Surrey
Guildford GU2 5XH, UK
J.Kittler@ee.surrey.ac.uk

Reinhard Klette
Dept. of Computer Science
The University of Auckland
Tamaki Campus
Private Bag 92019
Auckland, New Zealand
r.klette@auckland.ac.nz

André S.E. Koster
Origin/Technical Automation
Bakenmonde 2
3434 KK Nieuwegein, The Netherlands
Andre.Koster@nl.origin-it.com

Ryszard Kozera
Dept. of Computer Science
The University of Western Australia
Nedlands 6907 WA, Australia
ryszard@cs.uwa.edu.au

Albert Liptay
Agriculture and Agri-Food Canada
Greenhouse and Processing Crops Centre
Harrow, Ontario, Canada, N0R 1G0
liptaya@em.agr.ca

Radek Mařík
ProTys s.r.o.
Americka 24
120 00 Praha 2
Vinohrady, Czech Republic
Rmarik@ra.rockwell.com

Bogdan Matei
Electrical and Computer Engineering Dept.
Rutgers University
94 Brett Road
Piscataway, NJ 08854-8058, USA
matei@caip.rutgers.edu

Peter Meer
Electrical and Computer Engineering Dept.
Rutgers University
94 Brett Road
Piscataway, NJ 08854-8058, USA
meer@caip.rutgers.edu

Wiro J. Niessen
Image Sciences Institute
University Medical Center Utrecht
room E01.334
Heidelberglaan 100
3584 CX Utrecht, The Netherlands
wiro@isi.uu.nl

Naoya Ohta
   Dept. of Computer Science
   Gunma University
   Kiryu, Gunma, 376-8515 Japan
   ohta@cs.gunma-u.ac.jp

Maria Petrou
   School of Electronic Engineering
   Information Technology and Mathematics
   University of Surrey
   Guildford GU2 5XH, UK
   m.petrou@ee.surrey.ac.uk

Jan Puzicha
   Institut für Informatik III
   Rheinische Friedrich-Wilhelms-Universität
   D-53117 Bonn, Germany
   jan@cs.uni-bonn.de

Detlef Richter
   Wiesbaden University of Applied Sciences
   Dept. of Computer Science
   D-65197 Wiesbaden, Germany
   richter@informatik.fh-wiesbaden.de

Karl Rohr
   Universität Hamburg
   FB Informatik
   AB Kognitive Systeme
   Vogt-Kölln-Str. 30
   D-22527 Hamburg, Germany
   rohr@informatik.uni-hamburg.de

H. Siegfried Stiehl
   Universität Hamburg
   FB Informatik
   AB Kognitive Systeme
   Vogt-Kölln-Str. 30
   D-22527 Hamburg, Germany
   stiehl@informatik.uni-hamburg.de

Judit Verestóy
Computer and Automation Research Institute
Kende u.13-17
Budapest, H-1111 Hungary
judit@leader.ipan.sztaki.hu

Max A. Viergever
Image Sciences Institute
University Medical Center Utrecht, E01.334
Heidelberglaan 100
3584 CX Utrecht, The Netherlands
max@isi.uu.nl

Koen L. Vincken
Image Sciences Institute
University Medical Center Utrecht, E01.334
Heidelberglaan 100
3584 CX Utrecht, The Netherlands
koen@isi.uu.nl

Liu Wenyin
Microsoft Research China
5F Sigma Center
#49 Zhichun Road
Beijing 100080, PR China
wyliu@microsoft.com

Feng Wu
Dept. of Computer Science
The University of Auckland
CITR, Tamaki Campus
Private Bag 92019
Auckland, New Zealand
feng@citr.auckland.ac.nz

Shao-Zheng Zhou
Dept. of Computer Science
The University of Auckland
CITR, Tamaki Campus
Private Bag 92019
Auckland, New Zealand
zheng@citr.auckland.ac.nz

Preface

This edited volume addresses a subject which has been discussed intensively in the computer vision community for several years. Performance characterization and evaluation of computer vision algorithms are of key importance, particularly with respect to the configuration of reliable and robust computer vision systems as well as the dissemination of reconfigurable systems in novel application domains. Although a plethora of literature on this subject is available for certain areas of computer vision, the research community still faces a lack of a well-grounded, generally accepted, and—eventually—standardized methods.

The range of fundamental problems encompasses the value of synthetic images in experimental computer vision, the selection of a representative set of real images related to specific domains and tasks, the definition of ground truth given different tasks and applications, the design of experimental testbeds, the analysis of algorithms with respect to general characteristics such as complexity, resource consumption, convergence, stability, or range of admissible input data, the definition and analysis of performance measures for classes of algorithms, the role of statistics-based performance measures, the generation of data sheets with performance measures of algorithms supporting the system engineer in his configuration problem, and the validity of model assumptions for specific applications of computer vision.

The plan to edit this book was conceived in March 1998 at the ninth meeting on "Theoretical Foundations of Computer Vision" which was held in the castle of Dagstuhl, Germany. Many of the chapters presented in this volume are extended and updated versions of lectures at the workshop. However, this volume cannot be called a Proceedings of the workshop, because it contains—in addition to a selection of the subjects presented at the workshop—several chapters which were solicited by the editors to give a more complete overview of the topic.

The chapters in this volume have been grouped in six parts as follows: General Issues; Methodical Aspects; Statistical Aspects; Comparative Studies; Selected Methods and Algorithms; and finally a domain-specific part on Evaluation in Medical Imaging. All chapters in this volume have been reviewed independently by three reviewers ad minimum.

The volume editors are indebted to the "Schloss Dagstuhl International Conference and Research Center for Computer Science" in Wadern, Germany for creating an inspiring and free-of-duty environment. The exchange of ideas and the discussions between participants of the Dagstuhl workshop have greatly contributed to the quality of the present volume. We thank our colleague Prof. R.M. (Bob) Haralick of Washington University, Seattle, for his contributions to the organization of the meeting. We furthermore acknowledge the enthusiasm of Dr. Paul Roos of Kluwer Academic Publishers for this book project, and the pleasant communication with him concerning editorial matters.

During the preparation of this book we learned with deep regret that our colleague Dr. Piero Zamperoni (Technical University Braunschweig, Germany) passed away in August 1998. He authored many journal papers and books on image processing and analysis. Dr. Zamperoni was recognized by the international community as a gifted lecturer and an enthusiastic promoter of engineering education in image processing.

Dr. Zamperoni contributed to the success of the 1998 Dagstuhl Seminar through his encouraging personality and his sharp comments. Because of his illness, it was not feasible for him to finalize his book chapter. We include in this volume the extended abstract which was written by him for the Dagstuhl Seminar report, as a token of appreciation of Dr. Zamperoni's contributions to the field of computer vision.

Reinhard Klette
H. Siegfried Stiehl
Max A. Viergever
Koen L. Vincken

Auckland, Hamburg, Utrecht, August 1999.

Part I

General Issues

EXPERIENCES WITH EMPIRICAL EVALUATION
OF COMPUTER VISION ALGORITHMS

KEVIN W. BOWYER
Computer Science & Engineering
University of South Florida
Tampa, Florida 33620-5399, USA

1. Introduction

The lack of a substantial experimental side to computer vision has been
pointed to at various times in the past as a serious problem that hinders
advancement of the field. My own favorite example quote on this theme is
the following:

> ... *What is more interesting is that we are willing to develop one more
> edge detector, but we do not want to develop objective and quantitative
> methods to evaluate the performance of an edge detector. About three
> decades of research on edge detection has produced N edge detectors
> without a solid basis to evaluate the performance. In most disciplines,
> researchers evaluate the performance of a technique by a controlled set
> of experiments and specify the performance in clear objective terms. ...*

(Jain, R. and Binford, T. (1991) Ignorance, Myopia and Naivete in
Computer Vision Systems, *CVGIP: Image Understanding*, 53(1):116.)

Judging from the interest in recent workshops related to performance
evaluation of vision algorithms, the topic seems to finally be coming of
age. Work in our lab related to this topic includes projects for empirical
evaluation of: region segmentation algorithms for range images (Hoover
et al., 1996; Powell *et al.*, 1998), edge detection algorithms using human
ratings of edge goodness (Heath *et al.*, 1997), edge-based perceptual grouping algorithms (Borra and Sarkar, 1997), edge detection algorithms using a structure-from-motion task (Shin *et al.*, 1998) and edge detection
algorithms using an ROC curve framework (Dougherty *et al.*, 1998).

R. Klette et al. (eds.), Performance Characterization in Computer Vision, 3–16.
© 2000 *Kluwer Academic Publishers.*

Our experience gained through these projects has sharpened our ideas
about what properties of an evaluation framework are important, and has
led to some interesting insights. The purpose of this chapter is to summarize
the results of some of the evaluation projects that we have completed so
far, and to present what seem to be the general lessons learned from this
experience.

2. Evaluation of Range Segmentation algorithms

The first detailed performance evaluation experiment that we undertook
focused on algorithms for segmenting range images into regions that represent planar surfaces in the scene (Hoover *et al.*, 1996). This experiment
was motivated by our work on a high-level vision research project, involving
recognition of objects by reasoning about functionality (Stark *et al.*, 1996).
The object recognition work involved creating 3D models of the scene from
range images taken by a mobile robot. Region segmentation of the range
image is the first step in creating the 3D model. At one point, we became
interested in comparing the performance of different range image segmentation algorithms, in order to have the most accurate segmentation possible,
in hopes of having better 3D models. We formulated an empirical evaluation
framework which involved (1) acquiring a representative set of images,
(2) creating a "ground truth" specification for the images, (3) defining
performance metrics for the results of segmentation and (4) implementing
a software tool to automatically compare machine segmentation results to
ground truth specifications and tabulate the performance metrics.

We acquired a total of 80 range images to use in the experiment. There
are 40 images from each of two different types of range sensor, a time-
of-flight system and a structured-light system (Hoover *et al.*, 1996). Each
set of 40 was divided into a set of 10 to use in training the algorithms
and a set of 30 to use in testing. Based on knowing the geometric models
of the objects in the scenes, and being able to view registered range and
intensity images of the scene, "ground truth" region specification was manually created for each of the images. This was naturally time-consuming
and involved the development of supporting software tools. Provision was
made for some special cases in the ground truth: "edge regions" which are
effectively an artifact of the image acquisition process for the time-of-flight
system, "shadow regions" which are an artifact of the image acquisition
process for the structured-light system, and others. The essential property
of the ground truth specification is that any "noise" in it must be far smaller
than in any segmentation algorithm to be analyzed. Experience suggests to
us that there is no problem with this assumption.

The terms "correctly segmented region," "oversegmentation," "undersegmentation," "noise region," and "missed region" were given formal definitions as performance metrics. The key parameter in the definitions of these metrics is the percent of mutual overlap between a given region in the machine segmentation compared to a region in the ground truth. This parameter reflects the strictness of the definition of "an instance of correct segmentation." At high enough values of this parameter, say ≥ 0.95, all algorithms fail to correctly segment a large fraction of the regions. Note that "an instance of oversegmentation" and "an instance of undersegmentation" involve many-to-one and one-to-many relations, respectively, between the machine segmentation and the ground truth. Next, a tool was created to compare the result of a machine segmentation of an image to the corresponding ground truth and score the result in terms of these metrics.

The performance comparison itself was done in a distributed fashion by collaborating research groups. A number of researchers who had published papers describing algorithms for range image segmentation were contacted and solicited to participate. At the end, four research groups returned results. Another four or five groups made some level of attempt to participate but ran into problems of one sort or another. Each group trained the parameters of their segmenter separately on each of the two training sets, tested their segmenter on the two corresponding test sets, reported the results, and made the implementation of their segmenter available as part of the web site documenting the project. Due to this organization of the project, the training process varied greatly across the segmenters. The final paper was jointly authored by all of the contributors (Hoover et al., 1996).

The results that this type of performance evaluation can produce are illustrated in Figure 1. This plot shows the average number of instances of correct segmentation as a function of the percent of mutual overlap parameter. Performance is computed as an average over 30 test images, using the parameter settings found from training on a separate set of 10 images. The images were acquired with the ABW structured-light range sensor. The acronyms on the plotted lines are USF = University of South Florida, UB = University of Bern, WSU = Washington State University and UE = University of Edinburgh. Similar plots were obtained for the other performance metrics, and for all the metrics for the other scanner.

The results of this study did suggest some interesting and possibly surprising conclusions. First, the relative performance of the different segmentation algorithms was much the same for either type of range sensor. Thus it seems that there is a fair degree of generality to such performance studies, or at least to the algorithms considered in this particular study. It may be that there are some algorithms whose performance is highly sensor-specific, but we did not see evidence of this in our study. Second,

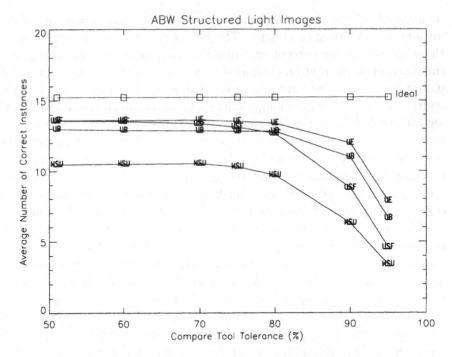

Figure 1. Average number of correctly segmented regions in range image.

the results suggest that there is still substantial room for improving the performance of algorithms which segment planar surfaces in range images. Small regions in the ground truth much more frequently participate in non-correct performance metrics that do large regions. But there were several examples of relatively large regions which none of the four algorithms correctly segmented at a tolerance of 80% mutual overlap with the ground truth.

The images, ground truth files, software tools, and segmentation algorithms used in this study are available through the web page
http://marathon.csee.usf.edu/range/seg-comp/SegComp.html

3. Edge Detector Evaluation Using Human Visual Ratings

The first approach to edge detector evaluation that we explored involves formalizing the typical subjective visual evaluation of edge images. In one experiment, we used a set of 20 images to evaluate the performance of 5 edge detectors (Heath *et al.*, 1997). To help ensure that any conclusions would not be specific to a certain type of subject matter in the images, the image set was balanced to have five images each of textured natural objects, textured man-made objects, non-textured natural objects and non-textured man-made objects. We do not claim that the different groups of five images are representative of the different classes of images, only that this composition of our set of 20 images should lead to greater generality in our conclusions. Images were taken specifically for this experiment, to have objects that were readily named by human observers centered in the scene and appearing in their natural context.

The evaluation was done through having observers rate the quality of a printed version of the edge image relative to the task of object recognition. Using statistical techniques from analysis of variance, we are able to check the rating data for overall consistency, and to make tests for statistical significance between the average ratings from different edge detectors. This type of experiment allows us to make statements of results such as those summarized in Table I.

TABLE I.   Edge detector ranking in visual evaluation experiment - adapted parameters.

Detector	Year	average rating
Canny	1986	4.80
Bergholm	1987	4.78
Rothwell	1995	4.76
Nalwa-Binford	1986	4.43
Iverson-Zucker	1995	4.26

These ratings are for the "adapted parameter" version of the experiment; that is, with edge detector parameters tuned on each image separately. The differences in average ratings of the Canny, Bergholm and Rothwell are not statistically significant. The difference between the Nalwa-Binford and Iverson-Zucker also are not statistically significant. However, the Canny, Bergholm and Rothwell average ratings are significantly higher than the Nalwa-Binford and Iverson-Zucker ratings. Interestingly, the relative rankings and the tests of statistical significance turned out differently when the data was analyzed for the "fixed parameter" scenario. In the fixed-parameter scenario, the edge detector is used with the same parameters across all images (Heath et al., 1997).

As an interesting aside, a simple comparison of the same edge detectors using synthetic images and noise also appears in (Heath *et al.*, 1997). In this comparison, all the detectors score essentially perfect! This suggests that evaluation experiments based on synthetic images and noise, at least of the simple type traditionally used in the computer vision literature, have no practical value.

The images used and additional information on this study can be found through the web page

`http://marathon.csee.usf.edu/edge/edgecompare_main.html`

4. Edge Detector Evaluation Using a SFM Task

A different evaluation experiment that we recently completed involves the use of the output of an edge detector as the input to a structure from motion algorithm (Shin *et al.*, 1998). The particular structure-from-motion algorithm that we use is that of Taylor and Kriegman (1995). In this project, the "ground truth" of the motion sequence is measured at the time that the image sequence is acquired, in terms of the motion between frames in a sequence and the structure (shape) of the object. The "best" edge detector is the one that allows recovery of the most accurate motion and structure estimates.

Three different image sequences were taken for each of two different types of scenes. The "scene type" here refers to the material used to construct the scene: wood blocks or colored plastic blocks. The actual objects in the scene were different for each of these original image sequences. An example image from one of the "lego house" image sequences in shown in Figure 2. Then, each of these original sequences was used to create two additional sequences with a greater amount of motion between frames. Thus, we had a total of 18 image sequences used in the experiment. An attempt was made to vary properties of the scene / image sequence such as the number of edges, the range of edge contrasts, the 3D angles of the edges and the amount of motion between frames.

The training process for this evaluation consisted of searching for a set of parameter values which produced the best result, in terms of minimum error in the structure or motion, on a given image sequence. The initial sampling of an edge detector's parameter space was five values uniformly distributed along the meaningful range of each parameter. The parameter value from this sampling which resulted in the minimum error became the center point for a local finer-grain sampling. The refined sampling was repeated a minimum of two iterations, and until the decrease in the error fell below 5%.

An sample of the type of result that we obtain in this evaluation frame-

Figure 2. Example image from a sequence of one of the "lego house" scenes.

work is shown in Figure 3. The mean error in recovered motion estimate on "lego house" image sequences is shown. With separate training and testing on 9 image sequences, there are 72 test trials. All four edge detectors converged in 48 of the 72 trials. The error shown here is the mean of these 48 trials. Results of the same style are given in (Shin *et al.*, 1998) for the error in recovered structure on sequences from this scene type, and for both error metrics for image sequences of the other scene type as well. The general trends in these other results are much the same.

Some of the detectors used in the human rating evaluation were not used in this work, and the Sarkar-Boyer detector (Sarkar and Boyer, 1991) was added. An interesting result from this experiment is that the Canny edge detector was the fastest in execution, gave edge maps which resulted in the highest rate of convergence in the SFM algorithm and gave on average the most accurate results on the test data. That is, there seemed to be no element of practical relative advantage for any of the other edge detectors considered in this study!

The images used and additional information on this study can be found through the web page

http://marathon.csee.usf.edu/edge/edgecompare_main.html

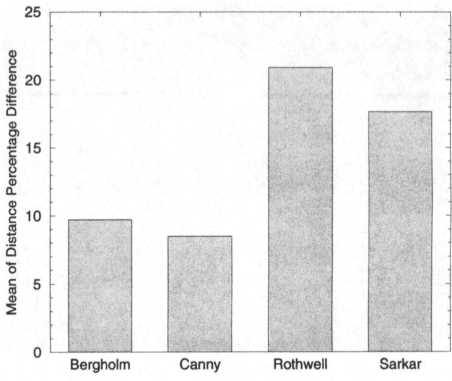

Figure 3.   SFM task comparison of edge detectors.

5. Edge Detector Evaluation Using ROC Curves

Yet another approach that we are still exploring involves the use of receiver operating characteristic (ROC) curves (Dougherty *et al.*, 1998). This approach requires that "ground truth" be specified for real images. One can argue that any manual specification of ground truth for real images is necessarily subjective. However, we believe that the ground truth specified is substantially more accurate that the current state-of-the-art in edge detection. Also, it seems unlikely that manually specified ground truth would be consistently biased for or against any particular edge detection algorithm.

The particular manner in which we specify ground truth templates for this study is to specify lines where we want the detector to find edges, regions within which we want the detector to not find edges, and allow any remaining unspecified portions of the image to be treated as "don't count" regions. We felt that the allowance for "don't count" regions was needed in order to be able to use real images and specify ground truth only where we could be highly confident that it was correct. For real images with

Figure 4.   An example image used in the ROC curve framework.

regions of substantial texture, it is tedious and error-prone to attempt to specify the ground truth edges in the texture regions. An example image used in this study appears in Figure 4, and its ground truth template appears in Figure 5. The black lines in the ground truth template represent "true edge" specifications. The white regions in the ground truth template represent "true no-edge region" specifications. The gray regions are "don't count" regions.

Given the ground truth specification for an image, we can run an edge detector on the image with many different settings of the edge detector's parameters. Each run of the edge detector produces an edge image which can be matched against the ground truth to obtain a potentially different performance result in terms of counts of "true positive" and "false positive" edge pixels. A "true positive" is a detected edge pixel which matches up to a line specified in the ground truth. A "false positive" is a detected edge pixel which occurs in a region marked as "no-edge" in the ground truth.

This approach allows us to produce performance results in terms of a receiver operating characteristic (ROC) curve. The ROC curve summarizes performance over a range of sensitivity to finding true positive edge pixels. A sample of this type of result ROC curve is shown in Figure 6. The ROC curves in this figure are obtained in "adapted parameter" mode; that is, with parameters tuned individually for each image. Also, the ROC curves represent an average performance over 40 images. It is also possible to use

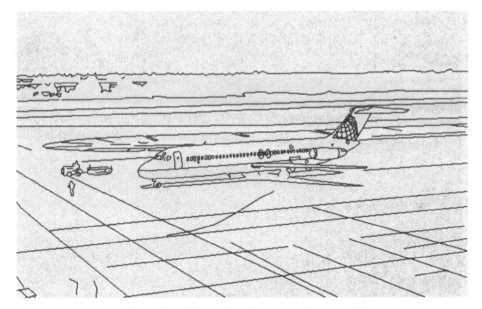

Figure 5.   Ground truth template for the airplane example image.

the parameter settings found on the ROC curve for one image to produce a "test" ROC curve for a different image, and to average such performance across a set of images. We are currently working on results of this type.

In all of our studies on edge detector performance (Heath *et al.*, 1997; Shin *et al.*, 1998; Dougherty *et al.*, 1998), we have tried to use implementations faithful to those of the original authors. We were able to obtain implementations from authors' web pages, as part of a software distribution from their lab, as part of the IUE, and by contacting individual authors. However, in the case of the Canny and the Sobel edge detectors, we used implementations written at USF. Our implementation of the Canny is a "vanilla" version with the standard hysteresis and non-maxima suppression; it has none of the "extra bells and whistles" alluded to in Canny's paper.

Again in this study, we are finding that the Canny edge detector generally performs better than the other detectors considered. Only the detector by Heitger (1995) shows any improvement in performance relative to the Canny detector (Canny, 1986). The images used and additional information on this study can be found through the web page
http://marathon.csee.usf.edu/edge/edgecompare_main.html

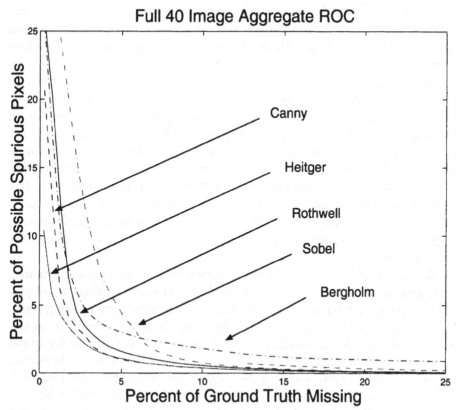

Figure 6. Empirical ROC curve comparison of edge detectors.

6. Discussion

We have found the development of meaningful performance evaluation paradigms for computer vision algorithms to be a substantial research effort in its own right. The emphasis of the research efforts in our group has been on empirical performance evaluation using real images. This style of research requires substantial effort in developing "experimental artifacts" such as image sets, ground truth files and supporting software tools. It also requires substantial attention to experimental detail. In this respect, we are fortunate to be able to collaborate, in our human visual evaluation studies, with a colleague from Psychology. Also, the style of research as in the range segmentation, SFM, and ROC studies requires truly enormous amounts of computer time.

We are continuing to expand our work in several directions. One effort is simply to expand the number of different edge detectors considered in our studies. Another effort is to use some known object recognition algorithm as a task for the evaluation of edge detectors, similar to the structure-from-motion study. A third effort is to expand the range segmentation comparison to include algorithms which segment images into curved-surface patches.

One emerging conclusion from our work is that the best performing algorithm is not necessarily the best known or the most recently published. Prior to the range segmentation performance study, the algorithms from the University of Bern and the University of Edinburgh were not the best known in the research community. Of course, given the results of the study, we expect that this is not true any longer. In the edge detection studies, the Canny algorithm probably is the best known in the community, but it is about 15 years old. Given the number of edge detector papers published in journals each year, a "consumer" of computer vision algorithms might reasonably expect that something should have emerged to offer better performance.

We can speculate that the historical lack of experimental performance evaluation in computer vision naturally led to the use of other techniques for measuring whether or not a new idea is an "advance" over existing ideas. If so, one dimension which the community have have consciously or unconsciously adopted for measuring progress is simply that of mathematical sophistication of an algorithm. In some sense, it is reasonable to think that a more mathematically sophisticated algorithm should be more powerful. More sophisticated mathematics is *by definition* more powerful in its own "abstract" or "ideal" world. However, the assumptions made in developing the mathematics of an algorithm do not necessarily correspond to the truth of any real world application. More sophisticated mathematics often makes more, and more specific, assumptions about the properties of the real application. If more sophisticated mathematics ends up meaning less accurate assumptions, then conceptually the situation may be as depicted in Figure 7. If this is the situation, then increasing mathematical sophistication may result in decreasing performance. It is important to understand that this would be due to assumptions not matching reality. The answer, then, would be to make assumptions which better correspond to reality. Measuring the correspondence to reality is a fundamentally empirical activity! In general, we cannot know which assumption best corresponds to reality unless we have cyclic feedback between theory and experiment. This was one of the simple and true messages in papers such as (Jain and Binford, 1991).

Acknowledgments

The work surveyed in this chapter was carried out by several talented students, both graduate and undergraduate, and in collaboration with some

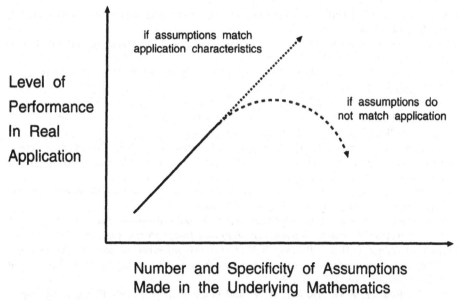

Figure 7.   Performance as a function of mathematical sophistication.

wonderful faculty colleagues. Collaborators at USF on the range segmentation comparison include Adam Hoover, Dmitry Goldgof and Gillian Jean-Baptiste. Collaborators on the human visual evaluation experiments include Mike Heath, Tom Sanocki and Sudeep Sarker. Collaborators on the structure-from-motion study include Min Shin and Dmitry Goldgof. Collaborators on the ROC curve study include Sean Dougherty and Christine Kranenburg.

The current projects in edge detector evaluation are supported by National Science Foundation IRI-9731821 and EIA-9729904 (equipment grant). Previous work was supported by National Science Foundation CDA9424214, CDA-92-00369, IRI-9120895 and National Aeronautics and Space Administration NGT-40015.

References

Bergholm, F. (1987) Edge Focusing, *IEEE PAMI*, 9:726–741.

Borra, S. and Sarkar, S. (1997) A framework for performance characterization of intermediate-level grouping modules, *IEEE PAMI*, 19(11):1306–1312.

Canny, J. (1986) A computational approach to edge detection, *IEEE PAMI*, 8(6):679–698.

Dougherty, S. and Bowyer, K.W. (1998) Objective evaluation of edge detectors using a formally defined framework, *Empirical Evaluation Techniques in Computer Vision*, Bowyer, K.W. and Phillips, P.J. (eds.), IEEE Computer Society Press, 211–234.

Heath, M., Sarkar, S., Sanocki, T. and Bowyer, K.W. (1997) A Robust Visual Method for Assessing the Relative Performance of Edge Detection Algorithms, *IEEE PAMI*, 19(12):1338–1359.

Heitger, F. (1995) Feature Detection using Suppression and Enhancement, TR 163, Image Science Lab, ETH-Zurich.

Hoover, A.W., Jean-Baptiste, J., Jiang, X., Flynn, P., Bunke, H., Goldgof, D., Bowyer, K.W., Eggert, D., Fitzgibbon, A. and Fisher, R. (1996) An experimental comparison of range image segmentation algorithms, *IEEE PAMI*, 18(7):673–689.

Jain, R. and Binford, T. (1991) *Ignorance, Myopia and Naivete in Computer Vision Systems, CVGIP: Image Understanding*, 53(1):116.

Powell, M., and Bowyer, K.W., Jiang, X. and Bunke, H. (1998) Comparing curved-surfaces range image segmenters, *International Conference on Computer Vision (ICCV '98)*, Bombay, India, 286–291.

Rothwell, C.A., Mundy, J.L., Hoffman, W. and Nguyen, V.D. (1995) Driving Vision by Topology, *Int. Symposium on Computer Vision*, 395–400.

Sarkar, S. and Boyer, K. (1991) Optimal Infinite Impulse Response Zero Crossing Based Edge Detection, *Computer Vision, Graphics and Image Processing*, 54(2):224–243.

Shin, M., Goldgof, D.B. and Bowyer, K.W. (1998) An objective comparison methodology of edge detection algorithms using a structure from motion task, *Computer Vision and Pattern Recognition '98*, 190–195.

Stark, L., Bowyer, K.W., Hoover, A.W. and Goldgof, D.B. (1996) Recognizing object function through reasoning about partial shape descriptions and dynamic physical properties, *Proceedings of the IEEE*, 84(11):1640–1656.

Taylor, C. and Kriegman, D. (1995) Structure and motion from line segments in multiple images, *IEEE PAMI*, 17(11):1021–1032.

EVALUATION AND VALIDATION OF COMPUTER VISION ALGORITHMS

A Perspective from a Vision Company

PATRICK COURTNEY
Visual Automation Ltd.
Stopford Building, Oxford Road
Manchester M13 9PT, UK

1. Introduction

Computer vision technology has the potential to address a broad range of tasks of significant economic and social value to mankind. However the construction of working systems present real difficulties, not just due to limitations of the technology, but also because these limitations are not well understood. This chapter describes some recent experiences, both positive and negative, in trying to apply computer vision technology. A contrast is made with practices in other engineering fields that have a solid record in building usable systems.

This chapter draws upon experience gained within the advanced technology division of a multi-national group specialising in image analysis solutions for the industrial automation, space and defence sectors, as well as the technology transfer unit attached to an academic research laboratory focussing on the medical and scientific equipment sectors. Although the examples are drawn from a commercial context, this should not be allowed to detract from the fact that they concern real applications and are an end-result of research work carried out by academic researchers.

Commercial end-users have always been under pressure to reduce costs (especially man power costs), to improve quality of products, services and data, and to reduce time to market. As a consequence, these end-users place a substantial value on systems that exhibit high degrees of autonomy and reliability. Being able to provide such systems, which are increasingly complex and incorporate different technologies is a generic requirement across

17

R. Klette et al. (eds.), Performance Characterization in Computer Vision, 17–28.

Figure 1.   The cable car of Grenoble, France.

the whole of engineering. It is worth examining how the other engineering disciplines provide these characteristics.

2. The engineering disciplines

2.1. CIVIL ENGINEERING

In the middle of the city of Grenoble in southeastern France, a cable car runs across the river Isère. Built in 1931, with a new cabin installed in 1951, the cable car possesses a span of 475m. By 1970, it had transported 11 million visitors a total distance of over 1 million kilometres. In 1976 the cabin was changed again to the present characteristic spheres and by 1996 it was transporting 230,000 visitors per year.

How is it that this complex structure of cables and moving parts has operated successfully in extreme environmental conditions[1] for so long? The answer lies in the fact that knowledge of the failure modes of such a system have been acquired and strategies developed for dealing with them. These failure modes have become known either through the failure of actual systems or through detailed analysis of designs. This knowledge has in turn driven the development of measures to reduce their occurrence. Experience has shown that among the most common causes of failure are:

– Design errors—actions to avoid these include design reviews with experienced staff and the application of design checks developed over
   time.

---

[1] Grenoble experiences a continental climate that can reach 40°C in summer and below −10°C in winter.

- Poor quality materials—may be reduced by the testing of samples. In the case of bridge construction, materials are routinely tested to six times the required limits. Another strategy is that of over-design, designing structures with a safety factor over the calculated stresses— bridge designers use a factor of three. Finally, it is accepted that single point failures may always occur and structures are designed to be resilient to such events where possible, by using additional cables, fixing bolts, etc.
- Uneven or excessive wear—will reduce the performance with respect to the specification. Detection requires planned maintenance by trained staff.
- Exceeding specified operating conditions—can be avoided by monitoring the conditions of use and taking appropriate action. In the case of the cable car this may mean limiting the number of passengers during peak times and closing it during severe weather.

This pairing of causes of failure with compensating measures has incorporated new knowledge and understanding over the millennia. As novel designs evolve, so new failure modes may arise. An example is the spectacular failure of the Tacoma narrows suspension bridge where wind caused torsion and ultimately the collapse of the road deck—an unexpected mode of behaviour. Once this failure mode had been identified, preventative measures could be developed. Aerodynamic shaping of the deck with validation in a wind tunnel were added as stages in the design process. At the other extreme, one has the example of the Eiffel tower, a structure which at the time was of sufficiently novelty to merit patenting. Though only intended to stand for the universal exhibition of 1889 and the three following years, it is still in use over a hundred years later.

Catastrophic failures are highly visible manifestations of new modes. However less spectacular observations during maintenance coupled with reporting to the profession have become increasingly important mechanisms for improvement as civil engineering has matured from a craft to a discipline.

2.2. AERONAUTICAL ENGINEERING

The city of Grenoble is famous for being the capital of the Alps and popular pastimes for its inhabitants include skiing and flying light aircraft. Some even combining these two activities to land their planes on glaciers. Despite the apparent risk of combining two dangerous activities, the accident rate is quite low and one is again led to wonder how this can be so. As with the cable car, airplanes are built and operated according to knowledge of failure modes and strategies for dealing with them:

- Design errors—design reviews and checks are a standard tool. In the case of novel designs and materials, the construction of reduced scale models and computer simulations are used. Furthermore, airframes are subject to certification by independent bodies. These will only issue a certificate of airworthiness after the airframe has been exhaustively tested, often to destruction.
- Poor quality materials—testing of materials and use of safety factors are again common practice. The effect of the failure of critical components is tempered by the presence of backup systems, be they power plants, radios or indicators.
- Uneven or excessive wear—regular maintenance is carried out following procedures defined by the manufacturer.
- Exceeding specified operating conditions—conditions such as loading and weather are carefully monitored and flights cancelled if the conditions are exceeded.

As in the case of civil engineering, the high visibility of catastrophic failures helps to reveal new failure modes. Indeed, black box recorders are a standard feature of the larger airplanes allowing failure data to be feed back into the design process.

2.3. ELECTRONIC SYSTEMS ENGINEERING

Down the road from Grenoble is the small town of Crolles, well known as home to a major VLSI manufacturing facility. Within plants such as these, systems of the most immense complexity, integrating many millions of transistors and connections are manufactured in huge numbers, ready for incorporation into all kind of equipment. Cost effective production is made all the more challenging by the rapidly changing nature of both the design and fabrication technology. As before, a solid understanding of the principal causes of failure is the key to making this work:

- Design errors—besides design reviews and design rules, system parameters such as circuit noise and delay budgets are managed and safety margins added. Design validation is further eased by the use of simulation tools.
- Failures in fabrication—fabrication defects are reduced by visual inspection and functional testing using test vector generators which guarantee a certain level of fault coverage. Specialised test circuits and test points are included to ensure testability.
- Failures during use—these follow a well understood curve that distinguishes infant mortality, random lifetime and end-of-life wearout failures. Infant failures are removed by pre-aging and final testing. The lifetime failure rate, expressed as FITS (failures in time), follows

a model which relates environmental parameters of temperature and voltage by simple exponentials derived from the underlying physics. Although an approximation for such complex systems, FITS is an essential reliability parameter that can be calculated, measured and propagated to produce overall system level parameters such as MTBF (Mean Time Between Failures).

- Exceeding specified operating conditions—special circuits protect against conditions such as overheating, static discharge, reverse polarity, etc.

With this strong culture of testing, validation and exploration of the parameters involved, it is perhaps no coincidence that the inspection of semiconductor devices has been one of the areas where machine vision has had the greatest commercial success.

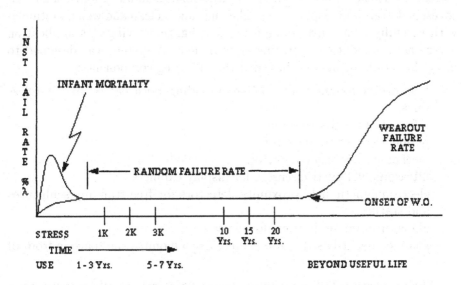

Figure 2.   Lifetime failure for an integrated circuit (Harris, 1998).

3. Computer vision applications

Having rapidly surveyed three successful engineering disciplines, one can now examine a number of vision case studies. The computer vision literature is rich in methods that purport to work and some applications that do work. There is little on performance evaluation and virtually nothing specifically on applications which were not made to work. It is perhaps natural that the emphasis be on working systems, but there is much to be learned from failure and the following sections discuss both positive and negative experiences in the construction of working vision applications.

3.1. VIDEO SURVEILLANCE

One particular application was based on a request from a museum for a system to detect disturbances to works of art. The museum in question already had a system to protect against intrusion with criminal intent, but it was looking for an early warning system to protect the works from damage due to handling by clumsy or over-curious visitors.

The system was to provide one level of protection to warn the visitors that they were too close and a second level to alert guards of persistent or serious disturbance, all at a high level of reliability. A wide range of works were to be protected from paintings to sculptures, statues, tapestries and pieces of furniture, in a diversity of situations including rooms, halls, alcoves, pedestals and display cases. The museum is clean and well maintained with carefully controlled temperature and lighting giving this application a very accommodating operating environment. A system was designed to meet the requirements and included the following components:

- a secure communication system providing both cabled and wireless links
- infrared proximity sensors
- piezoelectric shock detectors
- mechanical vibration detectors
- ultrasonic volumetric sensors for display cabinets
- electromagnetic field proximity detectors for free standing sculptures and statues
- 2D laser scanning barriers for alcoves
- passive imager-based motion detectors to monitor the space in front of paintings

The proposed solution included three particularly novel components: a secure wireless communication system, an electromagnetic field proximity detector (both from an external supplier) and a passive imager-based motion detector (which was to be developed internally). It is instructive to contrast the ease with which these non-vision and vision technologies were integrated into the system.

As part of the proposal, a detailed data sheet had to be produced indicating the principal characteristics of each component. This was easily prepared for the conventional detectors. For the secure wireless communication system and the electromagnetic field proximity detector, the suppliers helped to draft these, lending samples when requested. For the motion detector, four PhD-level engineers worked to develop a proof-of-concept prototype but were unable to produce a working detector, despite their combined experience in the subject and the relatively convivial operating environment. When the complete surveillance system was demonstrated to the client, the overall concept was accepted but without the motion detectors.

The success of the novel communications and sensing components resulted in financial resources flowing back to the developer of these non-vision technologies. This experience, when repeated over time and across different industrial sectors (and there is anecdotal evidence to suggest that this is what has been happening) provides a net differential disadvantage to computer vision in terms of the allocation of industrial development resources. This will ultimately be expressed as a corresponding reduction in research funding.

3.2. HIGH SPEED INSPECTION TEST BENCH

In another application, a tyre manufacturer issued an invitation to tender for an outdoor test bed to measure tyre contact area, wheel angle and position in three dimensions. This had to be carried out at high speed on an uninstrumented wheel—suggesting a vision-based solution. The client gave information on the operating and environmental conditions and was, unusually, able to provide detailed precision and accuracy requirements.

Proposing a feasible solution necessitated determining values for the sub-pixel precision of both feature detection and calibration stages. Previous experience on the algorithms provided rough values under laboratory conditions, but extrapolation to the conditions of the application to obtain overall system performance proved problematic. The situation is aggravated by the lack of information concerning the pixel response of the high speed cameras required.

Figure 3 illustrates the response of an individual photosite as a laser spot is traced across. As can be seen, the response is broadly gaussian along one axis, but highly non-gaussian along the other. Since the sub-pixel interpolation methods in the literature assume a monatonic profile, the precision obtained would be unpredictable. Because of this and related concerns, it was not felt possible to suggest a workable solution which could be guaranteed to fulfill the requirements.

3.3. AIRCRAFT TRACKING

Another application required being able to locate and track aircraft captured on high-speed film. A semi-automatic workstation capable of processing multiple film and aircraft types was to be produced. The key question in this project was which algorithms to use.

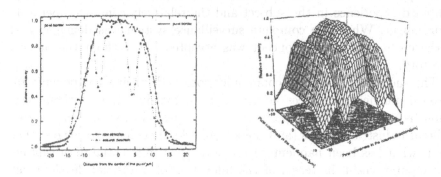

Figure 3.   Pixel response curve for a certain sensor (VTT, 1996).

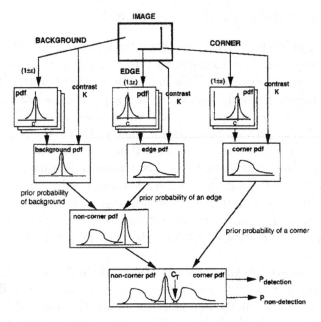

Figure 4.   Scheme for establishing corner detection reliability (Courtney and Skordas, 1996).

One of the candidates was corner detection to locate aircraft nose and wing tips. Initial tests were disappointing with corner detection proving totally unreliable. Further examination revealed that the problem lay in setting the detection threshold and that detection reliability and precision were linked to image contrast, image noise and feature scale. Without detailed understanding of the relationship between these parameters it would not be possible to use this algorithm with any confidence. A further study provided the required information and suggested that a signal to noise ratio of at least 22dB is required for 95% detection, and that noise filtering trades reliability for precision (Courtney and Skordas, 1996). This is in line with the results of other studies of feature detection reliability and precision.

3.4. SATELLITE TRACKING

For many years now the space agencies have been considering the use of computer vision techniques as a way of providing the autonomy needed for future space missions. For computer vision technology to be accepted it is necessary to assess the reliability and performance levels of precision and accuracy which can be expected.

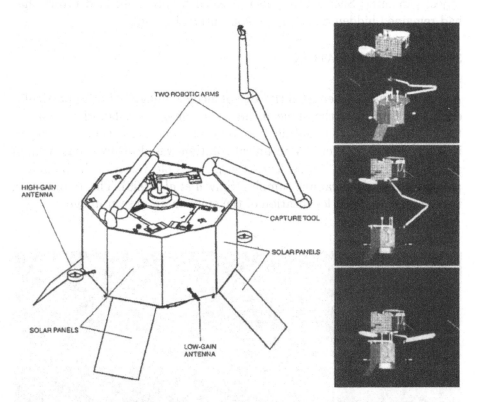

Figure 5. Geostationary Service Vehicle (left); final approach & capture (right). Reprinted from (de Peuter *et al.*, 1994).

One particular project under consideration is the Geostationary Service Vehicle (de Peuter *et al.*, 1994). This is a robotic vehicle that would patrol the commercially valuable geostationary orbit to remove dead communication satellites and repair damaged ones.

One of the key functional components of such a system would be a module to estimate and track a free flying object. Algorithms to perform this task have been developed and refined to the point that they seem to provide high levels of precision and reliability (Daucher *et al.*, 1993). However, since these algorithms employ statistically robust methods, the end result is a system that is rather brittle in the sense that it fails unpredictably.

A detailed analysis of the performance characteristics of one such tracking algorithm was carried out in (Courtney and Lapresté, 1997). Since the overall system is quite reliable individual modules were tested using a monte carlo approach. This relies upon a knowledge of the internal structure of the algorithms (glass box approach). The individual results were then combined to determine overall system reliability in terms of signal to noise ratio and object geometry. Such testing also revealed deeply embedded errors that had remained hidden during more conventional testing.

3.5. SPINE LOCALISATION

A final example is taken from the area of medical imaging. In this particular case, localisation of the spine in an X-ray image is a laborious manual task, essential for the quantification, diagnosis and evaluation of therapies in many spine disorders. A technical solution was developed based upon active shape models. These learn the permissible variation in boundary points from a set of training samples (Smyth *et al.*, 1996). This information is then used to guide localisation of the spine in an unseen image.

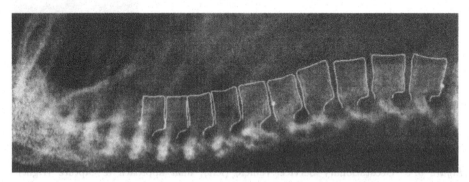

Figure 6.   Localised spine in X-ray image outlined in white.

Validation is carried out by comparing the performance with that of experienced radiologists. The lack of objective ground truth is not regarded as a problem once acceptable inter-observer variation can be measured.

4. Axioms for developing working vision systems

It is now possible to draw upon these examples to infer a set of design axioms which would facilitate the engineering of working vision systems:

1. Encourage modularity—provide multiple levels of abstraction and reusable blocks.
2. Assess module characteristics—define conditions of use in data sheets that express parameters in generic terms such as pdfs and receiver operating curves.
3. Develop tools for detecting design errors—be they at the algorithm, the code implementation or the machine execution level. Develop appropriate design checks and guidelines. Develop test environments providing known levels of fault coverage. Use computer simulations using synthetically generated data.
4. Quantify the design margins—the different branches of engineering use different factors but these safety margins are always required to produce reliable systems.
5. Obtain a good understanding of system failure modes—quantifiable failure models may be approximate. But they must be verifiable by empirical methods and should allow failure rates at the level of parts per million to be deduced.
6. Understand the limits of use—monitor the conditions and take appropriate action when they are exceeded.

It might be argued that computer vision technology is not comparable to the other engineering disciplines mentioned. That civil engineering grew out of a very ancient craft, that aeronautical engineering is tightly regulated for safety, and that electronics has vast resources at its disposal, and that computer vision is a software subject with a different set of problems and solutions. Whilst it is true that both computer vision and computer science are young fields, modern solid state electronics is less than 50 years old. Resources come with maturity and certification from responsibility. Computer vision suffers greatly from the immaturity of software development with its moving baseline of languages and tools. Although the construction and testing of hypotheses is a central tenet of the scientific method, the reluctance to test is endemic in computer science (Tichy, 1998). Computer vision would do well to emulate other engineering disciplines in order make the transition of ideas, from demos that can work to systems that will work.

Evaluation of vision systems is already carried out by end-user communities, from medicine to the entertainment industries. The result is often a negative one for computer vision. Unexplained failures and lack of trust characterised an earlier period of machine vision. But by careful application of the scientific method and an engineering methodology, it can be shown that many computer vision techniques are sound and can deliver benefits. It is up to all developers, both academic and industrial, to provide this proof since computer vision is in competition with other technologies that are not shy of using this approach.

Acknowledgements

The opinions expressed here are those of the author alone and do not represent those of any organisation. The author wishes to express his thanks to the researchers and engineers, too numerous to mention, who have been involved in the projects described, and to those who gave their consent for their figures to be reproduced.

References

Courtney, P. and Skordas, T. (1996) Caractèrisation de performances des algorithmes de Vision—un exemple : le détecteur de coins, *10th AFCET-RFIA*, Rennes, France, 953–962.

Courtney, P. and Lapresté, J.T. (1997) Performance Evaluation of a 3D Tracking System for Space Applications, *DAGM Workshop on Performance Characteristics and Quality of Computer Vision Algorithms*, Technical University of Brunswick, Germany.

Daucher, N., Dhome, M., Lapresté, J.T. and Rives, G. (1993) 3D Object Location and Tracking by Monocular Vision, *Procs. Workshop on Computer Vision for Space Applictions*, Antibes, France, 261–272.

Harris Semiconductor (1998) *Quality and Reliability Manual*, http://rel.semi.harris.com.

Petroski, H. (1994) Design Paradigms: Case Histories of Error and Judgement in Engineering, Cambridge University Press.

de Peuter, W., Visentin, G., Fehse, W., Elfving, A., Brown, D.L. and Ashford, E. (1994) Satellite Servicing in GEO by Robotic Service Vehicle, *ESA Bulletin*, 78:33–39.

Smyth, P.S., Taylor, C.J. and Adams, J.E. (1996) Automatic Measurement of Vertebral Shape using Active Shape Models, *Procs. BMVC.*

Tichy, W.F. (1998) Should Computer Scientists Experiment More? *IEEE Computer*, 31(5):32–40.

VTT Annual Report (1996) Finland, http://www.vtt.fi.

DATABASES FOR PERFORMANCE CHARACTERIZATION

ADRIAN F. CLARK
VASE Laboratory
University of Essex
Colchester CO4 3SQ, UK

PATRICK COURTNEY
Visual Automation
Stopford Building, Oxford Road
Manchester M13 9PT, UK

1. Introduction

The principal aim of machine vision is, naturally, to develop techniques and systems that allow computers to be aware of their surroundings and take actions consequent on what is seen. Many man-years of effort have been expended on this goal; although significant progress has been made, we are arguably not much closer to solving the basic problem. While it is undoubtedly an extremely difficult goal, we are all hampered to some extent by the fact that we do not necessarily know which technique works best in which situation. The realization that this problem needs to be addressed in order for vision to become an engineering discipline rather than purely a research area has been long in coming; and this idea of knowing what to use and when is the underlying tenet of *performance characterization*.

Although rarely discussed in the literature, there are many subjective assessments of performance: "Canny's edge finder is the best," is a common example, one that has been written in books. "Canny's edge finder is poor at detecting corners" is another. Although such assessments are useful, their subjectiveness makes them difficult to confirm—and still harder to build into some kind of system. Performance must be quantified in order for objective comparisons to be made. However, objective performance measures should not be compared blindly: image coding, for example, has long used the mean-square error between uncoded and coded images to

29

R. Klette et al. (eds.), Performance Characterization in Computer Vision, 29–40.
© 2000 *Kluwer Academic Publishers.*

estimate 'quality' and this has led to the design of coders that have excellent objective performance but poor visual results—and *vice versa*. It is essential that objective performance measures really do measure useful quantities, and mean-square error does not assess 'quality' in the same way as the human eye.

Progress is being made into the methodology of characterizing performance and into the performance of particular algorithms. As things stand today, the best approach is to apply vision techniques to the same sets of data and then to ascertain which performs better. (This latter requirement is considered further in section 5.) Hence, a central factor in characterizing the performance of vision algorithms is the use of common databases and common measures of performance.

The use of common datasets for comparing performance has been long-established in some areas of image processing: for example, the "Lenna" image scanned from *Playboy* magazine[1] has been used as a benchmark for comparing image processing performance. It turns out that the Lenna image is by no means typical of images in general (there are fairly large homogeneous areas and comparatively little texture), and it has been found that algorithms that work wonderfully on Lenna do not work nearly as well on more representative images. Hence, the use of databases in performance characterization is actually a rather important issue, and for this reason the authors have been conducting a survey of the use of databases in this context on behalf of ECVnet, the European "network of excellence" in computer vision.

The following section describes the nature of the ECVnet survey and outlines the its main findings. section 3 then gives some examples of where databases have been or are being valuable in characterizing performance. The following two sections discuss the design of databases and experiments to characterize performance, and section 6 gives some concluding remarks.

2. The ECVnet Survey

The authors have carried out a survey of what databases are being used to characterize performance in the computer vision community under the ægis of the ECVnet benchmarking committee, which was headed by the second author. The authors both have an active interest in performance characterization (*e.g.*, (Courtney *et al.*, 1997)) in both academic and industrial contexts.

---

[1] This means it is an infringement of copyright—though not as serious an infringement as the whole-scale scanning of Brodatz textures by many parties in the last 30 years.

The ECVnet survey took place during Feb–Oct 1997. It comprised two phases:

1. the gathering of information concerning the availability of databases, both free and commercial, for characterizing vision algorithms;
2. in-depth examinations of databases in two or three key areas.

Information concerning the availability of databases was collected primarily by means of a form on the World-Wide Web:

`http://peipa.essex.ac.uk/benchmark/`

the existence of which was announced in the `Vision-List` and `Pixel` digests and the newsgroup `sci.image.processing`. The response to requests of this nature is inevitably poor, so this has been backed up by Web searches, personal contact, and examination of published works by the authors. Even though the information we have gathered is representative, we consider it to be far from comprehensive. The 15 or so responses to the survey may be perused via the above URL. Note, however, that the information is all held in a database and converted to HTML for display; this will facilitate searching as the number of datasets in the database grows.

On the basis of this survey, the most popular type of database appears to comprise faces. This probably reflects both the high level of interest in face recognition in recent years and the comparative ease of collection of face images.

3. Databases and Performance Characterization

3.1. DATASETS FOR CHARACTER RECOGNITION AND DOCUMENT UNDERSTANDING SYSTEMS

In recent years there have been a number of initiatives to assess the performance of systems which extract information from images of text, as characters or words, either machine printed or handwritten. As part of these efforts, some groups have prepared datasets containing image data and "ground truth" results and made these available to the wider community (Guyon *et al.*, 1996). Here, we survey these activities in order to identify how this experience could assist in the development of datasets for other areas.

3.1.1. *Printed character and word recognition*
The Information Science Research Institute of the University of Nevada at Las Vegas carried out studies into the comparative performance of OCR

page readers. As part of this work, ground-truthed datasets were prepared for internal use. An initial set of 132 pages of English language government documents were collected, rising to 800 pages in later collections. Data entry was carried out over a period of four years by a group of paid undergraduates and managed by a full-time OCR expert. A format was specified for the ground truth (ISRI format) and the ground truth assigned by independently entering the data four times with difference resolved by the expert. The cost of preparation of good quality data was estimated at $15–$25 per page for English text, more for Japanese or Chinese. These performance studies were reported at an annual ASDAIR symposium (Rice et al., 1995; Rice et al., 1996).

3.1.2. *Handwritten character and word recognition*
The CENPARMI dataset consists of manually isolated handwritten digits within ZIP codes collected from live mail at one US post office. The dataset was naturalistic and unbiased in the sense that the mail was real mail and the sender did not know that it would be used for automatic recognition.

CEDAR, the Centre of Excellence for Document Analysis and Recognition at SUNY, Buffalo, New York, developed a dataset of handwritten character and words again from live mail captured in a working post office. This time the dataset contained high resolution images of words (towns and ZIP codes) (Hull, 1994).

A comparative study on the performance of form readers was carried out by the NIST (National Institute of Standards and Technology) for the US Census Bureau (Garris, 1993; Wilson, 1993). A set of special forms were designed containing random characters and digits for a writer to transcribe into a box. A group of Census Bureau employees were requested to complete these forms which were then scanned in and checked for correct transcription. These data were used as a training set, and a further set completed by high school students formed a test set. A first test was carried out on isolated digits and characters on 47 systems from 29 groups and reported at a workshop. A further set of tests examined the performance on fields of characters. The datasets were primarily for internal use but were made available on CD-ROM for other interested parties. A total of 50 institutions from 8 countries have participated.

3.1.3. *Understanding of machine printed documents*
The University of Washington compiled a set of CD-ROMs containing various document pages under DARPA funding to evaluate OCR systems (Phillips, 1998). The documents were English and Japanese technical journals and memos, copied and scanned. A specification of the ground truth giving image zones and attributes was prepared. This was validated by

members of the research group and a refined consistent version produced (DAFS: Document Attribute Format Specification). A group of undergraduates was hired to carry out the mainstream preparation, under the supervision of experienced staff. The first CD-ROM took a year and a half to produce. A workshop of OCR researchers was held and gave valuable feedback.

The main problems encountered were felt to be in managing the people, managing the data and validating the ground truth. The principal recommendations were for independent generation of two sets of ground truth followed by cross-checking, clarity in the specification and instructions for ground truth generation, and careful selection of relevant images by taking input from algorithms developers.

3.1.4. *Online handwriting recognition—the UNIPEN project*

TC11 of the IAPR initiated the UNIPEN project to collate datasets of online handwriting in order to encourage advances in the field (Guyon *et al.*, 1994a). Holders of datasets were encouraged to donate their personal datasets to a pool which would be shared by other workers, with the eventual aim of carrying out a quantitative evaluation of handwriting recognition algorithms. A working group developed the specification of a common format which allowed data specifying pen pressure, time and other parameters. This was distributed via `ftp` in the form of a call for participation (Guyon *et al.*, 1994b) and offered payment for large donations of quality data. The call was managed in collaboration with NIST and others. A total of 36 institutes provided 54 datasets making a total of nearly 5 million characters. So far no benchmark testing has taken place since the participants have not yet stated their readiness. The amount and diversity of the datasets may be causing difficulty.

3.1.5. *Theoretical work*

In parallel with the preparation of datasets, theoretical studies have been carried out on the design of datasets for (i) testing recognition rate and (ii) inter-system comparison. Dataset parameters of size and coverage are shown to be related to recognition rate, data variance and confidence level sought. Other work has examined the issue of the ratio of classifiers training data to testing data (Guyon *et al.*, 1998).

3.1.6. *Lessons to be learned*

The number of initiatives indicates that the OCR community has accepted that datasets have a role to play in assessing the performance of systems and algorithms. The response from commercial suppliers of OCR technology is that the use of ground-truthed datasets form part of the normal development process. The cost of collecting quality data is high and it makes sense to share quality data where possible. Companies have acquired their own very large and challenging datasets as part of their internal resources.

The best successes in the use of datasets seem to have been when a very precise task has been addressed with the support of an end-user— either the user of a system or the researchers themselves—to ensure that the effort is relevant to their needs. Great attention must be paid to the quality of the data and the ground truth if the data are to be of use. Although the task of assigning ground truth to isolated characters and words may seem simple, identifying characters within cursive script or zones within documents is much harder. Quality control becomes a very real issue for large datasets. This makes it vital to carefully develop and independently validate a specification of ground truth. Sufficient resources must be dedicated to the collection and verification process. Workshops are an important mechanism for obtaining feedback. Such initiatives require continued support over several years.

3.2. OPTICAL FLOW

Perhaps the most significant piece of genuine performance characterization in this area is that undertaken on optical flow by Barron and colleagues (Barron *et al.*, 1994; Beauchemin and Barron, 1995). In this work, most of the major approaches to optical flow were implemented and evaluated on the same image sequences. What is most significant about this work is not just that the methods have been implemented and compared, but that *both the data and the source code* are available on the Internet (Barron, 1993); about 300 people have downloaded the code. This serves two purposes:

- other researchers may verify that they reproduce the published results on their own hardware and software;
- researchers may compare their own algorithms with these 'benchmark' ones;
- improvements to the algorithms may be fed back to the community via updates to the code (though this does not appear to have happened in practice).

A further interesting fact emerged from this work: Barron *et al.* were unable to produce working implementation of some published approaches. The obvious implication from this is that the published accounts of the techniques are in some way inadequate: the principal purpose of publication is, after all, to provide sufficient detail for subsequent workers to reproduce the work.

An extension of this argument suggests that vision researchers should be much more ready to publish their work in a form that makes it more accessible. As recounted in a recent article (Clark and Courtney, 1996), the best way to achieve this is likely to be via an "electronic" journal in which authors are encouraged to submit both their software and data. In fact, the first issue of such a journal has recently appeared (MIT Press, 1996).[2]

3.3. FACES

The most widely-collected database appears to be of faces. The major factor in this is probably the ease of collection: cameras, room illumination and capture systems are all designed to with the observation of people in mind; and it is very easy to capture images of a few tens of people in a University group or research institution. This is what has generally been done, from (Sakai et al., 1972) onwards.

Conversely, large-scale (thousands of individuals, say) collection of databases is harder. People in research groups are used to acting as 'guinea pigs' and their permission may be assumed implicitly. However, larger-scale collection necessarily involves the general public, at which point some care is needed to verify that the data are collected legally. In the UK for example, the constraints of the *Data Protection Act* requires that individuals are aware of the location of the database; and they must be able to access, and perhaps change, the data that describe them.

A number of popular databases are compared in Table I. It will be apparent from this that, even though most of the databases are intended to be used for face recognition, there is a wide variation in image size, presence or absence of colour, number of subjects, and so on.

A recent comparison of results obtained using the Olivetti database is described in (Lucas, 1997) and summarized in Table II (which is taken from the paper). As well as showing a reasonable spread in error rates, the table indicates a wide variation in both training time and classification (*i.e.,* execution) time. The latter figures, which are rarely quoted in the literature, are actually rather important: many face recognition tasks need to run in near-real-time and any technique that takes longer than, say, ten seconds per face is unlikely to find practical use.

At the time of writing, the FERET database (Phillips et al., 1997) is by far the most comprehensive. It has the largest number of individuals, though even FERET is an order of magnitude smaller than would be required by, say, the UK Police. Associated with the database there is a testing protocol, discussed in (Phillips et al., 1997). Indeed, there are two distinct FERET evaluations, performed on the same datasets: one is completely automatic, while the second provides eye locations. One aspect of the testing procedure

---

[2] See http://mitpress.mit.edu/e-journals/Videre/

involves testing on totally unseen images; this is particularly valuable as it emulates what would happen operationally.

TABLE I. Characteristics of Popular Face Databases

Name	#subjects	#images	Image size	Comments
Bern	30	450	512×342	frontal and profile views
CMU	507	130	various	used for face detection
Essex CS	398	7960	196×196	JPEG coded
Essex ESE	10	4000	360×288	motion sequences
FERET	1199	14126	384×256	monochrome; requires license
Leiden	578	1156	175×270	19th century portrait photos
Manchester	30	690	512×512	monochrome
MIT	16	432	480×512	monochrome
M2VTS	37	185	286×350	has audio
Olivetti	40	400	92×112	monochrome
Weizmann	28	842	512×352	includes 3 expressions

TABLE II. Comparison of Recognition Results from Olivetti Database

Method	Error rate (%)	Training time	Classification time
PDBNN	4.0	20 min	< 0.1 sec
SOM+CN	3.8	4 hour	< 0.5 sec
top-down HMM	13.0	n/a	n/a
pseudo-2D HMM	5.0	n/a	240 sec
eigenface	10.0	n/a	n/a
n-tuple	14.0	0.9 sec	0.025 sec
continuous n-tuple	2.7	0.9 sec	0.33 sec
nearest-neighbour	3.7	0 sec	1 sec

Despite the extensive collection of images in the FERET database, it is not without shortcomings: Asian face types are well-represented but apparently negro types are not. Subjects do not wear spectacles. Although such shortcomings are fairly easily rectified, they are indicative of the magnitude of the task of collecting a representative database that does not prejudice the evaluation procedure.

4. The Need to Design Databases

The previous section illustrates an important principle in the use of databases for meaningful performance characterization: *databases must be representative of the problem.* For example, the comparatively poor representation of particular ethnic types in the FERET database may not be a problem in the context of face recognition in north America but it would be in, say, Zimbabwe.

As well as comprising appropriate types of imagery, databases need to have representative training and test components. Concentrating on face databases for the moment, UK law (as enshrined in the *Police and Criminal Evidence Act*) constrains the number of images of an individual that may be held by police authorities—and only images of convicted people may be retained following criminal proceedings. In designing a vision system to search an online database, it is important that the system is developed so as to use a small number of images for training (assuming training is required at all, of course: some face recognition techniques do not), and this impacts upon the database that is used.

The size of database is also an important factor that is often overlooked. In the first author's work on the recognition of remotely-sensed spectra, for example, a technique based on genetic optimization that attempted to identify a test spectrum as a mixture of seven laboratory-measured 'template' spectra was found to be very effective. However, when the number of spectra was increased to a more realistic 160, the genetic optimization failed to converge to acceptable values within a reasonable amount of time (Clark and Clark, 1997). In the context of, say, face recognition, a technique needs to be able to identify a reasonable (and yet reasonably small) number of matches in a database comprising hundreds of thousands (Essex Police has a database of roughly 50,000 people). This is well beyond anything that has been tried in the research community. There has been some recent work (Guyon *et al.*, 1998) exploring the size of database that is needed to give particular error rates but it is certain that more research into this topic is required.

It will be apparent from this discussion that thought needs to be given to the *design of databases* if they are to be used for realistic performance characterization. No longer will we be able to capture a few images of our colleagues or digitize a few textures from a book and use them to prove the effectiveness of a vision technique. Moreover, the database that is used must be representative of the problem being addressed, in terms of the overall size, the constituencies sampled, and the proportion available for training.

5. The Need to Design Experiments

Hand in hand with the need to design databases in the context of the problem being addressed goes the need *to design experiments* that will provide unequivocal evidence of the success or otherwise of a technique. In the vision community, there is a welcome move towards quoting measures such as false alarm rates (*i.e.*, the numbers of false negatives, false positives, etc) and showing ROC curves when assessing techniques; but comparisons of these measures for different algorithms assessed on the same datasets are still largely subjective.

There is, however, a large body of literature—and well-established techniques—on how such comparisons should be designed and performed, much of it concerned with medicine and the social sciences. Typically, one starts with the null hypothesis (*i.e.*, that the new technique is no better, on the average, than the old) and uses statistical arguments based on experiments to indicate the likelihood of the hypothesis (*e.g.*, (Manly, 1991)). Although a number of vision techniques include these types of considerations, the authors have seen very few (e.g., (Wilson, 1993; Guyon *et al.*, 1998)) where null-hypothesis testing is used to justify the claim that a new technique improves (or, indeed, does not improve) upon an established one; and this is in direct comparison to most other areas of science where statistical testing plays a rôle.

To be able to make such comparisons sensibly and in a realistic timescale, software tools are required to automate the process. Such a tool, HATE, is described in (Courtney *et al.*, 1997), though the statistical information gathered during the testing process needs to be improved. The most important point, however, is that a protocol that involves such a tool both lays down the methodology for conducting experiments *and*, by providing standard test cases, defines the yardstick by which techniques are measured and compared. This is quite a responsibility!

6. Concluding Remarks

The use of databases of test imagery is an essential component of any scheme to carry out meaningful comparisons of vision techniques, a fact that is now becoming apparent in the vision community. A survey of available image databases is under way and this chapter provides preliminary findings from it. An area where the use of databases of test imagery has proven valuable is discussed and one area in which databases are currently proving helpful is described. It certainly seems that the OCR community has the most experience in both gathering significant databases and using them to evaluate vision systems.

Even when the characterization of the performance of vision algorithms by means of evaluation on common data becomes well-established, there will be a need to treat the comparisons with care. Experience from other image-related disciplines indicates that simple objective measures do not necessarily measure what one wants; and it is important that the database used provides an acceptable model of a real problem. Moreover, the comparisons of techniques should be carried out using statistically-based techniques developed in other disciplines and practiced widely throughout science.

Finally, it must be pointed out that any comparisons of computer vision techniques actually compare the *software implementations of techniques* and not the mathematical descriptions of techniques: there is a tendency to assume these two things are equivalent—but they are not, due to the finite arithmetic of computers if nothing else. Comparing a careful implementation of a new technique with a hasty and inadequate implementation of an established one is pointless. The development of a common set of software implementations of vision techniques that can be used by the entire community is an important factor in the viability of carrying out comparisons of performance. The *Image Understanding Environment* project, though initiated for quite different reasons, may have much to offer here.

Acknowledgements

Thanks go to Tom Nartker (University of Nevada at Las Vegas), Mike Garris and Stan Janet (NIST), Tapas Kanungo (Caere) and Isabelle Guyon, all of whom were kind enough to respond in detail to our questions about the evaluation of OCR systems. This work was funded by the EU via ECVnet (project EP 8212).

References

Barron, J.L. (1993) Software for the analysis of optical flow techniques, ftp://csd.uwo.ca/pub/vision/.

Barron, J.L., Fleet, D.J. and Beauchemin, S.S. (1994) Performance of optical flow techniques, *International Journal of Computer Vision*, 12(1):43–77.

Beauchemin, S.S. and Barron, J.L. (1995) The computation of optical flow, *ACM Computing Surveys*, 27(3):433–467.

Clark, A.F. and Courtney, P. (1996) Vision online: Electronic publishing for computer vision, http://peipa.essex.ac.uk/vision-online/.

Clark, C. and Clark, A.F. (1997) Automatic spectral classification of imaging spectrometer data, *Proceedings of the International Conference on Image Processing and its Applications*, Dublin.

Courtney, P., Thacker, N.A. and Clark, A.F. (1997) Algorithmic modelling for performance evaluation, *Machine Vision and Applications*, 9:219–228.

Garris, M.D. (1993) Methods for evaluating the performance of systems intended to recognize characters from image data scanned from forms, Technical report, NIST, Gaithersburg, Maryland, USA, available at
http://www.itl.nist.gov/div894/vip/pubs.html#ocr.

Guyon, I., Schomaker, L., Plamondon, R., Liberman, M. and Janet, S. (1994a) UNIPEN project of on-line data exchange and benchmarks, In *International Conference on Pattern Recognition ICPR94*, Jerusalem, Israel, IEEE Computer Society Press, 29–33.

Guyon, I., Schomaker, L., Janet, S., Liberman, M. and Plamondon, R. (1994b) First UNIPEN benchmark of on-line handwriting recognizers organized by NIST, Technical report, ATT Bell Laboratories.

Guyon, I., Haralick, R.M., Hull, J. and Phillips, I. (1996) *Data sets for OCR and document image understanding*, World Scientific Publishing Company.

Guyon, I., Makhoul, J., Schwartz, R. and Vapnik, V. (1998) What size test set gives good error rates? *IEEE PAMI*, 20(1):52–64.

Hull, J.J. (1994) A database for handwritten text recognition research, *IEEE PAMI*, 16(5):550–554.

Lucas, S.M. (1997) Face recognition with the continuous n-tuple classifier, Clark, A.F. (ed.), *Proceedings of the British Machine Vision Conference, BMVC97*, BMVA, 222–231.

Manly, B.F.J. (1991) *Randomization and Monte Carlo Methods in Biology*, Chapman and Hall.

MIT Press (1996) Videre: Call for papers, http://peipa.essex.ac.uk/videre/.

Phillips, P.J., Moon, H., Rauss, P. and Rizvi, S. (1997) The FERET September 1996 database and evaluation procedure, In: Bigun, J., Chollet, G. and Borgefors, G. (eds.), *First International Conference on Audio- and Video-Based Biometric Person Authentication*, Springer-Verlag, volume LNCS 1206, 395–402.

Phillips, I.T. (1998) *Methodologies for Using UW Databases for OCR and Image Understanding Systems*.

Rice, S.V., Jenkins, F.R. and Nartker, T.A. (1995) The fouth annual test of OCR accuracy, Technical Report ISRI TR-95-04, Information Science Research Institute, University of Nevada, Las Vegas.

Rice, S.V., Jenkins, F.R. and Nartker, T.A. (1996) The fifth annual test of OCR accuracy, Technical Report ISRI TR-96-01, Information Science Research Institute, University of Nevada, Las Vegas.

Sakai, T., Nagao, M. and Kanade, T. (1972) Computer analysis and classification of photographs of human faces, In *Proc. First USA-Japan Computer Conference*, 55–62.

Wilson, C.L. (1993) Evaluation of character recognition systems, In *Neural networks for signal processing III*, New York, USA, IEEE, 485–496, available at
http://www.itl.nist.gov/div894/vip/pubs.html#ocr.

QUALITY IN COMPUTER VISION

RADEK MAŘÍK
ProTys s.r.o.
Americka 24, 120 00 Praha 2
Vinohrady, Czech Republic

1. Introduction

Computer vision as any other scientific field can be divided into theoretical and experimental parts. A set of reasoned ideas proposed in the theoretical part is verified by experiments. Furthermore, discernible discrepancies between theory and real-world facts and events are discovered during experiments. Thus, both theoretical and experimental parts are coupled creating a spiral on which a theoretical model is improved in the sense that discrepancies become smaller and smaller. The discrepancies are often measured by differences between theoretical and measured quantities if both are well established as they are in physics. However, we are still searching for such simple quantities in a number of fields including computer vision. The traditional solution is to define a set of performance indices and interpretation rules. From this point of view, it sounds rather curiously that performance evaluation of computer vision algorithms measuring discrepancies is not wide supported and must be still justified (Forstner, 1996).

Another aspect of theory is its preparedness to be applied. We are usually interested if a theory can be simplified according to a given precision and accuracy and if we are able to estimate cost of application. In real world, the application is also driven by customers who set their own priorities. The notion of quality can be used in these cases where we consider both performance of products and customer's point of view. Theory of quality used mainly in manufacturing has been developed significantly during the last ten years (Garvin, 1996; Hall and Wilson, 1997; Khattree, 1996; Kolarik, 1995; Logothetis and Wynn, 1989; Montgomery, 1991; Morisio and Tsoukias, 1997; Phadke, 1989; Ross, 1988; Taguchi, 1986; Taguchi *et al.*, 1989).

R. Klette et al. (eds.), Performance Characterization in Computer Vision, 41–51.

It is not difficult to demonstrate that even a simple task in computer vision leads to rather complex performance analysis evaluating a given algorithm using notions such as time and memory complexity, possible configurations of algorithms, precision, accuracy, numerical precision, resolution, scale, sensitivity to variations, recognition rate, evaluation of non-differentiable techniques, reliability, dependency on cooperating modules, detection of systematic errors, and tuning of control parameters (Pyle, 1996a; Pyle, 1996b; Trivedi et al., 1993; Woodside, 1993). In fact, any manufacturing process is designed under very similar conditions. One must evaluate and optimize a production line consisting of many different components as we do for complex vision algorithms.

Quality of manufacturing processes is assessed using theory of quality. However, not many people of computer vision community are aware about theory of quality. It could be used as a *top level framework* for performance analysis in computer vision. Thus, the main contribution of the theory to computer computer vision would be top-down methodology how to assess performance of complex configurations of computer vision algorithms. The important point is that differentiable functions (Haralick, 1994) or special approaches to non-linear cases using for example ROC technique are not assumed, at least at the top level of treatment. Better communication between researchers and practitioners supported by the theory and its unified concept is also considerable.

In this chapter the main idea of theory of quality is explained using simple examples applied to computer vision. We will present briefly selected notions and demonstrate how performance analysis of computer vision algorithms could benefit from clearly defined results and concepts of theory of quality. The presented methodology is intended to simplify design and using of performance indices. That is achieved by separation of objective (theory) and subjective (customer) inputs. Details can be found in the provided references. The presentation of the theory follows mainly the book by Kolarik (1995).

2. Concept of Quality

It is possible to find a number of definitions of quality (Kolarik, 1995). All of them try to express that **ideal quality** that a customer can expect is that every product delivers the target performance each time the product is used, under all intended operating conditions, and throughout its intended life, with no harmful side effects. A notion of **customer** defined as anyone or anything who receives or is affected by the product or process is the important part of the definition of quality. Thus, users or integrators of computer vision algorithms can be consider as an example of customers.

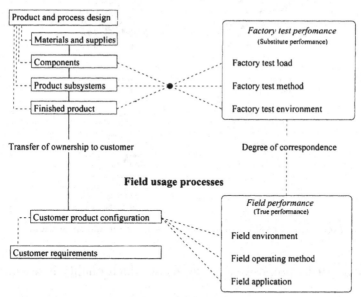

Figure 1. Concept of performance

Following Taguchi (1986), we measure the quality of a product in terms of the total loss to society due to functional variation and harmful side effects.

Figure 1 depicts both producer's world as well as the customer's field world. **True product performance** is determined in the field by the customer. That means, customers, by definition, determine true performance as a result of their field applications, environment, and methods of operation. On the other hand, producers, in computer vision researchers-developers, determine **substitute performance** based on their test loads, test environments, and test methods.

It is difficult to measure true performance directly as each individual customer would measure performance. Therefore, substitute performance measures, both qualitative and quantitative, are typically used. In computer vision field researchers often call these substitute measures as performance indices. To be able to measure performance, it must be clearly defined in terms of a measurable entity or entities, usually expressed in technical language. Furthermore, sensors must exist to measure the level of performance or models must exist to predict the level of performance. Two general types of performance measures are

— variables measure, either continuous or discrete,

— and attributes measure, for example such as classification labels to be edge or non-edge.

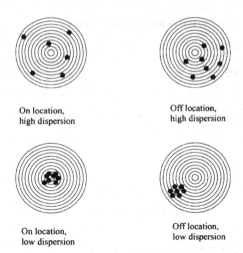

Figure 2.   Possible configurations of location and dispersion.

Taguchi (1989) proposes three levels at which quality is designed into products:

- **System design** applies to the functional level where relevant product or processes technologies and approaches are identified. In computer vision, we could say that at this level one selects or proposes a method with a necessary technical support.
- At the second level, so called **parameter design**, we focus on determining a "best" level, or target, for the design parameters identified and selected at the system design level. These parameters are free, undetermined parameters of a product. For example, one needs to choose a size of a filter mask even its coefficients are designed in an optimal way at the system design level.
- **Tolerance design** is the final step, where the parameter tolerances are set. The point is to recognize that production costs excalate at nonlinear rates, as tolerances are tightened. Published papers in computer vision usually do not exploit this step. Its omission results in difficulties during searching for a right configuration of free parameters because their tolerances are too narrow.

So called **target values** and **cost-performance calculation** are used to guide tolerancing when possible. **The ideal case** is to produce close to target with a small enough variation such that we can virtually eliminate sorting inspection. Performance measurement (to target) involves two critical parameters: location, relative to a specific point, and dispersion, relative to the center of measurements. Figure 2 illustrates possible configurations of location and dispersion. Of course, the on location, low dispersion case is the most desirable case. Therefore, it is declared as the case of the high-

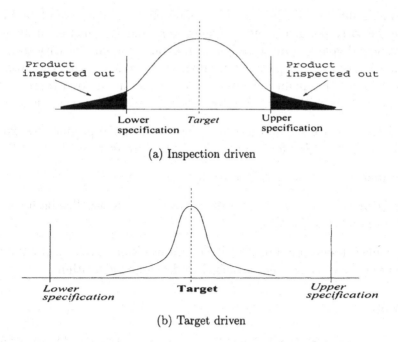

(a) Inspection driven

(b) Target driven

Figure 3. Production strategy

est performance. For example, in an ideal case a color based recognition system would classify correctly a yellow ball under changing illumination conditions.

It was shown that it is better to develop a production focused on explicit targets, rather than on broad plus-minus specification, see Figure 3. In plus-minus specifications, called usually **the goal post strategy**, we emphasize sorting and inspecting items out of the "tails" beyond the specification limits. Corner detectors, based on construction of a measure expressing how an tested part of an image is close to ideal corner, are examples of the goal post strategy. In **the target case**, we may still use specifications. However, we focus on the location of the distribution, or center portion, while reducing or controlling the dispersion. A true six-sigma process, an example of the target oriented strategy, introduced by Motorola will yield 2 defects per billion assuming normal distribution. In practice, it is usually stated 3.4 or fewer defect per million opportunities. This case includes a $\pm$ 1.5 - sigma shift in the mean.

The fundamental principle of Taguchi's **robust design** is to improve the quality of a product by minimizing the effect of the causes of variation without eliminating the causes. The first goal is to reduce the variation of a product's function in the customer's environment. The second goal is to ensure the correspondence between laboratory and customer environments. The principal goal of robust design is to exploit the nonlinearity to find a combination of product parameter values that gives the smallest variation in the value of the quality characteristic around the desired target value. One manipulates with three kinds of factors to reach the optimum setting:

Signal factors are set by the user of operator of the product to express the intended value for the response of the product.

Noise factors cannot be controlled by the designer.

Control factors can be specified freely by the designer. The designer can determine their best values.

Thus, robust design could be used in computer vision to reduce or eliminate a number of free parameters attached to developed algorithms.

3. Tools

There are a number of tools used to solve quality-related problems. Besides design of experiments and response surface theory, the most famous tools are old Japanese tools and new tools. Seven old tools, i.e. cause-effect diagram, stratification analysis, check sheet, histogram, scatter diagram, Pareto diagram, and control charts are said to solve that as much as 95 percent of the problems.

Seven new tools, i.e. relations diagram, affinity diagram, systematic diagram, matrix diagram, matrix data analysis, process decision program chart, and arrow diagram impact more strategic quality planning. They support developmental efforts in formulating strategic quality plans, as well as they provide a forum and a format that encourage communication and consensus building.

Some of the old tools, such as histogram, scatter diagram, check sheet, or stratification are already used in computer vision in everyday work. However, computer vision community could also utilize the others as well.

3.1. CAUSE-EFFECT DIAGRAM

Cause-effect diagram, sometimes referred to as a "fish-bone" diagram, is a diagram, where the effect is contained in a box on the right side and its causes appear on the left side. It promotes better communication. It forces us to discover, even someti_nes through speculation, many possible causes for a specific effect. In our opinion, the important point is, that the causes are *immediately visible* and understandable. The author of a

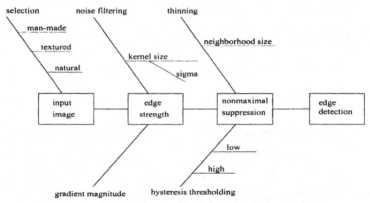

Figure 4. Cause-effect diagram made for Canny detector

diagram is pushed to state in open way what effect and causes he deals with. The cause-effect diagram made for Canny algorithm based on the discussion in (Heath *et al.*, 1997)is depicted on Figure 4. We can find there the main effects in the boxes and their dependence on main causes and their parameters.

3.2. AFFINITY DIAGRAM

The new Japanese tools are intended to be useful in high-level quality planning. **Affinity diagram** as a collection of facts, opinions, and ideas is an excellent tool to use to start out a cross-functional team effort, where

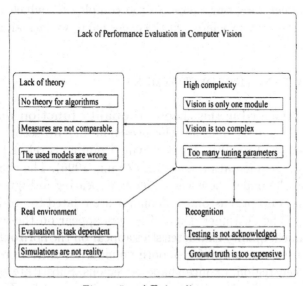

Figure 5. Affinity diagram

          R. Mařík

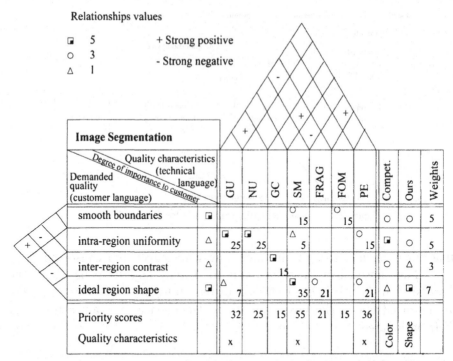

Figure 6. Quality function deployment

the team has a broad theme. To illustrate it, we tried to group the section titles of the paper (Forstner, 1996), see Figure 5. A simple interpretation of the conclusion could be the following one: we deal with real, natural environment. Therefore, our tasks are too complex for which there is not sufficient recognition by society. On the other hand, we lack an appropriate theory.

3.3. QUALITY FUNCTION DEPLOYMENT

The last tool presented in this chapter is **quality function deployment** that is based on matrix diagram (Franceschini and Rossetto, 1997). It is often called house of quality. The following example is related to Zhang's survey on image segmentation methods (Zhang, 1996). The characteristics are taken from the paper, however numbers appearing in Figure 6 are fabricated. In this concept, customers demands are related to product quality characteristics. The customer demand factors appear on the vertical axis, while the technical quality characteristics appear on the horizontal axis. Let us state the customer can prefer smooth boundaries, uniform regions, high contrast between region, or nice shape of regions. Substitute performance measures can be defined as it is proposed in the paper by Zhang (1996).

We choose only their subset: the gray-level uniformity GU, the normalized uniformity NU, the gray-level contrast measure GC, the shape measure SM, the fragmentation FRAG, the mean square distance figure of merit FOM, and the probability error PE.

General relationships are indicated in the rectangular body of the matrix. The strength of the relationships is represented by graphical symbols with associated weights. The triangular relationships matrices at the top and on the left side serve to document the interrelationships between quality characteristics.

At first, this diagram can be used to discuss the correspondence between substitute performance and true performance. Secondly, we can estimate constraints for a new algorithm. The diagram contains the preference of the customer and a competitor algorithm, for instance the current best algorithm. We can define our preference and assign the weights to it as it is shown in the last column. In this example, we can call the competitor strategy as color-focused because it supports segmentation resulting in nice uniform regions. Our preference addresses the spatial domain. Let us call it a shape-focused strategy. Now we can calculate a score for each cell as the result of multiplication of relationship weights by preference weights. Then we can sum down each column to obtain its quality characteristic priority score. We can conclude that our new algorithm must be very good in technical indices SM, GU, and PE(marked by the cross) by comparing of the result priority scores. Alternatively, this pattern of indices can be used for the selection of the best known algorithm solving our task.

4. Conclusions

In this chapter, we presented basic principles of theory of quality. It was not our goal to present here other parts of the theory like error propagation, factor analysis, design of experiments, ANOVA, response surface and reliability serving mainly for *quantification of the presented concepts* (Allan, 1993; Clifford, 1973; Nedialkov, 1994). It is a pity that the strategies recommended by theory of quality are followed only partially in a number of cases of vision algorithms designs. For example, results are often presented without confidence intervals. Although, theory of quality is used mainly in industrial environment, its results could be reflected into computer vision fields. It does not solve performance analysis of computer vision algorithms entirely. However, we could accept many well founded notions and trends. Thus, the development of vision algorithms could be speed up. Furthermore, the description of algorithms would be much closer to accepted standards in industrial environment.

References

Allan, A.L. (1993) *Practical Surveying and Computations*, Butterworth-Heinemann Ltd, Oxford OX2 8DP, second edition.

Clifford, A.A. (1973) *Multivariate Error Analysis*, Applied Science Publishers Ltd, Ripple Road, Barking Essex, England.

Forstner, W. (1996) 10 pros and cons against performance characterization of vision algorithms, Christensen, H.I., Forstner, W. and Madsen, C.B. (eds.), *Workshop on Performance Characteristics of Vision Algorithms, Proceedings*, April 19, Cambridge, UK, 13–29, http://www.vision.auc.dk/~hic/performance-ws.html. Sponsored by European Network of Excellence in Computer Vision, http://afrodite.dist.unige.it.

Franceschini, F. and Rossetto, S. (1997) Design for quality: Selecting a products technical features. *Quality Engineering*, 9(4):681–688.

Garvin, D.A. (1996) Competing on the eight dimensions of quality, *IEEE Engineering Managament Review*, pages 15–23, Spring 1996.

Hall, T. and Wilson, D. (1997) Views of software quality: a field report, *IEE Proceedings Software Engineering*, 144(2):111–118.

Haralick, R.M. (1994) Propagating covariance in computer vision, *12th International Conference on Pattern Recognition* (Jerusalem, Israel), volume I, IEEE Computer Society Press, Washington, DC, 493–498.

Heath, M.D., Sarkar, S., Sanocki, T. and Bowyer, K.W. (1997) A robust visual method for assessing the relative performance of edge-detection algorithms, *IEEE PAMI*, 19(12):1338–1369.

Khattree R. (1996) Robust parameter design: A response surface approach, *Journal of Quality Technology*, 28(2):187–198.

Kolarik, W.J. (1995) *Creating Quality: Concepts, Systems, Strategies, and Tools*, McGraw-Hill, Inc.

Logothetis, N. and Wynn, H.P. (1989) *Quality through Design, Experimental Design, Off-line Quality Control and Taguchi's Contributions*, Clarendon Press, Oxford.

Montgomery, D.C. (1991) *Design and Analysis of Experiments*, John Wiley and Sons, third edition.

Morisio, M. and Tsoukias, A. (1997) IusWare: a methodology for the evaluation and selection of software products, *IEE Proceedings Software Engineering*, 144(3):162–174.

Nedialkov, N.S. (1994) Precision control and exception handling in scientific computing, Master's thesis, University of Toronto, Department of Computer Science.

Phadke, M.S. (1989) *Quality Engineering using Robust Design*, Prentice-Hall International, Inc.

Pyle, I. (1996a) Performance considerations in COMPLEMENT, *IEEE Symposium and Workshop on Engineering of Computer-Based Systems*, IEEE Computer Society Press, 206–213.

Pyle, I. (1996b) Quality in software based systems, *IEEE Symposium and Workshop on Engineering of Computer-Based Systems*, IEEE Computer Society Press, 214–218.

Ross, P.J. (1988) *Taguchi Techniques for Quality Engineering, Loss Function, Orthogonal Experiments, Parameter and Tolerance Design*, McGraw-Hill Book Company.

Taguchi, G. (1986) *Introduction to Quality Engineering*, Asian Productivity Organization, 4-14, Akasaka 8-chome, Minato-ku, Tokyo 107, Japan.

Taguchi, G., Elsayed, E.A. and Hsiang, T.C. (1989) *Quality Engineering in Production Systems*, McGraw-Hill Book Company.

Trivedi, K.S., Ciardo, G., Malhotra, M. and Sahner, R.A. (1993) Dependability and Perfomability Analysis, Donatiello, L. and Nelson, R. (eds.), *Performance Evaluation of Computer and Communication Systems*, Joint Tutorial Papers of Performance '93 and Sigmetrics '93, Springer-Verlag, 587–612.

Woodside, C.M. (1993) Performance Engineering of Client-Server Systems, Donatiello, L. and Nelson, R. (eds.), *Performance Evaluation of Computer and Communication Systems*, Joint Tutorial Papers of Performance '93 and Sigmetrics '93, Springer-Verlag, 394–410.

Zhang, Y.J. (1996) A survey on evaluation methods for image segmentation, *PR*, 29(8):1335–1346.

Part II

Methodical Aspects

THE ROLE OF THEORY IN THE EVALUATION OF IMAGE MOTION ALGORITHMS

STEVEN S. BEAUCHEMIN and RUZENA BAJCSY
GRASP Laboratory
Dept. of Engineering and Information Sciences
University of Pennsylvania
Philadelphia PA 19104-6228, USA

1. Introduction

Undeniably, the numerical evaluation of Computer Vision algorithms is of utmost importance. However, often neglected is the role of theoretical knowledge to interpret the numerical performance of those algorithms. In addition, the lack of theoretical research in Computer Vision has long been recognized. In this contribution, we demonstrate that extended theoretical knowledge of a phenomenon enables one to design algorithms that are better suited for the task at hand and to evaluate the theoretical assumptions of other, similar algorithms. For instance, the problem posed by multiple image motions was poorly understood in the frequency domain yet frequency-based multiple motions algorithms were developed. We present algorithms for computing multiple image motions arising from occlusion and translucency which are capable of extracting the information-content of occlusion boundaries and distinguish between those and additive translucency phenomena. These algorithms are based on recent theoretical results on occlusion in the frequency domain and demonstrate that a complete theoretical understanding of a phenomenon is required in order to design adequate algorithms. We conclude by proposing an evaluation protocol which includes theoretical considerations and their influence on the numerical evaluation of algorithms.

1.1. IMAGE MOTION

The importance of motion in image processing cannot be understated: in particular, approximations to image motion may be used to estimate 3D scene properties and motion parameters from a moving visual sensor

R. Klette et al. (eds.), Performance Characterization in Computer Vision, 55–67.
© 2000 *Kluwer Academic Publishers.*

(Longuet-Higgins, 1981), to perform motion segmentation (Murray and Buxton, 1987), to compute the focus of expansion and time-to-collision (Overington, 1987), to perform motion-compensated image encoding (Musmann *et al.*, 1985), to compute stereo disparity (Jenkin *et al.*, 1991) and to measure biological parameters in medical imagery (Prince and McVeigh, 1992).

Based on recent theoretical developments in discontinuous motion, we devise multiple motion algorithms. We consider 1D and 2D signals, adopt a constant model of velocity and use a robust statistical procedure to extract multiple motions from local frequency spectra. The motion information provided by the algorithms includes single velocity, multiple (2) velocities, assessment of occlusion and, upon occlusion events, the orientation of the occlusion boundary and the identification of the occluding signal.

1.2. LITERATURE SURVEY

Computing multiple motions is a complex and rarely undertaken task. Indeed, most of the existing optical flow methods that have appeared in the literature make an explicit use of the single motion hypothesis. However, at motion discontinuities, where the information content of a signal mostly resides, the hypothesis is violated. Area-based and feature-based correlation techniques are equally sensitive to occlusion as local image structures and features appear and disappear from one image to the next. To further complicate matters, regularization techniques which impose a degree of continuity to optical flow are also clearly inadequate over occlusion boundaries. However, in the more recent research in optical flow, the non-linear, discontinuous and multiple-valued nature of image motion in the coordinates of the image plane has been recognized (Beauchemin and Barron, 1995).

In order to allow multiple motion events in optical flow estimation processes, a number of strategies have been devised, such as strong intensity gradients acting as inhibitors of flow coherence (Nagel, 1987) and robust estimators designed to capture dominant motions (Black, 1991). Other techniques such as clustering (Schunck, 1989), superposed motion layers and distributions (Shizawa and Mase, 1991; Wang and Adelson, 1993), parametric models of motion with discontinuous functions (Negahdaripour and Lee, 1992; Black and Jepson, 1994) and mixtures of probability densities (Jepson and Black, 1993) have appeared.

Our approach emanates from recent theoretical results (Beauchemin and Barron, 1997a; Beauchemin and Barron, 1997b; Beauchemin *et al.*, 1997) describing the Fourier structure of occlusion and translucency phenomena for constant and linear models of optical flow and points to an evaluation protocol capable of assessing the impact of theoretical considerations onto the numerical evaluation of algorithms.

2. Structure of Occlusion

We proceed to describe the structure of occlusion events in the frequency domain for 1D and 2D signals composed of an arbitrary number of distinct frequencies.

Let $\mathbf{I}_1(x)$ and $\mathbf{I}_2(x)$ be 1D functions satisfying Dirichlet conditions such that they may be expressed as complex exponential series expansions

$$\mathbf{I}_1(x) = \sum_{n=-\infty}^{\infty} c_{1n} e^{ink_1 x} \quad \text{and} \quad \mathbf{I}_2(x) = \sum_{n=-\infty}^{\infty} c_{2n} e^{ink_2 x}, \tag{1}$$

where n is integer, c_{1n} and c_{2n} are complex coefficients and k_1 and k_2 are the fundamental frequencies of both signals.

Let $\mathbf{I}_1(x,t) = \mathbf{I}_1(v_1(x,t))$ and $\mathbf{I}_2(x,t) = \mathbf{I}_2(v_2(x,t))$, where $v_i = x - a_i t$. The frequency spectrum of the occlusion is

$$
\begin{aligned}
\hat{\mathbf{I}}(k,\omega) = {} & \pi \sum_{n=i-\infty}^{\infty} c_{1n} \delta(k - nk_1, \omega + nk_1 a_1) \\
& + (1 - \pi) \sum_{n=-\infty}^{\infty} c_{2n} \delta(k - nk_2, \omega + nk_2 a_2) \\
& + i \sum_{n=-\infty}^{\infty} \left(\frac{c_{2n} \delta(ka_1 + \omega - nk_2 \Delta a)}{(k - nk_2)} - \frac{c_{1n} \delta(ka_1 + \omega)}{(k - nk_1)} \right),
\end{aligned}
\tag{2}
$$

where $\Delta a = a_1 - a_2$.

In the 1D case, equation (2) reveals that the frequency spectra of both signals are preserved to within scaling factors. In addition, the Dirac delta functions $\delta(ka_{12} + \omega)$ and $\delta(ka_1 + \omega - k_2 \Delta a)$ constitute linear spectra, intersecting the frequencies of both the occluding and occluded signals, and are oriented in the direction of the constraint line pertaining to the occluding signal. Figure 1 shows a typical example with 1D translating sinusoids in an occlusion scene.

Similarly, The frequency spectra for 2D signals are planar and preserved to within scaling factors under occlusion. In addition, the distortion cast by the occlusion boundary fits oriented lines parallel to the planar spectrum of the occluding signal.

Equation (2) me bay generalized to 2D image signals: Let $\mathbf{I}_1(\mathbf{x})$ and $\mathbf{I}_2(\mathbf{x})$ be 2D functions satisfying Dirichlet conditions such that they may be expressed as complex exponential series expansions

$$\mathbf{I}_1(\mathbf{x}) = \sum_{n=-\infty}^{\infty} c_{1n} e^{i\mathbf{x}^T N \mathbf{k}_1} \quad \text{and} \quad \mathbf{I}_2(\mathbf{x}) = \sum_{n=-\infty}^{\infty} c_{2n} e^{i\mathbf{x}^T N \mathbf{k}_2}, \quad (3)$$

where $\mathbf{n} = (n_x, n_y)^T$ and $N = \mathbf{n}^T I$ are integers, $\mathbf{x}$ are spatial coordinates, $\mathbf{k}_1 = (k_{1x}, k_{1y})^T$ and $\mathbf{k}_2 = (k_{2x}, k_{2y})^T$ are fundamental frequencies and c_{1n} and c_{2n} are complex coefficients. Let $\mathbf{I}_1(\mathbf{x}, t) = \mathbf{I}_1(\mathbf{v}_1(\mathbf{x}, t))$, $\mathbf{I}_2(\mathbf{x}, t) = \mathbf{I}_2(\mathbf{v}_2(\mathbf{x}, t))$, where $\mathbf{v}_i = \mathbf{x} - \mathbf{a}_i t$, and the occluding boundary be locally represented by:

$$\mathbf{U}(\mathbf{x}) = \begin{cases} 1 & \text{if } \mathbf{x}^T \mathbf{n}_1 \geq 0 \\ 0 & \text{otherwise,} \end{cases} \quad (4)$$

where $\mathbf{n}_1$ is a vector normal to the occluding boundary. The frequency spectrum of the occlusion is

$$\hat{\mathbf{I}}(\mathbf{k}, \omega) = \pi \sum_{n=-\infty}^{\infty} c_{1n} \delta(\mathbf{k} - N\mathbf{k}_1, \omega + \mathbf{a}_1^T N \mathbf{k}_1)$$

$$+ (1-\pi) \sum_{n=-\infty}^{\infty} c_{2n} \delta(\mathbf{k} - N\mathbf{k}_2, \omega + \mathbf{a}_2^T N \mathbf{k}_2)$$

$$+ i \sum_{n=-\infty}^{\infty,} \left(\frac{c_{2n} \delta((\mathbf{k} - N\mathbf{k}_2)^T \mathbf{n}_1^{\perp}, \mathbf{k}^T \mathbf{a}_1 + \omega - \Delta\mathbf{a}^T N \mathbf{k}_2)}{(\mathbf{k} - N\mathbf{k}_2)^T \mathbf{n}_1} \right.$$

$$\left. - \frac{c_{1n} \delta((\mathbf{k} - N\mathbf{k}_1)^T \mathbf{n}_1^{\perp}, \mathbf{k}^T \mathbf{a}_1 + \omega)}{(\mathbf{k} - N\mathbf{k}_1)^T \mathbf{n}_1} \right), \quad (5)$$

where $\Delta\mathbf{a} = \mathbf{a}_1 - \mathbf{a}_2$.

Equation (5) is a generalization of equation (2) from 1D to 2D signals and its geometric interpretation is similar. For instance, frequencies $(N\mathbf{k}_1, -\mathbf{a}_1^T N\mathbf{k}_1)$ and $(N\mathbf{k}_2, -\mathbf{a}_2^T N\mathbf{k}_2)$ fit the constraint planes of the occluding and occluded signals, defined as $\mathbf{k}_1^T \mathbf{a}_1 + \omega = 0$ and $\mathbf{k}^T \mathbf{a}_2 + \omega = 0$. In the distortion term, the Dirac δ function with arguments $(\mathbf{k} - N\mathbf{k}_2)^T \mathbf{n}_1^{\perp}$ and $\mathbf{k}^T \mathbf{a}_1 + \omega - \Delta\mathbf{a}^T N\mathbf{k}_2$ represent a set of lines parallel to the constraint plane of the occluding signal $\mathbf{k}^T \mathbf{a}_1 + \omega = 0$ and, for every discrete frequency $N\mathbf{k}_1$ and $N\mathbf{k}_2$ exhibited by both signals, there is a frequency spectrum fitting the lines given by the intersection of planes $\mathbf{k}^T \mathbf{a}_1 + \omega - \Delta\mathbf{a}^T N\mathbf{k}_2 = 0$ and $(\mathbf{k} - N\mathbf{k}_1)^T \mathbf{n}_1^{\perp} = 0$. The magnitudes of these spectra are determined by their corresponding scaling functions $c_{1n}[(\mathbf{k} - N\mathbf{k}_1)^T \mathbf{n}_1]^{-1}$ and $c_{2n}[(\mathbf{k} - N\mathbf{k}_2)^T \mathbf{n}_1]^{-1}$.

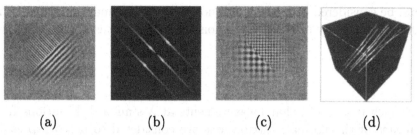

$$(a) \qquad (b) \qquad (c) \qquad (d)$$

Figure 1. **(a)** Gaussian-windowed 1D signal with sinusoidals acting as occluding and occluded surfaces. The occluding signal has spatial frequency $k_1 = \frac{2\pi}{16}$ and velocity $v_1 = (1,1)$. The occluded signal has frequency $k_2 = \frac{2\pi}{8}$ and velocity $v_2 = (-1,1)$; **(b)** Fourier spectrum of (a); **(c)** Gaussian-windowed 2D signal with sinusoidals acting as occluding and occluded surfaces. The occluding signal has spatial frequency $\mathbf{k}_1 = (\frac{2\pi}{16}, \frac{2\pi}{16})$ and velocity $\mathbf{v}_1 = (1,1,1)$. The occluded signal has frequency $\mathbf{k}_2 = (\frac{2\pi}{8}, \frac{2\pi}{8})$ and velocity $\mathbf{v}_2 = (-1,-1,1)$; **(d)** Fourier spectrum of (c).

3. Estimation of Multiple Image Motion

Equations (2) and (5) provide a model of the Fourier spectrum at an occlusion boundary. We devise, for both 1D and 2D image signals, algorithms capable of extracting multiple velocity measurements along with the information-content of occlusion boundaries.

3.1. 1D ALGORITHM

Given a frequency measurement $\hat{\mathbf{m}}_j = (\hat{k}_j, \hat{\omega}_j)^T$, its corresponding velocity estimate is given by $\hat{\mathbf{v}}_i = (-\hat{\omega}_j/\hat{k}_j, 1)^T$ and an error metric corresponding to the angular deviation between a measurement $\hat{\mathbf{m}}_j$ and an estimate of the ith velocity $\hat{\mathbf{v}}_i$, under the assumption that $\theta \approx \sin\theta$, may be defined as (Jepson and Black, 1993):

$$\xi(\hat{\mathbf{m}}_j, \hat{\mathbf{v}}_i) = \frac{\hat{\mathbf{m}}_j^T \hat{\mathbf{v}}_i}{\|\hat{\mathbf{m}}_j\|_2 \|\hat{\mathbf{v}}_i\|_2}. \tag{6}$$

Under the assumption that angular errors are normally distributed, we define a mixture of normal distributions to account for multiple motions as

$$G(\hat{\mathbf{m}}_j) = \sum_{i=0}^{2} \pi_i f_i(\hat{\mathbf{m}}_j, \hat{\mathbf{v}}_i), \tag{7}$$

which is the PDF for measurement $\hat{\mathbf{m}}_j$ and where π_i is a mixture probability. Aside from posing homoscedasticity, we use a uniform outlier distribution. Measurements at a predetermined distance from other distributions should be considered as outliers and not enter the estimation process. The constant probability of observing a noisy measurement is expressed as

$$\frac{1}{\sqrt{2\pi}\sigma_v}e^{\frac{-\lambda^2}{2\sigma_n^2}}, \tag{8}$$

from which it is noted that measurements at λ standard deviations from the means of the normal distributions are considered to be corrupted by noise.

With the hypothesis of homoscedasticity, constant standard deviation and uniform distribution of noisy measurements, we establish the iterative equations for the Expectation-Maximization algorithm. The expectation step is the computation of posterior probabilities, which we write as

$$\hat{\tau}_{ij}^{(k)} = \frac{\hat{\pi}_i^{(k)}e^{\frac{-1}{2\sigma_v^2}\xi^2(\hat{\mathbf{m}}_j, \hat{\mathbf{v}}_i)}}{\sum_{t=1}^{2}\hat{\pi}_t^{(k)}e^{\frac{-1}{2\sigma_v^2}\xi^2(\hat{\mathbf{m}}_j, \hat{\mathbf{v}}_t)} + \hat{\pi}_0^{(k)}e^{\frac{-\lambda^2}{2\sigma_n^2}}} \tag{9}$$

for $i = 1, 2$, the number of normal distributions and $j = 1, \ldots, n$ the number of measurements. For the uniform distribution of noisy measurements we write

$$\hat{\tau}_{0j}^{(k)} = \frac{\hat{\pi}_0^{(k)}e^{\frac{-\lambda^2}{2\sigma_v^2}}}{\sum_{t=1}^{2}\hat{\pi}_t^{(k)}e^{\frac{-1}{2\sigma_v^2}\xi^2(\hat{\mathbf{m}}_j, \hat{\mathbf{v}}_t)} + \hat{\pi}_0^{(k)}e^{\frac{-\lambda^2}{2\sigma_n^2}}} \tag{10}$$

for $j = 1, \ldots, n$. The equations for the maximization step, in which the velocities and mixture probabilities are updated, are written as

$$\hat{\mathbf{v}}_i^{(k+1)} = \frac{\sum_{j=1}^{n}\hat{\tau}_{ij}^{(k)}\kappa(\hat{\mathbf{m}}_j)\hat{\mathbf{m}}_j^{\perp}}{\hat{\pi}_i^{(k)}\sum_{j=1}^{n}\kappa(\hat{\mathbf{m}}_j)} \qquad \hat{\pi}_i^{(k+1)} = \frac{\sum_{j=1}^{n}\kappa(\hat{\mathbf{m}}_j)\hat{\tau}_{ij}^{(k)}}{\sum_{j=1}^{n}\kappa(\hat{\mathbf{m}}_j)}, \tag{11}$$

where $\kappa(\hat{\mathbf{m}}_j)$ is the magnitude of $\hat{\mathbf{m}}_j$ and $\hat{\mathbf{m}}_j^{\perp}$ is its negative reciprocal.

In order to identify the spectra associated with occluding boundaries, we first find peak frequency measurements for both signals. That is to say, we find for signal t, the frequency $\hat{\mathbf{m}}_t$ such that $\tau_{tk} > \tau_{ik}$ for $t \neq i$ and $\kappa(\hat{\mathbf{m}}_t)$ is maximal and determine the strength of measurements $\hat{\mathbf{m}}_j$ along the direction perpendicular to the hypothesized occluding velocity at the peak frequency of the hypothesized occluded signal.

To test for the signal corresponding to velocity $\mathbf{v}_i$ as occluding, the procedure is to first consider only those measurements $\hat{\mathbf{m}}_j$ belonging to the uniform distribution of the mixture: $\tau_{0j} > \tau_{ij}$, for $i = 1, 2$ and $j = 1 \ldots n$, as determined by the EM algorithm and the peak frequency of the signal corresponding to velocity $\mathbf{v}_t$, where $t \neq i$. We then proceed with the computation of the strengths of measurements confirming this hypothesis, once again using mixture probabilities.

Among measurements belonging to the uniform noise distribution, we compute their posterior probability of being part of the distortion spectra cast by the hypothesized occlusion and we also determine the posterior probabilities of the measurements to be from the uniform noise distribution to the exclusion of the spectra of the occlusion. Mixture proportions may be obtained from these posterior probabilities that assess the hypothesis under test. Thus, if velocity $\hat{v}_i$ is occluding, then the strengths of measurements confirming this hypothesis outnumber those pertaining to its contrary. This hypothesis-testing method is applied to determine the image events giving rise to multiple velocities.

3.2. 2D ALGORITHM

The algorithm for 2D signals is essentially similar to the 1D algorithm we described. The measurements $\hat{\mathbf{m}}_j = (k_{xj}, k_{yj}, \omega_j)^T$ and velocity estimates $\hat{\mathbf{v}}_i = (v_x, v_y, v_t)^T$ are used in the error metric (6) to deterimine the posterior probabilities τ_{ij}, as is the case with the 1D algorithm. However, the choice of velocity estimates differs substantially. In the case of 2D signals, the velocity estimates at each EM iteration must maximize the numerator exponential of (9). In this case, we follow the approach adopted by Jepson and Black (1993), and consider the square of the error metric (6) as the equation for which the solutions yield velocity estimates. We observe that $\xi^2(\hat{\mathbf{m}}_j, \hat{\mathbf{v}}_i)$ may be written in matrix form as

$$(\mathbf{m}_j^T \mathbf{v}_i)^2 = \mathbf{v}_i^T M_j \mathbf{v}_i, \qquad (12)$$

where $M_j = \hat{\mathbf{m}}_j \hat{\mathbf{m}}_j^T$. By selecting the eigenvector corresponding to the minimum eigenvalue of M_j for $\mathbf{v}_i$, we minimize (12). Since M_j is real and symmetric, its eigenvalues are real and non-degenerate and the eigenvectors form an orthogonal basis in the space of measurements. In light of these observations, we define

$$\Sigma_i^{(k+1)} = \frac{\sum_{j=1}^{n} \tau_{ij}^{(k)} \kappa(\hat{\mathbf{m}}_j) M_j}{\sum_{j=1}^{n} \kappa(\hat{\mathbf{m}}_j)} \qquad (13)$$

as the matrix from which the velocity estimate $\mathbf{v}_i^{(k+1)}$ is to be obtained in the form of the eigenvector $\mathbf{e}_i^{(k+1)}$ corresponding to the minimum eigenvalue $e_i^{(k+1)}$ of Σ_i. The minimum eigenvalue holds information about the velocity estimate obtained from its corresponding eigenvector. A zero value for e_i indicates that the velocity measurement is normal, whereas a non-zero value indicates a full velocity measurement (Jahne, 1990). To see this, consider a set of observations consisting of collinear measurements, consistent with a normal velocity. It is observed that in such circumstances, the lines of matrix Σ_i are linearly dependent, leading to a minimum eigenvalue of value zero. The final eigenvalues e_i contain information on the nature of the measured velocities that is very relevant in most uses of image velocity.

Under the hypothesis of a straight-edged occlusion boundary, its normal may be estimated from the frequency structure of the occlusion. To perform this estimation, the algorithm must recover the orientation of the spectrum cast by the occlusion about the maximum frequency of the occluded signal, within a plane parallel to that of the occluding signal. To perform this estimation, it is necessary to include an EM iteration which converges to this linear orientation within the specified constraint plane.

We consider only those measurements which are consistent with the plane containing the peak frequency $\hat{\mathbf{m}}_t$ of the occluded signal and perpendicular to the occluding velocity $\mathbf{v}_i$, that is to say, we find $\hat{\mathbf{m}}_j - \hat{\mathbf{m}}_t$ such that $\tau_{ik} > \tau_{tk}$, for $t \neq k$. We proceed with the computation of posterior probabilities given an initial estimate $\hat{\mathbf{n}}^{(0)}$ of the orientation of the linear spectra cast by the occlusion as

$$\hat{\tau}_{ij}^{(k)} = \frac{\hat{\pi}_i^{(k)} e^{\frac{-1}{2\sigma_v^2}\theta^2((\hat{\mathbf{m}}_j - \hat{\mathbf{m}}_t), \hat{\mathbf{n}})}}{\sum_{t=1}^{g} \hat{\pi}_t^{(k)} e^{\frac{-1}{2\sigma_v^2}\theta^2((\hat{\mathbf{m}}_j - \hat{\mathbf{m}}_t), \hat{\mathbf{n}})} + \hat{\pi}_0^{(k)} e^{\frac{-\lambda^2}{2\sigma_n^2}}}. \tag{14}$$

$$\hat{\tau}_{0j}^{(k)} = \frac{\hat{\pi}_0^{(k)} e^{\frac{-\lambda^2}{2\sigma_v^2}}}{\sum_{t=1}^{g} \hat{\pi}_t^{(k)} e^{\frac{-1}{2\sigma_v^2}\theta^2((\hat{\mathbf{m}}_j - \hat{\mathbf{m}}_t), \hat{\mathbf{n}})} + \hat{\pi}_0^{(k)} e^{\frac{-\lambda^2}{2\sigma_n^2}}}, \tag{15}$$

where θ is the error measure (6). The estimate of the spectral orientation and the mixture proportions are updated as

$$\hat{\mathbf{n}}^{(k+1)} = \frac{\sum_{j=1}^{n} \hat{\tau}_{ij}^{(k)} \kappa(\hat{\mathbf{m}}_j)(\hat{\mathbf{m}}_j - \hat{\mathbf{m}}_t)}{\hat{\pi}_i^{(k)} \sum_{j=1}^{n} \kappa(\hat{\mathbf{m}}_j)} \quad \text{and} \quad \hat{\pi}_i^{(k+1)} = \frac{\sum_{j=1}^{n} \hat{\tau}_{ij}^{(k)} \kappa(\hat{\mathbf{m}}_j)}{\sum_{j=1}^{n} \kappa(\hat{\mathbf{m}}_j)}. \tag{16}$$

4. Experiments

We report two sets of numerical experiments on synthetic sinusoidal imagery composed of 1D and 2D occlusion scenes. The images used for these experiments are noiseless and so are the computed optical flow fields reported in section 4.1. The fist set of experiments is to verify and demonstrate the correctness of the underlying theoretical results while the sec-

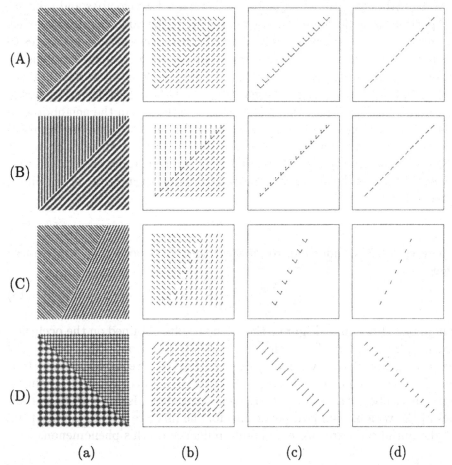

Figure 2. Synthetic imagery and results with $\mathbf{k}_1$ and $\mathbf{v}_1$ occluding. *Top to bottom:* 1D imagery **(A)** $k_1 = \frac{2\pi}{16}$, $k_2 = \frac{2\pi}{8}$, $\mathbf{v}_1 = (1,1)$ and $\mathbf{v}_2 = (-1,1)$; **(B)** $k_1 = \frac{2\pi}{16}$, $k_2 = \frac{2\pi}{8}$, $\mathbf{v}_1 = (1,1)$ and $\mathbf{v}_2 = (0,1)$; **(C)** $k_1 = k_2 = \frac{2\pi}{16}$, $\mathbf{v}_1 = (0.5,1)$ and $\mathbf{v}_2 = (-1,1)$; **(D)** 2D imagery $\mathbf{k}_1 = (\frac{2\pi}{16}, \frac{2\pi}{16})$, $\mathbf{k}_2 = (\frac{2\pi}{8}, \frac{2\pi}{8})$ $\mathbf{v}_1 = (1,1,1)$ and $\mathbf{v}_2 = (-1,-1,1)$. *Left to right:* **(a)** Synthetic image; **(b)** Optical flow; **(c)** Multiple velocities; **(d)** Occluding velocities.

ond set of experiments in section 4.2 exemplifies our proposed evaluation protocol for optical flow algorithms.

4.1. NUMERICAL VALIDATION

We performed numerical experiments on synthetic sinusoidal imagery composed of four 1D occlusion scenes and one 2D occlusion sequence, as described by Figure 2. Local frequency measurements are obtained for an image location by computing a local Fast Fourier Transform within a region of side size 32. We observed that 30 iterations were sufficient for the

EM algorithm to converge. The initial estimates for velocities and mixture proportions may be chosen randomly, but we prefer to have initial velocity estimates set as apart as possible to avoid convergence of both estimates to a single peak. When the EM iterations begin, we set σ_v to 0.2618 radians, or 15 degrees. At each step, we decrease σ_v to obtain a final value of 0.01745, or 1 degree. It is observed that a larger value for the standard deviation during the first iterations brings the initial velocity estimates in the neighborhood of the true parameters while a smaller value for the last iterations improves the accuracy of the final estimates. A value of 2.5 for λ and 1.0 for σ_n are chosen for the uniform distributions. It was experimentally determined that in order to assess the presence of multiple motions, the mixture probabilities must satisfy

$$\frac{\pi_i}{\pi_0} > \epsilon_1, \tag{17}$$

where $\epsilon_1 = 0.3$. In addition, to label velocity $\hat{\mathbf{v}}_i$ as occluding, we required that

$$\left| \frac{\pi_i(\hat{\mathbf{v}}_i)}{\pi_0(\hat{\mathbf{v}}_i)} - \frac{\pi_i(\hat{\mathbf{v}}_t)}{\pi_0(\hat{\mathbf{v}}_t)} \right| > \epsilon_2, \tag{18}$$

where $\epsilon_2 = 1.0 \times 10^{-3}$. Figure 2 shows the results obtained on the occlusion scenes. These optical flow fields are virtually free from error, due to the perfect nature of the synthetic imagery. However, we have observed that multiple velocities must at least be 15 degrees apart in orientation for the algorithms to be capable of correctly identifying them. Issues such as the values of the various standard deviations for the mixture and the orientations of the initial estimates have a definite influence on this phenomenon.

4.2. EXPERIMENTAL PROTOCOL

The nature of image motion, most particularly discontinuous motion in frequency space, has long been unclear. The algorithms proposed herein are based on a firm theoretical framework which describes the coherent behavior of occlusion events in frequency space. Indeed, we strongly believe that further developments in the field of optical flow and motion analysis ought to be based on firmly established theoretical backgrounds rather than incidental evidence, as is sometimes the case (Jain and Binford, 1991).

In light of this, we propose a novel evaluation protocol which includes theoretical considerations and their impact on evaluation of algorithms. By considering the theoretical knowledge about a phonomenon, such as image motion for instance, one is able to assess the quantitative and qualitative consequences of each part of the theoretical model in terms of numerical accuracy and of the type of information provided by the corresponding algorithms. For example, Figure 3 and Table I show our second set of exper-

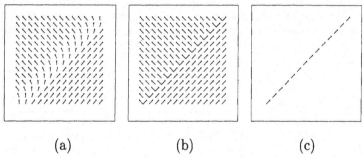

(a)   (b)   (c)

Figure 3.   Quantitative and qualitative impacts of extended theoretical knowledge:
(a) The optical flow on a sinusoidal occlusion scene produced with the MFFC SM1
algorithm. The average magnitude error is 0.2475 percent; **(b)** The optical flow obtained
this time with the MMFC EM1 algorithm. The average magnitude error is 0.0 percent;
(c) Extraction of the occluding velocity with algorithm MMFC EM2.

iments in which various hypotheses for the 1D algorithm are quantitatively
and qualitatively compared with the complete algorithm as described, thus
assessing the gain provided by more complete theoretical models. The cycle
in which this protocol operates may be defined by the following steps:

— *Incrementally incorporate theoretical knowledge of the phenomenon under study into a descriptive, computational model.* In the example of
  Figure 3, we used the *Motion From Fourier Components (MFFC)*
  hypothesis, which is the assumption of the presence of one motion
  only, followed by the use of the *Mutiple Motions from Fourier Components (MMFC)* hypothesis, and the spectral analysis of occlusion, as
  described for the 1D algorithm.

— *Derive the corresponding algorithms based on the computational model.*
  For each of our models, we derived a coresponding algorithm. For
  the MFFC principle, we posed that the Fourier components emanated
  from a single motion (SM algorithm) and simply computed an average
  velocity of the space of measurements. The EM1 algorithm implements
  the multiple motion hypothesis and the spectral analysis, implemented
  with algorithm EM2, encompasses the statistical tests for occluding
  velocities and related properties such as the computation of the normal
  to the occluding edge.

— *Numerically evaluate these algorithms on an appropriate set of images
  and assess their accuracy.* We proceeded to the numerical evaluation
  of each flow field obtained with the various algorithms. We also determined the qualititive gains made by each addition to the computational
  models, as reported in Table I.

— *Repeat the steps until the computational model is entirely compliant
  with the current body of applicable theoretical knowledge about the phe-*

TABLE I.   *The quantitative and qualitative impacts of the incremental addition of theoretical knowledge and implementation of correspondiong algorithms for optical flow in the frequency domain. Both quantitative and qualitative gains are made from SM to EM1, while only qualitative gains are obtained from EM1 to EM2.*

MODEL	ALGORITHM	AVERAGE ERROR	AVAIL. INFORMATION
MFFC	SM	0.2475	One motion
MMFC	EM1	0.0000	Two motions
MMFC	EM2	0.0000	Two motions, occluding velocity and boundary normal

nomenon under study. The three algorithms (SM, EM1 and EM2) represent our iterations towards a complete model of discontinuous optical flow in Fourier space with corresponding algorithms.

This iterative protocol allows to assess the impact that the addition of theoretical knowledge to computational models and algorithms generates and we believe it to be of importance because of its ability to provide the necessary insights pertaining to observed differences in numerical performances of various optical flow algorithms. By proposing such a protocol, we merely suggest to include the usual comparative numerical evaluations within this framework to understand the impact of computational models derived from various aspects of theoretical knowledge. We believe this to be an effective protocol to determine the causes of performance variations between different optical flow algorithms.

References

Beauchemin, S.S. and Barron, J.L. (1995) The computation of optical flow, *ACM Computing Surveys*, 27(3):433–467.

Beauchemin, S.S. and Barron, J.L. (1997a) A theoretical framework for discontinuous optical flow, submitted.

Beauchemin, S.S. and Barron, J.L. (1997b) The local frequency structure of 1D occluding image signals, submitted.

Beauchemin, S.S., Chalifour, A. and Barron, J.L. (1997) Discontinuous optical flow: Recent theoretical results, *Vision Interface*, Kelowna, Canada, 57–64.

Black, M.J. (1991) A robust gradient-method for determining optical flow, Technical Report YALEU/DCS/RR-891, Yale University, New-Haven, CT.

Black, M.J. and Jepson, A. (1994) Estimating optical flow in segmented images using variable-order parametric models with local deformations, Technical Report SPL-94-053, Xerox Systems and Practices Laboratory, Palo Alto, California.

Jahne, B. (1990) Motion determination in space-time images, *Proceedings of ECCV*, Antibes, France, 161–173.

Jain, R.C. and Binford, T.O. (1991). Ignorance, myopia and naivete in computer vision systems, *CVGIP:IU*, 53:112–117.

Jenkin, M.R.M., Jepson, A.D. and Tsotsos, J.K. (1991) Techniques for disparity measurement, *CVGIP*, 53(1):14–30.

Jepson, A.D. and Black, M. (1993) Mixture models for optical flow computation, *IEEE Proceedings of CVPR*, New York, 760–761.

Longuet-Higgins, H.C. (1981) A computer algorithm for reconstructing a scene from two projections, *Nature*, 223:133–135.

Murray, D.W. and Buxton, B.F. (1987) Scene segmentation from visual motion using global optimization, *IEEE PAMI*, 9(2):220–228.

Musmann, H.G., Pirsch, P. and Grallert, H.J. (1985) Advances in picture coding, *Proc of IEEE*, 73(4):523–548.

Nagel H.-H. (1987) On the estimation of optical flow: Relations between different approaches and some new results, *Artificial Intelligence*, 33:299–324.

Negahdaripour, S. and Lee, S. (1992) Motion recovery from image sequences using only first order optical flow information, *IJCV*, 9(3):163–184.

Overington, I. (1987) Gradient-based flow segmentation and location of the focus of expansion, *Alvey Vision Conference*, University of Cambridge, England, 860–870,

Prince, J.L. and McVeigh, E.R. (1992) Motion estimation from tagged MR image sequences, *IEEE Trans. on Medical Images*, 11(2):238–249.

Schunck, B.G. (1989) Image flow segmentation and estimation by constraint line clustering, *IEEE PAMI*, 11(10):1010–1027.

Shizawa, M. and Mase, K. (1991) Principle of superposition: A common computational framework for analysis of multiple motion, *IEEE Proceedings of Workshop on Visual Motion*, Princeton, New Jersey, 164–172.

Wang, J.Y.A. and Adelson, E.H. (1993) Layered representation for motion analysis, *Proceedings of CVPR'93*, 361–366.

MOTION EXTRACTION

An Approach Based on Duality and Gauge Theory

LUC FLORACK
Dept. of Computer Science
Utrecht University
PO Box 80089
3508 TB Utrecht, The Netherlands

1. Introduction

Vicious circularities pervade the field of image analysis. For instance, features like "edges" only exist by virtue of a fiducial "edge detector". In turn, such a detector is typically constructed with the aim to extract those features one is inclined to classify as "edges".

The paradox arises from abuse of terminology. The polysemous term "edge" can be used in two distinct meanings: as an operationally defined concept (output of an edge detector), or as a heuristic feature pertaining to our intuition. In the former case the design of edge detection filters is—*strictu sensu*—merely a convention for imposing structure on raw data. In the latter case it is our expectation of what an "edge" should be like that begs the question of appropriate detector design. The keyword then becomes interpretation.

Clearly all low-level image concepts pertain to structure as well as interpretation. Once defined, structure becomes evidence. Interpretation amounts to a selection among all possible hypotheses consistent with this evidence. Clarity may be served by a manifest segregation of the two. A convenient way to achieve this is to embed "structure" into a framework of *duality* and to model "interpretation" by a hermeneutic circle driven by external insight constraining the class of *a priori* feasible interpretations (*gauge conditions*, respectively *gauge invariance*).

Here the proposed framework is applied to motion analysis. Duality accounts for the role of preprocessing filters. The so-called "aperture problem"

R. Klette et al. (eds.), Performance Characterization in Computer Vision, 69–80.
© 2000 *Kluwer Academic Publishers.*

arises from an intrinsic local invariance (or gauge invariance), which cannot be resolved on the exclusive basis of image evidence. Gauge conditions reflect external knowledge for disambiguation.

Technical details of the motion extraction schemes used here can be found elsewhere (Florack *et al.*, 1998). Here we focus on aspects of validation and evaluation. To this end we carry out several simulation experiments on synthetic as well as popular benchmark sequences, and compare results with theoretical predictions and with figures reported in the literature.

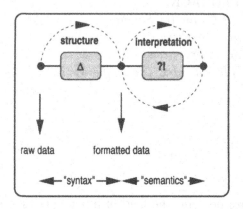

Figure 1. Manifest segregation of structural and semantic representations.

In line with the duality approach sketched above two stages can be distinguished in an error analysis of the outcome. There are errors of the obvious kind, caused by inadequate modelling ("semantical errors", or "mistakes"), which one would like to remove altogether, and subtle but inevitable errors propagated by any structural representation of data of intrinsically finite tolerance. Indeed, the flexibility to alter the gauge (re-interpret the data) and the possibility to carry out a rigorous error propagation study for the data formatting stage is a major rationale behind the current framework, *cf.* Figure 1 and 2.

2. Theory

Duality paradigms account for the inner workings of the filtering stage used to define data format. As such they should be contrasted with conventional "preprocessing" or "regularisation" techniques, in which the emphasis is on suitable preparation of data for subsequent processing. Rigidity of a fixed preprocessing or regularisation stage conflicts with the plasticity required for solving specific tasks of which all details cannot possibly be known in advance. Modelling image structure by duality principles on the other hand manifestly captures the public facts that one always needs a filtering stage to define the basic structural degrees of freedom driving image algorithms (*necessity*), and that outcome always depends crucially on the details of this stage (*criticality*). The latter observation is reflected in the way filters are handled in a dualistic approach, *viz.* as free (albeit mandatory) arguments to algorithms. This view makes the role of filters transparent.

The concept of duality leaves ample leeway for implementation. One of the simplest options is "topological duality". It is basically linear filtering with smooth, essentially compact filters, though one should always keep in mind that it is not output in itself ("black box") but in connection to its production ("glass box") that is of interest. Originally proposed by Schwartz (1966) as a mathematical formalism it may serve as a generic framework for many linear image processing filters used today. Topological duality subjected to a few plausible constraints produces the familiar Gaussian scale-space paradigm (*viz.* postulate a unique, positive filter consistent with Schwartz' theory and require algebraic closure (Florack, 1997)). In section 2.1 it is extended to cope with motion.

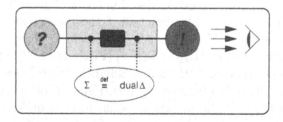

Figure 2.   In a duality formalism "structure" means "operationally defined structure". Degrees of freedom captured by raw data $f \in \Sigma$ are identified with probes of a fiducial filter class Δ, *i.e.* with mappings "dual Δ" : $\Delta \longrightarrow \mathbb{R}$ induced by the raw data through exposure to all members $\phi \in \Delta$. In particular, if two source configurations induce identical mappings they are considered equivalent ("metamerism"). This can be exploited so as to hide irrelevant grid details and alleviate the impact of noise (robustness).

Once a generic data format has been established, solutions to particular tasks typically depend on fewer degrees of freedom than actually available (provided one has sufficient data and knowledge). Indeed, genericity encourages redundancy, but at the same time has the potential of facilitating the selection of degrees of freedom that are relevant to a specific problem.

Gauge invariant representations—common in physics—are characterised by pointwise redundancies induced by the deliberate use of nonphysical variables (auxiliaries). The idea is that models may become most parsimonious in terms of redundant systems with constraints that cancel the effect of nonphysical degrees of freedom. Variables could be isolated such that the additional constraints (gauge conditions) become obsolete, but only at the price of an increase of model complexity. Gauge theoretical principles and their use in the context of motion are further discussed in section 2.2.

2.1. DUALITY IN THE CONTEXT OF MOTION

An *a priori* condition for the definition of a dense motion field is local conservation. Some well-defined local characteristic must retain its identity in order to enable us to monitor point trajectories over time. This condition is necessary but does not suffice to define unambiguous motion.

Since conservation is a generic principle data format can be defined so as to incorporate it *a priori* ("kinematic structure"). That is, the basic elements in the analysis are of a kinematic nature, encapsulating the "proto-semantics" that enjoys public consensus[1]. Further disambiguation of motion requires specific models, depending on task, image formation details, *et cetera* (the "aperture problem"). In view of specificity this is best left as an interpretation task. In this section only structural aspects are discussed.

Local conservation principles are often stated in terms of a vanishing Lie derivative, which can in turn be expressed in terms of an ordinary derivative and a vector field. For a scalar function f the Lie derivative is given by $L_v f = \nabla f \cdot v$, in which ∇ denotes the spatiotemporal gradient operator. For a density field ϱ one has $L_v \varrho = \nabla(\varrho \cdot v)$ (Fitzpatrick, 1988). The original "Horn & Schunck equation" (Horn and Schunck, 1981; Horn and Schunck, 1993; Schunck, 1984) is obtained by identifying f or ϱ with the image function and setting its Lie derivative equal to zero under the additional assumption that the temporal component of the vector field equals one.

Classical derivatives are ill-posed. Their counterparts in the setting of topological duality are not only well-posed but also operationally well-defined. If $f[\phi]$ denotes a linear sample obtained from "raw image" f by linear filtering with filter ϕ, then a derivative sample is defined as

$$\nabla f[\phi] \stackrel{\text{def}}{=} f[\nabla^{\text{T}} \phi],$$

in which A^{T} denotes the transposed of a linear operator A. Generalisation to higher orders is straightforward. The base point associated with such a sample is the filter's centre of gravity, while resolution is the inverse of the filter's width. In any case, derivatives are defined by virtue of a filter

---

[1] The premiss is that one agrees on the quantity that is actually conserved. A direct link with image data requires a careful acquisition protocol and a quantitative reconstruction, *e.g.* proton density cine-MR.

paradigm. This allows us to define a Lie derivative as follows:

$$L_v f[\phi] \stackrel{\text{def}}{=} f[L_v^T \phi] \,.$$

Again, the definition cannot be unconfounded from a fiducial filter class. It follows that motion, if defined along the lines of Horn & Schunck, has no existence on its own, but only relative to the filter paradigm in use.

According to a famous theorem a linear continuous sample $f[\phi]$ can be written in integral form as follows:

$$f[\phi] = \int f(x)\,\phi(x)\,dx \,,$$

from which it follows that transposition of a derivative brings in a minus sign: $\nabla^T = -\nabla$ and $L_v^T = -L_v$. A subtlety arises in the case of transposing Lie derivatives: If f is a scalar, then ϕ behaves as a density, *vice versa*. Under the assumption of homogeneity the transition from local samples to images is trivial, and leads to similar expressions with spacetime correlations—or, if one prefers, convolutions, in which case the minus signs are absorbed— instead of scalar products. The resulting motion constraint equation is homogeneous and trilinear with respect to input data f (whether scalar or density), correlation filter ϕ, and spacetime vector v.

2.2. GAUGE THEORY IN THE CONTEXT OF MOTION

Let v be the desired motion field satisfying the motion constraint equation:

$$L_v f[\phi] = 0 \,.$$

In principle this fixes 1 component of v per base point, leaving n undefined in $(n+1)$-dimensional spacetime (typically $n = 2$ or 3). In the terminology introduced previously one may say that v is a gauge field with 1 physical and n auxiliary components. It would complicate matters greatly if one would choose to dispense with the auxiliaries beforehand, and in fact could even obscure the very motion concept completely, since this is a semantical concept that requires additional knowledge in conjunction with the above constraint equation. Rather, the natural way to proceed is to enforce additional constraints to disambiguate the solution. Such gauge conditions reflect knowledge inspired by the application and other external factors.

However, along with the above equation one additional hypothesis is always tacitly adopted. One could describe it as *conservation of topological detail*. It entails that one takes for granted that the flow induced by v is transversal to spatial frames, so that (by virtue of homogeneity) one can always scale the temporal component to unity: $v = (1; \vec{v})$, say. It is the

spatial part $\vec{v}$ that is commonly associated with the optic flow or motion
vector. One explanation of this "temporal gauge" is that whatever it is that
moves cannot reverse its temporal sense and "travel backward in time". But
there is an alternative and more natural one, which at the same time shows
that the temporal gauge is not self-evident, and even unrealistic if strictly
enforced: A time-reversal of a spacetime trajectory can always be given the
causal interpretation of a creation or annihilation event. In this way one
can *e.g.* account for enhancement of extrema in a scalar image sequence
that would otherwise turn into spurious flow singularities.

All validation studies of section 3 adhere to the usual temporal gauge.
In section 3.1 the consequences of this are discussed for the case where it is
not appropriate to do so, while section 3.2 presents a simulation where it
is. Since semantics is de-emphasised the "canonical gauge" will be adopted
expressing the normal flow condition. The $n-1$ normal flow equations may
be replaced by physical conditions without technical difficulties. (This is
done in section 3.3.) Recall that this semantical flexibility lies at the core
of gauge theoretical formalisms.

3. Validation

In the validation study outlined below one of the aims is to isolate the effect
of semantical weaknesses. Errors due to measurement noise and numerical
approximations of image derivatives are not quantified in the tables (but
of course may contribute significantly to the results listed). Such intrinsic
errors set a lower bound on overall errors beyond which no improvement is
theoretically possible.

In conformity with scale-space theory all experiments are based on
the Gaussian filter family (Koenderink and van Doorn, 1990), a complete,
proper subset of Schwartz' space. For an analysis of error propagation in
computing Gaussian derivatives the reader is referred to Blom *et al.* (1993).
Below "error" is defined as "deviation from the model". No attempt is made
to relate it quantitatively to a theoretical prediction of the aforementioned
fundamental limitation. To compensate for this two related experiments are
carried out on synthetic data. The first simulates an intentionally deficient
model containing a feasible semantical error (section 3.1). The second is
set up without this deficiency, so that the only potential source of error
affecting the solution stems from data noise and numerical manipulations
(section 3.2). Both simulations are analytically tractable, so that numerical
results can be compared with theoretical predictions. In a third study,
which is carried out on real image data, there is no direct control over

the stimulus, but in this case external knowledge of scene configuration and image formation enables the formulation of analytical gauge conditions (section 3.3).

3.1. SIMULATION STUDY: DENSITY STIMULUS, SCALAR PARADIGM

Imagine a bell-shaped stimulus with oscillating radius somewhere in the middle of the image. If its amplitude covaries in such a way that its spatial integral ("mass") remains constant over time, then the sequence simulates density motion. Think of proton density cine-MR by way of example.

Let us endow the motion constraint equation with the following gauge conditions: (i) the normal flow condition, *in casu* the requirement that the motion field is radial, and (ii) the usual temporal gauge. With the blob centred at the coordinate origin we then have $v \propto (1; \vec{r}/\|\vec{r}\|)$, in which the proportionality factor depends on $\|\vec{r}\|$. If motion is well-defined in the first place this constant should have no singularities, and in view of symmetry the only reasonable motion vector to expect at the origin is the null vector, regardless of the filter paradigm.

Suppose, however, that we make the mistake of modelling the image sequence as a time-varying *scalar* field. Such a misinterpretation is not far-fetched in practice for several reasons. Firstly one may lack adequate knowledge of image formation, so that one does not know whether the image captures a density field at all. Even if it does, one may not understand the exact relation between image values and physical density. Secondly there will be deviations from any definite geometric paradigm, either due to plain noise or to the fact that the paradigm is merely an idealization. In particular some motion sequences are neither densities nor scalars, *e.g.* (typical) shading in optical projection imagery.

For the simulated density the consequence of the scalarity assumption is the appearance of a spurious motion singularity at the centre of the blob. Apart from this there are other qualitative discrepancies between visual percept (one observes alternating contractions and expansions) and prediction (simultaneous inward and outward flow on two sides of a circle oscillating in phase with the blob). Theoretical predictions are in quantitative agreement with numerical computations carried out on a digital rendering of the density sequence, *cf.* Figure 3. Two numerical schemes have been used, a 0-th and a 1-st order one, the details of which are given in the appendix. Errors turn out to be largest in the immediate neighbourhood of the singularity. It is clear that in realistic sequences with complex topological structure there will be many such problematic neighbourhoods.

If one retains faith in conservation, there are two legitimate explanations for model failure. Either the scalarity assumption fails, or one must allow

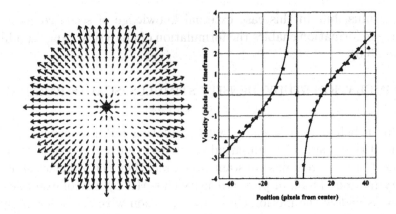

Figure 3. Flow field obtained for the density stimulus (left) and flow magnitudes along a horizontal scanline through the centre (right) showing analytical (solid line), 0-th (triangles) and 1-st order results (stars). Note the singularity and the flow inversion.

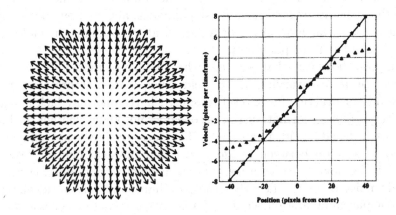

Figure 4. Flow field obtained for the scalar stimulus (left) and flow magnitudes along a horizontal scanline through the centre (right) showing analytical (solid line), 0-th (triangles) and 1-st order results (stars). Note that the field is everywhere well-defined and has no inversions (in agreement with perceptual impression).

for point sources and sink-holes, *i.e.* give up the temporal gauge. Note that the numerical schemes yield accurate estimates; failure does *not* have a computational cause. In fact, computations turn out to be quite robust.

3.2. SIMULATION STUDY: SCALAR STIMULUS, SCALAR PARADIGM

One would expect no problems if the motion constraint equation had been used in the appropriate form applicable to densities. Likewise, no singularities should emerge if we adhere to the scalar model but slightly adapt

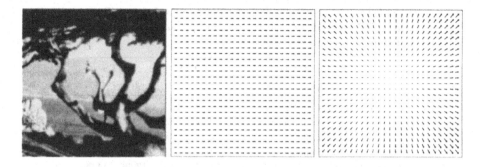

Figure 5.   Textured plane and vector field for translation (TTS) and divergence (DTS).

the stimulus by taking the blob's amplitude to be constant. Theory then predicts a motion field that (for a harmonically oscillating Gaussian blob) varies linearly with eccentricity. Again, this is confirmed numerically: Figure 4.

3.3. A COMPARATIVE STUDY

We subject the motion paradigm to a final test to check whether it has any practical advantages over alternative schemes proposed in the literature. To this end we fully exploit the flexibility of semantical modelling enabled by the manifest segregation of stages (Figure 1), as well as the theoretical properties of the filter paradigm (Figure 2). In the concrete, we (i) endow the basic structural equations (the motion constraint equation in temporal gauge) with additional spatial constraints reflecting *a priori* knowledge of camera motion and scenery—this should be contrasted with generic schemes that do not incorporate such specific knowledge—and (ii) exploit the scale degree of freedom of the Gaussian family by *scale selection*.

The motion algorithm derived from the theory is the first order scheme detailed in the appendix, in which filter scales are selected so as to (pixel-wise) minimize the Frobenius norm of the resulting linear system. It is run on benchmark sequences known as the *translating* and the *diverging tree sequence* ("TTS", respectively "DTS"): Figure 5. Outcome is compared to the comprehensive study of Barron *et al.* (1994) using the same error criterion. The tentative gauges reflect the hypothesis that vertical motion is absent, respectively that the focus of expansion is known. (The "hermeneutic principle" relies on the existence of consistent cues conspiring to produce such tentative hypotheses, and on the possibility to test and refine them.) Results are listed in Table I (dense flow estimation) and Table II (sparse flow estimation discarding uncertain estimates).

TABLE I.   Comparison with best performing techniques (Barron *et al.*, 1994) with dense velocity estimates; μ and σ denote mean and standard deviation of error.

Implementation method	TTS		DTS	
	μ	σ	μ	σ
Modified Horn & Schunck	2.02	2.27	2.55	3.67
Uras *et al.* (unthresholded)	0.62	0.52	4.64	3.48
Nagel	2.44	3.06	2.94	3.23
Anandan	4.54	3.10	7.64	4.96
Singh (step 1, $n = 2, w = 2, N = 4$)	1.64	2.44	17.66	14.25
Singh (step 2, $n = 2, w = 2, N = 4$)	1.25	3.29	8.60	5.60
Florack *et al.* ($M = 1$, scale selection)	0.49	1.92	1.15	3.32

TABLE II.   Comparison with best performing techniques (Barron *et al.*, 1994) discarding uncertain velocity estimates; μ and σ denote mean and standard deviation of error, ϱ indicates pixel fraction with motion estimates.

Implementation method	TTS			DTS		
	μ	σ	ϱ (%)	μ	σ	ϱ (%)
Modified Horn & Schunck	1.89	2.40	53.2	1.94	3.89	32.9
Lucas and Kanade ($\lambda_2 \geq 1.0$)	0.66	0.67	39.8	1.94	2.06	48.2
Lucas and Kanade ($\lambda_2 \geq 5.0$)	0.56	0.58	13.1	1.65	1.48	24.3
Uras *et al.* ($\det(H) \geq 1.0$)	0.46	0.35	41.8	3.83	2.19	60.2
Nagel $\|\nabla L\|_2 \geq 5.0$	2.24	3.31	53.2	3.21	3.43	53.5
Singh (step 1, $n = 2, w = 2, \lambda_1 \leq 5.0, N = 4$)	0.72	0.75	41.4	7.09	6.59	3.3
Heeger	4.53	2.41	57.8	4.49	3.10	74.2
Fleet & Jepson ($\tau = 2.0$)	0.23	0.19	49.7	0.80	0.73	46.5
Fleet & Jepson ($\tau = 1.0$)	0.25	0.21	26.8	0.73	0.46	28.2
Florack *et al.* ($M = 1$, scale selection)	0.16	0.18	60.0	0.79	1.13	60.0
Florack *et al.* ($M = 1$, scale selection)	0.14	0.13	40.0	0.43	0.40	40.0

4. Conclusion

The strength of duality is that the role of filters is made transparent, thus facilitating the exploitation of filter properties. In the case at hand Gaussian scale-space filters have been used and scale selection has been applied successfully for robust motion extraction (note that the filtering procedure is continuous with respect to the initial image data in L^1 sense).

The gauge field paradigm encourages clarity and parsimony. It has been applied here for a manifest segregation of data evidence (gauge invariant system) and external models (gauge conditions), and has led to a flexible operational scheme for combining motion evidence with prior knowledge. Numerical results vote in favour of the proposed line of approach.

Acknowledgements

Experiments have been carried out by Wiro Niessen at the Image Sciences Institute, Utrecht, The Netherlands.

A. Numerical Schemes for Motion Extraction

The $k = 0$ approximation is based on a zeroth order polynomial vector field

$$(u_0(t; x, y), v_0(t; x, y)) = (u, v),$$

and amounts to the inversion of

$$\begin{cases} u f_x + v f_y & = -f_t \\ -v f_x + u f_y & = 0, \end{cases}$$

which is the same as the traditional OFCE for normal flow. Here, f_x is shorthand notation for the linear filter output $-f[\phi_x]$, i.e. the distributional derivative of the raw image based on a Gaussian filter ϕ; likewise for the other coefficients. They have been computed using FFT in the straightforward way. For $k = 1$ we have

$$(u_1(t; x, y), v_1(t; x, y)) = (u + u_t t + u_x x + u_y y, v + v_t t + v_x x + v_y y),$$

and obtain instead

$$\begin{cases} u f_x + v f_y + u_t f_{xt} + v_t f_{yt} + u_x f_{xx} + v_x f_{xy} + u_y f_{xy} + v_y f_{yy} & = -f_t \\ u f_{xt} + v f_{yt} + u_t (f_x + f_{xtt}) + v_t (f_y + f_{ytt}) + u_x f_{xxt} + v_x f_{xyt} + u_y f_{xyt} + v_y f_{yyt} & = -f_{tt} \\ u f_{xx} + v f_{xy} + u_t f_{xxt} + v_t f_{xyt} + u_x (f_x + f_{xxx}) + v_x (f_y + f_{xxy}) + u_y f_{xxy} + v_y f_{xyy} & = -f_{xt} \\ u f_{xy} + v f_{yy} + u_t f_{xyt} + v_t f_{yyt} + u_x f_{xxy} + v_x f_{xyy} + u_y (f_x + f_{xyy}) + v_y (f_y + f_{yyy}) & = -f_{yt} \\ u f_y - v f_x + u_t f_{yt} - v_t f_{xt} + u_x f_{xy} - v_x f_{xx} + u_y f_{yy} - v_y f_{xy} & = 0 \\ u f_{yt} - v f_{xt} + u_t (f_y + f_{ytt}) - v_t (f_x + f_{xtt}) + u_x f_{xyt} - v_x f_{xxt} + u_y f_{yyt} - v_y f_{xyt} & = 0 \\ u f_{xy} - v f_{xx} + u_t f_{xyt} - v_t f_{xxt} + u_x (f_y + f_{xxy}) - v_x (f_x + f_{xxx}) + u_y f_{xyy} - v_y f_{xxy} & = 0 \\ u f_{yy} - v f_{xy} + u_t f_{yyt} - v_t f_{xyt} + u_x f_{xyy} - v_x f_{xxy} + u_y (f_y + f_{yyy}) - v_y (f_x + f_{xyy}) & = 0. \end{cases}$$

The lowest order system has $1 + 1$ equations in 2 unknowns, u, v, and is determined in terms of the image's first order derivatives ($1 + 2$ equations in 3 unknowns if temporal gauge is made explicit). The first order system comprises $4 + 4$ equations in $2 + 6$ unknowns, $u, v, u_x, u_y, u_t, v_x, v_y, v_t$, and requires derivatives of orders $1, 2, 3$ ($4 + 8$ equations in $3 + 9$ unknowns, respectively). Note that these parameters are *not* the flow field's partial derivatives; for example, the parameters u, v arising from the latter system differ from, and generally refine those of the former (an order tag has been left out for notational simplicity).

For the construction of linear systems for motion extraction to arbitrary orders of approximation, and of the above ones in particular, the reader is referred to the literature (Florack *et al.*, 1998). Both systems have been solved numerically by pixel-wise "LU decomposition" as described in Numerical Recipes (Press *et al.*, 1988, section 2.3).

References

Barron, J.L., Fleet, D.J., and Beauchemin, S.S. (1994) Performance of optical flow techniques, *International Journal of Computer Vision*, 12(1):43–77.

Blom, J., ter Haar Romeny, B.M., Bel, A. and Koenderink, J.J. (1993) Spatial derivatives and the propagation of noise in Gaussian scale-space, *Journal of Visual Communication and Image Representation*, 4(1):1–13.

Fitzpatrick, J.M. (1988) The existence of geometrical density-image transformations corresponding to object motion, *CVGIP: Image Understanding*, 44:155–174.

Florack, L.M.J. (1997) *Image Structure*, volume 10 of *Computational Imaging and Vision Series*, Kluwer Academic Publishers, Dordrecht, The Netherlands.

Florack, L.M.J., Niessen, W.J. and Nielsen, M. (1998) The intrinsic structure of optic flow incorporating measurement duality, *International Journal of Computer Vision*, 27(3):263–286.

Horn, B.K.P. and Schunck, B.G. (1981) Determining optical flow, *Artificial Intelligence*, 17:185–203.

Horn, B.K.P. and Schunck, B.G. (1993) Determining optical flow: a retrospective, *Artificial Intelligence*, 59:81–87.

Koenderink, J.J. and van Doorn, A.J. (1990) Receptive field families, *Biological Cybernetics*, 63:291–298.

Press, W.H., Flannery, B.P., Teukolsky, S.A. and Vetterling, W.T. (1988) *Numerical Recipes in C; the Art of Scientific Computing*, Cambridge University Press, Cambridge.

Schunck, B.G. (1984) The motion constraint equation for optical flow, *Proceedings of the 7th International Conference on Pattern Recognition*, Montreal, Canada, 20–22.

Schwartz, L. (1966) *Théorie des Distributions*. Publications de l'Institut Mathématique de l'Université de Strasbourg. Hermann, Paris, second edition.

PRINCIPLES OF CONSTRUCTING A PERFORMANCE EVALUATION PROTOCOL FOR GRAPHICS RECOGNITION ALGORITHMS

LIU WENYIN
Microsoft Research China
5F Sigma Center
#49 Zhichun Road
Beijing 100080, PR China

DOV DORI
Faculty of Industrial Engineering and Management
Technion—Israel Institute of Technology
Haifa 32000, Israel

1. Introduction

Graphics recognition is a process that takes as input a raster level image consisting of pixels or a vector level drawing consisting of symbolic primitives. It groups primitives on the input into higher order graphic entities, and identifies them with known objects on the basis of the matching basic features while allowing for parameter variation. The graphic objects that may be recognized from the input include text (character) regions, lines of various shapes (e.g., circular arcs and polylines) and styles (e.g., dashed lines and dash-dotted lines), special symbols, dimension sets, etc. Graphics recognition techniques have been developed for many years. However, the performance of most of these techniques are at best known only from the reports of their developers, based on their own perceptual, subjective, and qualitative human vision evaluation. Objective evaluations and quantitative comparisons among them are not available. This is due to the lack of protocols that provide for quantitative measurements of their interesting metrics, a sound methodology for acquiring appropriate ground truth data, and adequate methods for matching the ground truths with the

R. Klette et al. (eds.), Performance Characterization in Computer Vision, 81–90.
© 2000 *Kluwer Academic Publishers.*

recognized graphic objects. To further advance the research on graphics recognition, to fully comprehend and reliably compare the performance of graphics recognition algorithms, and to help select, improve, and even design new algorithms to be applied in new systems designed for some specific application, the establishment of objective and comprehensive evaluation protocols and a resulting performance evaluation methodology are strongly required. Groups that have reported research on performance evaluation of graphics recognition algorithms include (Kong *et al.*, 1996; Hori and Doermann, 1996; Liu and Dori, 1997; Liu and Dori, 1998a) and (Philips *et al.*, 1998). However, their researches are only on performance evaluation of recognition algorithms for some specific classes of graphic objects. The protocols of (Kong *et al.*, 1996; Hori and Doermann, 1996; Liu and Dori, 1997) are aimed at performance evaluation of line detection algorithms. Liu and Dori (1998a) propose a protocol for text segmentation evaluation. Philips *et al.* (1998) propose a performance evaluation protocol for engineering drawings recognition systems, which includes performance evaluation of both line detection and text segmentation capabilities. There is no common methodology that abstracts the performance genericity of graphics recognition algorithms and can be generally applied to their performance evaluation. Based on the observed genericity of graphics recognition (Ablameyko, 1996; Liu and Dori, 1998b) we propose a methodology for performance evaluation of graphics recognition algorithms. The methodology materializes an objective-driven evaluation philosophy that is based on definitions of a matching degree and comprehensive performance metrics.

2. The Performance Evaluation Protocol

We view the performance as a set of metrics of interest on the output data that a system implementing a set of one or more algorithms produces with respect to the expected, ground truth data. Usually, the metrics are expressed in terms of the difference between the expected output and the actual output of the system. The metrics should be represented by quantitative indices based on accepted definitions to avoid subjectivity. Moreover, the entire performance of an algorithm should be reflected by a comprehensive metric. Appropriate analysis of relevant metrics should help compare, select, improve, and even design new methods to be applied in new systems targeted at specific applications. To evaluate the performance of a graphics recognition algorithm, we need three elements. First of all, we need to know the expected output the ground truthsuch that it can be compared with the actual outputthe recognition results. Therefore, a sound methodology of acquiring the appropriate ground truth data is required. Secondly, Since both the ground truth data and the recognition results consist of many graphic objects, individual comparison of each ground truth object to its matching recognized object should be done in the first place. To do this, each ground truth graphic object must first be matched with one or more objects from the recognized objects set. Hence, a sound matching method is needed. Finally, representative metrics of interest should be selected, and quantitative indices that measure these metrics should be defined uniformly. In summary, the three essential performance evaluation elements are (1) ground truth acquisition; (2) matching procedure; and (3) quantitative metrics definition. A performance evaluation protocol for a graphics recognition system therefore consists of these three parts. While the ground truth acquisition methodology is widely accepted, the definitions of matching between ground truth objects and recognized ones, as well as the selection of the appropriate performance metrics are still controversial issues. In this sense, standards based on large amount of experiments, including the evaluation of performance evaluation protocols themselves, are strongly needed. A complete and reasonable evaluation protocol should be objective, comprehensive, and should include specific indices and an overall index of the algorithm performance. The three performance evaluation protocol elements are respectively discussed in detail in the following three sections.

3. Ground Truth Acquisition

Ground truth acquisition is the process that generates both the actual input for the evaluated system and the expected output (ground truth) for comparison with the actual output. To comprehensively and thoroughly evaluate an algorithm on real-life drawings, real-life ground truth is highly desirable. However, this type of ground truth is hard to obtain, as it requires manual measurements, which are labor intensive and error-prone. Moreover, manual ground truth input is somewhat subjective and may vary from one human to another. However, this seems to be the only method to acquire the ground truth for real-life input drawings. This is so since if we would have been able to find an automatic way to obtain the ground truth of real life inputs, it would be the ultimate graphics recognition algorithm, making any other algorithm useless. While large amount of manual work is required to build databases of real life input and their ground truths, we are especially short of ground truths of scanned real life paper drawing, and due to the reasons discussed above this situation is likely to stay. A second best alternative to real-life ground truth is synthetic input. For this input type, the ground truth is relatively easy to obtain, since the ground truth is known before the synthetic image/drawing is generated by incorporating a ground truth generating code into the synthetic drawing program. Another advantage of synthetic ground truth is that any type of "programmed noise" can be added to the actual input. The noise can model real life noise of real life input data. This procedure is usually referred to as degradation. It is especially useful in testing the robustness of the algorithm, since random perturbations on the input usually result in imperfections of the recognition and we want the effect of noise on the recognition rate to be as small as possible. Additive noise can also be used to train and improve existing algorithms. Since the expected output and the actual output are to be compared with each other, they should be in the same format. Usually, the actual output is represented in vector forms. In that case, the ground truth should also be represented in the same vector form. Hence, the ground truthing procedure is usually as follows: Generate ground truth graphic objects in vector form at an abstraction level that is identical to the abstraction level at which the expected output graphic objects are represented. For example, in engineering drawing recognition systems, if we expect dimension sets to be output by the graphics recognition algorithm, the ground truth should also be in the form of dimension sets. Decompose the compound ground truth graphic objects into their components, which are lower order graphic objects used as input to the evaluated graphics recognition algorithm. The immediate components may be recursively decomposed until they cannot be further decomposed in vector form. Lowest level objects can even be further decomposed into pixel-based units, as long as the evaluated graphics recognition algorithm can accept them as input. In that case, the input can be an image bitmap generated from the vectors. Optional degradation can be applied to the synthesized input, so that the evaluated graphics recognition algorithm can be tested with the desired level of noise that simulates real life noise. The above procedure has been used by (Kong et al., 1996; Hori and Doermann, 1996; Liu and Dori, 1997; Philips et al., 1998) in their performance evaluation protocols. Document image degradation has been modeled and simulated by (Baird, 1990; Baird, 1993) and (Kanungo et al., 1993; Kanungo et al., 1994; Kanungo et al., 1995), and used by (Haralick, 1992; Kong et al., 1996), and (Hori and Doermann, 1996) in their protocols. The noise has been applied at the pixel level. However, noise models at the vector level have generally not been studied. The only group known to us that addressed this issue is that of Madej and Sokolowski (1993), who proposed a statistical model of variations of parcel (land registry) parameters, including length, angle, etc., in ground truthing cadastral maps for performance evaluation of map recognition and understanding systems. Further research should be conducted on real life noise model of graphic objects, such as line width variation, graphics/text connectivity, and component redundancy and deficiency.

4. Matching Recognized with Ground Truth Objects

To measure the difference between actual and recognized objects, ground truth objects should be matched with the recognized ones. Concerns in this procedure are how to match and what can be considered as a match (match acceptance). There is no universal way to define the matching criteria. People may define them from different aspects of performance, some of which may be controversial. We propose the following principles for defining the matching method and criteria. We first note that the absolute difference between two entities is usually less meaningful than the relative difference, which is the ratio between the absolute difference and one of the compared entities. We therefore advocate the use of relative difference. In this sense, the ground truth and the recognized entity are not symmetrical. As a matching procedure, we propose that the recognition result be matched with the ground truth and not vice versa. The reason is that the ground truth is what the recognition is intended to reveal. The ground truth is to be used as the basis for comparison. In particular, relative difference measurement should make use of the ground truth as the base, as done by (Liu and Dori, 1997; Liu and Dori, 1998a). Match acceptance concerns what can be considered as matched or not. For this, we propose to use *a continuous match value* rather than a binary, threshold-based decision, as (Hori and Doermann, 1996; Kong et al., 1996; Philips et al., 1998) do. The continuous match value serves to indicate the level of matching of a pair of a ground truth and a recognized object. This is contrasted with judging a pair as matched or not in a binary fashion. One reason for using a continuous value for the matching degree is that it is better to recognize a ground truth object with low score, i.e., poor quality recognition, than not to recognize it at all. This is analogous to a near-sighted person, who cannot recognize an object well, but his recognition is by far preferable over total lack of recognition of a blind person. Figure 1 shows two examples of matching of a pair of an arc (ground truth, g) and its recognition (k). In Figure 1a, although the recognition (k) is not precise, the binary matching method would give a match value of 1. However, the continuous matching method would give a value of 0.6. While in Figure 1b, the arc is recognized as a bar. In this case, the binary matching method would consider it is not a match and give the value of 0, while the continuous matching method would give a value of 0.4 or less, because it is much better than finding nothing.

Another advantage of the continuous value approach is its usefulness in measuring multiple matching, especially when recognition of fragmentation and/or combined objects occurs. Since the recognition is frequently not perfect, it is likely that a ground truth object is recognized as several

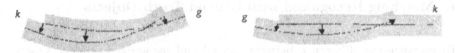

Figure 1. Examples of matching of a pair of an arc and its possible recognition results.

Figure 2. Example of recognition fragmentation/combination.

objects, and that several ground truth objects may be recognized as one object. These two cases are referred to by Liu and Dori (1997) as *recognition fragmentation and combination*. To evaluate these aspects of graphic recognition, the multiple matching problem should be considered. A ground truth object should be matched with several recognized objects and a recognized object may be matched with several ground truth objects. For example, in Figure 2, if the ground truth is a string of "W AB", it is most likely recognized as two strings of "W" and "AB". While if the ground truths are two strings of "W" and "AB", they are also likely recognized as one string of "W AB" or "WAB". Both cases should be considered as matched and given reasonable match values.

The definition of the matching degree may vary from one class of graphic objects to another, and from a method devised by one person to one proposed by another. In any case, it should involve the matched (usually overlapping) part of a pair of a ground truth and a recognized object. It may be defined in terms of the most important attributes of simple pattern graphic objects, such as, length for lines, and area for textboxes. In the first case, the ratio between the overlapping length and the ground truth length is used as the line matching degree (Liu and Dori, 1997), and in the second case, the ratio between the overlapping area and the ground truth area is used as the textbox matching degree (Liu and Dori, 1998a). The matching degree of a compound graphic object can be some combination of the matching degrees of its components. The matching degree of an object pair is weighted in the overall performance index of a single compound graphic object, as discussed in the next section.

5. Principles of Metrics Definition

The metrics definition is another controversial issue in performance evaluation. We propose the following principles in metrics definition.

1. *The metrics should be objective-driven.*

   The performance depends on the objective of the graphics recognition system. For instances, we want the coarse vectorisation to preserve the original line shape as much as possible. Hence, the shape preservation capability, which can be measured at the pixel level, is the metric of coarse vectorisation that should be evaluated (Liu and Dori, 1997). Following fine line detection, we want the vector attributes of lines (such as style, width, endpoints, etc.) to be as precise as possible. Hence, vector attribute value correspondence is used to evaluate line detection algorithms (Liu and Dori, 1997). Chhabra and Philips (1998) wants the engineering drawings recognition system to produce a result that requires the least effort for manual correction. Hence, the edit cost is used as the overall metric of the evaluated algorithms/systems. The purpose of text segmentation is twofold: recognition and layer separation. For recognition, the character box, called charbox, which is the minimal area that bounds the characters image, should be found so that the image within it can be input into an optical character recognition (OCR) module. To ensure the OCR accuracy, the charbox should be bounded such that all the black pixels belonging to the character and only these pixels are included within it. To improve text understanding at a higher level, all the characters belonging to the same string (word, number, or phrase) should also be grouped within a bounding box, called textbox. The purpose of layer separation is to clear the document image so that only graphics are left for further processing. In this case, the charboxes need not be as precise as they need to be for OCR. Hence, the performance criteria for the same text segmentation algorithm may be different for two different purposes.

2. *The performance evaluation should be comprehensive.*

   Performance evaluation comprehensiveness entails that all the targets of the graphics recognition system are considered. General principles of graphics recognition are starting to emerge. Ablameyko (1996) has discovered the graphics recognition principles "from simple to complex" and "from local to global". Liu and Dori (1998b) formulated the stepwise component recovery principle. Likewise, we claim here that as a principle, the performance evaluation of graphics recognition algorithms should include powerful indices for attribute recognition of simple graphic object and for component recognition of compound graphic objects. Thus, line width recognition capability and endpoint detection accuracy should be considered for a line, while for a dimension set issues, like textbox and arrowhead segmentation, accuracy has to be considered. The overall recognition performance value of the matched part between a pair of a ground truth and a recognized object is the combination of these indices. Combining the individual indices into a single comprehensive one is a complex issue. While the arithmetic mean is usually the easiest function to be used as the overall index, it may result in distorted outcomes due to simple averaging. Instead, we propose to use the geometric (possibly weighted) mean of the indices as the overall index of the recognition quality of a graphic object, since we consider that the correct recognition of each attribute is dominant in the recognition of the entire object. Using geometric mean, some poorly recognized attributes cause the overall recognition to be of low overall quality (Liu and Dori, 1997; Liu and Dori, 1998a). As noted, recognition fragmentation and combination should also be evaluated. The more fragmentary and the more equally broken the recognized objects are, the lower is the recognition performance. One possible function that can be used for measuring recognition fragmentation of a ground truth is the square root of the sum of the squared matching degrees between the ground truth and all its matching recognized objects, as done by Liu and Dori (1997). The same principle is used in the combination evaluation. The overall recognition quality of an individual graphic object should include the recognition fragmentation/combination index and the overall attribute recognition index, which is the matching degree weighted sum of the overall recognition performance value of the matched parts of the individual graphic object. The overall recognition quality of the entire input data is a combination of the recognition qualities of all the individual objects. The performance of recognition algorithms is usually reflected by two rates: true positive and false positive (Nalwa, 1993). True positive rate, or recognition rate in the case of graphics recognition, is the rate of positive responses in the presence of instances of the feature, i.e., the ratio of the number of correctly recognized features to the total number of ground truths. False positive rate, or false alarm rate, is the rate of positive responses in the absence of the feature, i.e., the ratio of the number of incorrectly recognized features to the total number of recognized features. These two rates are used together because it is desired that the true positive rate is maximized while the false alarm rate is minimized. We also propose that two similar indices be used in the performance evaluation of graphics recognition algorithms. However, since we do not use binary acceptance values of matching, we calculate them as the matching degree weighted sum of the individual terms. Normally, adjusting the parameters within an algorithm that increases the true positive rate is often accompanied by increase of the false alarm rate. A tradeoff between them has to be accounted for. We therefore recommend that some single index that combines the true positive rate and the false alarm rate, such as, their (possibly weighted) average may be useful as an overall and parameter-independent performance indicator of graphics recognition system performance.

3. *The metrics definition should be quantitative, normative, objective, and compatible with the human vision evaluation.*
    Quantitative metrics are outcomes of the calculation of the performance indices. The metrics definition should be objective rather than arbitrary. We mean that the metrics definition should be accepted by most people and be based on large amount of experiments. The metrics should also be normalized to a uniform range of values, e.g., from 0, which is the worst, to 1, which is the best. Moreover, they should be compatible with human vision evaluation. The performance value given to a recognition result is compatible with the value that a professional human or group would assign as a score. Although the values given by different professionals may be different, the difference should be small. For instance, if one evaluates a result as good, the quantitative measurement should be around 0.8.

6. Summary

We have proposed principles for establishing a sound performance evaluation protocol for graphics recognition algorithms. A protocol should consist of three elements: ground truthing methodology, matching definition, and performance contents and metrics. The systems should be tested with both real life data and synthetic data. The effect of random noise input on the algorithms output should also be evaluated. The matching degree is proposed instead of a binary matching result. Ground truth is used as the basis for relative difference evaluation. The performance contents should be objective-driven and comprehensive, and the metrics should be objective, quantitative, normalized, and compatible with the human vision evaluation. The proposed principles in this chapter can be used as a framework for performance evaluation of the recognition of all special classes of graphic objects. People can gear it to the performance evaluation of a special class of algorithms, with some matching and metrics definitions, as done by (Liu and Dori, 1997; Liu and Dori, 1998a).

References

Ablameyko, S.V. (1996) Recognition of Graphic Images, Institute of Engineering Cybernetics, Minsk.

Baird, H.S. (1990) Document image defect models, *Proc. of IAPR Workshop on Syntactic and Structural Pattern Recognition*, Murray Hill, NJ, 38–46.

Baird, H.S. (1993) Calibration of document image defect models, *Proc. of Second Annual Symposium on Document Analysis and Information Retrieval*, Las Vegas, Nevada, 1–16.

Chhabra, A. and Phillips, I.T. (1998) The Second International Graphics Recognition Contest—Raster to Vector Conversion: A Report, Tombre, K. and Chhabra, A. (eds.), *Graphics Recognition—Algorithms and Systems, (Lecture Notes in Computer Science)*, Springer, 1389:390–410.

Haralick, R.M. (1989) Performance assessment of near perfect machines, *Machine vision and applications*, 2:1–16.

Haralick, R.M. (1992) Performance Characterization in Image Analysis—Thinning, a Case in Point, *Pattern Recognition Letters*, 13:5–12.

Hori, O. and Doermann, D.S. (1996) Quantitative Measurement of the Performance of Raster-to-Vector Conversion Algorithms, *Graphics Recognition—Methods and Applications (Lecture Notes in Computer Science)*, Kasturi, R. and Tombre, K. (eds), Springer, 1072:57–68.

Kanungo, T., Haralick, R.M. and Phillips, I.T. (1993) Global and local document degradation models, *Proc. of Second International Conference on Document Analysis and Recognition*, Tsukuba, Japan, 730–734.

Kanungo, T., Haralick, R.M. and Phillips, I.T. (1994) Nonlinear local and global document degradation models, *Int. Journal of Imaging Systems and Technology*, 5(4):220–230.

Kanungo, T., Baird, H.S. and Haralick, R.M. (1995) Estimation and validation of document degradation models, *Proc. of Fourth Annual Symposium on Document Analysis and Information Retrieval*, Las Vegas, Nevada, 217–228.

Kong, B., Phillips, I.T., Haralick, R.M., Prasad, A. and Kasturi, R. (1996) A Benchmark: Performance Evaluation of Dashed-Line Detection Algorithms, *Graphics Recognition—Methods and Applications (Lecture Notes in Computer Science)*, Kasturi, R. and Tombre, K. (eds), Springer, 1072:270–285.

Liu, W. and Dori, D. (1997) A Protocol for Performance Evaluation of Line Detection Algorithms, *Machine Vision Applications*, 9:240–250.

Liu, W. and Dori, D. (1998a) Performance Evaluation of Graphics/Text Separation, *Graphics Recognition—Algorithms and Systems, (Lecture Notes in Computer Science)*, Tombre, K. and Chhabra, A. (eds.), Springer, 1389:359–371.

Liu, W. and Dori, D. (1998b) Genericity in Graphics Recognition Algorithms, *Graphics Recognition—Algorithms and Systems, (Lecture Notes in Computer Science)*, Tombre, K. and Chhabra, A. (eds.), Springer, 1389:9–21.

Madej, D. and Sokolowski, A. (1993) Towards automatic evaluation of drawing analysis performance: A statistical model of cadastral map, *Proc. of Int. Conf. on Document Analysis and Recognition*, Tsukuba, Japan, 890–893.

Nalwa, V.S. (1993) A Guided Tour of Computer Vision, Addison-Wesley, New York.

Phillips, I.T., Liang, J., Chhabra, A. and Haralick, R.M. (1998) A Performance Evaluation Protocol for Graphics Recognition Systems, *Graphics Recognition—Algorithms and Systems, (Lecture Notes in Computer Science)*, Tombre, K. and Chhabra, A. (eds.), Springer, 1389:372–389.

DISSIMILARITY MEASURES BETWEEN GRAY-SCALE IMAGES AS A TOOL FOR PERFORMANCE ASSESSMENT

PIERO ZAMPERONI
Technische Universität Braunschweig
Institut für Nachrichtentechnik
Braunschweig, Germany

The *measure of dissimilarity* $D(A, B)$ between arbitrary gray-scale images A and B presented in this contribution is useful for a quantitative performance evaluation of image restoration, edge detection, thresholding and segmentation methods, see (Zamperoni and Starovoitov, 1998).

The performances of such methods are ranked on the basis of the lowest dissimilarity between the processed image and a ground truth, e.g. the original image or a-priori known edge maps. Further applications of the $D(A, B)$ measure are:

(i) Quantitative evaluation of the cumulative dissimilarity caused by small amounts of shift, rotation, affine deformations, illumination changes and different types of noise.

(ii) Selection, from an image database, of the most similar images with respect to a given comparison image.

After an overview on the state of the art in gray-scale image comparison approaches, this contribution examines a set of properties that D should have, in order to cope with the tasks mentioned above.

Then it proposes a multi-stage dissimilarity measure, in which each stage, i.e. point-to-point, point-to-image, local image-to-image and global image-to-image can be realized by means of different distance measures, thus originating a manifold of variants of D.

Some properties of these variants, related to the requirements posed to D and to the nature of the compared images, are examined and made the object of experimental verification.

Numerous experimental results, obtained with real-world images and with widespread operators to be assessed, illustrate the performances of the proposed measure in relation with the following tasks or desired properties:

R. Klette et al. (eds.), Performance Characterization in Computer Vision, 91–92.

  (i) Shift and rotation mesurements,
 (ii) Edge-preserving smoothing operators,
(iii) Edge detection operators,
 (iv) Image segmentation by labeling,
  (v) Binarization with automatic threshold selection,
 (vi) Robustness with respect to spike noise and to varying scene illumination,
(vii) Selection of the "most similar images" from a database, and
(viii) Face recognition.

References

Zamperoni, P. and Starovoitov, V. (1996) On measures of dissimilarity between arbitrary grey-scale images, *Int. Journal of Shape Modeling*, 2:189–213.

Part III

Statistical Aspects

PROPAGATING COVARIANCE IN COMPUTER VISION

ROBERT M. HARALICK
Intelligent Systems Laboratory
Dept. of Electrical Engineering
University of Washington
Seattle, WA 98195, USA

1. Introduction

Each real computer vision problem begins with one or more noisy images and has many algorithmic steps. Development of the best algorithm requires understanding how the uncertainty due to the random perturbation affecting the input image(s) propagates through the different algorithmic steps and results in a perturbation on whatever quantities are finally computed. Perhaps a more accurate statement would be that the quantities finally computed must really be considered to be estimated quantities.

Once we have the perspective that what we compute are estimates, then it becomes clear that even though the different ways of estimating the same quantity typically yield the same result if the input quantities are not affected by a random perturbation, it is certainly not the case that the different ways of estimating the same quantities yield an estimate with the same distribution when the input is perturbed by a random perturbation. It is clearly the case that the distribution of the estimate depends on the distribution of the input random perturbation and the method or type of estimate.

With this in mind, it is then important to understand how to propagate a random perturbation through any algorithm step in a vision problem. The difficulty is that the steps are not necessarily linear computations, the random perturbations are not necessarily additive, and the appropriate kinds of perturbations change from algorithm step to algorithm step. Nevertheless, there are many computer vision and image analysis algorithm steps in which the appropriate kind of random perturbation is additive or approximately additive. For these kinds of steps one basic measure of the

95

R. Klette et al. (eds.), Performance Characterization in Computer Vision, 95–114.

size of the random perturbation is given by the covariance matrix of the estimate.

In this chapter, we describe how to propagate the covariance matrix of an input random perturbation through any kind of a calculation (linear or non-linear) that extremizes an implicit scalar function, with or without constraints, of the perturbed input quantity and the calculated output estimate. The only assumption is that the scalar function to be extremized have finite first and second order partial derivatives and that the random perturbations are small enough so that the relationship between the scalar function evaluated at the ideal but unknown input and output quantities and the observed input quantity and perturbed output quantity can be approximated sufficiently well by a first order Taylor series expansion. The propagation relationships do not depend on what algorithm is used to extremize the given scalar function.

As a related case, the given propagation relationships also show how to propagate the covariance of the coefficients of a function for which we wish to find a zero to the covariance of any zero we can find.

The analysis techniques of propagation of errors is well known in the photogrammetry literature. The Manual of Photogrammetry (Slama, 1980) has a section showing how to determine the variance of Y where $Y = F(X)$ from the variance of X. The generalization of this to find the covariance matrix for Y given the covariance matrix for X is rather straightforward. Just expand F around the mean of X in a first order Taylor expansion and consider that Y is a linear function T of X. Once the coefficients of the linear combination is known, so that the randomness of Y can be approximated by $Y - \mu_Y = T(X - \mu_X)$, then the covariance matrix Σ_Y of Y is easily seen to be given in terms of T and the covariance matrix Σ_X of X by $\Sigma_Y = T\Sigma_X T'$ (Mikhail, 1976; Koch, 1987). This only works well for cases where the function F can be given explicitly. The problem we discuss here is one in which the function F is not given explicitly, but Y is related to X in a specific way. The techniques we employ are well-known in statistical and engineering communities. There is nothing sophisticated in the derivation. However, this technique is perhaps not so well known in the computer vision community. There are many recent vision-related papers that could be cited to illustrate this. See for example (Weng *et al.*, 1992; Wu and Wang, 1993; Williams and Shah, 1993).

The chapter concludes with a discussion of how to validate that the software which we use to accomplish the calculation we desire actually works. We argue that this validation can be done by comparing the predicted statistical behavior with the experimentally observed statistical behavior in a set of controlled experiments.

2. The Abstract Model

The abstract model has three kinds of objects. The first kind of object relates to the measurable quantities or data. There is the unobserved $N \times 1$ vector X of the ideal unperturbed measurable quantities. We assume that each component of X is some real number. Added to this unobserved ideal unperturbed vector is an $N \times 1$ unobserved random vector $\triangle X$ of noise. The observed quantity is the randomly perturbed vector $X + \triangle X$.

The second kind of object relates to the unknown parameters. There is the unobserved $K \times 1$ vector Θ. We assume that each component of Θ is some real number. Added to this ideal unperturbed vector is a $K \times 1$ unobserved vector $\triangle \Theta$ that is the random perturbation on Θ induced by the random perturbation $\triangle X$ on X. The calculated quantity is the randomly perturbed parameter vector $\hat{\Theta} = \Theta + \triangle \Theta$.

The meaning of the data vector X and the parameter vector Θ is that there is a physical process which produces X on the basis of Θ. The law governing this production process is known. The third kind of object directly relates to this law. It is a continuous non-negative scalar valued function F which relates the unobserved vectors X and Θ: $F(X, \Theta) = 0$. Since F is non-negative, this is the smallest value that F can take. Therefore, for a given X, the corresponding Θ must minimize $F(X, \Theta)$.

Of course neither X nor Θ are observed. Rather only $\hat{X}$, the randomly perturbed value of X is observed. From it we desire to infer the value for Θ. But because $\hat{X} = X + \triangle X$ is random, the inferred value $\hat{\Theta} = \Theta + \triangle \Theta$ that we compute for Θ will be random. It will not be the case that $F(\hat{X}, \hat{\Theta}) = 0$. However, the estimation problem that we set up to infer a value $\hat{\Theta}$ for Θ will minimize $F(\hat{X}, \hat{\Theta})$. Therefore, in this situation it is natural to require that the function F to have finite first and second partial derivatives with respect to each component of Θ and X, including all second mixed partial derivatives taken with respect to a component of Θ and with respect to a component of X.

The basic inference problem is: given $\hat{X} = X + \triangle X$, determine a $\hat{\Theta} = \Theta + \triangle \Theta$ to minimize $F(\hat{X}, \hat{\Theta})$ given the fact that Θ minimizes $F(X, \Theta)$. For this estimate $\hat{\Theta}$ we want to compute its covariance matrix.

If $\hat{\Theta}$ is computed by an explicit function h, so that $\hat{\Theta} = h(\hat{X})$, the function F is just given by $F(X, \Theta) = (\Theta - h(X))'(\Theta - h(x))$. However, our development will handle as well the determining of the covariance of a $\hat{\Theta}$ which is known to minimize $F(\hat{X}, \hat{\Theta})$, without requiring any knowledge of how the minimizing $\hat{\Theta}$ was computed.

It is not unusual for some computer vision problems to be constrained problems. In this case the parameter vector Θ satisfies some constraints which we represent as $s(\Theta) = 0$. The unobserved ideal Θ, satisfying the constraints $s(\Theta) = 0$, and the unobserved ideal X minimize the scalar function F. In the constrained problem, $\hat{X} = X + \triangle X$ is observed and the problem is to determine that $\hat{\Theta} = \Theta + \triangle\Theta$ satisfying the constraints $s(\hat{\Theta}) = 0$ which minimizes $F(\hat{X}, \hat{\Theta})$.

We will see that the covariance matrix for $\hat{\Theta}$ will be a function of the unobserved unperturbed X and Θ, the covariance matrix for the perturbation $\triangle X$, and the partial derivatives of F evaluated at X and Θ. We will be able to develop estimates for this covariance matrix in terms of the observed $\hat{X}$, the inferred $\hat{\Theta}$, the covariance matrix for the perturbation $\triangle X$, and the partial derivatives of F evaluated at $\hat{X}$ and $\hat{\Theta}$.

Finally, we say what this abstract model is not. It is not a model for the general problem in which the covariance matrix for $\hat{X}$ is known and the inferred value for $\hat{\Theta}$ minimizes a non-negative $F(\hat{X}, \hat{\Theta})$. It is not a model for this problem because this problem does not have the assumption that there is an ideal X and Θ and the ideal Θ minimizes $F(X, \Theta)$ and this minimum value of F is 0.

3. Example Computer Vision Problems

There is a rich variety of computer vision problems which fit the form of the abstract model. In this section we outline a few of them, specifically: curve fitting (Koch, 1987), coordinated curve fitting, local feature extraction, exterior orientation, and relative orientation. Other kinds of calculations in computer vision such as calculation of curvature, invariants, vanishing points, or points at which two or more curves intersect, or problems such as motion recovery (Jerian and Jain, 1984) are all examples of problems which can be put in the abstract form as given above.

3.1. CURVE FITTING

In the general curve fitting scenario, there is the unknown free parameter vector, Θ, of the curve and the set of unknown ideal points on the curve $\{x_1, \ldots, x_N\}$. Each of the ideal points is then perturbed. If $\triangle x_n$ is the random noise perturbation of the nth point, then the observed point n^{th} point is $\hat{x}_n = x_n + \triangle x_n$. The form of the curve is given by a known function f which relates a point on the curve to the parameters of the curve. That is, for each ideal point x_n we have $f(x_n, \Theta) = 0$. We also assume that the parameters of the curve satisfy its own set of constraint equations: $h(\Theta) = 0$. The curve fitting problem is then to find an estimate $\hat{\Theta}$ to minimize $\Sigma_{n=1}^{N} f^2(\hat{x}_n, \hat{\Theta})$ subject to $h(\hat{\Theta}) = 0$. To put this problem in the form of the abstract problem we let

$$X = (x_1, \ldots, x_N)$$

$$\hat{X} = (x_1 + \triangle x_1, \ldots, x_n + \triangle x_N)$$
$$F(X, \Theta, \Lambda) = \Sigma_{n=1}^{N} f^2(x_n, \psi) + h(\Theta)' \Lambda$$

Then the curve fitting problem is to find $\hat{\Theta}$ and $\hat{\Lambda}$ to minimize $F(\hat{X}, \hat{\Theta}, \hat{\Lambda})$ where $F(X, \Theta, \Lambda) = 0$.

3.2. COORDINATED CURVE FITTING

In the coordinated curve fitting problem, multiple curves have to be fit on independent data, but the fitted curves have to satisfy some joint constraint. We illustrate the discussion in this section with a coordinated fitting of two curves and a constraint that the two curves must have some common point at which they are tangent.

Let $(x_1, \ldots, x_I)$ be the ideal points which are associated with the first curve whose parameters are ψ_1 and whose constraint is $h_1(\psi_1) = 0$. Each point x_i satisfies $f_1(x_i, \psi_1) = 0$, $i = 1, \ldots, I$.

Likewise, let $(y_1, \ldots, y_J)$ be the ideal points which are associated with the second curve whose parameters are ψ_2 and whose constraint is $h_2(\psi_2) = 0$. Each point y_j satisfies $f_2(y_j, \psi_2) = 0$, $j = 1, \ldots, J$.

The coordinated constraint is that for some unknown z,

$$f_1(z, \psi_1) = 0$$
$$f_2(z, \psi_2) = 0$$
$$\frac{\partial f_1}{\partial z}(z, \psi_1) = \frac{\partial f_2}{\partial z}(z, \psi_2)$$

The observed points $\hat{x}_i$ and $\hat{y}_j$ are related to the corresponding ideal points by

$$\hat{x}_i = x_i + \triangle x_i$$
$$\hat{y}_j = y_j + \triangle y_j$$

To put this problem in the framework of the abstract model, we take

$$\hat{X} = (\hat{x}_1, \ldots, \hat{x}_I, \hat{y}_1, \ldots, \hat{y}_J)$$
$$\hat{\Theta} = (\hat{\psi}_1, \hat{\psi}_2, \hat{z})$$
$$\hat{\Lambda} = (\hat{\lambda}_1, \hat{\lambda}_2, \hat{\lambda}_3, \hat{\lambda}_4, \hat{\lambda}_5)$$

and define

$$F(\hat{X}, \hat{\Theta}, \hat{\Lambda}) = \Sigma_{i=1}^{I} f_1^2(\hat{x}_i, \hat{\psi}_1) + \Sigma_{j=1}^{J} f_2^2(y_j, \psi_2) + \hat{\lambda}_1 h_1(\hat{\psi}_1) + \hat{\lambda}_2 h_2(\hat{\psi}_2)$$
$$+ \hat{\lambda}_3 f_1(z, \hat{\psi}_1) + \hat{\lambda}_4 f_2(z, \hat{\psi}_2) + \hat{\lambda}_5 [\frac{\partial f_1}{\partial z}(z, \psi_1) - \frac{\partial f_2}{\partial z}(z, \psi_2)]$$

The coordinated curve fitting problem is then to determine a $\hat{\Theta}$ and $\hat{\Lambda}$ to minimize $F(\hat{X}, \hat{\Theta}, \hat{\Lambda})$, where the perturbed $\hat{\Theta}$ is considered related to the ideal Θ by $\hat{\Theta} = \Theta + \triangle\Theta$.

3.3. LOCAL FEATURE EXTRACTION

There are a variety of local features that can be extracted from an image. Examples include edges, corners, ridges, valleys, flats, saddles, slopes, hillsides, saddle hillsides, etc. Each local feature involves the calculation of some quantities assuming that the neighborhood has the feature and then a detection is performed based on the calculated quantities. For example, in the simple gradient edge feature, the quantity calculated is the gradient magnitude and the edge feature is detected if the calculated gradient magnitude is high enough. Here we concentrate on the calculation of the quantities associated with the feature and not the detection of the feature itself.

To put this problem in the setting of the abstract problem, we let Θ be the vector of unknown free parameters of the feature and X be the unobserved neighborhood array of noiseless brightness values. We let $\hat{X}$ be the perturbed observed neighborhood array of brightness values, $\hat{X} = X + \triangle X$, and $\hat{\Theta}$ be the calculation of the required quantities from the perturbed brightness values $\hat{X}$. The form the of feature is given by the known function f which satisfies that $f(X, \Theta) = 0$. The feature extraction problem is then to find the estimate $\hat{\Theta}$ to minimize $F(\hat{X}, \Theta) = f^2(\hat{X}, \hat{\Theta})$.

3.4. EXTERIOR ORIENTATION

In the exterior orientation problem, there is a known 3D object model having points $(x_n, y_n, z_n), n = 1, \ldots, N$. The unobserved noiseless perspective projection of the point (x_n, y_n, z_n) is given by (u_n, v_n). The relationship between a 3D model point and its corresponding perspective projection is given by a rotation and translation of the object model point, to put it in the reference frame of the camera, followed by a perspective projection. So if ψ represents the triple of tilt angle, pan angle, and swing angle of the rotation, t represents the x-y-z-translation vector, and k represents the camera constant (the focal length of the camera lens), we can write:

$$(u_n, v_n)' = \frac{k}{r_n}(p_n, q_n)' \text{ where}$$
$$(p_n, q_n, r_n)' = R(\psi)(x_n, y_n, z_n)' + t$$

and where $R(\psi)$ is the 3×3 rotation matrix corresponding to the rotation angle vector ψ.

The function to be minimized can then be written as:

$$f_n(u_n, v_n, \psi, t) = f(u_n, v_n, x_n, y_n, z_n, \psi, t) \text{ where}$$

$$f(u_n, v_n, x_n, y_n, z_n, \psi, t) = [u_n - k\frac{(1,0,0)(R(\psi)(x_n, y_n, z_n)' + t)}{(0,0,1)(R(\psi)(x_n, y_n, z_n)' + t)}]^2$$

$$+ [v_n - k\frac{(0,1,0)(R(\psi)(x_n, y_n, z_n)' + t)}{(0,0,1)(R(\psi)(x_n, y_n, z_n)' + t)}]^2$$

To put this problem in the form of the abstract description we take

$$X = (u_1, v_1, \ldots, u_n, v_n)$$
$$\hat{X} = (\hat{u}_1, \hat{v}_1, \ldots \hat{u}_n, \hat{v}_n)$$
$$\Theta = (\psi, t)$$
$$\hat{\Theta} = (\hat{\psi}, \hat{t})$$

and define

$$F(\hat{X}, \hat{\Theta}) = \Sigma_{n=1}^N f_n^2(\hat{u}_n, \hat{v}_n, \hat{\Theta})$$

The exterior orientation problem is then to find a $\hat{\Theta}$ to minimize $F(\hat{X}, \hat{\Theta})$, given that $F(X, \Theta) = 0$. Because F is non-negative it must be that Θ minimizes $F(X, \Theta)$.

3.5. RELATIVE ORIENTATION

The relative orientation problem can be put into the form of the abstract problem in a similar way to the exterior orientation problem. We let the perspective projection of the nth point on the left image be (u_{nL}, v_{nL}) and the perspective projection of the nth point on the right image be (u_{nR}, v_{nR}). Then we can write that

$$(u_{nL}, v_{nL})' = \frac{k}{z_n}(x_n, y_n)' \text{ and that}$$

$$(u_{nR}, v_{nR})' = \frac{k}{r_n}(p_n, q_n)$$

where (p_n, q_n, r_n) is the rotated and translated model point as given in the description of the exterior orientation problem.

The observed perspective projection of the nth model point is noisy and represented as $(\hat{u}_n, \hat{v}_n) = (u_n + \triangle u_n, v_n + \triangle v_n)$. Then taking

$$X = (u_{1L}, v_{1L}, u_{1R}, v_{1R}, \ldots, u_{NL}, v_{NL}, u_{NR}, v_{NR})$$

$$\hat{X} = (\hat{u}_{1L}, \hat{v}_{1L}, \hat{u}_{1R}, \hat{v}_{1R}, \ldots, \hat{u}_{NL}, \hat{v}_{NL}, \hat{u}_{NR}, \hat{v}_{NR})$$

$$\Theta = (x_1, y_1, z_1, \ldots, x_N, y_N, z_N, \psi, t)$$

$$\hat{\Theta} = (\hat{x}_1, \hat{y}_1, \hat{z}_1, \ldots, \hat{x}_N \hat{y}_N, \hat{z}_N, \hat{\psi}, \hat{t})$$

the relative orientation problem is to find $\hat{\Theta}$ to minimize

$$F(\hat{X}, \hat{\Theta}) = \Sigma_{n=1}^N f(u_{nR}, v_{nR}, x_n, y_n, z_n, \psi, t) + f(u_{nl}, v_{nL}, x_n, y_n, z_n, 0, 0)$$

4. Zero Finding

Zero finding such as finding the zero of a polynomial in one or more variables occurs in a number of vision problems. Two examples are the three
point perspective resection problem and some of the techniques for motion
recovery. The zero finding problem is precisely in the form required for
computing the covariance matrix $\Sigma_{\triangle\Theta}$ as described in the solution section.
Let X be the ideal input vector and $\hat{X}$ be the observed perturbed input
vector. Let Θ be a $K \times 1$ vector zeroing the $K \times 1$ function $g(X, \Theta)$; that is,
$g(X, \Theta) = 0$. Finally, let $\hat{\Theta}$ be the computed vector zeroing $g(\hat{X}, \hat{\Theta})$; that
is, $g(\hat{X}, \hat{\Theta}) = 0$.

5. Solution: Unconstrained Case

For the purpose of covariance determination of the computed $\hat{\Theta} = \Theta + \triangle\Theta$,
the technique used to solve the extremization problem is not important,
provided that there are no singularities or near singularities in the numerical
computation procedure itself.

To understand how the random perturbation $\triangle X$ acting on the unobserved vector X to produce the observed vector $\hat{X} = X + \triangle X$ propagates to
the random perturbation $\triangle\Theta$ on the true but unknown parameter vector Θ
to produce the computed parameter vector $\hat{\Theta} = \Theta + \triangle\Theta$, we can take partial
derivatives of F with respect to each of the K components of Θ forming
the gradient vector g of f. The gradient g is a $K \times 1$ vector function.

$$g(X, \Theta) = \frac{\partial F}{\partial \Theta}(X, \Theta)$$

The solution $\hat{\Theta} = \Theta + \triangle\Theta$ extremizing $F(X + \triangle X, \Theta + \triangle\Theta)$, however it is
calculated, must be a zero of $g(X + \triangle X, \Theta + \triangle\Theta)$. Now taking a Taylor series
expansion of g around (X, Θ) we obtain to a first order approximation:

$$g^{K \times 1}(X + \triangle X, \Theta + \triangle\Theta) = g^{K \times 1}(X, \Theta) + \frac{\partial g}{\partial X}'^{K \times N}(X, \Theta)\triangle X^{N \times 1}$$

$$+\frac{\partial g}{\partial \Theta}'\overset{K \times K}{(X, \Theta)}\Delta\Theta^{K \times 1}$$

But since $\Theta + \Delta\Theta$ extremizes $F(X+\Delta X, \Theta+\Delta\Theta)$, $g(X+\Delta X, \Theta+\Delta\Theta) = 0$. Also, since Θ extremizes $F(X, \Theta)$, $g(X, \Theta) = 0$. Thus to a first order approximation,

$$0 = \frac{\partial g}{\partial X}'(X, \Theta)\Delta X + \frac{\partial g}{\partial \Theta}'(X, \Theta)\Delta\Theta$$

Since the relative extremum of F is a relative minimum, the $K \times K$ matrix

$$\frac{\partial g}{\partial \Theta}(X, \Theta) = \frac{\partial f^2}{\partial^2 \Theta}(X, \Theta)$$

must be positive definite for all (X, Θ). This implies that $\frac{\partial g}{\partial \Theta}(X, \Theta)$ is non-singular. Hence $(\frac{\partial g}{\partial \Theta})^{-1}$ exists and since it is symmetric we can write:

$$\Delta\Theta = -\{\frac{\partial g}{\partial \Theta}(X, \Theta)\}^{-1}\frac{\partial g}{\partial X}'(X, \Theta)\Delta X$$

This relation states how the random perturbation ΔX on X propagates to the random perturbation $\Delta\Theta$ on Θ. If the expected value of ΔX, $E[\Delta X]$, is zero, then from this relation we see the $E[\Delta\Theta]$ will also be zero, to a first order approximation.

This relation also permits us to calculate the covariance of the random perturbation $\Delta\Theta$.

$$
\begin{aligned}
\Sigma_{\Delta\Theta} &= E[\Delta\Theta\Delta\Theta'] \\
&= E[-(\frac{\partial g}{\partial \Theta})^{-1}\frac{\partial g}{\partial X}'\Delta X(-(\frac{\partial g}{\partial \Theta})^{-1}\frac{\partial g}{\partial X}'\Delta X)'] \\
&= (\frac{\partial g}{\partial \Theta})^{-1}\frac{\partial g}{\partial X}'E[\Delta X\Delta X']\frac{\partial g}{\partial X}(\frac{\partial g}{\partial \Theta})^{-1}{}' \\
&= (\frac{\partial g}{\partial \Theta})^{-1}\frac{\partial g}{\partial X}'\Sigma_{\Delta X}\frac{\partial g}{\partial X}(\frac{\partial g}{\partial \Theta})^{-1}
\end{aligned}
$$

Thus to the extent that the first order approximation is good, (i.e. $E[\Delta\Theta] = 0$), then

$$\Sigma_{\hat{\Theta}} = \Sigma_{\Delta\Theta}$$

The way in which we have derived the covariance matrix for $\Delta\Theta$ based on the covariance matrix for ΔX requires that the matrices

$$\frac{\partial g}{\partial \Theta}(X, \Theta) \text{ and } \frac{\partial g}{\partial X}(X, \Theta)$$

be known. But X and Θ are not observed. $X + \triangle X$ is observed and by some means $\Theta + \triangle\Theta$ is then calculated. So if we want to determine an estimate $\hat{\Sigma}_{\hat{\Theta}}$ for the covariance matrix $\Sigma_{\hat{\Theta}}$, we can proceed by expanding $g(X, \Theta)$ around $g(X + \triangle X, \Theta + \triangle\Theta)$.

$$g(X,\Theta) = g(X + \triangle X, \Theta + \triangle\Theta) - \frac{\partial g}{\partial X}'(X + \triangle X, \Theta + \triangle\Theta)\triangle X$$
$$- \frac{\partial g}{\partial\Theta}'(X + \triangle X, \Theta + \triangle\Theta)\triangle\Theta$$

Here we find in a similar manner,

$$\triangle\Theta = -(\frac{\partial g}{\partial\Theta}(X + \triangle X, \Theta + \triangle\Theta))^{-1}\frac{\partial g}{\partial X}(X + \triangle X, \Theta + \triangle\Theta)\triangle X$$

This motivates the estimator $\hat{\Sigma}_{\triangle\Theta}$ for $\Sigma_{\triangle\Theta}$ defined by

$$\hat{\Sigma}_{\triangle\Theta} = (\frac{\partial g}{\partial\Theta}(\hat{X},\hat{\Theta})^{-1}\frac{\partial g}{\partial X}'(\hat{X},\hat{\Theta})\Sigma_{\triangle X}\frac{\partial g}{\partial X}(\hat{X},\hat{\Theta})(\frac{\partial g}{\partial\Theta}(\hat{X},\hat{\Theta})^{-1}$$

So to the extent that the first order approximation is good, $\hat{\Sigma}_{\hat{\Theta}} = \hat{\Sigma}_{\triangle\Theta}$. The relation giving the estimate $\hat{\Sigma}_{\hat{\Theta}}$ in terms of the computable

$$\frac{\partial g}{\partial\Theta}(\hat{X},\hat{\Theta}) \text{ and } \frac{\partial g}{\partial X}(\hat{X},\hat{\Theta})$$

means that an estimated covariance matrix for the computed $\hat{\Theta} = \Theta + \triangle\Theta$ can also be calculated at the same time that the estimate $\hat{\Theta}$ of Θ is calculated.

5.1. BAYESIAN MEAN ESTIMATION

Consider the case when we observe a random vector $\hat{X}$ which is known to come from a Normal distribution with unknown mean Θ and known covariance matrix $\Sigma_{\hat{X}}$. The prior distribution on Θ has mean 0 and known covariance matrix Σ_Θ. From the observation $\hat{X}$ we are to find $\hat{\Theta}$, the most probable value for the mean Θ. In this case the function F to be minimized by choice of $\hat{\Theta}$ is:

$$F(\hat{X},\hat{\Theta}) = (\hat{X} - \hat{\Theta})'\Sigma_{\hat{X}}^{-1}(\hat{X} - \hat{\Theta}) + \hat{\Theta}'\Sigma_\Theta^{-1}\hat{\Theta}$$

In this case we can compute

$$g(\hat{X},\hat{\Theta}) = \frac{\partial F}{\partial\Theta}$$
$$= -2\Sigma_{\hat{X}}(\hat{X} - \Theta)' + 2\Sigma_\Theta\Theta$$

We can find the optimal value for $\hat{\Theta}$ by solving for that $\hat{\Theta}$ that makes $g(\hat{X}, \hat{\Theta}) = 0$. We find that

$$\hat{\Theta} = (\Sigma_{\hat{X}} + \Sigma_{\Theta})^{-1} \Sigma_{\hat{X}} \hat{X}$$

From this it is easy to explicitly determine $\Sigma_{\hat{\Theta}}$.

$$\Sigma_{\hat{\Theta}} = (\Sigma_{\hat{X}} + \Sigma_{\Theta})^{-1} \Sigma_{\hat{X}} (\Sigma_{\hat{X}} + \Sigma_{\Theta})^{-1}$$

Proceeding to compute the covariance matrix of $\hat{X}$ implicitly, we have

$$\frac{\partial g}{\partial \Theta} = 2\Sigma_{\hat{X}} + 2\Sigma_{\Theta}$$

and

$$\frac{\partial g}{\partial X} = -2\Sigma_{\hat{X}}$$

Now substituting into the equation for the implicit computation of $\Sigma_{\hat{\Theta}}$ there results

$$\begin{aligned} \Sigma_{\hat{\Theta}} &= (2\Sigma_{\hat{X}} + 2\Sigma_{\Theta})^{-1}(-2\Sigma_{\hat{X}})\Sigma_{\hat{X}}(-2\Sigma_{\hat{X}})(2\Sigma_{\hat{X}} + 2\Sigma_{\Theta})^{-1} \\ &= (\Sigma_{\hat{X}} + \Sigma_{\Theta})^{-1}\Sigma_{\hat{X}}(\Sigma_{\hat{X}} + \Sigma_{\Theta})^{-1} \end{aligned}$$

Notice that in this case the covariance matrix for the estimate $\hat{\Theta}$ does not depend on the ideal, non-observed value for X. But this is not always the case as our next example shows.

5.2. REGRESSION

As a special and classic case of the unconstrained optimization, we consider the regression problem of finding Θ to minimize $F(X, \Theta) = (X - J\Theta)' \Sigma_X^{-1} (X - J\Theta)$. For this F,

$$g(X, \Theta) = \frac{\partial F}{\partial \Theta} = -2J' \Sigma_X^{-1} J\Theta$$

Hence,

$$\frac{\partial g}{\partial \Theta} = 2J' \Sigma_X^{-1} J$$

and

$$\frac{\partial g}{\partial X} = -2\Sigma_X^{-1} J$$

Then,

$$\begin{aligned} \Sigma_{\Theta} &= (2J'\Sigma_X^{-1}J)^{-1}(-2\Sigma_X^{-1}J)\Sigma_X(-2\Sigma_X^{-1}J)'(2J'\Sigma_X^{-1}J)^{-1} \\ &= (J'\Sigma_X^{-1}J)^{-1} \end{aligned}$$

5.3. LINE FITTING

Another special case of the unconstrained optimization problem is the general line-fitting problem, which we illustrate for two-dimensional data. Assume that the unobserved points unperturbed points (x_n, y_n), $n = 1, \ldots, N$, lie on a line $x_n \cos\theta + y_n \sin\theta - \rho = 0$. In the line-fitting problem, we observe $(\hat{x}_n, \hat{y}_n)$, noisy instances of (x_n, y_n). $(\hat{x}_n, \hat{y}_n)$ are related to (x_n, y_n) by the noise model:

$$\begin{pmatrix} \hat{x}_n \\ \hat{y}_n \end{pmatrix} = \begin{pmatrix} x_n \\ y_n \end{pmatrix} + \xi_n \begin{pmatrix} \cos\theta \\ \sin\theta \end{pmatrix}$$

where ξ_n are independent and identically distributed as $N(0, \sigma^2)$.

To estimate the best fitting line parameters $(\hat{\theta}, \hat{\rho})$ using the least squares method, we use the criterion function which is the sum of the squared distances between the observed points and the fitted line:

$$F(X, \Theta) = \sum_{n=1}^{N} (x_n \cos\theta + y_n \sin\theta - \rho)^2$$

where $X = (x_1, y_1, \ldots, x_N, y_N)$ and $\Theta = (\theta, \rho)$. Now,

$$g^{2 \times 1}(X, \Theta) = \frac{\partial F}{\partial \Theta} = \begin{pmatrix} \frac{\partial F}{\partial \theta} \\ \frac{\partial F}{\partial \rho} \end{pmatrix}$$

Letting

$$\mu_x = \frac{1}{N} \sum_{n=1}^{N} x_n$$

$$\mu_y = \frac{1}{N} \sum_{n=1}^{N} y_n$$

$$S_x^2 = \sum_{n=1}^{N} (x_n - \mu_x)^2$$

$$S_y^2 = \sum_{n=1}^{N} (y_n - \mu_y)^2$$

$$S_{xy} = \sum_{n=1}^{N} (x_n - \mu_x)(y_n - \mu_y);$$

we can compute

$$\frac{\partial F}{\partial \theta} = (S_y^2 - S_x^2 + N(\mu_y^2 - \mu_x^2)) \sin 2\theta + 2(S_{xy} + N\mu_x\mu_y) \cos 2\theta$$
$$+ 2N\rho(\mu_x \sin\theta - \mu_y \cos\theta)$$

$$\frac{\partial F}{\partial \rho} = -2N(\mu_x \cos\theta + \mu_y \sin\theta - \rho)$$

Then,

$$\frac{\partial g}{\partial \Theta}^{2\times 2} = \begin{pmatrix} \frac{\partial g}{\partial \theta} \\ \frac{\partial g}{\partial \rho} \end{pmatrix} = \begin{pmatrix} \frac{\partial^2 F}{\partial \theta^2} & \frac{\partial^2 F}{\partial \theta \partial \rho} \\ \frac{\partial^2 F}{\partial \rho \partial \theta} & \frac{\partial^2 F}{\partial \rho^2} \end{pmatrix}$$

where

$$\frac{\partial^2 F}{\partial \theta^2} = 2[S_y^2 - S_x^2 + N(\mu_y^2 - \mu_x^2)] \cos 2\theta - 4(S_{xy} + N\mu_x\mu_y) \sin 2\theta$$
$$+ 2N\rho(\mu_x \cos\theta + \mu_y \sin\theta)$$

$$\frac{\partial^2 F}{\partial \rho^2} = 2N$$

$$\frac{\partial^2 F}{\partial \theta \partial \rho} = \frac{\partial^2 F}{\partial \rho \partial \theta} = 2N(\mu_x \sin\theta - \mu_y \cos\theta)$$

and

$$\frac{\partial g}{\partial X}^{'\,2\times 2N} = \begin{pmatrix} \frac{\partial^2 F}{\partial \theta \partial x_1} & \frac{\partial^2 F}{\partial \theta \partial y_1} & \frac{\partial^2 F}{\partial \theta \partial x_2} & \frac{\partial^2 F}{\partial \theta \partial y_2} & \frac{\partial^2 F}{\partial \theta \partial x_n} & \cdots & \frac{\partial^2 F}{\partial \theta \partial y_n} \\ \frac{\partial^2 F}{\partial \rho \partial x_1} & \frac{\partial^2 F}{\partial \rho \partial y_1} & \frac{\partial^2 F}{\partial \rho \partial x_2} & \frac{\partial^2 F}{\partial \rho \partial y_2} & \cdots & \frac{\partial^2 F}{\partial \rho \partial x_N} & \frac{\partial^2 F}{\partial \rho \partial y_N} \end{pmatrix}$$

$$\underbrace{\qquad\qquad\qquad\qquad\qquad\qquad\qquad\qquad\qquad\qquad}_{2\times 2N}$$

where

$$\frac{\partial^2 F}{\partial \theta \partial x_n} = 2[-x_n \sin 2\theta + y_n \cos 2\theta + \rho \sin\theta]$$

$$\frac{\partial^2 F}{\partial \theta \partial y_n} = 2[x_n \cos 2\theta + y_n \sin 2\theta - \rho \cos\theta]$$

$$\frac{\partial^2 F}{\partial \rho \partial x_n} = -2\cos\theta$$

$$\frac{\partial^2 F}{\partial \rho \partial y_n} = -2\sin\theta$$

Since the parametric equation of the line is given by

$$\begin{pmatrix} x_n \\ y_n \end{pmatrix} = \rho \begin{pmatrix} \cos\theta \\ \sin\theta \end{pmatrix} + \lambda_n \begin{pmatrix} -\sin\theta \\ \cos\theta \end{pmatrix}$$

substituting the above expressions for x_n and y_n into the partial derivatives, we obtain

$$\frac{\partial^2 F}{\partial\theta\partial x_n} = 2\lambda_n \cos\theta$$

$$\frac{\partial^2 F}{\partial\theta\partial y_n} = 2\lambda_n \sin\theta$$

$$\frac{\partial^2 F}{\partial\rho\partial x_n} = -2\cos\theta$$

$$\frac{\partial^2 F}{\partial\rho\partial y_n} = -2\sin\theta$$

For the given noise model, the covariance matrix Σ_X is given by:

$$\Sigma_X = \sigma^2 \begin{pmatrix} \cos^2\theta & \sin\theta\cos\theta & \cdots & 0 & 0 & 0 \\ \sin\theta\cos\theta & \sin^2\theta & 0 & \cdots & 0 & 0 \\ 0 & 0 & \cos^2\theta & \sin\theta\cos\theta & \cdots & 0 \\ 0 & 0 & \sin\theta\cos\theta & \sin^2\theta & \cdots & 0 \\ \vdots & & & & & \\ 0 & 0 & \cdots & 0 & \cos^2\theta & \sin\theta\cos\theta \\ 0 & 0 & 0 & \cdots & \sin\theta\cos\theta & \sin^2\theta \end{pmatrix}$$

Now we can easily do the required multiplications.

$$\frac{\partial g}{\partial X}' \Sigma_x \frac{\partial g}{\partial X} = 4\sigma^2 \begin{pmatrix} \sum_{n=1}^{N}\lambda_n^2 & -\sum_{n=1}^{N}\lambda_n \\ -\sum_{n=1}^{N}\lambda_n & N \end{pmatrix}$$

Define

$$\mu_\lambda = \frac{1}{N}\sum_{n=1}^{N}\lambda_n$$

$$S_\lambda^2 = \sum_{n=1}^{N}(\lambda_n - \mu_\lambda)^2$$

Then we have that

$$\mu_x = \rho\cos\theta - \mu_\lambda\sin\theta$$
$$\mu_y = \rho\sin\theta + \mu_\lambda\cos\theta$$
$$S_x^2 = \sin^2\theta S_\lambda^2$$
$$S_y^2 = \cos^2\theta S_\lambda^2$$
$$S_{xy} = -\sin\theta\cos\theta S_\lambda^2$$

Thus,

$$\mu_y^2 - mu_x^2 = (\mu_\lambda^2 - \rho^2)\cos 2\theta + 2\rho\mu_\lambda\sin 2\theta$$
$$\mu_x\mu_y = \frac{\rho^2 - \mu_\lambda^2}{2}\sin 2\theta + \rho\mu_\lambda\cos 2\theta$$
$$\mu_x\cos\theta + \mu_y\sin\theta = \rho$$

Then, after substituting these expressions and simplifying,

$$\begin{pmatrix}\frac{\partial^2 F}{\partial\theta^2} & \frac{\partial^2 F}{\partial\theta\rho}\\ \frac{\partial^2 F}{\partial\rho\theta} & \frac{\partial^2 F}{\partial\rho^2}\end{pmatrix} = \begin{pmatrix} 2(S_\lambda^2 + \mu_\lambda^2) & -2N\mu_\lambda\\ -2N\mu_\lambda & 2N\end{pmatrix}$$

Hence,

$$\begin{pmatrix}\frac{\partial^2 F}{\partial\theta^2} & \frac{\partial^2 F}{\partial\theta\rho}\\ \frac{\partial^2 F}{\partial\rho\theta} & \frac{\partial^2 F}{\partial\rho^2}\end{pmatrix}^{-1} = \frac{1}{2NS_\lambda^2}\begin{pmatrix} N & N\mu_\lambda\\ N\mu_\lambda & S_\lambda^2 + N\mu_\lambda^2\end{pmatrix}$$

Using these expressions, the covariance matrix of Θ, Σ_Θ, can be computed as:

$$\Sigma_\Theta^{2\times 2} = \begin{pmatrix}\sigma_{\theta\theta} & \sigma_{\theta\rho}\\ \sigma_{\rho\theta} & \sigma_{\rho\rho}\end{pmatrix}$$
$$= \frac{\partial g}{\partial\Theta}^{-1}(X,\Theta)\frac{\partial g}{\partial X}'(X,\Theta)\Sigma_X\frac{\partial g}{\partial X}(X,\Theta)\frac{\partial g}{\partial\Theta}^{-1}(X,\Theta)$$

We will find that

$$\Sigma_\Theta = \begin{pmatrix}\frac{1}{S_\lambda^2} & \frac{\mu_\lambda}{S_\lambda^2}\\ \frac{\mu_\lambda}{S_\lambda^2} & \frac{1}{N}+\frac{\mu_\lambda^2}{S_\lambda^2}\end{pmatrix}$$

This result has a simple geometric interpretation. In the coordinate system of the line where 0 is the point on the line closest to the origin, μ_λ

is the mean position of the points and S_λ^2 is the scatter of the points. The value of μ_λ acts like a length of an arm relative to a moment calculation. If the mean position of the points on the line is a distance of $|\mu_\lambda|$ from the origin on the line, then the variance of the estimated ρ increases by $\mu_\lambda^2 \sigma^2 / S_\lambda^2$. This says that the variance of the estimate ρ is not invariant to the translation of the coordinate system, a fact that is typically overlooked.

An immediate application of having the covariance of the estimated parameters of fitted lines is for grouping. One of the grouping questions is whether or not two fitted line segments should be grouped together because they are part of the same line. Depending on the grouping application, it may make a difference how far apart the line segments are. However the issue of whether the fitted line segments could have arisen from the same underlying line can in either case be answered using the covariance of the fitted parameters.

Let $\hat{\Theta}_1$ be the (θ, ρ) estimated line parameters from the first line segment and let $\hat{\Theta}_2$ be the estimated line parameters from the second line segment. Let $\Sigma_{\hat{\Theta}_1}$ be the covariance matrix associated with $\hat{\Theta}_1$ and let $\Sigma_{\hat{\Theta}_2}$ be the covariance matrix associated with $\hat{\Theta}_2$. The hypothesis to be tested is that $\Theta_1 = \Theta_2$. A test statistic for this hypothesis is

$$\chi^2 = (\hat{\Theta}_1 - \hat{\Theta}_2)'(\Sigma_{\hat{\Theta}_1} + \Sigma_{\hat{\Theta}_2})^{-1}(\hat{\Theta}_1 - \hat{\Theta}_2)$$

Under the null hypothesis, χ^2 has a Chi-square distribution with 1 degree of freedom. We can reject the null hypothesis that $\Theta_1 = \Theta_2$ at the α significance level if $\chi^2 < T_\alpha$ where the probability that a χ^2 variate with 1 degree of freedom is less than α is T_α.

6. Solution: Constrained Case

The constrained problem is: given $\hat{X}$, determine that $\hat{\Theta}$ satifying the constraints $s(\hat{\Theta}) = 0$ which minimizes the function $F(\hat{X}, \hat{\Theta})$. Using the Lagrange multiplier method, the function to be minimized is $F(\hat{X}, \hat{\Theta}) + s(\hat{\Theta})'\hat{\Lambda}$. As before, we define $g(X, \Theta) = \frac{\partial}{\partial \Theta} F(X, \Theta)$. We must have at the minimizing $(\hat{X}, \hat{\Theta})$,

$$\frac{\partial}{\partial \Theta}(F(\hat{X}, \hat{\Theta}) + s(\hat{\Theta})'\hat{\Lambda}) = 0$$

In the case of no noise with the squared criterion function as we have been considering, $F(X, \Theta) = 0$. This is certainly the smallest F can be given that F is a squared criterion function. Hence it must be that $g(X, \Theta) = \frac{\partial F}{\partial \Theta}(X, \Theta) = 0$. This implies that $\frac{\partial s}{\partial \Theta}(\Theta)\Lambda = 0$, which will only happen when $\Lambda = 0$ since we expect $\frac{\partial s}{\partial \Theta}$, a $K \times L$ matrix where $K > L$, to be of full rank.

Define

$$S(X,\Theta,\Lambda) = \begin{pmatrix} g(X,\Theta) + \frac{\partial s}{\partial \Theta}\Lambda \\ s(\Theta) \end{pmatrix}$$

Taking a Taylor series expansion of S,

$$S(X,\Theta,\Lambda) = S(X+\Delta X, \Theta+\Delta\Theta, \Lambda+\Delta\Lambda) - \frac{\partial S'}{\partial X}\Delta X - \frac{\partial S'}{\partial \Theta}\Delta\Theta - \frac{\partial S'}{\partial \Lambda}\Delta\Lambda$$

Because Θ satifies the constraints $s(\Theta) = 0$ and the pair (X,Θ) minimizes $F(x,\Theta)$, it follows that $S(X,\Theta,\Lambda) = 0$. Furthermore, at the computed $\hat{\Theta} = \Theta + \Delta\Theta$ and $\hat{\Lambda} = \Lambda + \Delta\Lambda$, $S(X+\Delta X, \Theta+\Delta\Theta, \Lambda+\Delta\Lambda) = 0$. Hence,

$$-\frac{\partial S'}{\partial X}\Delta X = \frac{\partial S'}{\partial \Theta}\Delta\Theta + \frac{\partial S'}{\partial \Lambda}\Delta\Lambda$$

Writing this equation out in terms of g and s, and using the fact that $\Lambda = 0$, there results

$$\begin{pmatrix} \frac{\partial g}{\partial \Theta} & \frac{\partial s}{\partial \Theta} \\ \frac{\partial s}{\partial \Theta} & 0 \end{pmatrix} \begin{pmatrix} \Delta\Theta \\ \Delta\Lambda \end{pmatrix} = \begin{pmatrix} -\frac{\partial g'}{\partial X} \\ 0 \end{pmatrix} \Delta X$$

From this it follows that

$$\Sigma_{\Delta\Theta,\Delta\Lambda} = A^{-1} B \Sigma_X B' A$$

where

$$A = \begin{pmatrix} \frac{\partial g}{\partial \Theta}, & \frac{\partial s}{\partial \Theta} \\ \frac{\partial s}{\partial \Theta} & 0 \end{pmatrix}$$

and

$$B = -\begin{pmatrix} \frac{\partial g'}{\partial X} \\ 0 \end{pmatrix}$$

and all functions are evaluated at Θ and X. For the estimated value $\hat{\Sigma}_{\Delta\Theta\Lambda}$ of $\Sigma_{\Delta\Theta\Lambda}$, we evaluate all functions at $\hat{\Theta}$ and $\hat{\Lambda}$.

As a special but classic case of this consider the constrained regression problem to find Θ minimizing

$$F(X,\Theta) = (X - J\Theta)'(X - J\Theta)$$

subject to $H'\Theta = 0$. In this case,

$$A = \begin{pmatrix} 2J'J & H \\ H' & 0 \end{pmatrix}$$

and

$$B = - \begin{pmatrix} 2J' \\ 0 \end{pmatrix}$$

Then

$$A^{-1} = \begin{pmatrix} (2J'J)^{-1}[I - H(H'(2J'J)^{-1}H)^{-1}H'(2JJ')^{-1}] & (2J'J)^{-1}H(H'(2J'J)^{-1}H)^{-1} \\ (H'(2J'J)^{-1}H)^{-1}H'(2J'J)^{-1} & -(H'(2J'J)^{-1}H)^{-1} \end{pmatrix}$$

and

$$A^{-1}B = - \begin{pmatrix} (2J'J)^{-1}[I - H(H'(2J'J)^{-1}H)^{-1}H'(2JJ')^{-1}]2J' \\ (H'(2J'J)^{-1}H)^{-1}H'(2J'J)^{-1}2J' \end{pmatrix}$$

From this it directly follows that if $\Sigma_X = \sigma^2 I$, then

$$\Sigma_\Theta = \sigma^2 (J'J)^{-1}[I - H(H'(JJ')^{-1}H)^{-1}H'(J'J)^{-1}]$$

7. Validation

There are two levels of validation. One level of validation is for the software. This can be tested by a large set of Monte-Carlo experiments off-line where we know what the correct answers are.

Another level of validation is on-line reliability. Here all that we have is the computed estimate and estimated covariance matrix for the estimate.

7.1. SOFTWARE AND ALGORITHM VALIDATION

Software for performing the optimization required to compute the estimate $\hat\Theta$ is often complicated and it is easy for there to be errors that are not immediately observable. For example, there we may have optimization software that produces correct answers on a few known examples but fails in a significant fraction of more difficult cases that we are not specifically trying out. One approach in testing that the software is producing the right answers is to test the statistical properties of the answers. That is, we can statistically test whether the statistical properties of its answers are similar to the statistical properties we expect. These expectations are whether the mean of the computed estimates is sufficiently close to the population mean and whether the estimated covariance matrix of the estimates is sufficiently close to the population covariance matrix. Rephrasing this more precisely the test is whether the computed estimates could have arisen from a population with given mean and covariance matrix.

Consider what happens in a hypothesis test: a significance level, α, is selected. When the test is run, a test statistic, say $\hat\phi$, is computed. The test statistic is typically designed so that in the case that the hypothesis is true, the test statistic will tend to have its values distributed around zero, in accordance with a known distribution. If the test statistic has a value say higher than a given ϕ_0, we reject the hypothesis that the computed estimate is statistically behaved as we expected it to be. If we do not reject, then in effect, we are tentatively accepting the hypothesis. The value of ϕ_0 is chosen so that the probability that we reject the hypothesis, given that is the hypothesis is true is less than the significance level α.

The key in using this kind of testing is that we can set up an experiment in which we know what the correct answer for the no noise ideal case would be. Then we can additively perturb the input data by a normally distributed vector from a population having zero mean and given covariance matrix. Then using the analytic propagation results derived earlier in the chapter, we can derive the covariance matrix of the estimates produced by software.

If we repeat this experiment many times just changing the perturbed realizations and leaving everything else the same, the experiment produces estimates $\theta_1, \ldots, \theta_N$ that will come from a normal population having mean θ, the correct answer for the ideal no noise case, and covariance matrix Σ, computed from the propagation equations. Now the hypothesis test is whether the observations $\theta_1, \ldots, \theta_N$ come fron a Normal population with mean θ and covariance matrix Σ. For this hypothesis test, there is a uniformly most powerful test. Let

$$B = \Sigma_{n=1}^{N}(\theta_n - \bar{\theta})(\theta_n - \bar{\theta})'$$

Define

$$\lambda = (e/N)^{pN/2}|B\Sigma^{-1}|^{N/2}$$
$$\times \, exp(-\frac{1}{2}[tr(B\Sigma^{-1}) + N(\bar{\theta} - \theta)'\Sigma^{-1}(\bar{\theta} - \theta)])$$

The test statistic is:

$$T = -2log\lambda$$

Under the hypothesis, T is distributed as:

$$\chi^2_{p(p+1)/2+p}$$

where p is the dimension of θ.

So to perform a test that the program's behavior is as expected we repeatedly generate the T statistic and compute its empirical distribution function. Then we test the hypothesis that T is distributed as the χ^2 variate using a Kolmogorov-Smirnov test.

7.2. ON-LINE RELIABILITY

For the on-line reliablity testing, the estimate is computed by minimizing the scalar objective function. Then based on the given covariance matrix of the input data, an estimated covariance matrix of the estimate is computed using the linearization around the estimate itself. Here a test can be done by testing whether the each of the diagonal entries of the estimated covariance matrix is sufficiently small.

8. Conclusion

Making a successful vision system for any particular application typically requires many steps, the optimal choice of which is not always apparent. To understand how to do the optimal design, a synthesis problem, requires that we first understand how to solve the analysis problem: given the steps of a particular algorithm, determine how to propagate the parameters of the perturbation process from the input to the parameters describing the perturbation process of the computed output. The first basic case of this sort of uncertainty propagation is the propagation of the covariance matrix of the input to the covariance matrix of the output. This is what this chapter has described.

This work does not come near to solving what is required for the general problem, because the general problem involves perturbations which are not additive. That is, in mid and high-level vision, the appropriate kinds of perturbations are perturbations of structures. Now, we are in the process of understanding some of the issues with these kinds of perturbations and expect to soon have some results in this area.

References

Jerian, C. and Jain, R. (1984) Determining Motion Parameters for Scenes with Translation and Rotation, *IEEE PAMI*, 6(4):523–530.

Koch, K. (1987) *Parameter Estimation and Hypothesis Testing in Linear Models*, Springer-Verlag, Berlin, 117,121.

Mikhail, E. (1976) *Observations and Least Squares*, IEP – A Dun-Donnelley Publisher, New York, 72–90.

Slama, C. (ed.) (1980) *The Manual of Photogrammetry*, The American Society of Photogrammetry, Falls Church, VA 22046, 73–74.

Weng, J., Cohen, P. and Herniou, M. (1992) Camera Calibration with Distortion Models and Accuracy Evaluation, *IEEE PAMI*, 14(10):965–980.

Williams, D. and Shah, M. (1993) Edge Characterization Using Normalized Edge Detector, *CVGIP: Graphical Models and Image Processing*, 55(4):311–318.

Wu, S.Y. and Wang, M.J. (1993) Detecting the Dominant Points by the Curvature-Based Polygonal Approximation, *CVGIP: Graphical Models and Image Processing*, 5(2):79–88.

INPUT GUIDED PERFORMANCE EVALUATION

PETER MEER and BOGDAN MATEI
Electrical and Computer Engineering Dept.
Rutgers University
94 Brett Road
Piscataway, NJ 08854-8058, USA

KYUJIN CHO
Software Business Team
Samsung SDS Co.
707-19 YokSam, KangNam
Seoul, Korea

1. Motivation

Performance evaluation is a difficult and very challenging task. In spite of many discussions in the literature, e.g., (Haralick *et al.*, 1994), and well understood goals, e.g., (Christensen and Förstner, 1997; Haralick, 1994), there is a wide gap between what performance assessment using simple, synthetic data predicts and what is obtained when the same algorithms are applied to real data.

The main factor for this discrepancy lies in the complexity of real images, where the variety of input configurations (even for a small, 5×5 gray-level neighborhood) largely exceeds what can be modeled and analyzed analytically. It was also shown several years ago that any performance evaluation protocol requires a prohibitively large number of input images to obtain statistically significant measures (Haralick, 1989). We do not know, however, how to establish equivalence classes over the space of real images relative to the task to be evaluated.

To execute a task of practical use, a vision system must contain interacting modules. For example, even the simplest stereo system must have smoothing, edge detection, feature recovery, matching, disparity computations. The user is interested in the the overall performance of the system

R. Klette et al. (eds.), Performance Characterization in Computer Vision, 115–124.

and not in that of the individual modules. To be able to predict the performance of moderately complex systems the traditional error propagation approach (Yi *et al.*, 1994) must incorporate simplifying assumptions, like homogeneous noise process, independent outputs at intermediate stages, continuous nature for the data etc. In the most sophisticated computer vision use of the error propagation approach e.g., (Ramesh and Haralick, 1994), a multistage feature extraction algorithm was analyzed. However, comparison of the empirical distributions derived from the annotated data with the theoretically obtained counterparts revealed significant differences.

Rigorous comparison of several algorithms executing the same task requires access to the ground truth, which for real data most often involves a huge effort as, for example, the evaluation of range image segmentation techniques (Hoover *et al.*, 1995) has shown. On the other hand, substituting the ground truth with the perceived quality of the processed image (Heath *et al.*, 1997), may emphasize too much the cognitive factors, i.e., the top-down information flow, which is seldom present in the algorithm.

Without denying the predictive power of a theoretical analysis, but recognizing its inherent weaknesses in the face of real data, in this chapter we present a new, very general performance assessment methodology based on the perturbation of the input in the context of the task (Figure 1). The basic idea is to slightly modify the relationship between the input and the computational procedure. Repeating this perturbation many times a distribution of the output is obtained from the *single* input, a distribution from which statically valid measures can be derived. If necessary, the input data obeying with high confidence the assumptions embedded into the computational procedure can be separated and an improved output obtained.

The new method is an extension of the *resampling paradigm* widely used

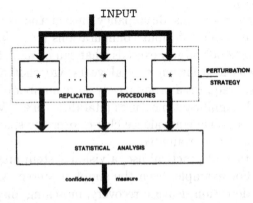

Figure 1. The proposed performance assessment paradigm.

in statistics, and has a solid theoretical basis. The method is entirely numerical and being data driven belongs to the class of empirical techniques. It retains the advantage of the empirical techniques (they are useful in real situations), but eliminates their often ad-hoc nature. When applied in analytically tractable cases it will reproduce (within the computational accuracy) the theoretically predicted results.

The resampling paradigm was first used for performance assessment in a low-level image understanding problem, edge detection (Cho *et al.*, 1997). The same idea was also successfully employed in an algorithm for gray-level image segmentation in which the goal was to reduce the inherent uncertainty of the original computational module (Cho and Meer, 1997).

There are several resampling methods used in statistics, but the most appropriate for performance evaluation appears to be the *bootstrap*. A short review of bootstrap is given in section 2. Application of the paradigm to edge detection is discussed in section 3, and to the comparison of rigid motion estimators in section 4.

2. Introduction to Bootstrap

The bootstrap was introduced in statistics by Bradley Efron in 1979. All the relevant material can be found in the books (Efron and Tibshirani, 1993; Davidson and Hinkley, 1997).

Let an estimate $\hat{\theta} = S\left[Z\right]$ be computed from the data $Z = [z_1, \cdots z_n]$. The data points z_i are assumed independent identically distributed (i.i.d.) from an unknown distribution F. The empirical distribution function $\hat{F}_n$ of Z is defined by associating equal probability $\frac{1}{n}$ with each measurement z_i. The bootstrap substitutes $\hat{F}_n$ for F. New data sets $Z^{*b} = \{z_1^{*b}, z_2^{*b}, \cdots, z_n^{*b}\}$ called *bootstrap replicates* are formed by sampling with replacement from Z. For each bootstrap sample Z^{*b}, $b = 1, 2, \ldots, B$, the estimate $\hat{\theta}^{*b} = S\left[Z^{*b}\right]$ is computed. The ensemble of $\hat{\theta}^{*b}$ is used instead of the sampling distribution of $\hat{\theta}$ and the accuracy of $\hat{\theta}$ as an estimator of θ is inferred from this ensemble. For example, the covariance matrix of $\hat{\theta}$ is computed as

$$\hat{C}_\theta = \frac{1}{B-1} \sum_{b=1}^{B} \left[\hat{\theta}^{*b} - \bar{\theta}^*\right] \left[\hat{\theta}^{*b} - \bar{\theta}^*\right]^\top, \quad \bar{\theta}^* = \frac{1}{B}\sum_{b=1}^{B} \hat{\theta}^{*b}. \quad (1)$$

In practice B should be at least 100 with higher values required if n is small (say less than 30). In confidence interval computations, where the tails of the sampling distribution have to be accurately estimated, larger values for B (in the range $1000 - 2000$) have to be used. It should be emphasized that the lower bound on B for satisfactory performance depends on the nature of $\hat{\theta}$ and the number of available measurements n.

In the case of linear regression, the most widely used method is to bootstrap the residuals. For example, in the classical regression, only the dependent variable is additively corrupted by noise

$$y_{io} = \alpha + \beta^\top x_{io}, \qquad x_{io} \in R^{p-1}, \quad y_{io} \in R, \qquad \Delta y_i \sim GI(0, \sigma^2) , \quad (2)$$

where $GI(\cdot)$ is a general distribution, and the errors are i.i.d. After the estimate $\hat{\theta} = \begin{bmatrix} \hat{\alpha} & \hat{\beta}^\top \end{bmatrix}^\top$ was obtained the residuals are computed as

$$\Delta \hat{y}_i = y_i - \hat{y}_i, \qquad \hat{y}_i = \hat{\alpha} + \hat{\beta}^\top x_i . \quad (3)$$

The residuals are centered (since should have a zero-mean distribution) and the bootstrap samples are constructed as

$$y_i^{*b} = \hat{y}_i + \widetilde{\Delta y_i}^{*b} , \quad (4)$$

where $\widetilde{\Delta y_i}^{*b}$ is obtained by sampling with replacement from the centered residuals.

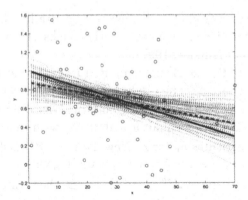

Figure 2.   An example of bootstrapped linear regression.

In Figure 2 a simple example is shown. The true fit (solid line) is $y = 1 - 0.01x$. The y coordinate of the 50 data points was corrupted with i.i.d., zero-mean, normal noise having standard deviation 0.5. Based on the least squares estimated fit (dashed line), $y = 0.88 - 0.0063x$, two hundred bootstrap replicates were generated (dotted lines). Beside the covariance matrix of the parameter estimates, the confidence in the corrected data points $\hat{y}_i$ can also be obtained. It is given by the envelope of the bootstrap replicate fits. Note how the potential leverage points (at the two end regions of the line segment) are associated with larger uncertainties, as expected from the theory.

In the following two sections we present two applications of the boot-strap methodology to performance evaluation of vision tasks.

3. Low-level Vision: Edge Detection

Paradoxically, evaluation of the low-level vision algorithms often can reveal much more than that of their middle-level counterparts. It can clearly show the inadequacy of the local image structure models on which these algorithms are based, and how strongly the cognitive factors in our perception of the image are biasing the expectation on the performance. Here we will concentrate on this issue, a more complete treatment of the performance evaluation of edge detection can be found in (Cho *et al.*, 1997).

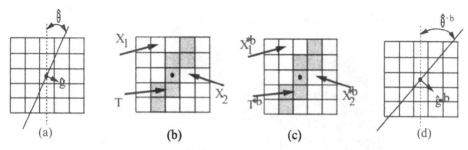

Figure 3.   Bootstrapping in edge detection. (a) The original gradient vector. (b) The derived neighborhood model. (c) Bootstrapped neighborhood. (d) Bootstrapped gradient vector.

Assume a simple step-edge model in a 5×5 neighborhood. The edge passes through the center of the neighborhood and is oriented at θ. Three regions can be distinguished. Two uniform regions, X_1 and X_2, in which the noisy pixel values are distributed around two constants, and the noisy planar transition region T between them (Figure 3b). The size of the transient region depends on θ. The model has an eight-fold symmetry.

When the the gradient vector $\hat{g}$ is computed for a given neighborhood (Figure 3a) the estimated orientation of the edge $\hat{\theta}$, is obtained. Based on the edge model, the neighborhood can be decomposed into the three regions. To generate a bootstrapped neighborhood, each region is processed independently. In the uniform regions sampling with replacement is used yielding X_1^{*b} and X_2^{*b}, while in the transition regions bootstrapping the residuals yields T^{*b} (Figure 3c). The gradient vector of the bootstrapped neighborhood, $\hat{g}^{*b}$, is then computed (Figure 3d). The standard deviation, $\hat{se}_\theta$ of the distribution of the bootstrapped edge directions $\hat{\theta}^{*b}$ was used as the performance measure. This measure has a weak dependency on the size of noisy step-edge and thus evaluates the presence of a step-edge *independent* of its magnitude.

The above described perturbation strategy was based on the hypothesis that the edge is located at the center of the neighborhood. Under the hypothesis of "no edge is present", the entire neighborhood should be resampled with replacement. Let performance measure computed under this hypothesis be $\hat{se}_\theta^{non}$. The two measures, derived under the two different hypotheses can be combined into a confidence in the presence of a step-edge in the center of the neighborhood.

$$confidence = 1 - \frac{\min(\hat{se}_\theta, \hat{se}_\theta^{non})}{\max(\hat{se}_\theta, \hat{se}_\theta^{non})} \ . \tag{5}$$

Values close to one validate the assumed model. Note that the confidence is computed independent of the step-edge magnitude.

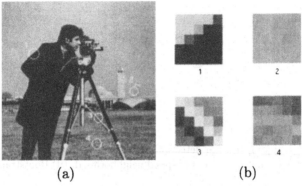

Figure 4.   The relation between gradient magnitude and the presence of the step-edge model. (a) The *cameraman* image. (b) Four representative 5 × 5 neighborhoods.

When applied to a real image (i.e., at every pixel), the notch sensitivity of the performance evaluation for step-edges, reveals disturbing facts. Take for example the well known *cameraman* image in which four representative neighborhoods were highlighted (Figure 4).

The "coat" (No. 1) corresponds to a local structure very similar to the model from which the gradient based step-edge detector is derived. So does the "small tower" (No. 2), however, the magnitude of the step edge is very small in spite of the feature being very significant semantically. As can be seen from Table I the neighborhood yields a gradient magnitude which is much less than that of the "lawn" (No. 4), a texture which is perceived as homogeneous and thus should not contain edges. A global, gradient magnitude based edge-detector cannot recover the tower while also removing the texture of the lawn. To complicate matters further, local structures which were *not taken into account* when designing the edge-detector can yield large gradient magnitudes. The bright line in the "tripod" (No. 3) is such an example.

We conclude that gradient based edge-detection with its underlying step-edge model cannot recover from an image only those edges which are considered significant by a human observer. It should be also emphasized, that several of the *desired* results are obtained by chance, the assumptions embedded into the algorithm do not cover such cases.

TABLE I.   Gradient Magnitude vs. Confidence

Neighborhood	1	2	3	4
Gradient Mag.	58.5579	3.6184	24.8354	4.9954
Confidence	0.9056	0.9032	0.5348	0.3194

4. Middle-level Vision: Rigid Motion Estimation

In the second example we compare the performance of two rigid motion estimators. For more details see (Matei *et al.*, 1998). A traditional approach to performance evaluation for this task is (Eggert *et al.*, 1997).

Middle-level vision tasks are best modeled by using the *linear, errors-in-variables (EIV)* model in which *all* the variables are corrupted by noise. Thus, if $z_{io} = \begin{bmatrix} x_{io}^\top & y_{io} \end{bmatrix}^\top$ the available measurements are

$$z_i = z_{io} + \Delta z_i, \qquad i = 1 \cdots n, \qquad \Delta z_i \sim GI(0, \sigma^2 I) . \tag{6}$$

In the applications most often we are interested in the recovered data points and thus assessing the confidence in the input space is of special importance. The EIV model is estimated using *total (orthogonal) least squares*, and it is well known that the uncertainty along the fit cannot be eliminated.

To visualize the uncertainty in the input space the confidence region for the corrected data $\hat{z}_i$ has to be determined. This is achieved in several steps.

1. Bootstrap the data and obtain $\hat{C}_\theta$ (1).
2. Define the confidence ellipsoid at level $(1-\delta)$ of $\hat{\theta}$, $\mathcal{D}_{1-\delta}$, as the $100(1-\delta)$ percentile of the distribution of the squared Mahalanobis distances

$$\begin{bmatrix} \hat{\theta}^* - \hat{\theta} \end{bmatrix}^\top \hat{C}_\theta^\# \begin{bmatrix} \hat{\theta}^* - \hat{\theta} \end{bmatrix} , \tag{7}$$

where $\hat{\theta}^*$ is a bootstrap estimate of $\hat{\theta}$, and $\#$ stands for the pseudoinverse.
3. Choose B_1 parameter vectors $\hat{\theta}^{*j} \in \mathcal{D}_{1-\delta}$.

4. Generate B_2 bootstrap replicates $\boldsymbol{Z}^{*b}$ from the residuals of $\hat{\boldsymbol{\theta}}$.
5. Project each $\boldsymbol{Z}^{*b}$ onto the hyperplane $\hat{\boldsymbol{\theta}}^{*j}$ to obtain $\hat{\boldsymbol{Z}}^{*jb}$.
6. Compute

$$\hat{\boldsymbol{C}}_{z_i} = \frac{1}{B_1 B_2} \sum_{b=1}^{B_2} \sum_{j=1}^{B_1} \left[\hat{z}_i^{*bj} - \hat{z}_i\right]\left[\hat{z}_i^{*bj} - \hat{z}_i\right]^\top, \quad i = 1, \cdots, n. \qquad (8)$$

7. With probability $(1 - \delta)(1 - \gamma)$ $z_{io} \in \Gamma_i$, the level $(1 - \gamma)$ confidence ellipsoid defined by the $100(1 - \gamma)$ percentile of the distribution of

$$(\hat{z}_i^* - \hat{z}_i)^\top \hat{\boldsymbol{C}}_{z_i}^{\#} (\hat{z}_i^* - \hat{z}_i) \qquad (9)$$

where $\hat{z}_i^*$ is a bootstrapped estimate of $\hat{z}_i$.

Note the inherently assumed elliptically symmetrical error distributions.

The motion estimation problem can be formulated as two sets of matched measurements in R^3

$$\boldsymbol{x}_i = \boldsymbol{x}_{io} + \Delta \boldsymbol{x}_i \qquad \boldsymbol{y}_i = \boldsymbol{y}_{io} + \Delta \boldsymbol{y}_i \qquad (10)$$

corrupted by zero-mean errors with covariances $\boldsymbol{C}_x = \sigma_x^2 \boldsymbol{I}$ and $\boldsymbol{C}_y = \sigma_y^2 \boldsymbol{I}$. The true data points satisfy

$$\boldsymbol{y}_{io} = \boldsymbol{R}\boldsymbol{x}_{io} + \boldsymbol{t}, \qquad i = 1, \cdots, n. \qquad (11)$$

Estimate the rotation matrix $\boldsymbol{R}$ and translation vector

Two methods are considered here. The *singular value decomposition* (SVD) based technique, e.g. (Umeyama, 1991), first recovers $\boldsymbol{R}$ from the centered data and then finds the value of $\boldsymbol{t}$. The *linear subspace* method first eliminates algebraically the rotation component and starts by estimating the translation (Wang and Jepson, 1994). The real image example in Figure 5 clearly reveals that the SVD method has superior performance.

5. Conclusions

Real images are complex and any image understanding algorithm of practical importance requires the interaction among several computational modules. Traditional performance evaluation methods based on error propagation, have only a limited use in such conditions since often the results obtained for simple, synthetic data do not extend to real images. A new performance evaluation paradigm was proposed which exploits a resampling technique very popular in statistics, the boostrap. The potential of the new paradigm was shown by employing it for a low-level task, edge detection, and a middle-level task, rigid motion estimation. The two examples shown in this chapter illustrates the potential of input guided performance evaluation. A lot of open questions remain, but the technique can become an important tool in closing the gap between academic research and practical applications.

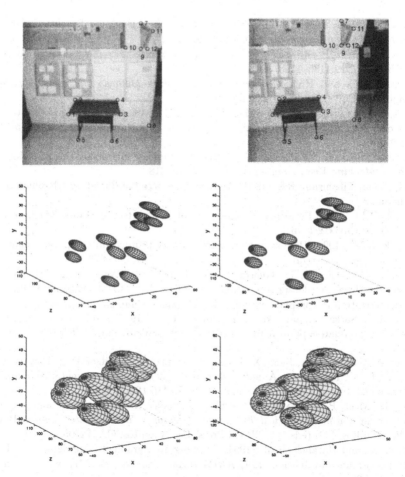

Figure 5.   An example of motion estimation evaluation. Top: two reflection images derived from a range image motion sequence with the matched points marked. Middle: Confidence ellipses for the points for the SVD method. Bottom: Confidence ellipses for the points for the linear subspace method.

Acknowledgments

The authors gratefully acknowledge the support by the National Science Foundation under grant IRI-9530546. The range images were obtained from the CESAR lab at Oak Ridge National Laboratory, and preprocessed by programs developed at Computer Vision Laboratory of the University of South Florida, Tampa.

References

Cho, K. and Meer, P. (1997) Image segmentation from consensus information, *Computer Vision and Image Understanding*, 68:72–89.

Cho, K. and Meer, P. and Cabrera, J. (1997) Performance assessment through bootstrap, *IEEE PAMI*, 19:1185–1198.

Davidson, A.C. and Hinkley, D.V. (1997) *Bootstrap Methods and their Application*, Cambridge University Press, Cambridge, UK.

Eggert, D.W., Lorusso, A. and Fisher, R.B. (1997) Estimating 3-D rigid body transformations: A comparison of four major algorithms., *Machine Vision and Applications*, 9:272–290.

Christensen, H.I. and Förstner, W. (1997) Performance characteristics of vision algorithms, *Machine Vision and Applications*, 9:215–218.

Efron, B. and Tibshirani, R.J. (1993) *An Introduction to the Bootstrap*, Chapman & Hall, London.

Haralick, R.M. (1989) Performance assessment of near-perfect machines, *Machine Vision and Applications*, 2:1–16.

Haralick, R.M. (1994) Performance characterization protocol in computer vision, *1994 ARPA Image Understanding Workshop*, Monterey, CA, 667–673.

Haralick, R.M.; Cinque, L., Guerra, C. and Levialdi, S.; Weng, J. and Huang, T.S.; Meer, P.; Shirai, Y.; Draper, B.A. and Beveridge, J.R. (1994) Dialogue: Performance characterization in computer vision, *CVGIP: Image Understanding*, 60:245–265.

Heath, M.D., Sarkar, S., Sanocki, T. and Bowyer, K.W. (1997) A robust visual method for assessing the relative performance of edge-detection algorithms, *IEEE PAMI*, 19:1338–1359.

Hoover, A., Gillian, J.-B., Jiang, X., Flynn, P.J., Bunke, H., Goldgof, D.B., Bowyer, K.W., Eggert, D.W., Fitzgibbon, A. and Fisher, R.B. (1996) An experimental comparison of range image segmentation algorithms, *IEEE PAMI*, 18:673–689.

Matei, B., Meer, P. and Tyler, D. (1998) Performance assessment by resampling: Rigid motion estimators, *Empirical Evaluation Techniques in Computer Vision*, Bowyer, K.W., Phillips, P.J. (eds.), IEEE CS Press, Los Alamitos, CA, 72–95.

Ramesh, V. and Haralick, R.M. (1994) An integrated gradient edge detector – Theory and performance evaluation, *1994 ARPA Image Understanding Workshop*, Monterey, CA, 689–702.

Umeyama, S. (1991) Least-squares estimation of transformation parameters between two point patterns, *IEEE PAMI*, 13:376–380.

Wang, Z. and Jepson, A. (1994) A new closed-form solution for absolute orientation, *IEEE Conference on Computer Vision and Pattern Recognition 1994*, Seattle, WA, 129–134.

Yi, S., Haralick, R.M. and Shapiro, L.G. (1994) Error propagation in machine vision, *Machine Vision and Applications*, 7:93–114.

UNCERTAINTY PROPAGATION IN SHAPE RECONSTRUCTION AND MOVING OBJECT DETECTION FROM OPTICAL FLOW

A Statistical Approach to Computer Vision Problems

NAOYA OHTA
Dept. of Computer Science
Gunma University
Kiryu
Gunma, 376-8515 Japan

1. Introduction

Computer vision systems often have to deal with information that is inherently uncertain. Consider, for example, an object detection system by vision. It usually consists of several modules which execute their specific tasks. Low-level modules in the system detect image primitives such as edges and textures. However, it is hopeless to expect those modules to perfectly achieve their tasks. One reason is the existence of noise. Noise contaminates input images and causes uncertainty to the results. The other reason is that image primitives have inherent uncertainty. Edges vary in strength from very weak ones to obvious ones, so the edge detection module can only output a fuzzy result. This situation is the same in the texture analyzing module. High-level modules, which are the object detection modules in the system, must make a decision based on information with uncertainty about the image primitives. Therefore, it is very important that these modules are so designed that they can handle the uncertainty and also propagate information about the uncertainty from the inputs to outputs.

Probability theory and statistics provide a theoretical base to systematically handle the uncertainty and make a decision based on the fuzzy information. The image primitive detection can be formalized as statistical estimation problems, with the uncertainty represented in terms of covari-

R. Klette et al. (eds.), Performance Characterization in Computer Vision, 125–135.

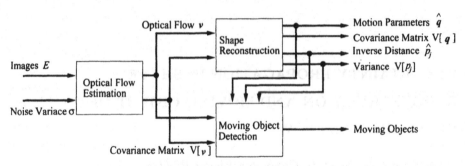

Figure 1.   Block diagram of the system.

ance matrices of the estimates. The decision for object detection is then made based on statistical decision rules.

In this chapter, we discuss a system which reconstructs object shapes and detects moving objects from optical flow. The system consists of 1) optical flow detection module, 2) shape reconstruction module, and 3) moving object detection module (Figure 1). The tasks that each module executes are defined as statistical problems. Covariance matrices are associated with all the information the modules input and output in order to propagate uncertainty.

In the following, we outline a fundamental framework of the statistical parameter estimation and then explain the algorithms for each module.

2. Statistical Parameter Eestimation

Here, we briefly review the maximum likelihood estimation and evaluation of the covariance matrix of an estimator.

Let $\bar{\boldsymbol{\theta}}$ be the parameter vector that we want to estimate and $\bar{\boldsymbol{\eta}}$ be the data that would be observed if noise were not present. The bars on the variables indicate that they are true values. The relation between $\bar{\boldsymbol{\theta}}$ and $\bar{\boldsymbol{\eta}}$ is expressed by a vector function $\boldsymbol{f}$ as follows:

$$\bar{\boldsymbol{\eta}} = \boldsymbol{f}(\bar{\boldsymbol{\theta}}). \tag{1}$$

A measurement $\boldsymbol{\eta}$ of $\bar{\boldsymbol{\eta}}$ is contaminated by additive noise $\Delta\boldsymbol{\eta}$. That is,

$$\boldsymbol{\eta} = \bar{\boldsymbol{\eta}} + \Delta\boldsymbol{\eta} = \boldsymbol{f}(\bar{\boldsymbol{\theta}}) + \Delta\boldsymbol{\eta}. \tag{2}$$

We assume $\Delta\boldsymbol{\eta}$ to be a zero mean Gaussian noise whose covariance matrix is $V[\boldsymbol{\eta}]$. The probability distribution of the measurement, $\Pr(\boldsymbol{\eta})$, is represented by

$$\Pr(\boldsymbol{\eta}) = \frac{1}{\sqrt{(2\pi)^n |V[\boldsymbol{\eta}]|}} \exp\left(-\frac{1}{2}(\boldsymbol{\eta} - \boldsymbol{f}(\bar{\boldsymbol{\theta}}))^{\top} V[\boldsymbol{\eta}]^{-1}(\boldsymbol{\eta} - \boldsymbol{f}(\bar{\boldsymbol{\theta}}))\right), \tag{3}$$

where n is the dimension of $\boldsymbol{\eta}$, $|\cdot|$ the determinant and T the transpose of a matrix. Given data $\boldsymbol{\eta}$, the **maximum likelihood estimator** $\hat{\boldsymbol{\theta}}$ of the parameter $\bar{\boldsymbol{\theta}}$ is defined as the value of $\bar{\boldsymbol{\theta}}$ which maximizes Eq. (3) or, equivalently, minimizes J, where

$$J = (\boldsymbol{\eta} - \boldsymbol{f}(\bar{\boldsymbol{\theta}}))^\mathsf{T} V[\boldsymbol{\eta}]^{-1}(\boldsymbol{\eta} - \boldsymbol{f}(\bar{\boldsymbol{\theta}})). \tag{4}$$

The covariance matrix $V[\boldsymbol{\theta}]$ of the estimator $\hat{\boldsymbol{\theta}}$ can be estimated by approximating function J by a quadratic form around the true values, $\bar{\boldsymbol{\eta}}$ and $\bar{\boldsymbol{\theta}}$. Noticing that $\bar{\boldsymbol{\eta}} - \boldsymbol{f}(\bar{\boldsymbol{\theta}}) = 0$, the quadratic form $\tilde{J}$ is

$$\tilde{J} = \left(\Delta\boldsymbol{\eta} - \frac{\partial \boldsymbol{f}}{\partial \boldsymbol{\theta}}\Delta\boldsymbol{\theta}\right)^\mathsf{T} V[\boldsymbol{\eta}]^{-1}\left(\Delta\boldsymbol{\eta} - \frac{\partial \boldsymbol{f}}{\partial \boldsymbol{\theta}}\Delta\boldsymbol{\theta}\right), \tag{5}$$

where $\Delta\boldsymbol{\theta}$ is a perturbation to $\bar{\boldsymbol{\theta}}$ and $\partial \boldsymbol{f}/\partial \boldsymbol{\theta}$ denotes the Jacobi matrix. Because the estimator $\hat{\boldsymbol{\theta}}$ is given as the minimum point of function J, differentiating $\tilde{J}$ with respect to $\Delta\boldsymbol{\theta}$ and setting it to zero, we obtain the following relation:

$$\Delta\boldsymbol{\theta} = \left(\frac{\partial \boldsymbol{f}}{\partial \boldsymbol{\theta}}^\mathsf{T} V[\boldsymbol{\eta}]^{-1}\frac{\partial \boldsymbol{f}}{\partial \boldsymbol{\theta}}\right)^{-1}\frac{\partial \boldsymbol{f}}{\partial \boldsymbol{\theta}}^\mathsf{T} V[\boldsymbol{\eta}]^{-1}\Delta\boldsymbol{\eta}. \tag{6}$$

Therefore, the (approximated) covariance matrix $V[\boldsymbol{\theta}]$ is given by

$$V[\boldsymbol{\theta}] = E[\Delta\boldsymbol{\theta}\Delta\boldsymbol{\theta}^\mathsf{T}] = \left(\frac{\partial \boldsymbol{f}}{\partial \boldsymbol{\theta}}^\mathsf{T} V[\boldsymbol{\eta}]^{-1}\frac{\partial \boldsymbol{f}}{\partial \boldsymbol{\theta}}\right)^{-1}, \tag{7}$$

where $E[\cdot]$ denotes the expectation. In practice, the Jacobi matrix $\partial \boldsymbol{f}/\partial \boldsymbol{\theta}$ is evaluated at the estimated value $\hat{\boldsymbol{\theta}}$ because the true value $\bar{\boldsymbol{\theta}}$ is not known. If the function $\boldsymbol{f}$ is linear, then Eq. (7) is exact.

3. Optical Flow Estimation

A lot of methods for optical flow computation have been proposed (Barron et al., 1994). We based our algorithm on one of the traditional differential methods, reported in (Lucas and Kanade, 1981), among the proposed methods.

The differential methods are based on the optical flow constraint equation.

$$E_{xi}\bar{u} + E_{yi}\bar{v} + E_{ti} = \Delta E_{ti}, \tag{8}$$

where (E_{xi}, E_{yi}, E_{ti}) is the intensity gradient at image point i, $(\bar{u}, \bar{v})$ is the optical flow at that point, and ΔE_{ti} is the error of the constraint. We consider a small region of the image and assume that the flow is constant within it. The optical flow is estimated by minimizing the sum of squared errors, $\sum \Delta E_{ti}^2$. This approach is referred to as the **least squares** (LS) method.

This procedure can be statistically justified by applying maximum likelihood estimation under the condition that the measurements are corrupted by Gaussian noise. We can rewrite Eq. (8) as

$$\bar{b} = M\bar{u}, \tag{9}$$

where

$$\bar{b} = \begin{pmatrix} -\bar{E}_{t1} \\ \vdots \\ -\bar{E}_{tn} \end{pmatrix}, \quad M = \begin{pmatrix} E_{x1} & E_{y1} \\ \vdots & \vdots \\ E_{xn} & E_{yn} \end{pmatrix}, \quad \bar{u} = \begin{pmatrix} \bar{u} \\ \bar{v} \end{pmatrix}. \tag{10}$$

Then we assume that the measurement of $\bar{b}$ is corrupted by Gaussian noise.

$$b = \bar{b} + \Delta b, \tag{11}$$

where

$$\Delta b = \begin{pmatrix} \Delta E_{t1} \\ \vdots \\ \Delta E_{tn} \end{pmatrix}. \tag{12}$$

Equations (9) and (11) correspond to Eqs. (1) and (2), respectively. If we assume that all the ΔE_{ti}'s are independent and have the same variance σ^2, the covariance matrix of Δb is $\sigma^2 I$, where I denotes the identity matrix. The cost function from Eq. (4) becomes

$$J_{of} = \Delta b^{\top}(\sigma^2 I)\Delta b = \sigma^2(b - M\bar{u})^{\top}(b - M\bar{u}). \tag{13}$$

The estimated flow $\hat{u}$, which minimizes J_{of}, is obtained by solving the **normal equation**. This gives

$$\hat{u} = (M^{\top}M)^{-1}M^{\top}b. \tag{14}$$

We note that $\hat{u}$ does not depend the magnitude of σ^2. From Eq. (7), the covariance matrix $V[u]$ of the flow $\hat{u}$ is given by

$$V[u] = \sigma^2(M^{\top}M)^{-1}. \tag{15}$$

An optical flow estimation result is shown in Figure 2a. In order to select reliable optical flow estimates, the largest eigenvalue of the covariance matrix $V[u]$ can be used (Ohta, 1991), because it represents the variance along the most uncertain direction. In Figure 2b, only flow estimates in which the largest eigenvalue is lower than some threshold are drawn.

Although this optical flow computation algorithm works reasonably well in practice, it is unrealistic to assume that only the time derivatives contain noise. If all the derivatives contain noise, the problem can be solved using the **total least squares** (TLS) method (Weber and Malik, 1993). A statistical formalization of TLS is found in (Ohta, 1997). In addition to LS and TLS, other noise models for the optical flow constraint equation have been proposed by Simoncelli *et al.* (1991) and Ohta (1996). The best noise model depends on the actual noise characteristics of the imaging system.

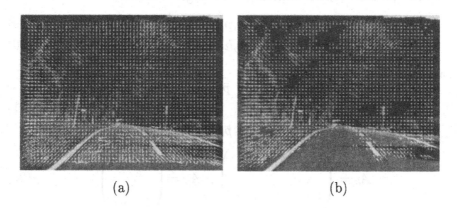

(a)   (b)

Figure 2.   (a) Detected optical flow. (b) Reliable optical flow.

4. Shape Reconstruction

The problem to compute shape of the environment and motion of the camera from optical flow is referred to as **structure from motion** problem. Many methods for the problem, as in optical flow computation, have been proposed. Here, we formalize this problem as a statistical estimation problem (Ohta, 1993), which enables the module to use the uncertainty information (the covariance matrices) of the input (the optical flow) and the output (the shape and motion parameter).

Suppose a camera is moving in a rigid environment. The observed optical flow depends on camera motion and the distance between the camera and the environment. Let $\bar{h}$ and $\bar{\omega}$ be the camera velocities in translation and rotation respectively, and $\bar{Z}_j$ be the distance along the optical axis from the camera to the environment, at image position (x_j, y_j). The pair of velocities, $\bar{q} = (\bar{h}^\top \ \bar{\omega}^\top)^\top$, is referred to as the (instantaneous) **motion parameters**. The observed optical flow $\bar{u}_j$ is expressed as follows (Heeger and Jepson, 1992).

$$\bar{u}_j = \bar{p}_j A_j \bar{h} + B_j \bar{\omega}, \tag{16}$$

where

$$\bar{p}_j = \frac{1}{\bar{Z}_j}, \quad A_j = \begin{pmatrix} -1 & 0 & x_j \\ 0 & -1 & y_j \end{pmatrix}, \tag{17}$$

$$B_j = \begin{pmatrix} x_j y_j & -(x_j^2 + 1) & y_j \\ y_j^2 + 1 & -x_j y_j & -x_j \end{pmatrix}. \tag{18}$$

If we stack all the optical flow vectors $\bar{u}_j$, where $j = 1, 2, \ldots, m$, into a single vector $\bar{v}$ then the bilinear form of Eq. (16) with respect to $\bar{h}$ and $\bar{p}_j$ gives two possible representations for $\bar{v}$, as given below:

$$\bar{v} = A_h \bar{p} + B\bar{\omega}, \tag{19}$$
$$\bar{v} = A_p \bar{h} + B\bar{\omega}, \tag{20}$$

where

$$\bar{v} = \begin{pmatrix} \bar{u}_1 \\ \vdots \\ \bar{u}_m \end{pmatrix}, \quad \bar{p} = \begin{pmatrix} \bar{p}_1 \\ \vdots \\ \bar{p}_m \end{pmatrix}, \quad B = \begin{pmatrix} B_1 \\ \vdots \\ B_m \end{pmatrix}, \tag{21}$$

$$A_h = \begin{pmatrix} A_1 \bar{h} & & 0 \\ & \ddots & \\ 0 & & A_m \bar{h} \end{pmatrix}, \quad A_p = \begin{pmatrix} \bar{p}_1 A_1 \\ \vdots \\ \bar{p}_m A_m \end{pmatrix}. \tag{22}$$

Equations (19) and (20) represent the relation between the parameters to be estimated and the expected measurement without noise. These equations correspond to Eq. (1).

Let Δu_j be a vector representing the noise in the measured optical flow u_j. The measurement vector v of the large optical flow vector $\bar{v}$ is expressed by

$$v = \bar{v} + \Delta v, \tag{23}$$

where

$$v = \begin{pmatrix} u_1 \\ \vdots \\ u_m \end{pmatrix}, \quad \Delta v = \begin{pmatrix} \Delta u_1 \\ \vdots \\ \Delta u_m \end{pmatrix}. \tag{24}$$

Equation (23) corresponds to Eq. (2). From Eq. (4), the quantity to be minimized, J_{sr}, is represented by the next two formulae.

$$J_{sr} = (v - A_h \bar{p} + B\bar{\omega})^\top V[v]^{-1} (v - A_h \bar{p} + B\bar{\omega}), \tag{25}$$
$$J_{sr} = (v - A_p \bar{h} + B\bar{\omega})^\top V[v]^{-1} (v - A_p \bar{h} + B\bar{\omega}), \tag{26}$$

where

$$V[v]^{-1} = \begin{pmatrix} V[u_1]^{-1} & & 0 \\ & \ddots & \\ 0 & & V[u_m]^{-1} \end{pmatrix}, \tag{27}$$

and $V[\boldsymbol{u}_j]$ is the covariance matrix of $\Delta \boldsymbol{u}_j$. Note that the minimal point of J_{sr} is not unique. If we multiply $\bar{\boldsymbol{h}}$ by an arbitrary constant and divide $\bar{\boldsymbol{p}}$ by the same constant, J_{sr} remains unchanged. To remove this extra freedom, we impose the constraint $\|\bar{\boldsymbol{h}}\|^2 = 1$.

The next step is the minimization of J_{sr}. Because of the bilinear structure of the problem, if $\bar{\boldsymbol{h}}$ is fixed then J_{sr} is represented by the quadratic form (25). Conversely, when $\bar{\boldsymbol{p}}$ is fixed then J_{sr} has the quadratic form given in (26). Therefore, J_{sr} can be minimized by repeating the two quadratic form minimizations. The minimizer $\hat{\boldsymbol{p}}$ of Eq. (25) is given by

$$\hat{\boldsymbol{p}} = (A_h^\top V[\boldsymbol{v}]^{-1} A_h)^{-1} A_h^\top V[\boldsymbol{v}]^{-1} (\boldsymbol{v} - B\bar{\boldsymbol{\omega}}). \qquad (28)$$

If $\hat{p}_j$ is the jth component of $\hat{\boldsymbol{p}}$ then it can be written as

$$\hat{p}_j = \frac{\bar{\boldsymbol{h}}^\top A_j^\top V[\boldsymbol{u}_j]^{-1} (\boldsymbol{u}_j - B_i \bar{\boldsymbol{\omega}})}{\bar{\boldsymbol{h}}^\top A_j^\top V[\boldsymbol{u}_j]^{-1} A_j \bar{\boldsymbol{h}}}. \qquad (29)$$

The minimizer $\hat{\boldsymbol{q}} = (\hat{\boldsymbol{h}}^\top \ \hat{\boldsymbol{\omega}}^\top)^\top$ of Eq. (26) is given by

$$\hat{\boldsymbol{q}} = (C^\top V[\boldsymbol{v}]^{-1} C)^{-1} C^\top V[\boldsymbol{v}]^{-1} \boldsymbol{v}, \qquad (30)$$

where we defined $C = (A_p | B)$. The overall minimization process is given by the following algorithm.

Step 1: Initialize $\hat{\boldsymbol{q}}$ to $(0 \ 0 \ 1 \ 0 \ 0 \ 0)^\top$ and go to **step 4**.

Step 2: Compute Eq. (28) or (29) by substituting the current value of $\hat{\boldsymbol{q}}$ for $\bar{\boldsymbol{q}} = (\bar{\boldsymbol{h}}^\top \ \bar{\boldsymbol{\omega}}^\top)^\top$.

Step 3: Normalize the length of $\hat{\boldsymbol{h}}$ in $\hat{\boldsymbol{q}}$ so that $\|\hat{\boldsymbol{h}}\|^2 = 1$.

Step 4: Compute Eq. (30) by substituting the current value of $\hat{\boldsymbol{p}}$ for $\bar{\boldsymbol{p}}$.

Step 5: Check for convergence. If not converged then go to **step 2**.

In order to compute the covariance matrix $V[\boldsymbol{q}, \boldsymbol{p}]$ of the estimated parameter $(\hat{\boldsymbol{q}}, \hat{\boldsymbol{p}})$, we could use Eq. (7). However, the matrix inside the parentheses in Eq. (7) is singular. This singularity originates from the fact that the length of the translation velocity, $\|\hat{\boldsymbol{h}}\|^2$, is indeterminable. In this case, to compute the covariance matrix we use the **generalized inverse** (Kanatani, 1996) instead:

$$V[\boldsymbol{q}, \boldsymbol{p}] = \begin{pmatrix} C^\top V[\boldsymbol{v}]^{-1} C & C^\top V[\boldsymbol{v}]^{-1} A_h \\ A_h^\top V[\boldsymbol{v}]^{-1} C & A_h^\top V[\boldsymbol{v}]^{-1} A_h \end{pmatrix}^-, \qquad (31)$$

where $(\cdot)^-$ denotes the generalized inverse of a matrix. The rank of $V[\boldsymbol{q}, \boldsymbol{p}]$ is $m + 5$, and the direction of its kernel is $(-\hat{\boldsymbol{h}}^\top \; \boldsymbol{0}^\top \; \hat{\boldsymbol{p}}^\top)^\top$.

The generalized inverse can be computed through an eigenvalue computation, which is not difficult even if the size of the matrix is large. However, if we need only the variance $V[p_j]$ of each component $\hat{p}_j$ of vector $\hat{\boldsymbol{p}}$, the easiest way to reduce the computation cost is to assume the estimated motion parameter to be correct and compute the variance by

$$V[p_j] = \frac{1}{\hat{\boldsymbol{h}}^\top A_j^\top V[\boldsymbol{u}_j]^{-1} A_j \hat{\boldsymbol{h}}}. \tag{32}$$

When the motion parameter is accurately estimated, this formula gives a good approximation. We adopted this approximation in the experiments.

The reconstructed shape from the optical flow given in Figure 2a is shown in Figure 3a. A light smoothing process was applied to the result, but we omit the details since it is not essential. The reliable regions shown in Figure 3b were selected by the value of $V[p_j]$ in Eq. (32).

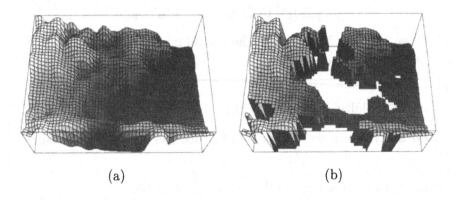

(a)   (b)

Figure 3.   (a) Reconstructed shape $(1/Z)$. (b) Reliable regions.

5. Moving Object Detection

In the shape reconstruction process described in the previous section, we assume that the environment was rigid and all optical flow was generated by the camera movement. In this section, we assume that some small moving objects are present and we consider an algorithm to detect them.

Assuming that the moving objects are small enough for the motion parameters $\hat{\boldsymbol{q}}$ to be reasonably estimated, the predicted optical flow $\bar{\boldsymbol{u}}_j$ represented by Eq. (16) is valid only in image regions corresponding to a rigid environment. In the moving object regions, it is expected that optical flow estimation will be inconsistent with Eq. (16). This conflict can be measured by a residual e_j^2 given by

$$e_j^2 = (\boldsymbol{u}_j - \hat{\boldsymbol{u}}_j)^\top V[\boldsymbol{u}_j]^{-1}(\boldsymbol{u}_j - \hat{\boldsymbol{u}}_j), \tag{33}$$

where $\hat{\boldsymbol{u}}_j$ is computed by substituting $\hat{\boldsymbol{h}}$, $\hat{\boldsymbol{\omega}}$ and $\hat{p}_j$ for $\bar{\boldsymbol{h}}$, $\bar{\boldsymbol{\omega}}$ and $\bar{p}_j$ in Eq. (16), respectively. The module concludes that moving objects are present where the value of e_j^2 is large.

This test is insufficient when an object moves in the same direction of the camera translation $\bar{\boldsymbol{h}}$, as it affects only $\hat{p}_j$ and yields no residual e_j^2. Thus, we also test that the estimated inverse distance, $\hat{p}_j$, has a physically achievable value, and if not then conclude that a moving object is present. The inverse distance $\hat{p}_j$ cannot be negative. In addition, if the maximum speed of the camera is below $\|\bar{\boldsymbol{h}}\|_{\max}$ and the minimum distance to the environment is above $\bar{Z}_{j\,\min}$, then the value of the computed $\hat{p}_j$, under the condition $\|\bar{\boldsymbol{h}}\| = 1$, cannot exceed $\|\bar{\boldsymbol{h}}\|_{\max}/\bar{Z}_{j\,\min}$.

The module detects moving objects using the following conditions.

1. The residual is large; i.e.

$$e_j^2 > \tau_e. \tag{34}$$

2. The estimated $\hat{p}_j$ is reliable but exhibits a physically unachievable value; i.e.

$$V[p_j] < \tau_p \text{ and } (\ \hat{p}_j < 0 \text{ or } \hat{p}_j > \frac{\|\bar{\boldsymbol{h}}\|_{\max}}{\bar{Z}_{j\,\min}}\ ). \tag{35}$$

In these conditions, τ_e and τ_p are the thresholds that adjust sensitivity. An experimental result of the moving object detection is shown in Figure 4. In the experiment, the thresholds τ_e and τ_p were empirically determined.

We can theoretically compute the threshold values too. The residual e_j^2 has an approximately χ^2 distribution, and so condition (34) could be regarded as a χ^2 test. More advanced solutions than the χ^2 test are to formulate the problem as a statistical model selection and to use criteria such as AIC and MDL. We have investigated using AIC for a moving object detection system in (Ohta et al., 1998).

6. Conclusions

We have discussed the uncertainty propagation by covariance matrices in the case of optical flow estimation, shape reconstruction and moving object detection tasks. Proper handling of uncertainty is essential in computer vision systems. We think we could demonstrate the advantages of formalizing computer vision tasks as statistical estimation and decision problems, and propagating uncertainty in terms of covariance matrices. This approach is

Figure 4.   Detected moving objects (darker areas).

applicable to other computer vision problems, some of which have been reported in (Kanatani, 1996; Ji and Haralick, 1998).

Acknowledgements

We thank Prof. Kenichi Kanatani of Gunma University, who gave us helpful suggestions and encouragements. We also thank Dr. Daniel Morris of Carnegie Mellon University and Dr. Du Huynh of Murdoch University, who discussed technical issues with us and helped to correct the English in this chapter.

References

Barron, J.L., Fleet, D.J. and Beauchemin, S.S. (1994) Performance of Optical Flow Techniques, *International Journal of Computer Vision*, 12(1):43–77.

Heeger, D.J. and Jepson, A.D. (1992) Subspace Methods for Recovering Rigid Motion I: Algorithm and Implementation, *International Journal of Computer Vision*, 7(2):95–117.

Ji, Q. and Haralick, R.M. (1998) Breakpoint Detection Using Covariance Propagation, *IEEE PAMI*, 20(8):845–851.

Kanatani, K. (1996) *Statistical Optimization for Geometric Computation: Theory and Practice*, Elsevier Science, Amsterdam.

Lucas, B. and Kanade, T. (1981) An Iterative Image Registration Technique with an Application to Stereo Vision, *Proceedings of 7th International Joint Conference on Artificial Intelligence*, Vancouver, Canada, 674–679.

Ohta, N. (1991) Image Movement Detection with Reliability Indices, *IEICE Transactions on Information and Systems*, E74(10):3379–3388.

Ohta, N. (1993) Structure from Motion with Confidence Measure and Its Application for Moving Object Detection (Japanese), *IEICE Transactions*, J76-D-II(8):1562–1571.

Ohta, N. (1996) Uncertainty Models of the Gradient Constraint for Optical Flow Computation, *IEICE Transactions on Information and Systems*, E79-D(7):958–964.

Ohta, N. (1997) Optical Flow Detection Using a General Noise Model for Gradient Constraint, *Proceedings of 7th International Conference on Computer Analysis of Images and Patterns*, Kiel, Germany, 669–676.

Ohta, N., Kanatani, K. and Kimura, K. (1998) Moving Object Detection from Optical Flow without Empirical Thresholds, *IEICE Transactions on Information and Systems*, E81-D(2):221–223.

Simoncelli, E.P., Adelson, E.H. and Heeger, D.J. (1991) Probability Distributions of Optical Flow, *Proceedings of International Conference on Computer Vision and Pattern Recognition*, Maui, Hawaii, 310–315.

Weber, J. and Malik, J. (1993) Robust Computation of Optical Flow in a Multi-Scale Differential Framework, *Proceedings of 4th International Joint Conference on Computer Vision*, Berlin, Germany, 12–20.

Part IV

Comparative Studies

PERFORMANCE CHARACTERISTICS OF LOW-LEVEL MOTION ESTIMATORS IN SPATIOTEMPORAL IMAGES

BERND JÄHNE and HORST HAUSSECKER
Research Group Image Processing
Interdisciplinary Center for Scientific Computing
University of Heidelberg
Im Neuenheimer Feld 368
69120 Heidelberg, Germany

1. Introduction

This chapter presents an analytical, numerical, and experimental study of the performance of low-level motion estimators in spatiotemporal images. Motivation for this work arose from scientific applications of image sequence processing within the frame of an interdisciplinary research unit. Here, the study of transport, exchange, and growth processes with various imaging techniques requires highly accurate velocity estimates (Jähne *et al.*, 1996; Jähne *et al.*, 1998). These high accuracy demands triggered a revisit of the fundamentals of motion estimation in spatiotemporal images. In this chapter only low-level motion estimators are discussed. This is only a part of the picture, but errors in low-level estimators propagate and thus cause also errors in higher-level features. Only a few systematic studies of the performance characteristics of low-level motion estimators are available in the literature. Kearney *et al.* (1987) performed an error analysis of optical flow estimation with gradient-based methods, while Simoncelli (1999) studied the error propagation of multi-scale differential optical flow. Barron *et al.* (1994) used a set of computer-generated and real image sequence to compare various approaches to optical flow computation. To study the performance of phase-based and energy-based techniques, Haglund and Fleet (1994) used an image sequence generated by warping a single natural image. Otte and Nagel (1994) were the first to verify motion estimators with a calibrated real-world sequence. Bainbridge-Smith and Lane (1997)

R. Klette et al. (eds.), Performance Characterization in Computer Vision, 139–152.

theoretically compared various first and second-order differential techniques and proved the results using a series of test sequences.

None of the above cited papers includes an analytical performance analysis of different techniques with typical deviations from ideal conditions as they occur in real-world sequences. This is the main contribution of this chapter. Section 2 gives a brief outline of differential, tensor-based, and phase-based techniques formulated in a unified framework as nonlinear filter operations in continuous spatiotemporal images. Section 3 discusses general ways to model motion fields and spatial grayscale variations. The main section of this chapter, Section 4, discusses the analytical studies. Finally, Section 5 deals with the errors caused by discretization and Section 6 shows some experimental verifications with computer generated and real world image sequences.

2. Motion estimation as nonlinear filtering

The basic expression for a unified approach to low-level motion estimation in spatiotemporal images contains the product of derivatives into the different coordinate directions averaged over a certain window (Jähne, 1993):

$$
\begin{aligned}
J_{pq}(\mathbf{x}, t) &= \int w(\mathbf{x} - \mathbf{x}', t - t') \partial_p g(\mathbf{x}', t') \partial_q g(\mathbf{x}', t') \mathrm{d}^2 x' \mathrm{d}t' \\
&= \langle \partial_p g(\mathbf{x}', t') \partial_q g(\mathbf{x}', t') \rangle .
\end{aligned}
\tag{1}
$$

This operation can be performed as a cascade of linear convolution and (nonlinear) point operations as $\mathcal{B}(\mathcal{D}_p \cdot \mathcal{D}_q)$, where $\mathcal{B}$ and $\mathcal{D}_p$ are a smoothing filter and a derivative filter into the directions p and q.

The standard *differential least squares approach* (Bainbridge-Smith and Lane, 1997; Kearney *et al.*, 1987; Lucas and Kanade, 1981; Simoncelli, 1993), results in the following linear equation system for the optical flow $\mathbf{f} = [f_x, f_y]^T$:

$$
\begin{bmatrix} J_{xx} & J_{xy} \\ J_{xy} & J_{yy} \end{bmatrix} \begin{bmatrix} f_x \\ f_y \end{bmatrix} = \begin{bmatrix} J_{xt} \\ J_{yt} \end{bmatrix} .
\tag{2}
$$

This equation system can be solved provided the inverse of the 2×2 matrix exists. If all gradient vectors within the local neighborhood are pointing into the same direction, the matrix gets singular. In this case only the normal flow

$$
\mathbf{f}_\perp(\mathbf{x}, t) = -\frac{g_t(\mathbf{x}, t)}{\|\nabla g(\mathbf{x}, t)\|^2} \nabla g(\mathbf{x}, t),
\tag{3}
$$

perpendicular to lines of constraint brightness can be estimated.

The *tensor method* (Bigün and Granlund, 1987; Haußecker and Spieß, 1999; Jähne, 1990) also uses the component J_{tt} to form the symmetric tensor

$$\mathbf{J} = \begin{bmatrix} J_{xx} & J_{xy} & J_{xt} \\ J_{xy} & J_{yy} & J_{yt} \\ J_{xt} & J_{yt} & J_{tt} \end{bmatrix}. \tag{4}$$

An eigenvalue analysis of this tensor is equivalent to a total least squares approach and yields the optical flow and a characterization of the spatial brightness structure. In case of a distributed spatial structure and a constant motion, only one eigenvalue of $\mathbf{J}$ is zero. The optical flow can then be computed from the corresponding eigenvector $\mathbf{e}_3 = [e_{3x}, e_{3y}, e_{3t}]^T$ as (Karlholm, 1996)

$$\mathbf{f} = \frac{1}{e_{3t}} \begin{bmatrix} e_{3x} \\ e_{3y} \end{bmatrix}. \tag{5}$$

For a spatially oriented structure (e. g. an edge), only the velocity component perpendicular to the oriented structure can be computed from the eigenvector to the largest eigenvalue $\mathbf{e}_1 = [e_{1x}, e_{1y}, e_{1t}]^T$ as

$$|\mathbf{f}_\perp| = \sqrt{\frac{e_{1t}^2}{e_{1x}^2 + e_{1y}^2}} = \sqrt{\frac{e_{1t}^2}{1 - e_{1t}^2}}. \tag{6}$$

The *phase method*, introduced by Fleet and Jepson (1990), deviates in as much from the previous methods that only component velocities are determined, i. e., normal velocities from image sequences filtered by a set of directional quadrate filters (q_+ and q_-). Then the component of the optical flow into the direction of the directional quadrature filter can be computed by

$$f_\perp = -\frac{q_+ \, \partial_t q_- - q_- \, \partial_t q_+}{q_+ \, \partial_x q_- - q_- \, \partial_x q_+}. \tag{7}$$

3. Modeling of motion fields and spatial grayscale variations

The analysis performed in this chapter is very general without making any specific assumptions about the types of gray value structures. It does not use Taylor expansions of the gray scale structure which give only approximate results. The following two classes of general continuous gray value structures are applied:

$$\text{planar wave, moving "edge"} \quad {}^I g(r) = g(\mathbf{k}\mathbf{x} - \omega t), \tag{8}$$
$$\text{constant 2-D motion, moving "corner"} \quad {}^{II} g(\mathbf{x}') = g(\mathbf{x} - \mathbf{u}t). \tag{9}$$

Note that r is a scalar variable and $\mathbf{x}'$ is a 2-D vector. The normal velocity in (8) is given by $\mathbf{f}_\perp = \mathbf{k}\omega/\|\mathbf{k}\|^2$. The gradient and temporal derivative of (8) and (9) are given by $\nabla^I g(r) = \mathbf{k}g_r$, $\partial_t{}^I g = -\omega\partial_r g$ and $\nabla^{II} g = \nabla g$, $\partial_t{}^{II} g = -\mathbf{u}\nabla g$, respectively. These two elementary classes are modified systematically by adding various types of deviations, e. g.:

$$\text{isotropic noise} \qquad g(\mathbf{x}, t) = g(\mathbf{x} - \mathbf{u}t) + n(\mathbf{x}, t), \qquad (10)$$

$$\text{accelerated motion} \qquad g(\mathbf{x}, t) = g(\mathbf{x} - \mathbf{u}t - 1/2\mathbf{a}t^2), \qquad (11)$$

$$\text{motion discontinuity} \qquad g_1(x + ut)\Pi(-x) + g_2(x - ut)\Pi(x), \qquad (12)$$

$$\text{motion superimposition} \qquad g_1(x + ut) + g_2(x - ut), \qquad (13)$$

$$\text{global illumination change} \qquad g(\mathbf{x}, t) = g(\mathbf{x} - \mathbf{u}t, t), \qquad (14)$$

where $\mathbf{a} = \partial \mathbf{u}/\partial t$ and $\Pi(x)$ is the step function.

4. Analytical studies of biases

In this section, we will analyze possible systematic errors of the three motion estimators discussed in Section 2. The analytical study of continuous signals does not include errors due to the discretization. This is discussed in Section 5. Often these two types of errors are mixed up in the literature.

4.1. IDEAL MOTION

The verification of the various techniques under ideal conditions gives further insight into their general properties and systematic biases.

Differential Method.   Using (9) we obtain

$$\mathbf{f} = -\left\langle \nabla^{II} g \nabla^{II} g^T \right\rangle^{-1} \left\langle \partial_t{}^{II} g \nabla g \right\rangle = -\left\langle \nabla g \nabla g^T \right\rangle^{-1} \left\langle -\mathbf{u}(\nabla g \nabla g^T) \right\rangle$$

$$= \mathbf{u} \left\langle \nabla g \nabla g^T \right\rangle^{-1} \left\langle \nabla g \nabla g^T \right\rangle \qquad = \mathbf{u},$$

provided that the inverse of $\left\langle \nabla g \nabla g^T \right\rangle$ exists. It is a widespread misconception that differential methods do not deliver accurate results if the spatial gray value structure cannot be adequately approximated by a first-order Taylor series (see, for example, (Kearney et al., 1987; Singh, 1991)). As shown above, exact results are obtained independent of the specific form of the grayscale structure as soon as the linear equation system can be solved at all. As we will discuss in Section 5, errors in the estimation of optical flow are only introduced by an inadequate discretization of the partial derivative operators to the extent that the discrete differential operators deviate from the transfer function of an ideal derivative operator.

In the case of a moving edge (8), the equation system gets singular and only the normal component $\mathbf{f}_\perp$ can be estimated according to (3).

Tensor Method. For an oriented pattern or planar wave (8), the structure tensor reduces to

$$\langle g_r^2 \rangle \begin{bmatrix} k_x^2 & k_x k_y & -k_x \omega \\ k_x k_y & k_y^2 & -k_y \omega \\ -k_x \omega & -k_y \omega & \omega^2 \end{bmatrix}. \tag{15}$$

Since all three row vectors are the same except for a constant factor, two eigenvalues are zero and the eigenvector of the nonzero eigenvalue is given by

$$\mathbf{e}_1 = \begin{bmatrix} -k_x \\ -k_y \\ \omega \end{bmatrix}, \tag{16}$$

which verifies (6). With a constant moving spatially distributed structure according to (9), the six independent components of the structure tensor are

$$\begin{aligned} J_{xx} &= \langle (\partial_x g)^2 \rangle, \quad J_{yy} = \langle (\partial_y g)^2 \rangle, \quad J_{xy} = \langle \partial_x g \, \partial_y g \rangle \\ J_{xt} &= -u_x \langle (\partial_x g)^2 \rangle - u_y \langle \partial_x g \partial_y g \rangle \\ J_{yt} &= -u_x \langle \partial_x g \, \partial_y g \rangle - u_y \langle (\partial_y g)^2 \rangle \\ J_{tt} &= u_x^2 \langle (\partial_x g)^2 \rangle + 2 u_x u_y \langle \partial_x g \, \partial_y g \rangle + u_y^2 \langle (\partial_y g)^2 \rangle. \end{aligned} \tag{17}$$

Evaluating the eigensystem of this tensor shows that one eigenvalue is zero and that the corresponding eigenvector has the form

$$\mathbf{e}_3 = \frac{1}{u_x^2 + u_y^2 + 1} \begin{bmatrix} u_x \\ u_y \\ 1 \end{bmatrix}, \tag{18}$$

verifying (5).

Phase Method. To verify the phase method, we apply a quadrature filter pair to an arbitrary 1-D spatial gray value structure moving with constant velocity and obtain $g_+(x - ut)$ and $g_-(x - ut)$. Then (7) results in

$$f = -\frac{\langle -u\, g_+ \partial_x g_- + u\, g_- \partial_x g_+ \rangle}{\langle g_+ \partial_x{}^\circ g_- - g_- \partial_x g_+ \rangle} = u\frac{\langle g_+ \partial_x g_- - g_- \partial_x g_+ \rangle}{\langle g_+ \partial_x g_- - g_- \partial_x g_+ \rangle} = u,$$

provided that $\langle g_+ \partial_x g_- - g_- \partial_x g_+ \rangle \neq 0$. This result is surprising because we do not make any use of the fact that g_- and g_+ are a quadrature pair. The phase method gives exact results with any pair of g_+ and g_- if only the requirement $\langle g_+ \partial_x g_- - g_- \partial_x g_+ \rangle \neq 0$ is met.

4.2. BIAS BY NOISE

We investigate this bias by adding *isotropic zero-mean noise* according to (10). We assume that the partial derivatives of the noise function are not correlated with themselves or the partial derivatives of the image:

$$\langle n \rangle = 0, \quad \langle \partial_p n \partial_q n \rangle = \delta(p-q)\sigma_n^2 \quad \langle \partial_p g \partial_q n \rangle = 0 \qquad (19)$$

Differential Method. A noisy image with the conditions as set up above gives the optical flow estimate for the differential method:

$$\mathbf{f} = \mathbf{u}(\langle \nabla g \nabla g^T \rangle + \langle \nabla n \nabla n^T \rangle)^{-1} \langle \nabla g \nabla g^T \rangle. \qquad (20)$$

The key to understanding this matrix equation is to observe that the noise matrix $(\nabla n \nabla n^T)$ is diagonal in any coordinate system, because of the conditions set by (19). Therefore, we can transform the equation into the principal-axes coordinate system in which $\nabla g \nabla g^T$ is diagonal. Then

$$\mathbf{f} = \left[u_x \frac{\langle g_{x'}{}^2 \rangle}{\langle g_{x'}{}^2 \rangle + \sigma_n^2}, \; u_y \frac{\langle g_{y'}{}^2 \rangle}{\langle g_{y'}{}^2 \rangle + \sigma_n^2} \right]^T \quad \text{for } \sigma_n^2 > 0. \qquad (21)$$

We *always* obtain a solution for nonzero noise and can thus no longer distinguish the noise-free image structures corresponding to rank 0, 1, and 2, matrices, i. e., constant neighborhoods, edge-like, and corner-like structures, respectively. Furthermore, the estimate are biased towards lower values.

Tensor Method. A spatiotemporal image consisting only of zero-mean normal-distributed and isotropic noise with the variance σ_n results in a diagonal inertia tensor in any coordinate system, $\sigma_n^2 \mathbf{I}$, where $\mathbf{I}$ is the unit diagonal tensor. The structure tensor of a noisy spatiotemporal image is therefore given by

$$\mathbf{J}' = \mathbf{J} + \sigma_n{}^2 \mathbf{I} = \begin{bmatrix} J_{xx} + \sigma_n{}^2 & J_{xy} & J_{xt} \\ J_{xy} & J_{yy} + \sigma_n{}^2 & J_{yt} \\ J_{xt} & J_{yt} & J_{tt} + \sigma_n{}^2 \end{bmatrix}.$$

Thus the eigenvectors for an ideal oriented structure with *isotropic* noise are the same as for the noise-free case and an unbiased estimate of orientation is obtained. If $\{\lambda_1, \lambda_2, \lambda_3\}$ is the set of eigenvalues of $\mathbf{J}$, the eigenvalues of $\mathbf{J}'$ are

$$\{\lambda_1 + \sigma_n^2, \lambda_2 + \sigma_n^2, \lambda_3 + \sigma_n^2\}. \qquad (22)$$

The tensor method has the significant advantage that in areas of constant motion ($\lambda_3 = 0$), the lowest eigenvalue gives directly the noise level.

Moreover regions with oriented spatial structure can—in contrast to the standard least squares approach (see above)—still be recognized, since then the second and third eigenvalue are equal to the noise level.

4.3. UNSTEADY MOTION

In this section we check the sensitivity of the optical flow estimation to changes in the motion field. Since motion results in oriented structures in space-time images, changes in the motion either by acceleration or by spatial changes lead to curved structures. By way of example, accelerated motion according to (11) is discussed. This modified model influences only the temporal derivative

$$\partial_t g' = -(u_1 + a_1 t)g_x - (u_2 + a_2 t)g_y = -(\mathbf{u} + \mathbf{a}t)\nabla g, \qquad (23)$$

With all techniques, weighted products of the derivatives appear. For example,

$$\langle \partial_x g \partial_t g \rangle = -\langle (\mathbf{u} + \mathbf{a}t)\nabla g \partial_x g \rangle = -\mathbf{u}\langle \nabla g \ \partial_x g \rangle - \mathbf{a}\langle t\nabla g \ \partial_x g \rangle \qquad (24)$$

and

$$\begin{aligned}
\langle (\partial_t g)^2 \rangle &= \langle [-(\mathbf{u} + \mathbf{a}t)\nabla g]^2 \rangle \\
&= u_1^2 \langle g_x^2 \rangle + 2u_1 u_2 \langle g_x g_y \rangle + u_2^2 \langle g_y^2 \rangle \\
&\quad + 2u_1 a_1 \langle t g_x^2 \rangle + 2(u_1 a_2 + u_2 a_1) \langle t g_x g_y \rangle + 2u_2 a_2 \langle t g_y^2 \rangle \\
&\quad + a_1^2 \langle t^2 g_x^2 \rangle + 2a_1 a_2 \langle t^2 g_x g_y \rangle + a_2^2 \langle t^2 g_y^2 \rangle .
\end{aligned} \qquad (25)$$

First, we have terms in which the time appears linearly in the averaging together with the corresponding derivatives. In the ideal case, when the spatial derivatives are evenly distributed over the averaged time, they all cancel out. The expression $\langle t \rangle$ is zero since the center of the coordinate system has been placed at the center pixel in (23). Now consider the converse case that the whole neighborhood over which we average contains only a singular steep spatial derivative at time t_0. Then, for instance, (24) reduces to

$$\langle \partial_x g \partial_t g \rangle = -(\mathbf{u} + \mathbf{a}t_0) \langle \nabla g \ \partial_x g \rangle . \qquad (26)$$

This equation means that the velocity obtained is not the velocity at time $t = 0$—as expected—but the velocity at time t_0. Thus the worst that could happen is that the optical flow estimate is biased to a value which is at the edge of the averaging neighborhood. If the spatial gray values are more equally distributed, the shift is of course less.

The discussion so far is valid for *all* methods, since the effect of the accelerated motion is simply that the correct velocity $\mathbf{u}$ has to be replaced by a biased velocity $\mathbf{u} + \mathbf{a} t_0$. The upper limit for t_0 is the temporal extension of the averaging mask. It is obvious that the same train of thought is valid for spatial variations of the velocity field. The velocity in the neighborhood is biased at most to a velocity value at the edge of the averaging neighborhood. Generally, we can conclude that the estimate of the optical flow is pulled to the values of regions with the steepest gradients.

One term remains to be discussed which appears only in the tensor method. It is $J_{tt} = \langle (\partial_t g)^2 \rangle$ (25). If we neglect the terms linear in t, terms that are quadratic in t still remain and (25) reduces to

$$
\begin{aligned}
\langle (\partial_t g)^2 \rangle &= u_x^2 \langle (\partial_x g)^2 \rangle + 2 u_x u_y \langle \partial_x g\, \partial_y g \rangle + u_y^2 \langle (\partial_y g)^2 \rangle \\
&+ a_x^2 \langle (t \partial_x g)^2 \rangle + 2 a_x a_y \langle t^2 \partial_x g\, \partial_y g \rangle + a_y^2 \langle (t \partial_y g)^2 \rangle .
\end{aligned}
$$

The terms quadratic in t appear as soon as the motion is accelerated. They contain a product of the squared acceleration and a measure of the temporal variance weighted with the steepness of the gray value changes. We illustrate this effect of an accelerated motion with the 2-D case. Then

$$
\langle (\partial_t g)^2 \rangle = u_x^2 \langle (\partial_x g)^2 \rangle + a_x^2 \langle (t \partial_x g)^2 \rangle \tag{27}
$$

and the 2-D structure tensor is

$$
\begin{bmatrix}
\langle (\partial_x g)^2 \rangle & -u_x \langle (\partial_x g)^2 \rangle \\
-u_x \langle (\partial_x g)^2 \rangle & u_x^2 \langle (\partial_x g)^2 \rangle + a_x^2 \langle (t \partial_x g)^2 \rangle .
\end{bmatrix} \tag{28}
$$

In the limit $a_x^2 \langle (t \partial_x g)^2 \rangle \ll (1 + u_x^2) \langle (\partial_x g)^2 \rangle$, the eigenvalues are

$$
\left\{ (1 + u_x^2) \langle (\partial_x g)^2 \rangle , a_x^2 \langle (t \partial_x g)^2 \rangle \right\} . \tag{29}
$$

In this approximation the eigenvector $\mathbf{e}_2$ of the smallest eigenvalue is no longer simply $[u_x, 1]^T$ but

$$
\mathbf{e}_2 = \left[u_x \left(1 + \frac{a_x^2 \langle (t \partial_x g)^2 \rangle}{(1 + u_x^2) \langle (\partial_x g)^2 \rangle} \right) , 1 \right]^T . \tag{30}
$$

Thus there is a small bias in the estimate of the optical flow which goes with the square of the acceleration. As an example we take $u_x = 1$, $a_x = 0.1$, and $\langle (t \partial_x g)^2 \rangle / \langle (\partial_x g)^2 \rangle = 4$. This means that the motion is changing by $\pm 20\,\%$ within the temporal width of the averaging window with a radius of 2. Even with this large relative velocity variation, the relative bias in the estimate of the optical flow is only $2\,\%$.

4.4. MOTION DISCONTINUITY AND MOTION SUPERIMPOSITION

We discuss only the case of a one-dimensional flow estimate for the tensor method. The neighborhood is either partitioned into two subareas with different velocities according to (12) or consists of two spatiotemporal structures g' and g'' moving in opposite direction according to (13). The equations for the estimation of the optical give the same results in both cases:

$$f \approx u \frac{\langle (\partial_x g')^2 \rangle - \langle (\partial_x g'')^2 \rangle}{\langle (\partial_x g')^2 \rangle + \langle (\partial_x g'')^2 \rangle}. \tag{31}$$

If the mean square gradient is equal in both spatiotemporal structures g' and g'', the estimated optical flow is zero, as expected.

In any case, a motion discontinuity at a straight line between two regions with random variations in the mean square gradient will not appear as a straight line in the optical flow image. It will rather become a wiggly line because of the bias caused by weighting. The deviation from the true discontinuity can be as much as half the mask size of the averaging filters. We seem to have reached a point in the analysis of motion that cannot be solved on the base of local information alone. At this point, global information must be considered, such as the smoothness of boundaries.

4.5. GLOBAL ILLUMINATION CHANGE

Finally, we discuss the influence of illumination changes using an explicit temporal dependence of the gray value according to (14). Then $\partial_x g = \partial_x g$ and $\partial_t g = -u \, \partial_x g + \partial_t g$, where $\partial_t g$ is the explicit temporal derivative. The estimate of the optical flow for the tensor method for a 2-D spatiotemporal image gives

$$f = \frac{u - \langle \partial_x g \, \partial_t g \rangle / \langle (\partial_x g)^2 \rangle}{1 - u^2 + 2u \langle \partial_x g \, \partial_t g \rangle / \langle (\partial_x g)^2 \rangle - \langle (\partial_t g)^2 \rangle / \langle (\partial_x g)^2 \rangle}. \tag{32}$$

Even if $\langle \partial_x g \, \partial_t g \rangle = 0$, the velocity estimate is biased towards higher velocities, as can be seen for $u \ll 1$:

$$f \approx \frac{u}{1 - \langle (\partial_t g)^2 \rangle / \langle (\partial_x g)^2 \rangle}. \tag{33}$$

This result is not surprising, since illumination changes occur as additional patterns with an orientation corresponding to infinite velocity.

From a phase-based method we would expect that global illumination changes are entirely suppressed since only the phase and not the amplitude of the signal is used for the determination of displacements.

After some algebra we obtain

$$f = u - \frac{\langle g_+ \partial_t g_- - g_- \partial_t g_+ \rangle}{\langle g_+ \partial_x g_- - g_- \partial_x g_+ \rangle}, \tag{34}$$

where $\partial_t g$ again means the *explicit* temporal derivative. The additional term vanishes when the explicit temporal derivative is directly proportional to the gray value. This is indeed the case for global illumination changes. Thus the phase method suppresses global illumination changes under very general assumptions.

5. Error by discretization

With discrete image sequences, motion estimation becomes biased since the differential operators are to be replaced by difference operators. We estimate here the error for the simplest case. With the standard differential least squares approach, the estimate of one component of the velocity can be written in the local principal coordinate system as

$$u' = \frac{\langle g_{x'} g_t \rangle}{\langle g_{x'}^2 \rangle} = \frac{\langle k\omega |\hat{g}|^2 \rangle}{\langle k^2 |\hat{g}|^2 \rangle}. \tag{35}$$

The second part of the equation is written in the Fourier domain. For difference operators the ideal transfer functions of the spatial and temporal derivatives has to be replaced by the transfer function of the corresponding difference operator, $\hat{D}_x$ and $\hat{D}_t$:

$$u' = \frac{\hat{D}_t(\omega)}{\hat{D}_x(k)} \tag{36}$$

for a narrow spectral distribution. For the simple symmetric difference filter $1/2\ [1\ 0\ \text{-}1]$ with the transfer function $\sin(\pi k)$ and $\sin(\pi\omega)$, the estimate becomes:

$$f = u + u\frac{\pi^2 k^2}{6}\left(1 - u^2\right). \tag{37}$$

The bias is zero for the velocities 0 and 1. In-between it is maximal. Experimental tests with a moving random pattern verify this behavior very nicely (Figure 1a). With the standard symmetric difference filter, large deviations up to 0.1 pixels/frame occur. With 3×3 Sobel-type filter that are specifically optimized to minimize the error in the *direction* of the gradient (Scharr *et al.*, 1997), the error is well suppressed below 0.005 pixels/frame (Figure 1b).

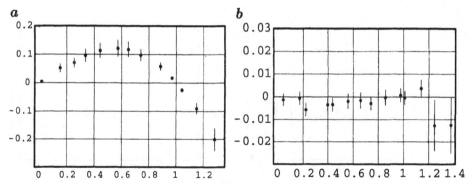

Figure 1.   Systematic error in the velocity estimate as a function of the interframe displacement measured with a moving random pattern. Derivatives computed with a **a** the symmetric difference filter 1/ 2 [1 0 -1] **b** an optimized Sobel filter (Scharr *et al.*, 1997).

6. Error analysis with computer-generated and real-world image sequences

In this last section, some results of experiments with computer-generated and real-world sequences are briefly discussed that verify some of the analytic studies discussed in this chapter. A much more detailed study is contained in Haußecker and Spieß (1999).

The bias of the standard differential least squares approach is verified in Figure 2a and b. If the variance of the noise is about the squared magnitude of the gradient, the estimated values are only about half of the true values. In contrast, the tensor approach does not show a bias (Figure 2c and d).

The effect of a static pattern caused by the photoresponse nonuniformity (PRNU) of the sensor is demonstrated in Figure 3. In all regions where (around dust particles) the gradients in the PRNU are steeper than that of the texture of the moving object, the motion estimate is biased towards lower values. Once the sensor is radiometrically calibrated, the effect disappears (Figure 4).

7. Conclusions

In this chapter we have shown that an analytical study of the performance characteristics of low-level motion estimation is possible under very general assumptions. This also includes a detailed analysis of biases in the motion estimate common in real-world image sequences and caused by noise, inhomogeneous and accelerated motion, motion discontinuities, motion superimposition, and global illumination changes. The analysis performed in this chapter can certainly carried on much further since it is using only

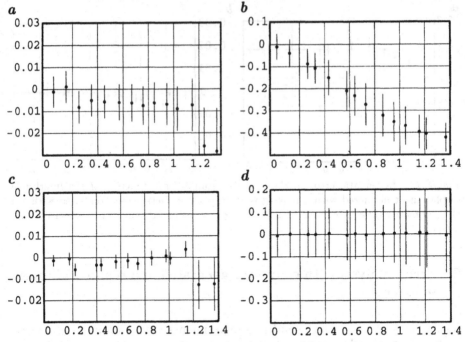

Figure 2. Systematic error in the velocity estimate with a moving random pattern using the least squares gradient method (**a** and **b**) and the tensor method (**c** and **d**) for velocities in x direction from 0 to 1.4 pixels/frame. The signal-to-noise ratio is 10 (**a** and **c**) and 1, (**b** and **d**) respectively.

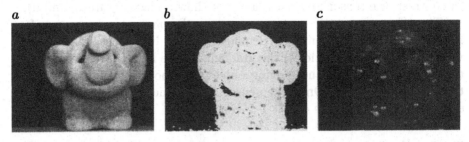

Figure 3. Motion analysis of an uncalibrated sequence: **a** Image of a sequence with constant motion of about 0.2 pixel/frame in x direction. **b** Motion field (x component) in grayscale coding. **c** Image of the smallest eigenvalue of the structure tensor.

quite simple mathematical tools so far. The significant results gained with rather simple techniques hopefully encourage analytical studies for other computer vision problems as well.

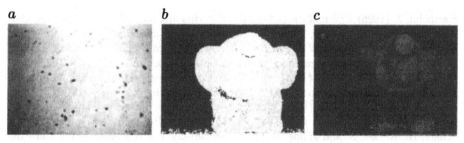

a   b   c

Figure 4.   Motion analysis with radiometrically calibrated sequence: **a** Contrast enhanced image of the sensor response. **b** Motion field (x component) in grayscale coding. **c** Image of the smallest eigenvalue of the structure tensor.

References

Bainbridge-Smith, A. and Lane, R.G. (1997) Determining optical flow using a differential method, *Image and Vision Computing*, 15:11–22.

Barron, J.L., Fleet, D.J. and Beauchemin, S. (1994)   Performance of optical flow techniques, *Int. J. Computer Vision*, 12(1):43–77.

Bigün, J. and Granlund, G.H. (1987) Optimal orientation detection of linear symmetry, *Proceedings ICCV'87*, London, IEEE Computer Society Press, Los Alamitos, 433–438.

Fleet, D.J. and Jepson, A.D. (1990)   Computation of component image velocity from local phase information, *Int. J. Comp. Vision*, 5:77–104.

Haglund, L. and Fleet, D.J. (1994) Stable estimation of image orientation, *Proceedings ICIP'94, Austin 1994, Vol. III*, IEEE Computer Society Press, Los Alamitos, 68–72.

Haußecker, H. and B. Jähne, (1997) A tensor approach for precise computation of dense displacement vector fields, Wahl, F. and Paulus, E. (eds.), *Proc. Mustererkennung 1997*, Braunschweig, Informatik Aktuell, Springer, Berlin, 15–17.

Haußecker, H. and Spieß, H. (1999) Motion, Jähne, B., Haußecker, H. and Geißler, P. (eds.), *Computer Vision and Applications*, Academic Press, San Diego, 2:309–396.

Jähne, B. (1990) Motion determination in space-time images, Faugeras, O. (ed.), *Proc. Computer Vision—ECCV'90*, Lecture Notes Computer Science 427, 161–173.

Jähne, B. (1993) *Spatio-Temporal Image Processing, Theory and Scientific Applications*, Lecture Notes in Computer Science 751, Springer, Berlin.

Jähne, B. (1997a) *Handbook of digital image processing for scientific applications*, CRC Press, Boca Raton, Florida.

Jähne, B. (1997b) *Digital Image Processing—Concepts, Algorithms, and Scientific Applications*, 4th completely revised edition, Springer, Berlin.

Jähne, B., Haußecker, H., Hering, F., Balschbach, G., Klinke, J., Lell, M., Schmundt, D., Schultz, M., Schurr, U., Stitt, M. and Platt, U. (1996) The role of active vision in exploring growth, transport, and exchange processes, Mertsching, B. (ed.), *Proc. Aktives Sehen in technischen und biologischen Systemen*, Workshop der GI-Fachgruppe 1.0.4. Bildverstehen Hamburg, Proc. in Artifical Intelligence 4, infix, Sankt Augustin, 194–202.

Jähne, B., Haußecker, H., Scharr, H., Spies, H., Schmundt, D. and Schurr, U. (1998) Study of dynamical processes with tensor-based spatiotemporal image processing techniques, Burkhardt, H. and Neumann, B. (eds.), *Computer Vision (ECCV'98), Proc. Vol. II*, Lecture Notes in Computer Science 1407, Springer-Verlag, Berlin, 322–335.

Karlholm, J. (1996) *Efficient Spatiotemporal Filtering and Modelling*, Linköping Studies in Science and Technology, Thesis No. 562, Linköping University, Sweden.

Kearney, J.K., Thompson, W.B. and Boley, D.L. (1987) Optical flow estimation: an error analysis of gradient-based methods with local optimization, *IEEE PAMI*, 9(2):229–244.

Lucas, B. and Kanade, T. (1981) An iterative image registration technique with an application to stereo vision, *DARPA Image Understanding Workshop*, 121–130.

Otte, M. and Nagel, H.-H. (1994) Optical flow estimation: advances and comparisons, Eklundh, J.O. (ed.), *Proc. ECCV'94, Vol. II*, Springer, Berlin, 51–60.

Scharr, H., Körkel, S. and Jähne, B. (1997) Numerische Isotropieoptimierung von FIR-Filtern mittels Querglättung, Wahl, F. and Paulus, E. (eds.), *Proc. Mustererkennung 1997*, Braunschweig, Informatik Aktuell, Springer, Berlin, 367–374.

Simoncelli, E.P. (1993) Distributed representation and analysis of visual motion, *Ph.D. dissertation*, Dept. of Electrical Engineering and Computer Science, MIT.

Simoncelli, E.P. (1999) Bayesian multi-scale differential optical flow, Jähne, B., Haußecker, H. and Geißler, P. (eds.), *Computer Vision and Applications*, Academic Press, San Diego, 2:397–422.

Singh, A. (1991) *Optic flow computation: a unified perspective*, IEEE Computer Society Press, Los Alamitos, CA.

EVALUATION OF NUMERICAL SOLUTION SCHEMES FOR DIFFERENTIAL EQUATIONS

RYSZARD KOZERA
Dept. of Computer Science
The University of Western Australia
Nedlands 6907 WA, Australia

REINHARD KLETTE
Dept. of Computer Science
The University of Auckland
Tamaki Campus, Private Bag 92019
Auckland, New Zealand

1. Introduction

Differential equations (ODEs or PDEs) appear in many computer vision fields. Shape from shading, optical flow, optics, and 3D motion are examples of such fields. Solving problems modeled by ODEs and PDEs can be accomplished by finding either an analytical solution, what is in general a difficult task, or by computing a numerical solution to the corresponding discrete scheme. Numerical solutions are usually more easily found with the aid of a computer.

In this chapter we consider the case of numerical schemes. The evaluation of numerical solution schemes may be based on

(i) theoretical criteria for the corresponding continuous problem,
(ii) theoretical criteria for the discrete numerical scheme, or
(iii) experimental measurements for the implemented numerical scheme.

Single-scheme analysis as well as a comparative analysis may be performed utilising any of these three types of criteria. *Well-posedness* questions for the corresponding continuous problems may be cited for type (i) evaluations. Upon derivation of a specific discrete numerical scheme (either sequential or parallel) *convergence and stability* issues need to be established.

R. Klette et al. (eds.), Performance Characterization in Computer Vision, 153–166.
© 2000 *Kluwer Academic Publishers.*

Most of the existing numerical schemes in computer vision (in areas such as shape from shading, optical flow, surface integration, or 3D motion) have been so-far neither supplemented by pertinent convergence and stability analysis nor compared by using an appropriate evaluation procedure.

The specification of *domains of influence* is a further example of type (ii) evaluations. Experimental analysis may be based on selected performance measures as different *error measures* within the domain of influence.

In this chapter we illustrate the study of numerical solution schemes for differential equations by discussing a special application. We report on theoretical and experimental results concerning the shape-from-shading problem in which the reflectance map is linear. The significance of this topic and the conclusions stemming out from this work is itemized in the closing section of this chapter. section 2 introduces a linear shape from shading problem being our example discourse area in this chapter. Then, section 3 provides the general model and a few related results for evaluations of numerical schemes in general. Section 4 reports about applying this general multigrid model for numerical schemes to the example of linear shape from shading. Further applications could be, eg., in optical flow calculations or 3D motion estimation.

In section 4 we discuss and compare four different two-layer finite-difference based schemes derived for the linear shape-from-shading problem specified in section 2. The schemes are based on the combination of forward- and backward- difference derivative approximations and operate over a rectangular fixed grid. The evaluation analysis is based on both theoretical (convergence, stability, domain of influence) and experimental (performance of implemented schemes) criteria.

Finally, section 5 informs about more general conclusions with respect to the model given in section 3.

2. Linear Shape from Shading

Linear shape-from-shading problems arose in the study of the maria of the moon (Horn, 1986, sections 10.9 and 11.1.2) and in a local shape-from-shading analysis (Pentland, 1990). If a small portion of an object surface, described by the graph of a function u, having reflectivity properties approximated by a linear reflectance map, is illuminated by a distant light source of unit intensity from direction $(a_1, a_2, -1)$, then the corresponding image function $\mathcal{E}(x_1, x_2)$ satisfies a *linear image irradiance equation* of the form

$$\left(a_1 \frac{\partial u}{\partial x_1}(x_1, x_2) + a_2 \frac{\partial u}{\partial x_2}(x_1, x_2) + 1 \right) (a_1^2 + a_2^2 + 1)^{-1/2} = \mathcal{E}(x_1, x_2), \quad (1)$$

over an image domain $\Omega = \{(x_1, x_2) \in \mathbf{R}^2 : \mathcal{E}(x_1, x_2) \geq 0\}$. The problem consists in reconstructing the object surface $graph(u)$ based on given irradiance values $\mathcal{E}(x_1, x_2)$ and based on given or calculated light source parameters a_1 and a_2. These parameters and the grid resolution along the x_1- and x_2- axes characterise a specific *discrete linear shape-from-shading problem*. More general shape-from-shading problems are studied in (Horn, 1986; Jähne *et al.*, 1998; Klette *et al.*, 1998; Sethian, 1996).

Letting $E(x_1, x_2) = \mathcal{E}(x_1, x_2)(a_1^2 + a_2^2 + 1)^{1/2} - 1$, one can rewrite (1) into a transformed linear image irradiance equation

$$a_1 \frac{\partial u}{\partial x_1}(x_1, x_2) + a_2 \frac{\partial u}{\partial x_2}(x_1, x_2) = E(x_1, x_2). \tag{2}$$

In this chapter we evaluate four finite-difference based schemes derived from (2). Critical to our approach is the assumption that u is given along some (not necessarily smooth) initial curve γ in the image domain Ω or at the boundary of Ω. A prior knowledge of pertinent boundary conditions is essential for other algorithms used in shape from shading and based on methods of *charactersitic strips* or *equal-height contour propagation* (Horn, 1986; Sethian, 1996). These boundary conditions can be obtained, for example if we combine a single image shape recovery with the *photometric stereo technique* (Klette *et al.*, 1998; Kozera, 1991; Kozera, 1992; Onn and Bruckstein, 1990). The latter is applicable only over the intersection of multiple images (*e.g.* over $\Omega = \Omega_1 \cap \Omega_2$) and does not require boundary conditions. As a side effect, apart from finding the function $u \in C^2(\Omega)$, missing Dirichlet boundary conditions are also recovered along the boundary $\partial\Omega$. These Dirichlet conditions constitute, in turn, a start-up curve γ for each discussed finite-difference scheme to recover the unknown shape over the remaining non-overlapping parts of images (*i.e.* over $\Omega_1 \setminus \Omega$ and $\Omega_2 \setminus \Omega$). Alternatively, in certain cases (when the object is positioned on the plane parallel to x_1x_2-plane and has the so-called occluding boundary over $\partial\Omega$), one can also assume that $u_{|\partial\Omega} \equiv const$ along $\partial\Omega$. All presented here schemes provide the numerical solution of the following Cauchy problem:

Object surfaces $u \in C(\bar{\Omega}) \cap C^2(\Omega)$ are considered over a rectangular image domain $\Omega = \{(x_1, x_2) \in \mathbf{R}^2 : -a \leq x_1 \leq a \text{ and } -b \leq x_2 \leq b\}$, with both a and b positive:

$$\begin{aligned} L(u(x_1, x_2)) &= E(x_1, x_2) \\ u(x_1, -b) &= f(x_1) \quad \text{for } -a \leq x_1 \leq a,\ sgn(a_1 a_2) \geq 0, \\ u(-a, x_2) &= g(x_2) \quad \text{for } -b \leq x_2 \leq b; \end{aligned} \tag{3}$$

where $Lu = a_1 u_{x_1} + a_2 u_{x_2}$, and the functions $f \in C([-a, a]) \cap C^2((-a, a))$ and $g \in C([-b, b]) \cap C^2((-b, b))$ satisfy $f(-a) = g(-b)$, $E \in C^2(\bar{\Omega})$, and a_1 and a_2 are light source parameters such that $(a_1, a_2) \neq (0, 0)$.

The case $sgn(a_1 a_2) \leq 0$ can be treated analogously. For details of this work, the interested reader is referred to (Kozera and Klette, 1997a; Kozera and Klette, 1997b).

3. Basic Notions and Theory for Finite-Difference Schemes

At first we recall some basic notions and results from the theory of finite-difference methods applied to PDEs (Van der Houwen, 1968, chapter 1).

Assume that an interval $I = [-T, T]$ and a domain $G = G_1 \times G_2 \times \ldots \times G_m \subset \mathbf{R}^m$ (where each G_i is a subinterval of $\mathbf{R}$) together with its boundary Γ and $\bar{G} = G \cup \Gamma$ are given and that $(E_0(\bar{G}), \| \|_{E_0})$, $(E(\bar{G}), \| \|_{\bar{G}})$, $(E(\Gamma), \| \|_{\Gamma})$, and $(E(G), \| \|_G)$ are linear normed spaces of scalar or vector-valued functions, defined respectively, on the set of points $\bar{G}$, $\bar{G} \times I$, $\Gamma \times I$, and $G \times I$. Consider now the following problem:

$$U_t(x, t) + \sum_{i=1}^{m} D_i(x, t) U_{x_i}(x, t) = H(x, t),$$
$$U(\Gamma \times I) = \Psi(\Gamma), \ U(x, -T) = U_0(x), \tag{4}$$

where $(x, t) \in G \times I$, the scalar functions $U_0 \in E_0(\bar{G})$, $\Psi \in E(\Gamma)$, and a vector function $F(x, t) = (H(x, t), D(x, t)) \in E(G)$, for $D(x, t) = (D_1(x, t), D_2(x, t), \ldots, D_n(x, t))$. A problem of finding the inverse of a given mapping $\mathcal{L} : D_{\mathcal{L}} \to \Delta_{\mathcal{L}}$ of an unknown function $U \in D_{\mathcal{L}} = (E(\bar{G}), \| \|_{\bar{G}})$ onto a known element

$$(U_0, F, \Psi) \in \Delta_{\mathcal{L}} = (E_0(\bar{G}) \times E(G) \times E(\Gamma), \| \|_\times),$$

where

$$\|(U_0, F, \Psi)\|_\times = \|U_0\|_{E_0} + \|F\|_G + \|\Psi\|_\Gamma,$$

is called *an initial boundary value problem*.

DEFINITION 13.1. *An initial boundary value problem* $\mathcal{L}U = (U_0, F, \Psi)$ *is said to be* well-posed *with respect to norms in* $E(\bar{G})$ *and in* $E_0(\bar{G}) \times E(G) \times E(\Gamma)$ *if* $\mathcal{L}$ *has a unique inverse* $\mathcal{L}^{-1}$ *which is continuous at the point* (U_0, F, Ψ).

Now we introduce *uniform grid sequences*. We replace the continuous interval $I = [-T, T]$ by a discrete set of points

$$[t_0 = -T, t_1, t_2, \ldots, t_M = T], \tag{5}$$

where $t_{k+1} - t_k = \Delta t$, for each $k \in [0, \ldots, M-1]$, and $M \Delta t = 2T$. Furthermore assume a finite set of points $\Gamma_{\Delta t} \subset \Gamma$ and of points $G_{\Delta t} \subset G$

such that the fixed distance Δx_i, for $i \in [1, \ldots, m]$, between two consecutive points in the x_i-axis direction satisfies $\Delta x_i = \mathcal{A}_i \Delta t$, where $\mathcal{A}_i$ is a scaling factor such that, for some integer N_i, we have $N_i \mathcal{A}_i \Delta t = \mu(G_i)$, where $\mu(G_i)$ denotes the measure of G_i.

These three sets $\{t_k\}_{k=0}^M$, $G_{\Delta t}$, and $\Gamma_{\Delta t}$ of points constitute *a grid* $Q_{\Delta t}$ in $\bar{G} \times I$, *i.e.* $Q_{\Delta t} = \bar{G}_{\Delta t} \times \{t_k\}_{k=0}^M$, where $\bar{G}_{\Delta t} = G_{\Delta t} \cup \Gamma_{\Delta t}$. We assume that *a sequence of grids* $Q_{\Delta t}$ is defined in such a way that $\{Q_{\Delta t}\}$ is *dense* in $\bar{G} \times I$. The last requirement is satisfied when

$$\lim_{\Delta t \to 0^+} \mathcal{N}_i \mathcal{A}_i \Delta t = 0,$$

for each $i \in [1, \ldots, m]$. Furthermore we introduce the corresponding normed grid spaces

$$(E_0(\bar{G}_{\Delta t}), \| \ \|_{E_{0\Delta t}}), \quad (E(\bar{G}_{\Delta t}), \| \ \|_{\bar{G}_{\Delta t}}),$$
$$(E(\Gamma_{\Delta t}), \| \ \|_{\Gamma_{\Delta t}}), \quad (E(G_{\Delta t}), \| \ \|_{G_{\Delta t}}) \tag{6}$$

defined on the sets $\bar{G}_{\Delta t}$, $\bar{G}_{\Delta t} \times \{t_k\}_{k=0}^M$, $\Gamma_{\Delta t} \times \{t_k\}_{k=0}^M$, and $G_{\Delta t} \times \{t_k\}_{k=0}^M$, respectively.

The elements of these spaces are called *grid functions* and are denoted by lower case letters u_0, u, ψ, and f.

A mapping $\mathcal{R}_{\Delta t}$ of an unknown grid function u of $(E(\bar{G}_{\Delta t}), \| \ \|_{\bar{G}_{\Delta t}})$ into the known element (u_0, f, ψ) of $(E_0(\bar{G}_{\Delta t}) \times E(G_{\Delta t}) \times E(\Gamma_{\Delta t}), \| \ \|_{\Delta t_x})$, where

$$\|(u_0, f, \psi)\|_{\Delta t_x} = \|u_0\|_{E_{0\Delta t}} + \|f\|_{G_{\Delta t}} + \|\psi\|_{\Gamma_{\Delta t}}$$

is defined for each grid $Q_{\Delta t}$, is called a *finite-difference scheme*.

Difference schemes can be described by the equation $\mathcal{R}_{\Delta t} u = (u_0, f, \psi)$, with the domain and range of $\mathcal{R}_{\Delta t}$ denoted by $D_{\mathcal{R}_{\Delta t}}$ (called as a *discrete domain of influence*) and $\Delta_{\mathcal{R}_{\Delta t}}$, respectively. It is assumed that both $D_{\mathcal{R}_{\Delta t}}$ and $\Delta_{\mathcal{R}_{\Delta t}}$ are linear spaces and $\mathcal{R}_{\Delta t}$ has a unique inverse $\mathcal{R}_{\Delta t}^{-1}$, which is continuous in $D_{\mathcal{R}_{\Delta t}}$ for every $\Delta t \neq 0$.

DEFINITION 13.2. *For a given initial boundary value problem, a grid sequence and an associated finite-difference scheme we define that a set* $D_I \subset \Omega$ *is called* domain of influence, *where* $D_I = cl\left(\bigcup D_{\mathcal{R}_{\Delta t}}\right)$.

Let us now introduce the *discretisation operator* $[\ ]_{d(\Delta t)}$ which transforms a function $U \in E(\bar{G})$ to its discrete analogue $[U]_{d(\Delta t)}$ defined as U reduced to the domain of the grid $Q_{\Delta t}$. In the same manner we define discretised elements $[U_0]_{d(\Delta t)} \in E_0(\bar{G}_{\Delta t})$, $[F]_{d(\Delta t)} \in E(G_{\Delta t})$, and $[\Psi]_{d(\Delta t)} \in E(\Gamma_{\Delta t})$. In this chapter we use the convention:

$$[U]_{d(\Delta t)} = u, [U_0]_{d(\Delta t)} = u_0, [F]_{d(\Delta t)} = f, \text{and} [\Psi]_{d(\Delta t)} = \psi, \tag{7}$$

where $f = (h, d)$. Moreover, it is also assumed that the norms on the grid sequence $\{Q_{\Delta t}\}$ *match* the corresponding norms from the related *continuous spaces i.e.*

$$\|u\|_{\bar{G}_{\Delta t}} \rightarrow \|U\|_{\bar{G}}, \quad \|u_0\|_{E_{0\Delta t}} \rightarrow \|U_0\|_{E_0},$$
$$\|f\|_{G_{\Delta t}} \rightarrow \|F\|_G, \quad \|\psi\|_{\Gamma_{\Delta t}} \rightarrow \|\Psi\|_\Gamma \tag{8}$$

as $\Delta t \rightarrow 0$.

Now we introduce the evaluation criteria for numerical solution schemes. Assume that $\tilde{U}$ is a solution to the initial boundary value problem $\mathcal{L}\tilde{U} = (U_0, F, \Psi)$, and that u is a solution to the corresponding discrete problem

$$\mathcal{R}_{\Delta t}u = (u_0, f, \psi). \tag{9}$$

If $\mathcal{R}_{\Delta t}$ is to be a "good approximation" of $\mathcal{L}$ we expect that the function $\tilde{u} = [\tilde{U}]_{d(\Delta t)}$, for some element $(\tilde{u}_0, \tilde{f}, \tilde{\psi})$, satisfies a finite-difference equation $\mathcal{R}_{\Delta t}\tilde{u} = (\tilde{u}_0, \tilde{f}, \tilde{\psi})$ which closely relates to (9).

DEFINITION 13.3.   *The value* $\|[\mathcal{L}\tilde{U}]_{d(\Delta t)} - \mathcal{R}_{\Delta t}\tilde{u}\|_{\Delta t_\times}$ *is called the* error of the approximation, *whereas the value* $\|u - \tilde{u}\|_{\bar{G}_{\Delta t}}$ *is, in turn, called the* discretisation error.

DEFINITION 13.4.   *We say that a difference scheme is* consistent *with an initial boundary value problem if the error of approximation converges to zero as* $\Delta t \rightarrow 0$.

DEFINITION 13.5.   *We say that a difference scheme is* convergent *to the solution u (if it exists) if the discretisation error converges to zero as* $\Delta t \rightarrow 0$.

DEFINITION 13.6.   *We say that a linear finite-difference scheme is* R-F stable *if operators* $\{\mathcal{R}_{\Delta t}^{-1}\}$ *are uniformly bounded as* $\Delta t \rightarrow 0$.

Combining the Definitions 5.3 and 6.2 with the Theorem 5.1 in (Van der Houwen, 1968, chapter 1) we have the following:

THEOREM 13.1.   *A consistent and R-F stable finite-difference scheme is convergent to the solution of* $\mathcal{L}\tilde{U} = (U_0, F, \Psi)$, *if such a solution exists.*

Of course, for a Cauchy problem (3) (with $a_2 \neq 0$), we have $m = 1$, $I = [-b, b]$, $x_2 = t$, $x_1 = x$, $G = (-a, a)$, $\Gamma = \{-a, a\}$ $U_0(x_1) = f(x_1)$, $\Psi(\Gamma \backslash \{a\}) = g(x_2)$, $H(x_1, x_2) = (1/a_2)E(x_1, x_2)$, and $D_1(x_1, x_2) = (a_1/a_2)$. If in turn, $a_2 = 0$ then the parameter t is assigned to x_1−variable and further analysis is analogous to the preceding case. The continuous and discrete normed spaces defined above, are assumed to be equipped here with standard *maximum norms* $\| \ \|_\infty$ clearly satisfying *compatibility conditions* (8) (Kozera and Klette, 1997a).

4. Evaluation of Different Finite-Difference Based Schemes

In this section we consider the problem (3) over a rectangle Ω with $a_2 \neq 0$. We assume a uniform grid $Q_{\Delta x_2}$ with $N_1 = M$, $\Delta x_2 = (2b/M)$ and $\Delta x_1 = (2a/M) = A_1\Delta x_2$, where $M \in [0,1,\ldots,\infty]$ and $A_1 = a/b$. It follows that

$$((a_1\Delta x_2)/(a_2 A_1)\Delta x_2)) = const. \tag{10}$$

In addition, we assume that a function u is a C^2 solution to (2), and lastly that problem (3) is *well-posed* (Kozera and Klette, 1997a). Note that a_1 and a_2 are the model parameters (light source parameters) of the linear problem.

4.1. FORWARD-FORWARD FINITE-DIFFERENCE SCHEME

Applying forward-difference derivative approximations together with Taylor's formula yields

$$\frac{\partial u}{\partial x_1}\bigg|_j^n = \frac{u_{j+1}^n - u_j^n}{\Delta x_1} + O(\Delta x_1) \quad \text{and} \quad \frac{\partial u}{\partial x_2}\bigg|_j^n = \frac{u_j^{n+1} - u_j^n}{\Delta x_2} + O(\Delta x_2), \tag{11}$$

for any $j,n \in \{1,\ldots,M-1\}$. Here u_j^n, $\frac{\partial u}{\partial x_1}\big|_j^n$, and $\frac{\partial u}{\partial x_2}\big|_j^n$ denote the values of u, $\frac{\partial u}{\partial x_1}$, and $\frac{\partial u}{\partial x_2}$, respectively, at the point (x_{1j}, x_{2n}) in the grid. Δx_1 and Δx_2 denote the distances between grid points in the respective directions. M denotes the grid resolution. By substituting (11) into (2) at each grid point (x_{1j}, x_{2n}), we get

$$a_1 \frac{u_{j+1}^n - u_j^n}{\Delta x_1} + a_2 \frac{u_j^{n+1} - u_j^n}{\Delta x_2} + O(\Delta x_1, \Delta x_2) = E_j^n. \tag{12}$$

Denoting by v an approximate of u, we obtain from (12) the following sequential two-level finite-difference *explicit* scheme

$$v_j^{n+1} = \left(1 + \frac{a_1\Delta x_2}{a_2\Delta x_1}\right)v_j^n - \frac{a_1\Delta x_2}{a_2\Delta x_1}v_{j+1}^n + \frac{\Delta x_2}{a_2}E_j^n, \tag{13}$$

with $j,n \in \{1,\ldots,M-1\}$. The following result holds (Kozera and Klette, 1997a):

THEOREM 13.2. *Let* $\alpha = (a_1\Delta x_2)(a_2\Delta x_1)^{-1}$ *be a fixed constant. Then, numerical scheme* (13) *is R-F stable, if and only if* $-1 \leq \alpha \leq 0$.

Consequently (by Theorem 13.1), for $-1 \leq \alpha \leq 0$, the sequence of functions $\{u_{\Delta x_2}\}$ (where each $u_{\Delta x_2}$ is a solution of (13) with Δx_2 temporarily fixed) is convergent to the solution of the Cauchy problem (3), while $\Delta x_2 \to 0$.

As mentioned before, given an initial boundary value problem (3), the scheme (13) recovers the unknown shape over a domain of influence D_I which, for $a_1 \neq 0$ and $N_1 = M$, coincides with

$$\Delta = \{(x_1, x_2) \in \mathbf{R}^2 : -a \leq x_1 \leq a, \text{ and } -b \leq x_2 \leq (-b/a)x_1\}, \quad (14)$$

and for $a_1 = 0$ with the entire $\bar{\Omega}$. The scheme (13) has been tested for $a = b = \sqrt{2}$, with grid resolution $N_1 = M = 64$, $\Delta x_1 / \Delta x_2 = 1.0$, $a_1 = -0.5$, and $a_2 = 1.0$, and therefore with $\alpha = -0.5$.

A *volcano-like surface* represented by the graph of the function $u_v(x, y) = (1/(4(1 + (1 - x^2 - y^2)^2)))$ (see Figure 1a) and a *mountain-like surface* represented by the graph of the function $u_m(x, y) = (1/(2(1 + x^2 + y^2)))$ (see Figure 1b) were taken as test surfaces.

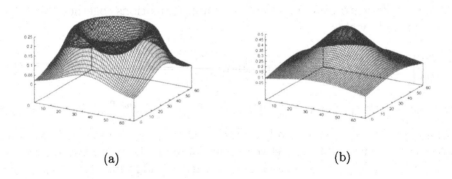

(a)   (b)

Figure 1.   (a) The graph of the function $u_v(x, y) = (1/(4(1 + (1 - x^2 - y^2)^2)))$ being a volcano-like surface. (b) The graph of the function $u_m(x, y) = (1/(2(1 + x^2 + y^2)))$ being a mountain-like surface.

The absolute errors between heights of the ideal and computed surfaces are presented in Figure 2. For $\alpha \notin [-1, 0]$ an implementation of numerical scheme (13) resulted in *instability* of (13) (Kozera and Klette, 1997a).

4.2. BACKWARD-FORWARD FINITE-DIFFERENCE SCHEME

Applying now a backward-difference derivative approximation to u_{x_1}

$$\left. \frac{\partial u}{\partial x_1} \right|_j^n = \frac{u_j^n - u_{j-1}^n}{\Delta x_1} + O(\Delta x_1),$$

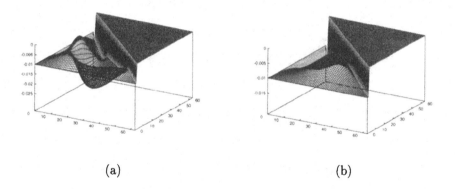

(a)   (b)

Figure 2.   (a) The absolute error between volcano-like and computed surface for the
forward-forward scheme. (b) The absolute error between mountain-like and computed
surface for the forward-forward scheme.

and a forward-difference derivative approximation to u_{x_2} leads to the corresponding two-level explicit finite-difference scheme

$$v_j^{n+1} = \left(1 - \frac{a_1 \Delta x_2}{a_2 \Delta x_1}\right) v_j^n + \frac{a_1 \Delta x_2}{a_2 \Delta x_1} v_{j-1}^n + \frac{\Delta x_2}{a_2} E_j^n, \qquad (15)$$

with $j, n \in \{1, \ldots, M - 1\}$. The following stability and convergence result
for the above finite-difference scheme holds (Kozera and Klette, 1997a):

THEOREM 13.3.   *Let* $\alpha = (a_1 \Delta x_2)(a_2 \Delta x_1)^{-1}$ *be a fixed constant. Then,*
numerical scheme (15) is R-F stable, if and only if $0 \leq \alpha \leq 1$.

Consequently (by Theorem 13.1), for $0 \leq \alpha \leq 1$, the sequence of functions
$\{u_{\Delta x_2}\}$ (where each $u_{\Delta x_2}$ is a solution of (15) with Δx_2 temporarily fixed)
is convergent to the solution of the Cauchy problem (3), while $\Delta x_2 \to 0$.
   As easily verified, the domain of influence D_I of scheme (15) coincides
with $\bar{\Omega}$, for arbitrary α. Thus, assuming the goal of global shape reconstruction, it is clear that (15) provides a better reconstruction opposed to
(13).
   The scheme (15) has been tested for the same shapes as in the previous
case. With $a = b = \sqrt{2}$, grid resolution $N_1 = M = 64$, $\Delta x_1 / \Delta x_2 = 1.0$,
$a_1 = 0.5$, $a_2 = 1.0$, and thus with $\alpha = 0.5$, the absolute errors between
heights of the ideal and computed surfaces are presented in Figure 3.

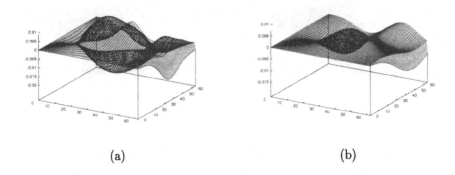

(a)   (b)

Figure 3. (a) The absolute error between volcano-like and computed surface for the backward-forward scheme. (b) The absolute error between mountain-like and computed surface for the backward-forward scheme.

4.3. FORWARD-BACKWARD FINITE-DIFFERENCE SCHEME

Applying now a forward-difference derivative approximation to u_{x_1} and a backward-difference derivative approximation to u_{x_2} leads to the following two-level explicit and *horizontal* finite-difference scheme:

$$v_{j+1}^n = \left(1 - \frac{a_2\Delta x_1}{a_1\Delta x_2}\right)v_j^n + \frac{a_2\Delta x_1}{a_1\Delta x_2}v_j^{n-1} + \frac{\Delta x_1}{a_1}E_j^n, \qquad (16)$$

(for $a_1 \neq 0$), or otherwise to the following *vertical* two-level explicit scheme:

$$v_j^n = v_j^{n-1} + \frac{\Delta x_2}{a_2}E_j^n, \qquad (17)$$

with $j, n \in \{1, \dots, M-1\}$. Observe that for the scheme (16) the role of increment step Δt is played by Δx_1, if an implicit scheme is not considered. Clearly, the shape reconstruction proceeds now sequentially along the x_1–axis direction (opposite to the previous cases). In a natural way, the boundary condition is represented by the function $f(x_1)$ and the corresponding initial condition by the function $g(x_2)$. We present now the next convergence result for the schemes (16) and (17) (Kozera and Klette, 1997a):

THEOREM 13.4. *Let $\tilde{\alpha} = (a_2\Delta x_1)(a_1\Delta x_2)^{-1}$ be a fixed constant. Then, numerical scheme (16) is R-F stable, if and only if $0 \leq \tilde{\alpha} \leq 1$. Moreover, numerical scheme (17) is unconditionally R-F stable.*

Consequently (by Theorem 13.1), for $0 \leq \tilde{\alpha} \leq 1$, the sequence of functions $\{u_{\Delta x_1}\}$, where each $u_{\Delta x_1}$ is a solution of (16) with Δx_1 temporarily fixed, is convergent to the solution of the Cauchy problem (3), while $\Delta x_1 \to 0$. Moreover, the sequence of computed solutions $\{u_{\Delta x_2}\}$ to (17) converges to the solution of the corresponding Cauchy problem (3), while $\Delta x_2 \to 0$.

For both schemes the respective domains of influence D_I coincide with $\bar{\Omega}$. We discuss here only the performance of the scheme (16). It has been tested for the same sample surfaces as in the previous cases. With $a = b = \sqrt{2}$, grid resolution $N_1 = M = 64$, $\Delta x_1/\Delta x_2 = 1.0$, $a_1 = 1.0$, $a_2 = 0.5$, and thus with $\tilde{\alpha} = 0.5$, the absolute errors between heights of the ideal and computed surfaces are presented in Figure 4.

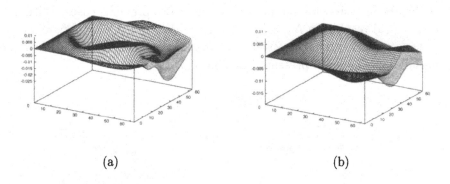

(a)   (b)

Figure 4. (a) The absolute error between volcano-like and computed surface for the forward-backward scheme. (b) The absolute error between mountain-like and computed surface for the forward-backward scheme.

4.4. BACKWARD-BACKWARD FINITE-DIFFERENCE SCHEME

Applying now backward-difference derivative approximations for both derivatives u_{x_1} and u_{x_2} we arrive at the following two-level *implicit* scheme:

$$v_j^n = \frac{1}{1+\alpha} v_j^{n-1} + \frac{\alpha}{1+\alpha} v_{j-1}^n + \frac{\Delta x_2}{a_2(1+\alpha)} E_j^n \qquad (18)$$

(for $\alpha \neq -1$), or otherwise at the following two-level *explicit* scheme:

$$v_{j-1}^n = u_j^{n-1} + \frac{\Delta x_2}{a_2} E_j^n, \qquad (19)$$

with $j, n \in \{1, \ldots, M-1\}$ and $\alpha = (a_1 \Delta x_2 / a_2 \Delta x_1)$.

It is clear that, as opposed to the last subsection, (18) cannot be reduced to the explicit iterative form by a mere change of the recovery direction. This can be achieved by using implicit approach (Kozera and Klette, 1997a, section 3.4). The following result for schemes (18) and (19) holds (Kozera and Klette, 1997a):

THEOREM 13.5. *Let* $\alpha = (a_1 \Delta x_2)(a_2 \Delta x_1)^{-1}$ *be a fixed constant. Then, numerical scheme* (18) *is R-F stable, if and only if* $\alpha \geq 0$. *Moreover, the numerical scheme* (19) *is unconditionally R-F stable.*

Consequently (by Theorem 13.1), for $\alpha \geq 0$, the sequence of functions $\{u_{\Delta x_2}\}$, where each $u_{\Delta x_2}$ is a solution of (18) with Δx_2 temporarily fixed, is convergent to the solution of the Cauchy problem (3), while $\Delta x_2 \to 0$. Moreover, the sequence of computed solutions $\{u_{\Delta x_2}\}$ to (19) converges to the solution of the corresponding Cauchy problem (3), while $\Delta x_2 \to 0$.

The corresponding domain of influence D_I for the scheme (18) covers the entire $\bar{\Omega}$, whereas for the scheme (19) coincides with (14). The scheme (18) has been tested for sample shapes as in the previous cases. With $a = b = \sqrt{2}$, grid resolution $N_1 = M = 64$, $\Delta x_1/\Delta x_2 = 1.0$, $a_1 = 0.5$, $a_2 = 1.0$, and thus with $\alpha = 0.5$, the absolute errors between heights of the ideal and computed surfaces are presented in Figure 5.

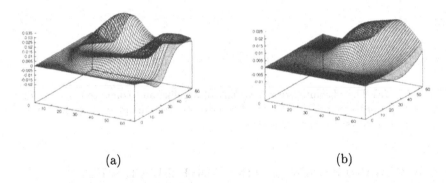

(a)   (b)

Figure 5. (a) The absolute error between volcano-like and computed surface for the backward-backward scheme. (b) The absolute error between mountain-like and computed surface for the backward-backward scheme.

5. Conclusions

Four two-layer finite-difference based schemes are discussed in this chapter and the experimental results for two sample surfaces, a volcano-like and a mountain-like surface, are presented. *Convergence, stability, domain of influence,* and *maximum relative errors* are considered here as algorithmic features used as evaluating criteria. The table below collates both theoretical and experimental results. The corresponding *relative errors* listed in the last two columns (for the volcano-like and the mountain-like surfaces) represent the maximum of the ratio of the difference of heights between computed and ideal surfaces devided by the height of the ideal surface (volcano and mountain-like, respectively), for grid points within the domain of influence.

Scheme	Stab./Conv.	Influence Domain	Error-V	Error-M
f-f	$-1 \leq \alpha \leq 0$	$D_I = \Delta$	$\leq 10\%$	$\leq 3\%$
b-f	$0 \leq \alpha \leq 1$	$D_I = \Omega$	$\leq 6\%$	$\leq 2\%$
f-b	$0 \leq \alpha^{-1} \leq 1$	$D_I = \Omega$	$\leq 8\%$	$\leq 3\%$
b-b	$0 \leq \alpha$	$D_I = \Omega$	$\leq 14\%$	$\leq 5\%$

Finally, we itemize a few aspects of the presented results:

- In choosing a proper scheme theoretical criteria such as *stability, convergence* and *domain of influence*, or experimental criteria such as *relative error* can be used as evaluation criteria. For experimental errors for optical flow calculations (another case of applying numerical schemes for solving differential equations) see also (Klette *et al.*, 1998).
- *Stability and convergence* are intrinsic properties of a given scheme.
- The *domain of influence* depends on the choice of a given scheme, the geometry of Ω and available Dirichlet boundary conditions.
- A *complete convergence and stability analysis* of all considered schemes is reported in this chapter (as opposed to approach (Horn, 1986) or flawed results (Pentland, 1990)). Stability analysis provides also means to discuss noisy camera-captured input images (Kozera and Klette, 1997a).
- *Well-posedness* of the corresponding continuous Cauchy problem (3) is also established (Kozera and Klette, 1997a).
- As opposed to the classical base characteristic strips method (John, 1971) applied in computer vision by Horn (1986), all *two-layer schemes* introduced here operate on *fixed rectangular grid. Three-layer schemes* can also be investigated in future research.
- A *linear model of reflectance maps* can be applied to the satellite image interpretation or to local shading analysis (Horn, 1986; Pentland, 1990).
- The *linear case* helps to understand *a non-linear case*. Finite-difference schemes can also be applied to the *non-linear PDEs* (Rosinger, 1982) and therefore to *non-linear reflectance maps*.
- The single image finite-difference technique can be combined with the multiple image photometric stereo technique, if Dirichlet conditions are not *a priori* available (see section 2).

A real image Ω may possess *invisible surface area i.e.* $\Omega_{black} \subset \Omega$, where $\mathcal{E} \equiv 0$. This work deals exclusively with the simulated images defined globally over Ω. In particular, negative values of image function $\mathcal{E}$ over Ω_{black}, were considered to be admissible according to the formula (1). If however, the simulated image function $\mathcal{E}$ is pre-defined as vanishing, whenever $a_1 u_{x_1} + a_2 u_{x_2} + 1 < 0$, the corresponding domain of influnece D_I is clearly diminished. It depends no longer exclusively on a given finite-difference scheme, the geometry of Ω and the corresponding Dirichlet boundary conditions, but also on the choice of the specific illumination direction as well as the surface $graph(u)$. Stability and convergence results remain unchanged.

References

Horn, B.K.P. (1986) *Robot Vision*, McGraw-Hill, New York, Cambridge, MA.

John, F. (1971) *Partial Differential Equations*, Springer-Verlag, New York.

Klette, R., Kozera, R. and Schlüns, K. (1998) Shape from shading and photometric stereo methods, *Handbook of Computer Vision and Applications*, Jähne, B., Haussecker, H. and Geissler, P. (eds.), Academic Press Inc., San Diego, California (in press).

Kozera, R. (1991) Existence and uniqueness in photometric stereo, *Applied Mathematics and Computation*, 44(1):1–104.

Kozera, R. (1992) On shape recovery from two shading patterns, *International Journal of Pattern Recognition and Artificial Intelligence*, 6(4):673–698.

Klette, R., Schlüns, K. and Koschan, A. (1998) *Computer Vision - Spatial Data from Images*, Springer, Singapore.

Kozera, R. and Klette, R. (1997a) Finite difference based algorithms for a linear shape from shading, *Machine Graphics and Vision*, 6(1/2):167–201.

Kozera, R. and Klette, R. (1997b) Evaluation of finite difference based algorithms for a linear shape-from-shading problem, *Proc. of 3rd IWVF'97*, Capri, Italy, 28-30 May, 330–339.

Onn, R. and Bruckstein, A. (1990) Integrability disambiguates surface recovery in two-image photometric stereo, *International Journal of Computer Vision*, 5(1):105–113.

Pentland, A. (1990) Linear shape from shading, *International Journal of Computer Vision*, 4(2)153–162.

Rosinger, E. (1982) *Nonlinear Equivalence, Reduction of PDEs to ODEs and Fast Convergent Numerical Methods*, Pitman Advanced Publishing Program, Boston.

Sethian, J. (1996) *Level Set Methods: Evolving Interfaces in Geometry, Fluid Mechanics and Material Science*, Cambridge University Press.

Houwen, P.J. van der (1968) *Finite Difference Methods for Solving Partial Differential Equations*, Mathematical Centre Tract, Mathematisch Centrum Amsterdam.

EXPERIMENTAL COMPARATIVE EVALUATION
OF FEATURE POINT TRACKING ALGORITHMS

JUDIT VERESTÓY and DMITRY CHETVERIKOV
Computer and Automation Research Institute
Kende u.13-17
Budapest, H-1111 Hungary

1. Introduction

We consider dynamic scenes with multiple, independently moving objects. The objects are represented by feature points whose motion is tracked in long image sequences. The feature points may temporarily disappear, enter and leave the view field. This situation is typical for surveillance, scene monitoring (Courtney, 1997) and some other applications.

Most of the existing approaches to feature point tracking (Sethi and Jain, 1987; Hwang, 1989; Salari and Sethi, 1990; Rangarajan and Shah, 1991) have limited capabilities in handling incomplete trajectories, especially when the number of points and their speeds are large, and trajectory ambiguities are frequent. Recently, we have proposed a new tracking algorithm (Chetverikov and Verestóy, 1997; Chetverikov and Verestóy, 1998), called IPAN Tracker, which efficiently resolves these ambiguities.

Let F_k, $k = 1, 2, \ldots, M$, be the kth frame of the motion sequence, where M is the total number of the frames. Assume feature points $P_{k,i}$, $i = 1, 2, \ldots, N_k$, have been detected in each F_k prior to tracking. The number of points in the kth frame, N_k, may vary from frame to frame. Denote by N the total number of distinct points that appear in the sequence. This number is equal to the total number of distinct trajectories T. (A temporarily occluded trajectory counts as one although it consists of several pieces.)

When a point enters or leaves the view field in any frame $k \neq 1, M$, the trajectory is called *partial*. A trajectory is *broken* if the point temporarily disappears within the view field, and later reappears again. In this case, we speak of *occlusion*, although feature points may, in general, become

R. Klette et al. (eds.), Performance Characterization in Computer Vision, 167–178.
© *2000 Kluwer Academic Publishers.*

undetectable for other reasons as well. If a trajectory is broken, partial, or both, it is called *incomplete*. Entries, exits and temporal occlusions are referred to as *events*.

A survey of feature point tracking approaches can be found in (Rangarajan and Shah, 1991). An up-to-date description of our algorithm is given in (Chetverikov and Verestóy, 1998). All tracking algorithms rely on the assumptions of smooth motion, limited—but, possibly, large—speeds, and short occlusions. They differ in admissible events, trajectory optimization strategies, and cost functions. A cost function evaluates the local deviation from smoothness and penalizes changes in both direction and magnitude of the velocity vector.

The tests reported in previous studies are not statistically relevant and usually consider only sparse point sets, e.g., 4–10 points per frame (Sethi and Jain, 1987; Rangarajan and Shah, 1991). We have recently initiated a systematic, comparative performance evaluation study of feature point tracking algorithms, similar to the one available for optical flow techniques (Barron *et al.*, 1994). As a part of this evaluation, experimental results are presented in this chapter for our algorithm (Chetverikov and Verestóy, 1998) and the algorithms by Sethi and Jain (1987), Hwang (1989), Salari and Sethi (1990) and Rangarajan and Shah (1991).

2. The Algorithms

In this section, we summarize the five algorithms considered. Each technique uses a smoothness based cost function defined for 3 points from 3 consecutive frames. Different linking strategies are applied to find the correspondences and optimize the trajectories. The reader is referred to the original papers (Sethi and Jain, 1987; Hwang, 1989; Salari and Sethi, 1990; Rangarajan and Shah, 1991; Chetverikov and Verestóy, 1998) for detailed, authentic presentation.

Sethi and Jain (1987) developed an iterative greedy exchange algorithm to find a suboptimal solution to the motion correspondence problem. This algorithm will be referred to as **SJ87**. The average local smoothness of the trajectory set is maximized. In each new frame the trajectories are extended by first establishing correspondences based on the nearest neighbor relationship, then exchanging those correspondence pairs which yield the largest gain in smoothness. This procedure is repeatedly applied in forward and backward directions until an equilibrium state is reached.

The computational load of SJ87 becomes very high as N grows. The iterative procedure converges slowly. As pointed out in (Rangarajan and Shah, 1991), it may occasionally not converge at all. SJ87 assumes that every trajectory extends through the whole sequence: entry and exit are not considered. Occlusion is only indicated in F_k when $N_{k-1} > N_k$. The $N_{k-1} - N_k$ occluded points of F_{k-1} are then identified, and their positions in F_k are found by extrapolation.

The assumption of no entry and exit is restrictive. Based on the idea of Sethi and Jain (1987), Salari and Sethi proposed later an improved algorithm (Salari and Sethi, 1990), denoted by **SS90**, in which partial trajectories are allowed for. SS90 uses a speed limit and a cost limit. A trajectory is split if the cost limit is exceeded. An occlusion also splits a trajectory into two partial ones: no occlusion processing is done. The iterative SS90 is again slow for large N, although it is somewhat faster than the original SJ87.

Hwang (1989) proposed a heuristic search algorithm denoted here by **HW89**. The algorithm extends the trajectory of a point by predicting its location in the new frame and examining the points lying in the vicinity of this location. A point may belong to several trajectories. For each point, the algorithm keeps track of the best few plausible trajectories. The valid trajectory is then selected based on heuristic reasoning.

HW89 uses a speed limit and indicates that a point has disappeared if a vicinity of the predicted location is empty. The vicinity is defined by the speed limit. This is sufficient but not necessary condition for occlusion, especially in dense point sets. The resulting trajectory set may contain superfluous trajectories, while some points may be assigned no trajectory at all. Exit is a non-admissible event, but entry is allowed.

The non-iterative algorithm by Rangarajan and Shah (1991) (**RS91**) uses the same assumptions as SJ87, that is, entry and exit are not admissible. In addition, the initial correspondences between F_1 and F_2 are assumed to be given, as smoothness alone is claimed to be insufficient. Given the initial links, RS91 maximizes the proximal uniformity of the trajectories, that is, prefers smooth trajectories and small displacements. Each individual correspondence is optimized for proximal uniformity while trying to keep the overall cost value close to the minimum as possible. The occlusion handling of RS91 is similar to that of SJ87.

In our experiments, the cost function of RS91 was modified to obtain better results at the relatively large displacements typical for our test sequences: the term penalizing large displacements was removed. (See (Rangarajan and Shah, 1991) for details.) The modified cost function performed consistently better even at low speeds.

Our recently proposed IPAN Tracker (Chetverikov and Verestóy, 1998), abbreviated as **IP97**, assumes that a speed limit and a cost limit are given. Occlusion, entry and exit are handled. (The maximum duration of an occlusion is two frames.) The cost function of SJ87 is used. After initialization, a non-iterative, competitive linking procedure is applied in forward direction. The procedure is based on repetitive hypothesis testing procedure which switches between three consecutive frames. The points that remain unlinked either close or open a trajectory. Then, post-processing is done which exploits the directional continuity of temporarily broken trajectories and attempts connecting these trajectories.

3. Experimental Protocol

A motion model called Point Set. Motion Generator (PSMG) is used to generate synthetic motion sequences for testing the tracking algorithms. Let us briefly overview and justify the PSMG whose more detailed description is given in (Chetverikov and Verestóy, 1997).

The randomly generated points move independently. The advantage of this solution is that different types of events and trajectory ambiguities appear with statistically controllable frequencies. In fact, the PSMG is a generator of these events and ambiguities as *disturbances* which efficiently 'test' the algorithms.

Later, simulations of assorted coherent motions will be added to test the capability to cope with correlated trajectories. Real motion sequences and detected feature points will also be considered. We believe that the disturbances that make the algorithms err will essentially remain the same. However, we understand that the occurrence probabilities of various disturbances depend on the test data. Since the algorithms may be sensitive to different disturbances in different ways, one should be cautious when interpreting the error rates presented in alternative experimental studies, including ours. Keeping this in mind, we still believe it is possible to assess the performances of the tracking techniques using the PSMG.

Each test sequence has $M = 20$ frames. The size of a frame is 200×200. In F_1, initial points are located randomly; random initial motion directions and Gaussian-distributed speeds with the mean v are assigned to them. In the subsequent frames, a limited Gaussian perturbation of the velocity vectors is introduced. The speeds are limited by $v_{max} = 2v$. The probability and the maximum duration of occlusions are specified. (The results shown below were obtained for single-frame occlusions.) Motion across the image borders is generated by applying the PSMG to a large area enclosing the view field.

The performance of the algorithms is evaluated by repeatedly generating trajectories with PSMG and comparing the tracking results to the ground truth. The varying parameters are the total number of trajectories T and the mean speed v. (Recall that $T = N$.) The generation of a trial data set is repeated until the desired T is obtained. For each setting of the varying parameters, 100 trials are done with independently generated data.

Three *merits of tracking performance* are calculated. The strict trajectory-based merit only accepts perfect trajectories: $M_{traj} = T_{corr}/T_{total}$, where T_{corr} is the number of the perfectly tracked trajectories. The relaxed trajectory-based criterion allows for local deviations from the ideal trajectory if the last point is connected to the correct initial point. Finally, the link-based criterion accounts for the partially tracked trajectories: $M_{link} = L_{corr}/L_{total}$, where L_{corr} is the number of the correct links, L_{total} the total links. (A correct link is a vector that connects the same two points of the two consecutive frames as the ideal trajectory.) The error plots given in this chapter show the error rates defined as $E_{traj} = 1 - M_{traj}$, etc.

Only IP97 can handle all events: occlusions, entries and exits. The other four algorithms have different sets of admissible events. The intersection of these sets is empty. (See section 2.) In our tests, each algorithm is compared, under its own conditions, to IP97.

4. Experimental Results

Two essentially different data sets are used in the evaluation. The sequences synthesized for SJ87 and RS91 contain no motion across image border, while the sequences generated for HW89, SS90 and IP97 contain border crossings. (For HW89, entry is only allowed.) It is important to emphasize that the *results for these two data sets should not be compared directly*. The reason is that the same number of trajectories in the two data sets does not mean the same average point density: when the points are allowed to exit and enter, many trajectories are short. When no motion across border is allowed, a generated trajectory is only accepted if it extends through the whole sequence, with a few possible occlusions. This higher average point density leads to more frequent groupings and ambiguities. The difference in density for the same T grows with the mean speed.

4.1. IP97 VERSUS RS91

Figure 1 shows the plots of E_{traj} and E_{link} against N (T) for low speeds $v = 3$ pixels. The plots compare RS91 to IP97. In this case, no entry/exit was allowed. The original cost function (Rangarajan and Shah, 1991) of RS91 was modified as discussed in section 2. Note that the algorithm RS91 needs the initial correspondences to be given, while IP97 is self-initializing. At low speeds, the performance of RS91 is better.

For high speeds $v = 12$ pixels (Figure 2), IP97 performs better, with the difference growing with N. At high densities $N > 40$, the performance of RS91 deteriorates fast. The difference between the strict and the relaxed criterion-based E_{traj} plots characterizes the self-correction capability of an

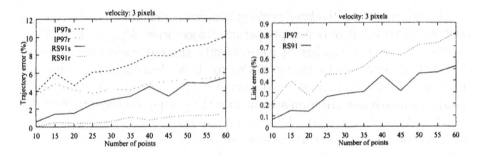

Figure 1.   IP97 versus RS91 for low speeds. Plots of trajectory error (left) and link error (right). 's' is the strict, 'r' the relaxed criterion.

algorithm. The self-correction capabilities of RS91 and IP97 are similar. A moderate improvement in the tracking performance is achieved when the initial correspondences are given to IP97 as well.

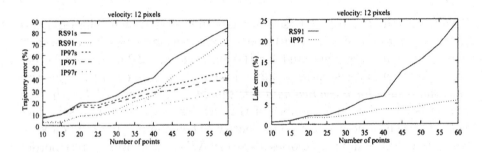

Figure 2.   IP97 versus RS91 for high speeds. 'i' is the strict criterion with the initial correspondences given.

4.2. IP97 VERSUS SJ87

No entry/exit was allowed. Here, we could only obtain tracking results for $N \le 45$, since for $N > 45$ the computational cost of the iterative SJ87 becomes prohibitive. At low speeds (Figure 3), the trajectory performance of SJ87 is better, while the link performances are very similar.

At high speeds (Figure 4), one observes an unusual behavior of the plots: the trajectory performance of SJ87 is still better, while the link performance is worse. In all other cases, the link error is consistent with the trajectory error. Analysis of SJ87 shows that, occasionally, the algorithm yields a few completely wrong trajectories with many invalid links, while the other trajectories are tracked properly.

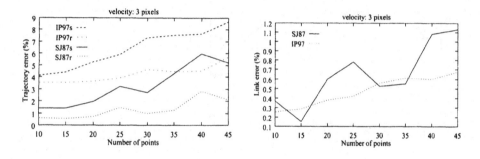

Figure 3.   IP97 versus SJ87 for low speeds.

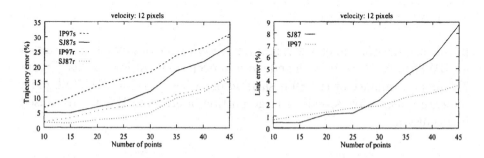

Figure 4.   IP97 versus SJ87 for high speeds.

4.3. IP97 VERSUS SS90

In this case, no occlusion was generated. The tracking performances of SS90 and IP97 for low speeds (Figure 5) are close. For high speeds (Figure 6), IP97 performs consistently better, especially at high point densities.

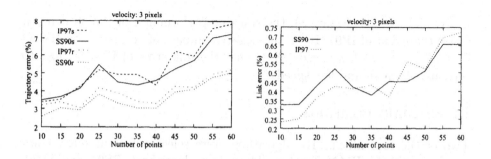

Figure 5.   IP97 versus SS90 for low speeds.

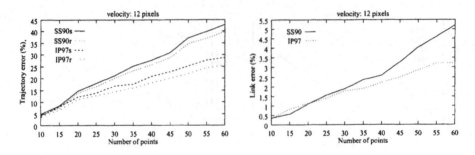

Figure 6.   IP97 versus SS90 for high speeds.

4.4. IP97 VERSUS HW89

In this comparison, no exit was allowed. Two link error plots were obtained for HW89 at each speed: with and without occlusions. At low speeds (Figure 7), the performance of HW89 is satisfactory when N is low. The link plots indicate that, at low speeds, a large portion of errors in HW89 are caused by occlusions.

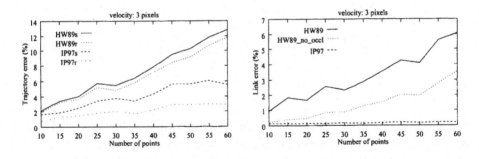

Figure 7.   IP97 versus HW89 for low speeds.

At high speeds (Figure 8), the tracking performance of HW89 is much worse than that of IP97. Here, the negative impact of occlusions on HW89 is smaller than at low speeds. Note that the link error of IP97 is close to zero at both high and low speeds.

4.5. SUMMARY COMPARISON

Two of the four alternative algorithms were selected for summary comparison with the IPAN Tracker. These two algorithms, RS91 and SS90, were judged to be both efficient and typical. Tables I and II summarize the tracking results obtained by IP97, RS91 and SS90 for the strict trajectory-based merit M_{traj}, in percents, defined in section 3. Each row shows M_{traj}

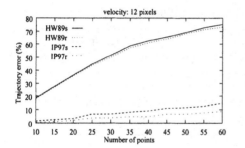 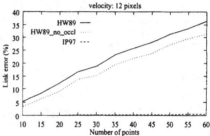

Figure 8.   IP97 versus HW89 for high speeds.

TABLE I.   Summary comparison of IP97 and RS91.

Alg.	Self-init.	Occl.	Low speed			High speed		
			$T = 20$	$T = 40$	$T = 60$	$T = 20$	$T = 40$	$T = 60$
IP97	+	+	95.35	92.07	89.98	82.70	67.55	54.56
IP97	+	−	95.60	92.92	91.20	85.70	74.02	62.45
IP97	−	+	97.50	94.10	92.28	83.95	72.05	61.26
RS91	−	+	98.50	95.52	94.58	81.15	59.47	16.61

for varying total number of trajectories and two different mean speeds, low and high, which are 3 and 12 pixels per frame, respectively.

The first three columns of the tables specify the algorithm and the conditions of the evaluation. In particular, '−' in the 'Self.-init.' column means that no self-initialization was done, that is, the initial correspondences were given. Two different data sets were used, as discussed earlier in this section. The sequences used to obtain Table I contain no entry and exit, while the sequences generated for Table II contain both.

The first two rows of Table I refer to IP97 in its standard self-initializing mode. One can see that the negative impact of occlusion on the tracking performance grows with v and T. In the third row, the proposed algorithm is given the initial correspondences. Apparently, the initialization can compensate for the negative effect of occlusion, since the corresponding values in the second and the third rows are quite close. Note that the differences between the first and the third rows only become significant for high speeds and many trajectories. Otherwise, self-initialization is possible and sufficient.

TABLE II.   Summary comparison of IP97 and SS90.

Alg.	Self-init.	Occl.	Low speed			High speed		
			$T = 20$	$T = 40$	$T = 60$	$T = 20$	$T = 40$	$T = 60$
IP97	+	+	95.02	94.18	90.51	79.45	68.78	58.82
IP97	+	−	95.77	95.64	92.16	87.92	79.06	71.17
SS90	+	−	95.87	95.39	92.75	85.35	72.33	57.20

The third and fourth rows show that the performance of RS91 is close to, or even slightly better than, that of IP97 for low speeds and/or sparse point sets. However, RS91 performs poorly at large speeds and medium-to-high densities.

Table II demonstrates that the proposed algorithm performs reasonably well in presence of all the events considered. Occlusion has the same impact here as in the previous case. Again, the alternative technique (SS90) can only compete with the IPAN Tracker until the motion conditions become severe.

4.6. PROCESSING TIMES

Table III shows typical average CPU times per sequence, in seconds, used by the algorithms for different numbers of points. The tests were run on an HP Visualize B132L workstation. Clearly, the execution times depend on implementation. Also, the average values do not reflect the large variations in the times used by the iterative algorithms SJ87 and SS90. Some general conclusions can be drawn anyway.

TABLE III.   Typical processing times.

Algorihm	10 points	30 points	45 points
SJ87	0.75	54.78	659.25
SS90	0.58	18.85	81.74
HW89	0.09	0.35	0.66
RS91	0.03	0.21	0.58
IP97	0.10	0.30	0.56

The iterative algorithms SJ87 and SS90 are much slower than the non-iterative HW89, RS91 and IP97. The difference in the worst case running times is even more striking as the iterative algorithms, especially SJ87, occasionally converge very slowly. As the number of points N grows, the running times of SJ87 and SS90 increase dramatically. A critical value of N is around 40, when SJ87 becomes practically impossible to systematically test.

5. Summary and Conclusion

We have presented current results of an ongoing systematic performance evaluation study of feature point tracking algorithms. Our experience can be summarized as follows.

- The admissible events of the algorithms are different. Currently, only IP97 can handle all events. The occlusion handling procedure of IP97 can be used in SS90, extending to all events the scope of SS90 as well. The other three algorithms have intrinsic limitations.
- N is a key parameter, with 40 trajectories per 200×200 size image being a critical value.
- For $N < 40$, SJ87 offers good trajectory performance at the expense of link performance and computational feasibility.
- HW89 may loose trajectories and gives multiple choices. The algorithm is better suited for slow motion and low densities. Otherwise, its performance is surprisingly poor.
- SS90 is less efficient at high speeds and densities. At less severe conditions, the performances of SS90 and IP97 are similar.
- RS91 performs reasonably well at low-to-moderate speeds. At high speeds and densities, its performance deteriorates fast.
- RS91 needs the initial correspondences which limits its application area. Rangarajan and Shah (1991) argue that prior knowledge of the initial correspondences is required for reliable tracking. We experienced that this might only be true when both speeds and densities are high. Otherwise, self-initialization is possible.
- IP97 is the most robust to high speeds and point densities.
- The non-iterative HW89, RS91 and IP97 are much faster than the iterative SJ87 and SS90.

Our performance evaluation study will proceed by considering more algorithms; analyzing trajectory ambiguities and estimating irreducible error rates; testing with coherent motion, natural image sequences and detected feature points. Finally, we intend to apply the IPAN Tracker to real problems, including digital particle image velocimetry, surveillance, scene monitoring, and detection of events and activities.

The tracking algorithms studied in this chapter are available for online testing over the Internet at the following URL:

http://visual.ipan.sztaki.hu/psmweb/psmweb.html.

Acknowledgments

This work is supported in part by grants OTKA T026592 and INCO-COPERNICUS CT96-0742. The authors are grateful to Gábor Pécsy, László Szűcs, Attila Rácz, Krisztina Viktor, András Erdei and Márton Fülöp for implementing the alternative tracking algorithms.

References

Barron, J., Fleet, D. and Beauchemin, S. (1994) Performance of optical flow techniques, *International Journal of Computer Vision*, 12(1):43–77.

Chetverikov, D. and Verestóy, J. (1997) Motion tracking of dense feature point sets, In *Proc. 21st Workshop of the Austrian Pattern Recognition Group*, Oldenbourg Verlag, 233–242.

Chetverikov, D. and Verestóy, J. (1998) Tracking feature points: A new algorithm, In *Proc. International Conf. on Pattern Recognition*, 1436–1438.

Courtney, J.D. (1997) Automatic video indexing via object motion analysis, *Pattern Recognition*, 30:607–625.

Hwang, V. (1989) Tracking feature points in time-varying images using an opportunistic selection approach, *Pattern Recognition*, 22:247–256.

Rangarajan, K. and Shah, M. (1991) Establishing motion correspondence, *CVGIP: Image Understanding*, 54:56–73.

Salari, V. and Sethi, I.K. (1990) Feature point correspondence in the presence of occlusion, *IEEE Trans. PAMI*, 12:87–91.

Sethi, I.K. and Jain, R. (1987) Finding trajectories of feature points in a monocular image sequence, *IEEE Trans. PAMI*, 9:56–73.

Part V

Selected Methods and Algorithms

EVALUATION OF AN OPTICAL FLOW METHOD FOR MEASURING 2D AND 3D CORN SEEDLING GROWTH

JOHN L. BARRON
The University of Western Ontario
Dept. of Computer Science
London, Ontario, Canada, N6A 5B7

ALBERT LIPTAY
Agriculture and Agri-Food Canada
Greenhouse and Processing Crops Centre
Harrow, Ontario, Canada, N0R 1G0

1. Introduction

We propose the use of optical flow as a means of accurately measuring 2D and 3D growth of young corn seedlings. Our method is ultra-sensitive and operates in a non-intrusive, non-contact manner and can measure motions whose magnitude is as minuscule as 5 microns/second. Our 2D analysis, started in 1994 (Barron and Liptay, 1994), uses a least squares integration method to locally integrate spatio-temporal image derivatives into an optical flow field (Lucas and Kanade, 1981). Thus the work described here is an evaluation and verification of just one optical flow method for the use in (accurately) measuring young corn seedling growth. The 2D plant motion is displayed as a vector field of nearly uniform 2D velocities. A key assumption of the 2D growth analysis is that growth motion occurs locally in a 3D plane and its accuracy depends on this assumption being satisfied. We observed that the plant sways in 3D space as it grows, so this assumption does not hold over long time intervals. To capture this swaying over longer time intervals we extended our optical flow approach to 3D (Barron and Liptay, 1997). We use a single least squares calculation to integrate all spatio-temporal image derivatives into a single 3D velocity. Each image in the sequence consists of two views of the same seedling; one view of the

181

R. Klette et al. (eds.), Performance Characterization in Computer Vision, 181–194.
© 2000 *Kluwer Academic Publishers.*

corn seedling is front-on while the second view is an orthogonal view (at 90 degrees) of the seedling made by projecting the plant's orthogonal image onto a mirror oriented at 45° with respect to the camera. We compute 3D optical flow at the corn seedling's tip by using a simple extension of the 2D motion constraint equation. Both the 2D and 3D methods assume orthographic projection, which holds locally in the image plane. This allowed motions in pixels/frame to be directly scaled to meters/second. We conclude this chapter by showing the accuracy of optical flow as a means of measuring 2D and 3D corn seedling growth.

2. Literature Survey

Measurement of minute increments in plant growth, using displacement transducers, has been used for a number of years (Lang, 1990; Luthen et al., 1990; Pasumarty et al., 1991). Using transducers, resolution of measurement of growth can be as sensitive as 10^{-6} meters. However, the transducer technique for growth measurement requires mechanical coupling of the transducer to the plant and the effect of this mechanical engagement has not been documented. A non-contact optical technique of growth measurement had also been demonstrated using interferometry (Fox and Puffer, 1976; Jiang and Staude, 1989). However, this method of measuring plant growth requires an elaborate setup with mirrors, lasers and other instruments. The use of optical flow, as advocated here, avoids these problems and required a simple setup with just a black and white camera, a frame grabber, at most one mirror (for 3D growth measurements) and a PC computer.

3. 2D Experimental Technique

We used an optical method we attribute to Lucas and Kanade (Lucas and Kanade, 1981; Barron et al., 1994) to approximate the local 2D image motion in a sequence of image of a growing corn seedling. Our choice of Lucas and Kanade's method was motivated by its ease of implementation, computational speed and good accuracy (Barron et al., 1994). As such, the work described here is a very careful experimental study of one optical flow method, rather than a comparative evaluation of many optical flow methods for our growth measurement task; see (Barron et al., 1994) for a comparative analysis of 9 optical flow methods.

The local motion measured via an optical flow computation corresponds directly with the 2D plant growth in the image. The instrumentation necessary for this technique is comprised of a black and white camera, frame grabber and computer with appropriate software. In our particular setup, a colour camera (a Sony 3 CCD camera, model DXC-327 with a zoom lens, model VCL-712BX, having a focal length range of 7.5-90 mm) was used and the 480×512 pixel colour images were converted to 150×150 grayvalue images by using a YIQ colour to grayvalue transformation and by partitioning out the same subareas of each of the images that contained the corn seedling before optical flow analysis. The Sony camera used in our experimentation has non-square pixels with a height of 9.8×10^{-6} meters and a width of 8.4×10^{-6} meters. To take this into account we scaled all the computed horizontal components of full velocity by $\frac{8.4}{9.8}$. This scaling has only a minor effect on the final computed full velocities as most unscaled full velocities were almost vertical. Corn seeds were sown singly in modified peat moss growing medium in black polyethylene tubes 10 cm long and of 1 cm inner diameter. A tube with a corn seedling at the primary leaf stage was inserted into a glass bottle containing water and coils from water baths set at various temperatures. In a first 2D experiment (Barron and Liptay, 1994), the seedling shoot was exposed to the ambient room air temperature of 24°C while the roots in the tube were exposed to the water bath temperature. The seedlings were grown initially at a temperature of 24°C for about 1 hour. Following this period the water temperature was reduced to 12°C, held at that temperature for a period and then raised back to room temperature. In a second 2D experiment (Liptay *et al.*, 1995), we use constant root temperature and measured corn seedling growth in long image sequence (over 3 days), where the motion of a leaf emerging from the coleoptile at the end of the second day was measured separately. Constant scene illumination was maintained during both growth sequences. The windows in the experimental room were also blocked so that the room was devoid of natural light. This setup results in the scene being illuminated by ambient light, thus ensuring constant spatio-temporal illumination for all visible parts of the scene. Surface reflectivity was minimized by using a deep nap black rayon velvet cloth behind the seedling as the image background and placing the camera with a macro lens in close proximity to the front of the seedling. An image was acquired every 2 minutes during this activity. This sampling rate was determined from trial and error.

3.1. 2D OPTICAL FLOW

We computed optical flow from spatiotemporal derivatives of filtered versions of the images in a sequence taken of a growing seedling. Such differential techniques are based on the *motion constraint equation*:

$$\nabla I(\mathbf{x}, t) \cdot \mathbf{v} + I_t(\mathbf{x}, t) = 0 , \qquad (1)$$

where $I_t(\mathbf{x}, t)$ denotes the partial time derivative of $I(\mathbf{x}, t)$, $\nabla I(\mathbf{x}, t) = (I_x(\mathbf{x}, t), I_y(\mathbf{x}, t))^T$ is the spatial intensity gradient and $\nabla I \cdot \mathbf{v}$ denotes

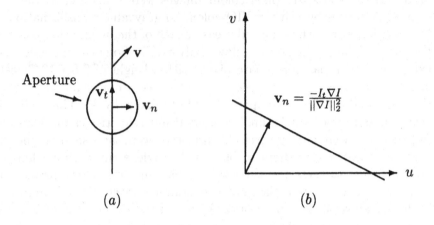

(a)　　　　　　　　　　(b)

Figure 1. **(a)** The aperture problem: only the component of velocity normal to the
line's orientation, v_n, can be recovered, the tangential component of velocity, v_t, cannot
be recovered; **(b)** The Motion Constraint Equation (1) yields a line in $\mathbf{v} = (u, v)$ space,
the velocity with the smallest magnitude on that line is $\mathbf{v}_n$. Another velocity on the line
is the correct full velocity $\mathbf{v}$.

the usual dot product. From this equation, we can see that constant scene
illumination is necessary, otherwise non-zero intensity derivatives due to
illumination changes may lead to the detection of "false" image motion
where none exists. Equation (1) yields the normal component of image
velocity relative to spatial contours of constant intensity. There are two
unknown components of full velocity $\mathbf{v}$ in (1), constrained by only one
linear equation. This is a consequence of the *aperture problem* (see Figure
1). The equation describes a line in velocity space. Any velocity on this
line satisfies (1). The velocity on the line with the smallest magnitude is
the normal velocity, which can be written as $\mathbf{v}_n = -\frac{I_t \nabla I(\mathbf{x},t)}{||\nabla I(\mathbf{x},t)||_2^2}$. Another
velocity on the line (at unknown location) is the correct full velocity $\mathbf{v}$.
Hence, further constraints in addition to (1) are necessary to solve for both
components of $\mathbf{v}$. One way to compute $\mathbf{v}$ is to use a local *constant velocity*
model (all velocities in a local neighbourhood are the same) in a frame-
work suggested by Lucas and Kanade (1981). We use their method with
thresholding modifications proposed by Simoncelli *et al.* (1991). A study
of various performance issues of this and other techniques is presented in
(Barron *et al.*, 1994) and those results led us to believe that optical flow
would be suitable for measuring plant growth. We implemented a weighted
least-squares fit of local first-order constraints (1) to a constant model for

$\mathbf{v}$ in each small spatial neighbourhood Ω by minimizing

$$\sum_{\mathbf{x}\in\Omega} W^2(\mathbf{x}) \left[\nabla I(\mathbf{x}, t) \cdot \mathbf{v} + I_t(\mathbf{x}, t)\right]^2 , \qquad (2)$$

where $W(\mathbf{x})$ denotes a window function that gives more influence to constraints at the centre of the neighbourhood than those at the periphery. Equation (2) can be minimized by solving

$$\mathbf{v} = [A^T W^2 A]^{-1} A^T W^2 \mathbf{b} \qquad (3)$$

where, for n points $\mathbf{x}_i \in \Omega$ at a single time t,

$$
\begin{aligned}
A &= [\nabla I(\mathbf{x}_1), ..., \nabla I(\mathbf{x}_n)]^T , \\
W &= \mathrm{diag}[W(\mathbf{x}_1), ..., W(\mathbf{x}_n)] , \\
\mathbf{b} &= -(I_t(\mathbf{x}_1), ..., I_t(\mathbf{x}_n))^T .
\end{aligned}
$$

Spatial neighbourhoods Ω are 5×5 pixels, and the window function $W^2(\mathbf{x})$ was separable and isotropic; its effective 1-d weights are $(0.0625, 0.25, 0.375, 0.25, 0.0625)$ as in (Simoncelli *et al.*, 1991). The solution to this system of equations is a least squares fit of a single full velocity to a local 5×5 neighbourhood of normal velocity measurements,

3.2. IMAGE PREFILTERING AND DIFFERENTIATION

Our implementation first smoothed each image in the sequence. This filtering helped to attenuate temporal aliasing and quantization effects in the input. We used **balanced** smoothing which involves using a 3D separable Gaussian filter with a standard deviation (σ) of 1.5 pixels-frame. Good digital approximations to Gaussians can be found using n coefficients, where n is the smallest odd integer greater than or equal to $6\sigma + 1$. For $\sigma = 1.5$, to produce one smoothed image at frame i we used images $i - 5$ to $i + 5$.

For balanced smoothed images, we computed I_x, I_y and I_t using 4-point central differences with mask coefficients of $\frac{1}{12}(-1, 8, 0, -8, 1)$. Hence the temporal support for a single flow computation was 15 frames (we used 5 smoothed adjacent images for differentiation and 11 images to produce one smoothed image), i.e. we used frames $i - 7$ to $i + 7$ to compute the flow for frame i.

3.3. FLOW THRESHOLDING

Following Simoncelli *et al.* (1991), unreliable velocity estimates were identified using the eigenvalues of $A^T W^2 A$, $\lambda_1 \geq \lambda_2$, which depended on the range of magnitudes and orientations of spatial gradients in local image neighbourhoods. The greater the range of magnitudes and orientation the larger λ_2 is and the more confident we can be in the computed velocity. If λ_2 is zero the matrix is singular and no velocity can be recovered. In the instance where there is little variation in the local normal velocities, λ_2 will be quite small, meaning full velocity cannot be reliably recovered. We used the value of λ_2 to ascertain the reliability of computed full velocities. In our implementation, if λ_2 (and hence λ_1) was greater than a threshold τ, then **v** was computed from (3), otherwise no full velocity was recoverable at that location. We have found in previous work (Barron *et al.*, 1994) that τ is a good threshold; large τ values produce accurate but sparse flow fields while small τ values produce inaccurate but dense flow fields. For the results in this chapter we used $\tau = 1.0$. This number is based on empirical observations (Barron *et al.*, 1994) made on a large number of synthetic and real image sequences, including the image data analyzed for this chapter.

Further thresholding of the computed flows was necessary to remove surviving outliers. We first remove all velocities with a negative vertical component (there were only a few of these). Second, we impose a similar velocity constraint on the computed flow on the basis that all velocities computed should be the same if the plant is growing uniformly for some short time interval. We do this using a number of thresholds. Viewing a velocity $\mathbf{v} = (u, v)^T$ as a 3 component vector, $\mathbf{v}_3 \equiv \frac{1}{\sqrt{u^2+v^2+1}}(u, v, 1)^T$ we can measure the angle between any two velocities, $\mathbf{v}_{31}$ and $\mathbf{v}_{32}$, as

$$\psi = \arccos(\mathbf{v}_{31} \cdot \mathbf{v}_{32}) . \tag{4}$$

This metric was used as an error measure in (Barron *et al.*, 1994). For the 2D results in this chapter, all velocities not within 3.5° of the average velocity in local 11×11 neighbourhoods (using (4) to measure the angles) were thresholded. Finally, we computed the average magnitude and angle plus standard deviations of the remaining velocities and removed all those velocities not within 1.0 standard deviation of these averages. The final result of all this thresholding was a flow field with nearly uniform velocities.

4. 2D Experimental Results

Our program computed the rate of growth in pixels per frame. We converted this to 10^{-4} meters per frame by imaging a metric ruler in the same 3D plane as the plant was in and computing the number of pixels per centimeter, we found that vertically 1 pixel corresponds to 7.853×10^{-5} meters. Since the images were acquired at 2 minute intervals, 1 pixel/frame is 6.544×10^{-7} meters per second. Figure 2a shows an image of the corn seedling, Figure 2b its normal flow field and Figure 2c the full flow field computed from the normal flow field after thresholding as described above.

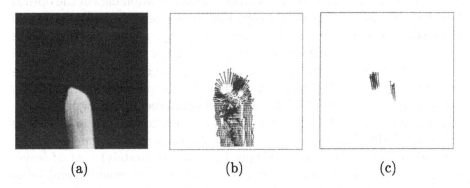

(a)   (b)   (c)

Figure 2. **(a)** An image of the corn seedling sequence; **(b)** Normal optical flow field; **(c)** Full optical flow field. The corn seedling's root temperature was 24°C, the normal and full flow fields were sampled by 2 and scaled by 50.0. The flows were computed using balanced smoothing and differentiation. The full flow (c) was computed from neighbourhoods of local normal flow (b) and then thresholded as described in the text.

The average rate of growth for this image (the average full velocity magnitude) was $1.982 \times 10^{-7} \pm 8.393 \times 10^{-9}$ meters/second with a density of 93 velocities. Note that full velocities can only be computed where there is sufficient variation in the normal velocities (as indicated by the magnitude of λ_2), i.e. at the tip of the seedling in this case as shown in Figure 2b. Figure

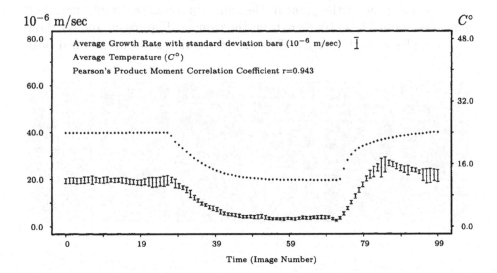

Figure 3. The growth rate plus standard deviation versus time (the solid disks) and the temperature versus the time for the corn seedling image sequence (the open circles). Flow was computed using Gaussian smoothing ($\sigma = 1.5$) and 4-point central differentiation.

3 shows the average magnitudes with standard deviation bars of the optical flow for each time (image) in the corn seedling sequence (as solid disks) and the seedling's root temperature versus time (as open circles) for a sequence of 100 images. Note that the growth rate and the temperature were well correlated (Pearson's product moment correlation coefficient, $r = 0.943$) as expected. These results show that optical flow is quite suitable under the circumstances described here for measuring corn seedling growth.

In further work (Liptay *et al.*, 1995), much longer image sequences (more than 2000 images) could be analyzed by optical flow and the growth not only of an original corn seedling but also (separately) that of leaves emerging from the coleoptile could be measured. The experimental setup and the optical method were the same as before.

One observation from these experiments is that a corn seedling only grew locally in a 3D plane (thus satisfying the assumptions made in using the motion constraint equation) but that over time the plant appeared to have significant 3D motion. This indicated the need to directly measure 3D growth.

5. 3D Experimental Technique

The experimental setup varies from the 2D growth study in one significant way: in order to obtain front and side views simultaneously we used a mirror situated about 10 centimeters from the plant and oriented at 45° to obtain a side view of the plant in the same image as the front view. The plant was about 15 centimeters from the camera. Figures 4a and 4d show two examples of such images. The corn seeds were sown in modified peat

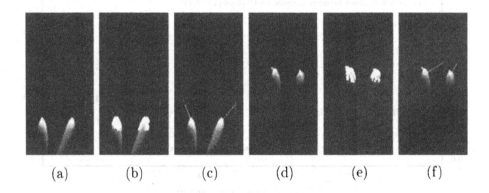

(a)	(b)	(c)	(d)	(e)	(f)

Figure 4. (a) and (d) Original images 10 and 400; (b) and (e) The highlighted image points contributing equations to the 3D velocity calculation for the images in (a) and (d); (c) and (f) The (u, v) and (v, w) velocity vectors superimposed at the corn seedling's tip for the front and side views of the corn seedling in the two images.

moss in black polyethylene tubes and exposed to a room temperature of about 20° celsius. The camera, plant/tube and mirror were contained in a wooden box, the inside of which was covered by a black velvet cloth to minimize illumination changes and specularities, to eliminate any room air currents and to keep the scene temperature constant (the box was illuminated internally by fiber optics).

6. 3D Optical Flow

In the computer vision literature the constant velocity model used in the 2D case to integrate normal velocities is known as an 0th order parametric model for image velocity (Bergen *et al.*, 1992). Other parametric models assume a more complex local distribution of image velocities (i.e. non-zero velocity derivatives) and are not considered here as the local constant velocity assumption is satisfied for our data. Using higher order parametric models in the computation of 3D optical flow would also require us to solve the correspondence problem, that is to find the same image points in the two plant views corresponding to the same 3D point, a difficult problem.

We replaced/modified the 3 steps we used in the computation of 2D optical flow to increase computational efficiency and accuracy. We use the balanced/matched filters for prefiltering and differentiation proposed by Simoncelli (1994). A simple averaging filter $[\frac{1}{4}, \frac{1}{2}, \frac{1}{4}]$ was used to slightly blur the images before prefiltering/differentiation. The prefiltering kernel's coefficients were (0.0356976, 0.2488746, 0.4308557, 0.2488746 and 0.0356976) while the differential kernel's coefficients were (−0.107663, −0.282671, 0.0, 0.282671 and 0.107663). For example, to compute I_x, we first convolve the prefiltering kernel in the t dimension, that convolve the prefiltering kernel on that result in the y dimension and finally convolve the differentiation kernel in the x dimension on that result.

It has been shown that derivative results (and hence, velocity calculations) obtained using his filters have about the same accuracy and are more dense but only use half as much image data as Gaussian smoothing and 4-point central differences (Simoncelli, 1994; Barron and Khurana, 1997). We performed the integration step in a single computation using all the normal velocities of the front and side views of the corn seedling to compute 3D velocity, (u, w, v), rather than computing (u, v) and (v, w) separately from local 5×5 neighbourhoods in the front and side images because, based on 2D results, neighbourhooding velocities are nearly always identical. This yields both computational efficiency and increased accuracy (as more data is being used). For normal velocities from the front view we used the given motion constraint equation for (u, v) in equation (1) while we use a slightly different form of equation (1) for the side image, $-I_x w + I_y v = -I_t$, to compute (v, w). Note that the minus sign in front of I_x is necessary as a negative x velocity in the front image is a positive z velocity in the side image. These two equations yield 2 equations in 3 unknowns (u, v, w). We measure I_x, I_y and I_t for the two views and use one of two forms of equation (1) to set up a linear system of equations which we can solve for in the least squares sense (we must have at least one derivative set from each of the views or a (u, v, w) calculation is not possible). Note here that because we are using a constant velocity model (all normal velocities emulate from the same 3D velocity) no correspondence between left and side views is needed; if the image of some 3D plant point contributes an equation for the front view it does not have to contribute an equation for the side view as well and vice versa. Also note that because the front and side views of the corn seedling are made under perspective projection, they have sightly different sizes because their effective distances from the camera are 15cm and 25cm respectively (in image 400 [Figure 4d] the front (left) view is about 4 pixels higher than the side (right) view, while in image 10 [Figure 4a] their heights are roughly the same). Taking the perspective difference into account by scaling has only very minimal actual effect on the computed velocities.

We perform the 3D computation using those image points in the front or side images where $\min(I_x, I_y) \geq \tau$ to obtain the front or side equations. We used $\tau = 2.0$ for the results reported here and Figures 4b and 4d shows those points in the front and side images that are used in the 3D velocity calculation for 2 images (note that they are all at the tip of the plant). Our scheme requires the solution of a $n \times 3$ system of equations

$$N_{n \times 3}(u, v, w)^T = B_{n \times 1}, \tag{5}$$

$n \geq 3$, where the row entries of N and B are determined using one of the two forms of equation (1). We use a weighted least squares calculation by computing a diagonal matrix $W_{i,i} = min(I_{xi}, I_{yi})$ and solving for (u, v, w) as

$$(u, v, w)^T = \left(N_{3 \times n}^T W_{n \times n}^2 N_{n \times 3}\right)^{-1} N_{3 \times n}^T W_{n \times n} B_{n \times 1}. \tag{6}$$

Solving this system of equation simply involves inverting a 3×3 matrix. We also solved systems of equations [the two forms of (1)] separately to obtain (u, v) for the front views of the corn seedling and (v, w) for the side views of the corn seedling in the images by solving simple $m_l \times 2$ and $m_r \times 2$ least squares systems of equations $(m_l + m_r = n)$. In this case, the 2D u and w values were almost identical to those in the 3D case while 3D v values are roughly the weighted average of the 2D v values (which are usually very close to start with).

7. 3D Experimental Results

We collected 506 images of a front/side view of a growing corn seedling and used them to obtain 500 3D growth vectors (u, v, w). Our program computes growth in pixels per frame, we converted this to meters per second by imaging a metric ruler in the same 3D plane as the plant is in and measuring the number of pixels per centimeter. We found that 1 pixel corresponded to 3.745×10^{-4} meters. Since images were acquired at 2 minute intervals, 1 pixel/frame motion corresponds to a speed of 3.112×10^{-6} meters/second.

We display the data as 2D plots of magnitude M:

$$M = ||(u, v, w)||_2 \tag{7}$$

and residual R:

$$R = \sqrt{\frac{\sum_{i=0}^{499} (W_{i,i}(B_i - N_i(u,v,w)^T))^2}{\sum_{i=0}^{499} W_{i,i}^2}} \tag{8}$$

against the image number i (time) in Figure 5. M is the magnitude of 3D growth while R indicates how good the least squares calculation at each time was. Furthermore, Figure 6 shows a 2D plot of the direction angles (θ and ϕ, see the definitions below), also against the image number i. Since $\vec{v}_{3D} = (u, v, w)$ is a 3D vector only two angles are needed to describe its orientation. We define θ as the angle from $0°$ to $360°$ counterclockwise about the line-of-axis $(0, 0, 1)$ as

$$\theta = acos(\hat{v}_P \cdot (0, 0, 1)), \tag{9}$$

where $\hat{v}_P = (u, 0, w)$ is $\vec{v}_{3D}$ projected onto the $x - z$ plane and normalized to 1. Thus θ is the amount of rotation of $\vec{v}_{3D}$ about the $(0, 1, 0)$ axis. ϕ is the angle of $\vec{v}_{3D}$ with respect to $(0, 1, 0)$ vertical axis, that is,

$$\phi = acos(\hat{v}_{3D} \cdot (0, 1, 0)). \tag{10}$$

θ and ϕ are converted from radians to degrees by multiplying by $180.0/\pi$.

The results showed that the growth on corn seedlings is not uniform but grows in fast and slow spurts as the plant tip rotates and sways in 3D space. To subjectively verify the correctness of our results we also made a movie of the plant growth with the growth measurements superimposed on the images and when visually viewed the computed growth measurements agree with the actual plant growth. Note that currently, we have no way of independently verifying the growth measurements by other means. However, we observe that the sum of the v values for the front and side view 2D velocity computations is 132.17 and 128.54 pixels respectively for the 500

3D Magnitude M (microns/second) and residual R (of 3D calculation)

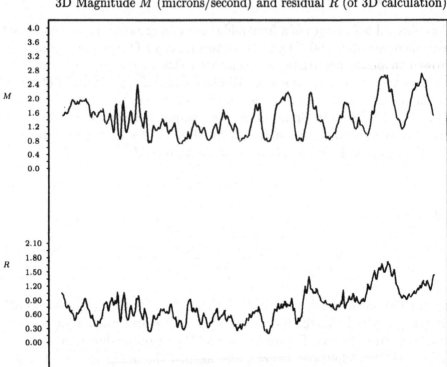

Figure 5. Plots of 3D magnitude (M) and residual R against time (image number) for 500 3D velocity calculations.

images while the difference in the front and side tip positions (computed as the center of masses of all points contributing normal velocity data to the 3D calculation) between the first and last images is 133.59 and 129.25 pixels respectively, relative differences of 1.06% and 0.96% between the tip positions and the velocity sums over the entire image sequence. We believe this is an indication of the accuracy we are obtaining.

We have imposed the (u, v) and (v, w) vectors on images 10 and 400 of the sequence (see Figures 4c and 4f). These show the growth is taking place in roughly the same direction as the corn seedling tip is pointing in Figure 4c but in a different direction in 4f (although, in general, we note that tip direction and 3D velocity direction can be quite different). Lastly, we point again out one important advantage of our technique: that the apparatus for the optical flow method is rather inexpensive as one only needs a black and white camera, a frame grabber, a mirror and a PC computer.

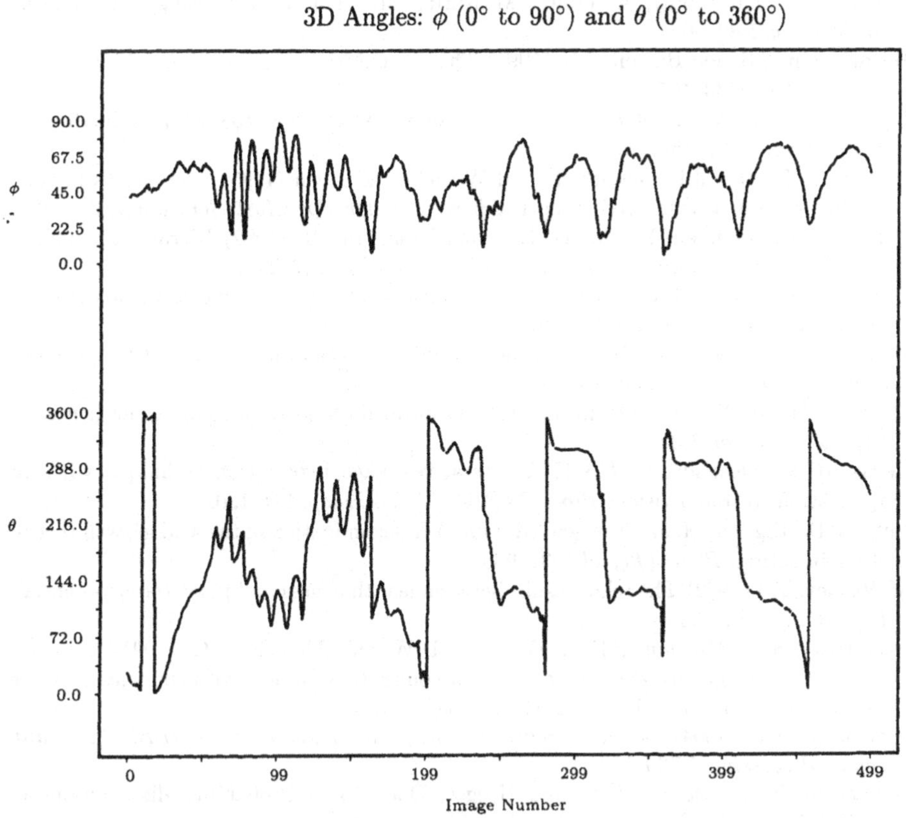

3D Angles: ϕ (0° to 90°) and θ (0° to 360°)

Figure 6.   Plots of the 3D angles θ and ϕ against time (image number) for 500 3D velocity calculations.

Acknowledgements

We thank Nick Dimenna for his technical assistance. This work has been supported in part by NSERC (Natural Sciences and Engineering Research Council of Canada) and Agriculture and Agri-Food Canada.

References

Barron, J.L., Fleet, D.J. and Beauchemin, S.S. (1994) Performance of optical flow techniques, *Int. J. of Comp. Vis.*, 12(1):43–77.

Barron, J.l. and Khurana, M. (1997) Determining optical flow for large motions using parametric models in a hierarchical framework, *Vision Interface*, 47–56.

Barron, J.L. and Liptay, A. (1994) Optic flow to measure minute increments in plant growth, *BioImaging*, 2(1):57–61.

Barron, J.L. and Liptay, A. (1997) Measuring 3D plant growth using optical flow, *BioImaging*, 5:82–86.

Beauchemin, S.S. and Barron, J.L. (1995) The computation of optical flow, *ACM Comp. Surveys*, 27(3):433–467.

Liptay, A. (1992) Air circulation in growth chambers stunts tomato seedling growth *Can. J. Plant Sci.*, 72:1275–1281.

Liptay, A., Barron, J.L., Jewett, T. and Wesenbeeck, I. van (1995) Oscillations in corn seedling growth as measured by optical flow, *J. Amer. Soc. Hort. Sci.*, 120(3):379–385.

Bergen, J.R., Anandan, P., Hanna, K.J. and Hingorani, R. (1992) Hierarchical model-based motion estimation, *European Conf. Comp. Vis.*, 237–252.

Fox, M.D. and Puffer, L.G. (1976) Analysis of transient plant movements by holographic interferometry, *Nature*, 261:488–490.

Jiang, Z. and Staude, W. (1989) An interferometric method for plant growth measurements, *J. Exp. Bot.*, 40:1169–1173.

Lang, A. (1990) Xylem, phloem and transpiration flows in developing apple fruits, *J. Exp. Bot.*, 41:645–651.

Lucas, B. and Kanade, T. (1981) An iterative image registration technique with an application to stereo vision, *Proc. DARPA IU Workshop*, 121–130.

Luthen, H., Bigdon, M. and Böttger, M. (1990) Re-examination of the acid growth theory of auxin action, *Plant Physiol.*, 931–939.

McBurney, T.J (1992) The relationship between leaf thickness and plant water potential, *Exp. Bot.*, 43:327–335.

Pasumarty, S.V., Minchin, P.E.H., Fountain, D.W. and Thomas, R.G. (1991) Influence of shade on the growth and sink activity of young flower heads and peduncles of white clover (trifolium repens L.), *J. Exp. Bot.*, 42:705–710.

Simoncelli, E.P. (1994) Design of multi-dimensional derivative filters, *IEEE Int. Conf. Image Processing*, 1:790–793.

Simoncelli, E.P., Adelson, E.H. and Heeger, D.J. (1991) Probability distributions of optical flow, *IEEE Proc. of CVPR*, 310–315.

UNSUPERVISED LEARNING FOR ROBUST TEXTURE SEGMENTATION

JOACHIM M. BUHMANN and JAN PUZICHA
Institut für Informatik III
Rheinische Friedrich-Wilhelms-Universität
D-53117 Bonn, Germany

1. Introduction

Robustness of computer vision algorithms requires stability of the computed results against variations in the input data caused by noise or modeling uncertainty. In unsupervised image processing tasks like texture segmentation the extracted image partition should provide reliable model estimates of the different texture types. These texture models represent typical properties of textures and they should not depend on the specific texture data available to the algorithm. Instead, the performance of the algorithms should be invariant to within-class texture fluctuations and sample fluctuations which are omnipresent in noisy images. Segmentation solutions have to generalize from the given texture samples to new instances of the same texture types.

The underlying evaluation methodology of this chapter is a two step process: first, computer vision algorithms are characterized by an appropriate optimization principle for the computer vision task; second, the noise sensitivity of these algorithms is measured by a large deviation analysis as known from Statistical Learning Theory. We demonstrate in an exemplary fashion how this methodology provides a systematic evaluation of algorithms. The unsupervised segmentation of texture images using histogram clustering is employed as a prototypical application. Histogram clustering is described in an abstract way in section 2.

A central question for all data analysis procedures is concerned with the significance of the extracted structures, i.e. the robustness of the induced image partition against within–class variability and noise. In the language of statistics, the expectation value w.r.t. the feature distribution of a given cluster measure is called the expected risk and its empirical mean evaluated

R. Klette et al. (eds.), Performance Characterization in Computer Vision, 195–209.
© 2000 *Kluwer Academic Publishers.*

for the particular texture sample at hand is known as empirical risk. A meaningful segmentation of textured images should not change when a homogeneously textured image region is replaced by a different texture sample of the same texture class. Strong dependencies on sample peculiarities, known as the overfitting phenomenon, can jeopardize supervised learning solutions and they also occur in unsupervised learning tasks such as image segmentation.

In this chapter, the asymmetric clustering model for texture segmentation is theoretically investigated in the framework of statistical learning theory (Vapnik, 1995). More specifically, we apply the *Empirical Risk Approximation* (ERA) induction principle (Buhmann, 1998) to derive a robust algorithm for histogram clustering (section 3). This induction principle provides estimators of the expected risk which are designed to avoid overfitting phenomena. It is a key observation in statistics that solutions of statistical inference problems with slightly different expected risk can not be reliably distinguished by observing the empirical risk which fluctuates around its expectation value. Therefore, the space of different solutions for e.g. texture segmentation is partitioned into equivalence classes of statistically indistinguishable solutions. Empirical risk approximation determines the equivalence class which contains the solution with minimal empirical risk and it averages over all solutions of this set. The size of this equivalence class is determined by a large deviation estimate based on Bernstein's inequality.

As the major contribution of this chapter, empirical risk approximation of the asymmetric clustering model is shown to be naturally implemented by a deterministic annealing algorithm with a finite stopping temperature. In essence, deterministic annealing returns a typical or *average* solution of a set of statistically indistinguishable solutions and thus avoids overfitting. The computational temperature thereby serves as a Lagrange parameter for the deviation of the empirical risk from the expected risk. The theoretical results are confirmed by a benchmark study on mondrians of Brodatz textures. Significant overfitting phenomena are observed for the minimal empirical risk estimator. It is demonstrated that deterministic annealing algorithms with finite stopping temperature are capable to substantially improve generalization performance (section 4).

2. Texture Segmentation Based on Feature Histograms

2.1. TEXTURE SEGMENTATION CONCEPTS

Most approaches in texture segmentation follow a two–stage procedure:

- First, features are extracted to describe the local textural characteristics of an image site. A broad variety of feature extraction schemes has

been proposed (Geman *et al.*, 1990; Jain and Farrokhnia, 1991; Mao and Jain, 1992; Hofmann *et al.*, 1998; Puzicha *et al.*, 1999).
- Second, similar objects are grouped or partitioned into classes according to a clustering criterion which favors homogeneous segments.

The clustering criterion measures the quality of a particular segmentation solution and can be interpreted as the underlying learning principle for the low level image analysis task. The underlying data type to represent textures—a vector, proximity or histogram data type—allows us to define categories of different segmentation methods, which are intrinsically connected to the notion of *texture similarity*. In the most common representation, texture features are interpreted as *vectors in an Euclidean space* which, in essence, amounts to fitting a Gaussian mixture model to the data. The clustering method of choice for vectorial data is the k–means algorithm and its variants, which have been exploited for texture segmentation e.g. in (Jain and Farrokhnia, 1991; Mao and Jain, 1992). A severe problem arises in cases where the Euclidean distances in feature space do not match the perceptual similarity judgment of humans since such mismatches lead to unexpected and inferior segmentation results.

Alternative approaches have employed *proximity data*, which are usually based on statistical tests to discriminate between the local feature distribution at two image sites. As a major advantage, these methods define similarity of textures by the *similarity of the respective feature distributions* rather than refering to a vector-space metric. For pairwise similarity data optimization approaches to graph partitioning (Geman *et al.*, 1990; Hofmann *et al.*, 1998; Shi and Malik, 1997) have been proposed in the texture segmentation context, which we refer to as *pairwise dissimilarity clustering* (PDC).

Recently, a novel technique known as *Asymmetric Clustering Model* (ACM) (Hofmann and Puzicha, 1998) has been proposed which is directly applicable to *histogram data* and empirical feature distributions (Puzicha *et al.*, 1999). This technique does not rely on pairwise comparison of histograms based on statistical tests as in (Geman *et al.*, 1990; Hofmann *et al.*, 1998) but instead exploits a statistical mixture model to estimate prototypical class distributions.

2.2. THE ASYMMETRIC CLUSTERING MODEL

To stress the generality of the proposed model for histogram clustering we temporarily detach the presentation from the specific problem of image segmentation and consider the following more abstract setting (Hofmann and Puzicha, 1998): Denote by $\mathcal{X} \times \mathcal{Y}$ the product space with elements $x_i \in \mathcal{X}, 1 \leq i \leq n$ and $y_j \in \mathcal{Y}, 1 \leq j \leq m$. Dyadic data are joint occurrences of objects from both spaces. These measurements $(x_i, y_j) \in \mathcal{X} \times \mathcal{Y}$ are characterized by a number of observations

$$\mathcal{Z} = \{(x_{i(r)}, y_{j(r)}), 1 \leq r \leq l\} . \tag{1}$$

The sufficient statistics of how often the pair (x_i, y_j) occurs in the data set $\mathcal{Z}$ is measured by the set of frequencies

$$n_{ij} = \frac{1}{l} \sum_{r=1}^{l} \Delta_{i,i(r)} \Delta_{j,j(r)} . \tag{2}$$

$\Delta_{i,j} = \begin{cases} 1 & \text{if } i = j \\ 0 & \text{if } i \neq j \end{cases}$ denotes the Kronecker function. n_{ij} is also known as the empirical distribution of the data $\mathcal{Z}$. Assuming a constant number l/n of observations for each object x_i, the histogram

$$n_{j|i} = n_{ij} / \sum_{j=1}^{m} n_{ij} = n \cdot n_{ij} \tag{3}$$

for each x_i defines an *empirical distribution* over $\mathcal{Y}$. This distribution denotes the frequency to observe object y_j given object x_i. The frequencies n_{ij} and $n_{j|i}$ are empirical estimates of the probabilities $\mathbf{P}^{\text{true}}\{x_i, y_j\}$ and $\mathbf{P}^{\text{true}}\{y_j | x_i\}$ based on the data $\mathcal{Z}$. The assumption that each object x_i is selected with probability $1/n$ implies the relation $\mathbf{P}^{\text{true}}\{x_i, y_j\} = \frac{1}{n}\mathbf{P}^{\text{true}}\{y_j | x_i\}$.

The proposed mixture model, which is referred to as Asymmetric Clustering Model (ACM), explains the observed data by a finite number of component probability distributions on the feature space. The generative model is defined by a three step process:

1. select an object (resp. image site) $x_i \in \mathcal{X}$ with uniform probability $1/n$,
2. choose the cluster (texture type) according to the cluster membership of x_i ($\alpha = m(i)$),
3. select $y_j \in \mathcal{Y}$ from the (texture-specific) conditional distribution $q_{j|\alpha}$.

The assignment function $m : \{1, \ldots, n\} \rightarrow \{1, \ldots, k\}$ maps each object x_i to a cluster $m(i)$. The data $\mathcal{Z}$ are assumed to be distributed according to the generative data model over $\mathcal{X} \times \mathcal{Y}$:

$$\mathbf{P}\{x_i, y_j | m, \vec{q}\} = \frac{1}{n} q_{j|m(i)} . \tag{4}$$

Learning the model requires to estimate the model parameters $(m, \vec{q})$ in (4) with $m(i) \in \{1, \ldots, k\}$ and $q_{j|\alpha} \in [0, 1]$, subject to the constraint $\sum_{j=1}^{m} q_{j|\alpha} = 1$.

Returning to the texture segmentation problem we can identify $\mathcal{X}$ with the set of image sites, whereas $\mathcal{Y}$ denotes the (discretized) domain of textural feature(s). Each class corresponds to a different texture which is characterized by a specific distribution $q_{j|\alpha}$ of features y_j. Since these component distributions of the mixture model are not constrained, they can virtually model any distribution of features. In particular, no further parametric restrictions on $q_{j|\alpha}$ are imposed. Note that typically the number of objects x_i scales with the number of observations since the number of measured (local) features per image site remains constant.

The log–likelihood function per sample of the generative model (4) is given by

$$\mathcal{L} = \frac{1}{l} \log \prod_{i=1}^{n} \prod_{j=1}^{m} \left(\mathbf{P}\left\{ x_i, y_j | m, \vec{q} \right\} \right)^{l n_{ij}}$$

$$= \sum_{i=1}^{n} \sum_{j=1}^{m} n_{ij} \log q_{j|m(i)} - \log n \ . \tag{5}$$

Maximum likelihood (ML) equations are derived from (5) by differentiation, using Lagrange parameters to ensure a proper normalization of the continuous model parameters $\vec{q}$. Let us introduce the index sets Λ_α, $1 \le \alpha \le k$ which enumerate all objects assigned to cluster α, $\Lambda_\alpha = \{i : \hat{m}(i) = \alpha\}$. The resulting stationary equations for the ML assignments $\hat{m}(i)$ and the ML probabilities $\hat{q}_{j|\alpha}$ are given by

$$\hat{q}_{j|\alpha} = \frac{1}{|\Lambda_\alpha|} \sum_{i \in \Lambda_\alpha} n_{j|i} \ , \tag{6}$$

$$\hat{m}(i) = \arg\min_{\nu} \left\{ -\sum_{j=1}^{m} n_{j|i} \log \hat{q}_{j|\nu} \right\} \ . \tag{7}$$

Solutions of (6,7) are found in an iterative fashion similar to the k-means algorithm. It is worth noting the similarity of (6) to the calculation of k-means in vectorial clustering. The ML probabilities $\hat{q}_{j|\alpha}$ are determined as means of the conditional frequencies $n_{j|i}$ for all object x_i which are assigned to cluster α.

2.3. DETERMINISTIC ANNEALING FOR ACM

A technique which allows us to improve the presented maximum likelihood estimation procedure is known as *deterministic annealing* (DA). The key idea is to introduce a temperature parameter T and to replace the minimization of a combinatorial objective function by a substitute known as the *generalized free energy*. Details on this topic in the context of data clustering can be found in (Rose *et al.*, 1990; Buhmann and Kühnel, 1993; Pereira *et al.*, 1993; Hofmann *et al.*, 1998). Minimization of the free energy corresponding to (5) yields the following equations for probabilistic assignments:

$$\mathbf{P}\{m(i) = \alpha\} \equiv \frac{\exp\left[\sum_{j=1}^{m} n_{j|i} \log q_{j|\alpha}/T\right]}{\sum_{\nu=1}^{k} \exp\left[\sum_{j=1}^{m} n_{j|i} \log q_{j|\nu}/T\right]}. \tag{8}$$

In DA the estimates $\mathbf{P}\{m(i) = \alpha\}$ are iterated with

$$q_{j|\alpha} = \sum_{i=1}^{n} \mathbf{P}\{m(i) = \alpha\} n_{j|i} \tag{9}$$

for fixed temperature T and, in an outer loop, T is gradually lowered down to the final temperature value. The partition of unity in (8) is a very intuitive generalization of the nearest neighbor rule in (7). For $T \to 0$ the arg–min operation in the nearest neighbor rule (7) is recovered. Deterministic annealing tracks solutions from high to low temperatures, which maximizes the log–likelihood in the limit $T = 0$. Notice that the DA procedure also generalizes the Expectation Maximization (EM) algorithm which is obtained for $T = 1$. In this case, (8) corresponds to the computation of posterior probabilities for hidden variables $m(i)$ in the E–step.

3. A Statistical Learning Theory for Histogram Clustering

3.1. RISK OF HISTOGRAM CLUSTERING

Maximizing the log-likelihood (5) can be rephrased in terms of minimizing statistical risk, i.e., searching for a maximum of $\mathcal{L}$ is equivalent to minimizing the average statistical loss of assigning object x_i to cluster $m(i)$. This loss is given for the Asymmetric Clustering Model (ACM) by

$$\mathrm{h}(x_i, y_j; m, \vec{q}) = -\log q_{j|m(i)} . \tag{10}$$

This loss function (10) has already been suggested by Fisher (1922; 1952) and later by Wald (1947) for density estimation. The Asymmetric Clustering Model clusters objects into groups with a prototypical feature distribution $q_{j|m(i)}$ per group $m(i) \in \{1, \ldots, k\}$. The set of all possible hypotheses for histogram clustering, known as the hypothesis class in statistical learning theory, is defined as

$$\mathcal{H} = \{-\log q_{j|m(i)} : m(i) \in \{1, \ldots, k\} \wedge q_{j|\alpha} \in \{1/l, 2/l, \ldots, 1\}\} \tag{11}$$

The conditional probabilities $q_{j|\alpha}$ are normalized ($\forall \alpha : \sum_{j=1}^{m} q_{j|\alpha} = 1$). The value $q_{j|\alpha} = 0$ has been excluded since it causes infinite expected risk for $\mathbf{P}^{\text{true}}\{y_j|x_i\} > 0$ – a case which could actually occur for ML–estimates.

The expectation value of the loss $h(x_i, y_j; m, \vec{q})$ defines the expected risk $\mathcal{R}(h)$ of ACM with

$$\mathcal{R}(h) = \sum_{i=1}^{n}\sum_{j=1}^{m} \mathbf{P}^{\text{true}}\{x_i, y_j\}\, h(x_i, y_j; m, \vec{q})$$

$$= -\sum_{i=1}^{n}\sum_{j=1}^{m} \frac{1}{n}\mathbf{P}^{\text{true}}\{y_j|x_i\} \log q_{j|m(i)} \ . \tag{12}$$

The nature of the expected risk is clarified by subtracting the conditional entropy of the data source $-\sum_{i=1}^{n}\sum_{j=1}^{m}\mathbf{P}^{\text{true}}\{y_j|x_i\}\log \mathbf{P}^{\text{true}}\{y_j|x_i\}$ from $\mathcal{R}(h)$. This adjustment of the risk scale does not change the inference process since the conditional entropy is independent on model parameters $m, \vec{q}$. The difference amounts to an equivalent expected risk

$$\mathcal{R}'(m, \vec{q}) = \sum_{i=1}^{n}\sum_{j=1}^{m} \frac{1}{n}\mathbf{P}^{\text{true}}\{y_j|x_i\}\left(h(x_i, y_j; m, \vec{q}) + \log \mathbf{P}^{\text{true}}\{y_j|x_i\}\right)$$

$$= \frac{1}{n}\sum_{i=1}^{n} \mathcal{D}^{KL}\left(\mathbf{P}^{\text{true}}\{y_j|x_i\}\,\|\,q_{j|m(i)}\right) \ , \tag{13}$$

where $\mathcal{D}^{KL}(.\|.)$ denotes the Kullback Leibler divergence between two feature distributions. According to (13) the expected risk equals the Kullback Leibler divergence between the true conditional distribution $\mathbf{P}^{\text{true}}\{y_j|x_i\}$ and the model distribution $q_{j|m(i)}$ averaged over all objects x_i.

To determine the *empirical risk* of ACM we insert the empirical distribution $n_{j|i}$ (2) into (12) which yields the term

$$\hat{\mathcal{R}}(h; \mathcal{Z}) = -\sum_{i=1}^{n}\sum_{j=1}^{m} n_{ij} \log\left(q_{j|m(i)}\right) = -\frac{1}{l}\sum_{r=1}^{l} \log\left(q_{j(r)|m(i(r))}\right) \ . \tag{14}$$

The empirical risk $\hat{\mathcal{R}}(h; \mathcal{Z})$ in (14) can be transformed into the negative log-likelihood $\mathcal{L}$ by subtraction of $l \log n$.

3.2. CONVERGENCE OF EMPIRICAL TO EXPECTED RISK

Vapnik and Chervonenkis (1971)—see also Vapnik (1982; 1995)—have analyzed in great detail the *Empirical Risk Minimization* (ERM) induction principle which selects a hypothesis $h(x_i, y_j; m, \vec{q})$ according to minimal empirical risk $\hat{\mathcal{R}}(h; \mathcal{Z})$ evaluated on the data set $\mathcal{Z}$. Let us denote by $\hat{h}^{\perp}(x) = \arg\min_{h \in \mathcal{H}} \hat{\mathcal{R}}(h; \mathcal{Z})$ and by $h^{\perp}(x) = \arg\min_{h \in \mathcal{H}} \mathcal{R}(h)$ the loss functions which minimize the empirical and the expected risk, respectively. The quality of the inference process is measured by the deviation of the empirically determined minimal risk on the data set from the minimal expected risk for the segmentation loss (10), i.e.,

$$\mathcal{R}(\hat{h}^{\perp}) - \inf_{h \in \mathcal{H}} \mathcal{R}(h) \ . \tag{15}$$

To determine the complexity of the learning problem we define a representative subset of loss functions $\mathcal{H}_{\gamma} = \{\tilde{h}_1, \dots, \tilde{h}_{\tilde{n}}\}$. These representative loss functions $\tilde{h}_i$ are chosen in such a way that all functions in the hypothesis class are elements of a function ball centered at $\tilde{h}_i$, $1 \le i \le \tilde{n}$. The function balls with radius γ are defined as the subsets

$$B_{\gamma}(\tilde{h}) := \left\{ h : \sum_{i=1}^{n} \sum_{j=1}^{m} \frac{1}{n} \mathbf{P}^{\text{true}} \{y_j | x_i\} \left| \log \frac{\tilde{q}_{j|\tilde{m}(i)}}{q_{j|m(i)}} \right| \le \gamma \right\} \ . \tag{16}$$

Distances between functions are measured by the $l_1(\mathbf{P}^{\text{true}}\{y_j|x_i\})$ distance (Devroye and Györfi, 1985). The set $\mathcal{H}_{\gamma}$ is known as a γ-cover of the hypothesis class $\mathcal{H}$, i.e.,

$$\mathcal{H} \subset \bigcup_{\tilde{h} \in \mathcal{H}_{\gamma}} B_{\gamma}(\tilde{h}) \ . \tag{17}$$

In the sequel $\mathcal{H}_{\gamma}$ denotes the minimal cover of the hypothesis class $\mathcal{H}$, i.e., $|\mathcal{H}_{\gamma}| \le |\mathcal{H}'_{\gamma}|$ for all other γ-covers $\mathcal{H}'_{\gamma}$.

We are interested in an approximation of the minimal expected risk $\inf_{h \in \mathcal{H}} \mathcal{R}(h)$ by that function $\hat{h}^*$ of the γ-cover $\mathcal{H}_{\gamma}$ which minimizes the empirical risk $\hat{\mathcal{R}}(h; \mathcal{Z})$ on the given frequencies $n_{j|i}$, i.e.,

$$\hat{h}^* = \arg\min_{h \in \mathcal{H}_{\gamma}} \hat{\mathcal{R}}(h; \mathcal{Z}) \ . \tag{18}$$

Using the cover property of the γ-cover yields the chain of bounds

$$\mathcal{R}(\hat{h}^{\perp}) - \inf_{h \in \mathcal{H}} \mathcal{R}(h) \le \mathcal{R}(\hat{h}^*) - \inf_{h \in \mathcal{H}_{\gamma}} \mathcal{R}(h) + \gamma$$

$$\le \mathcal{R}(\hat{h}^*) - \hat{\mathcal{R}}(\hat{h}^*) + \gamma + \sup_{h \in \mathcal{H}_{\gamma}} |\hat{\mathcal{R}}(h) - \mathcal{R}(h)|$$

$$\le 2 \sup_{h \in \mathcal{H}_{\gamma}} |\hat{\mathcal{R}}(h) - \mathcal{R}(h)| + \gamma \ . \tag{19}$$

In the following, deviations of the empirical risk from the expected risk are measured on the scale of the maximal standard deviation

$$\sigma^\top := \sup_{h \in \mathcal{H}_\gamma} \sqrt{\mathbf{V}\{h\}}. \tag{20}$$

The probability that a solution of poor quality is selected by the ERM principle is bounded by Bernstein's inequality[1] (van der Vaart and Wellner, 1996), i.e.,

$$\mathbf{P}\left\{\mathcal{R}(\hat{h}^\perp) - \inf_{h \in \mathcal{H}} \mathcal{R}(h) > \epsilon\sigma^\top\right\} \leq \mathbf{P}\left\{\sup_{h \in \mathcal{H}_\gamma} |\hat{\mathcal{R}}(h) - \mathcal{R}(h)| \geq \frac{1}{2}\left(\epsilon\sigma^\top - \gamma\right)\right\}$$

$$\leq \sum_{h \in \mathcal{H}_\gamma} 2 \exp\left(-\frac{l\left(\epsilon\sigma^\top - \gamma\right)^2}{8\mathbf{V}\{h\} + 4\tau\sqrt{\mathbf{V}\{h\}}(\epsilon\sigma^\top - \gamma)}\right)$$

$$\leq 2|\mathcal{H}_\gamma| \exp\left(-\frac{l\left(\epsilon - \frac{\gamma}{\sigma^\top}\right)^2}{8 + 4\tau(\epsilon - \frac{\gamma}{\sigma^\top})}\right) \equiv \delta. \tag{21}$$

The last inequality results from an upper bound of $\sqrt{\mathbf{V}\{h\}} \leq \sigma^\top$. The probability of large deviations (21) is bounded by the cardinality $|\mathcal{H}_\gamma|$ times an exponential factor. With probability $(1 - \delta)$ deviations of the empirical risk $\hat{\mathcal{R}}(h; \mathcal{Z})$ from the expected risk $\mathcal{R}(h)$ are bounded by $\gamma^{\mathrm{app}} := \frac{1}{2}(\epsilon\sigma^\top - \gamma)$. The empirical risk of the best loss function $h^\perp$ (in the sense of minimal expected risk) exceeds the minimal empirical risk not by more than $2\gamma^{\mathrm{app}}$, i.e.,

$$\hat{\mathcal{R}}(h^\perp) - \hat{\mathcal{R}}(\hat{h}^\perp) \leq \mathcal{R}(h^\perp) + \gamma^{\mathrm{app}} - (\mathcal{R}(\hat{h}^\perp) - \gamma^{\mathrm{app}}) \leq 2\gamma^{\mathrm{app}} \tag{22}$$

since $\mathcal{R}(h^\perp) \leq \mathcal{R}(\hat{h}^\perp)$. Averaging over all functions with an empirical risk difference smaller than $2\gamma^{\mathrm{app}}$ from the empirical minimizer yields a hypothesis which represents the statistically significant structure in the data.

The key computational task is to calculate an upper bound of the cardinality $|\mathcal{H}_\gamma|$ of the γ–cover and, thereby, to determine the approximation bound γ^{app}. $|\mathcal{H}_\gamma|$ is bounded by the fraction of the cardinality of the complete hypothesis class divided by the minimal cardinality of a function ball with center $\tilde{h} \in \mathcal{H}$, i.e.,

$$|\mathcal{H}_\gamma| \leq \frac{|\mathcal{H}|}{\min\limits_{h \in \mathcal{H}} |\mathcal{B}_\gamma(h)|}. \tag{23}$$

---

[1] It is assumed that the tails of the data distribution vanish sufficiently fast, i.e., τ is a distribution dependent parameter to enforce the moment constraint $\forall h \in \mathcal{H}, \forall r > 2 :$ $\mathbf{E}_{\mathbf{P}^{\mathrm{true}}\{y_j|x_i\}}\{|h(x_i, y_j; m, \vec{q}) - \mathcal{R}(h)|^r\} \leq r!\tau^{r-2}\mathbf{V}_{\mathbf{P}^{\mathrm{true}}\{y_j|x_i\}}\{h(x_i, y_j; m, \vec{q})\}.$

A tighter bound than (23) can be derived if we restrict the ball centers to the γ-cover $\mathcal{H}_\gamma$, i.e., $\mathrm{h} \in \mathcal{H}_\gamma$.

The cardinality of a function ball with radius γ can be approximated by adopting techniques from statistical physics and asymptotic analysis (Bruijn, 1958):

$$\left| \mathcal{B}_\gamma(\tilde{\mathrm{h}}) \right| = \sum_{\{m\}} \sum_{\{q_{j|\alpha}\}} \Theta \left(\gamma - \sum_{i=1}^{n} \sum_{j=1}^{m} \frac{1}{n} \mathbf{P}^{\mathrm{true}} \{y_j | x_i\} \left| \log \frac{q_{j|m(i)}}{\tilde{q}_{j|\tilde{m}(i)}} \right| \right) \quad (24)$$

$$= \frac{k^n l^{k(m-1)}}{(2\pi)^k} \int_0^1 \cdots \int_0^1 \prod_{j=1}^{m} \prod_{\nu=1}^{k} dq_{j|\nu} \int_{-i\infty}^{+i\infty} \cdots \int_{-i\infty}^{+i\infty} dQ_\nu \int_{-i\infty}^{+i\infty} \frac{d\hat{x}}{2\pi\hat{x}} \exp\left(nS(\vec{q}, \mathbf{Q}, \hat{x}) \right),$$

with $\Theta(x) = \begin{cases} 1 & \text{if } x \geq 0 \\ 0 & \text{if } x < 0 \end{cases}$. The entropy S is given by

$$S(\vec{q}, \mathbf{Q}, \hat{x}) = \hat{x}\gamma - \sum_{\nu=1}^{k} Q_\nu \left(\sum_{j=1}^{m} q_{j|\nu} - 1 \right) +$$

$$\frac{1}{n} \sum_{i=1}^{n} \log \sum_{\rho=1}^{k} \exp\left(-\hat{x} \sum_{j=1}^{m} \mathbf{P}^{\mathrm{true}} \{y_j | x_i\} \left| \log \frac{q_{j|\rho}}{\tilde{q}_{j|\tilde{m}(i)}} \right| \right). \quad (25)$$

The auxiliary variables $\mathbf{Q} = (Q_\nu)_{\nu \in \{1,...,k\}}$ are Lagrange parameters to enforce the constraint $\sum_{j=1}^{m} q_{j|\nu} = 1$. Choosing

$$\tilde{q}_{j|m(i)} = \begin{cases} 1 - (m-1)/l & \text{for } \tilde{j}(i) := \arg\min_{j'} \mathbf{P}^{\mathrm{true}} \{y_{j'} | x_i\}, \\ 1/l & \text{else}, \end{cases} \quad (26)$$

we obtain a lower bound on the entropy and therefore a bound on the integral, which is independent of $\tilde{\mathrm{h}}$. Using the abbreviations

$$\kappa_{i\nu} := \sum_{j \neq \tilde{j}(i)} \mathbf{P}^{\mathrm{true}} \{y_j | x_i\} (\log q_{j|\nu} + \log l)$$

$$+ \mathbf{P}^{\mathrm{true}} \left\{ y_{\tilde{j}(i)} | x_i \right\} (\log(1 - \frac{m-1}{l}) - \log q_{\tilde{j}(i)|\nu}), \quad (27)$$

$$\mathbf{P}_{i\alpha} = \frac{\exp(-\hat{x}\kappa_{i\alpha})}{\sum_{\mu=1}^{k} \exp(-\hat{x}\kappa_{i\mu})}, \quad (28)$$

the following saddle point approximations are obtained:

$$q_{j|\gamma} = \frac{\sum_{i=1}^{n} \mathbf{P}^{\mathrm{true}} \{y_j | x_i\} \mathbf{P}_{i\gamma}}{\sum_{l=1, l \neq \tilde{j}}^{m} \sum_{i=1}^{n} \mathbf{P}^{\mathrm{true}} \{y_l | x_i\} \mathbf{P}_{i\gamma}}, \; \forall j \neq \tilde{j} \quad \wedge \quad q_{\tilde{j}(i)|\gamma} = 0 \; (29)$$

$$\gamma = \frac{1}{n} \sum_{i=1}^{n} \sum_{\mu=1}^{k} \mathbf{P}_{i\mu} \sum_{j=1}^{m} \mathbf{P}^{\mathrm{true}} \{y_j | x_i\} \kappa_{j|\mu}. \quad (30)$$

The entropy S evaluated at the saddle point in combination with the Laplace approximation yields an estimate for the cardinality of the γ-cover

(23)

$$\log |\mathcal{H}_\gamma| = \frac{1}{2}\log n + \frac{1}{2}\log |A^{\text{sp}}| + n(\log k - \mathcal{S}) , \qquad (31)$$

where $|A^{\text{sp}}|$ denotes the determinant of the Hessian matrix of the entropy $\mathcal{S}$ evaluated at the saddle point. The reader should note that γ is related to the auxiliary variable $\hat{x}$ by (30).

3.3. SAMPLE COMPLEXITY

The right-hand-side of Bernstein's inequality is abbreviated as confidence δ with $1 - \delta$ being the probability that an estimate is ϵ-typical. This equation determines the required number of samples l_0 for fixed precision ϵ and confidence δ if we consider the hypothesis class $\mathcal{H}_\gamma$, i.e., the sample complexity is given by

$$n(\log k - \mathcal{S}) + \frac{1}{2}\log n + \frac{1}{2}\log |A^{\text{sp}}| - \frac{l_0\left(\epsilon - \frac{\gamma}{\sigma^\top}\right)^2}{8 + 4\tau(\epsilon - \frac{\gamma}{\sigma^\top})} + \log\frac{2}{\delta} \le 0 . \qquad (32)$$

The bound (21) becomes non-trivial for $\epsilon \ge \gamma/\sigma^\top$ since a cover of a function space limits the finite achievable precision. Equality in (32) yields a functional relationship between the precision ϵ and the approximation quality γ for fixed sample size l_0 and confidence δ. Qualitative insight is gained in the relation (ϵ, γ) if we neglect the factor $4\tau(\epsilon - \frac{\gamma}{\sigma^\top})$ in the bound (32) essentially assuming that the tails of the data distribution is bounded by a Gaussian. Under this assumption the precision ϵ depends on γ in a non-monotone fashion, i.e.,

$$\epsilon(\gamma) = \frac{\gamma}{\sigma^\top} + 2\sqrt{\frac{2}{l_0}}\sqrt{n(\log k - \mathcal{S}) + \frac{1}{2}\log n + \frac{1}{2}\log |A^{\text{sp}}| + \log\frac{2}{\delta}} . \qquad (33)$$

Decreasing γ obviously decreases the fraction $\gamma/\sigma^\top$ but it increases the term $(\log k - \mathcal{S})$ in the square root. The minimum of the function $\epsilon(\gamma)$ defines a compromise between uncertainty originating from empirical fluctuations and the loss of precision due to the approximation by an γ–cover. Differentiating with respect to γ and setting the result to zero yields as upper bound for the inverse temperature (assuming that $\frac{\partial \log |A^{\text{sp}}|}{\partial \gamma} \approx 0$).

$$\hat{x} \le \frac{1}{\sigma^\top}\sqrt{\frac{l_0}{2n}}\sqrt{(\log k - \mathcal{S}) + \frac{1}{2n}\left(\log n + \log |A^{\text{sp}}| + 2\log\frac{2}{\delta}\right)} . \qquad (34)$$

The inverse temperature $\hat{x}$ is bounded from above which prevents the inference algorithm from cooling down to a too low temperature. We like to emphasize that this inequality prevents the learning algorithm to select noise sensitive loss functions.

4. Texture Segmentation Results

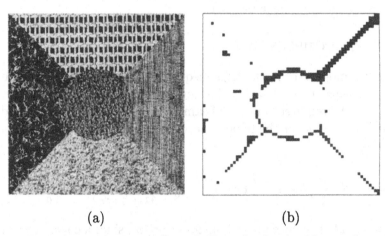

(a)   (b)

Figure 1. Typical segmentation results with $K = 5$ for the algorithms under examination: (a) original image, (b) annealed ACM. Misclassified blocks w.r.t. ground truth are depicted in black.

Algorithms which incorporate information from distributions of features have been successfully used in texture analysis (Geman *et al.*, 1990; Hofmann *et al.*, 1998). In the experiments we have followed (Jain and Farrokhnia, 1991; Hofmann *et al.*, 1998; Puzicha and Buhmann, 2000) and utilized an image representation based on the modulus of complex Gabor filters. All experiments are performed with a multiscale image representation using a Gabor filter bank with four orientations at three scales separated by octaves. Each filter channel has been discretized using 20 equally sized bins, which have been adapted to the dynamical range of the filter. The resulting feature space expands in 240 dimensions. Image sites are located on a regular grid of size 64×64 and 128×128 to reduce the computational complexity of the clustering algorithm. Local histograms of the feature distribution have been estimated in a square neighborhood of a size proportional to the filter scale, starting with a size of 8×8 pixels for the highest frequency. The ratio of data to image sites is chosen as $l/n = 5376$ in the segmentation experiments. In Figure 1 we illustrate the typical performance of ACM–based texture segmentation algorithms. The ACM exhibits excellent performance. Errors mostly occur on texture boundaries. More examples are documented in (Puzicha *et al.*, 1999).

The central question which we empirically examine in this chapter is concerned with the generalization performance of solutions computed by deterministic annealing with finite stopping temperature. To measure the expected risk, mondrians with five different textures taken from the Brodatz album as depicted in Figure 1 have been selected to estimate class parameters $q_{i|\nu}^{T}, \nu = 1, \ldots, 5$ for different temperatures T using DA. Then 43 test images have been generated using different instances of the same 5 texture types. On these test images a segmentation $m^{T}(i)$ has been computed by assigning each local histogram $n_{j|i}$ in the test image to the nearest texture prototype $q_{j|\alpha}^{T}$ according to

$$m^{T}(i) = \arg\min_{\nu} \left[-\sum_{j=1}^{m} n_{j|i} \log q_{j|\nu}^{T} \right] . \qquad (35)$$

This result is then compared with the known ground truth segmentation and the number of incorrectly segmented sites is determined. As the expected generalization we report the median number of incorrectly classified sites over all 43 images. In addition, the median negative log–likelihood over 43 images according to (5) is reported. In Figure 2 results are presented for three different examples. The overfitting effect is clearly visible in all three examples. As illustrated by the example in Figure 2c the gain in performance by choosing the optimal stopping temperature can be substantial.

5. Conclusion

As the major contribution, a theoretical justification of deterministic annealing for robust clustering and robust texture segmentation was derived. Monte Carlo or analytical estimates of probabilistic assignments and cluster parameters can be interpreted as averages of loss functions with a pre-determined approximation accuracy. ϵ-entropies in solution space motivate an annealing scheme with finite stopping temperature and result in improved generalization performance. The qualitative behavior of approximations with finite precision have been confirmed in a benchmark study on mondrians of Brodatz textures. Texture models estimated for a too low temperature do not generalize well from one texture image to another texture image of the same type compared to segmentation solutions which are calculated with the optimal stopping temperature.

The asymmetric clustering model can be naturally generalized to a hierarchical grouping procedure. A heuristic tree topology is induced by the diagram of successive phase transitions or cluster splits which occur when

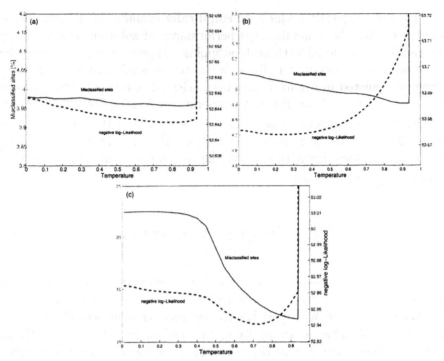

Figure 2. Typical examples of generalization performance of the ACM model. The ACM has been estimated on an image 512×512 pixels for (a) and 256×256 pixels for (b) and (c). The generalization performance has been estimated on 43 images each of which consisted of a mixture a different instances of the same 5 texture types.

lowering the temperature T. If not artificially bounded the number of clusters k approaches the number of objects n for $T \to 0$. In this context, robust inference provides a natural bound on the depth of the hierarchy that can be reliably estimated. An extension to hierarchical texture segmentation will be presented in a forthcoming paper.

References

de Bruijn, N.G. (1958) *Asymptotic Methods in Analysis*, North-Holland Publishing Co. (repr. Dover 1981), Amsterdam.

Buhmann, J.M. (1998) Empirical Risk Approximation: An Induction Principle for Unsupervised Learning, IAI-TR 98-3, Institut für Informatik III, University of Bonn.

Buhmann, J.M. and Kühnel, H. (1993) Vector Quantization with Complexity Costs, *IEEE Transactions on Information Theory*, 39:1133–1145.

Devroye, L. and Györfi, L. (1985) *Nonparametric Density Estimation: The L_1 View*, John Wiley & Sons.

Fisher, R.A. (1922) On the mathematical foundation of theoretical statistics, *Philos. Trans. Roy. Soc. London (Ser. A)*, 222:309–368.

Fisher, R.A. (1952) *Contributions to Mathematical Statistics*, John Wiley & Sons, New York.

Geman, D., Geman, S., Graffigne, C. and Dong, P. (1990) Boundary Detection by Constrained Optimization, *IEEE PAMI*, 12(7):609–628.

Hofmann, T. and Puzicha, J. (1998) Statistical Models for Co-occurrence Data, AI–MEMO 1625, MIT.

Hofmann, T., Puzicha, J. and Buhmann, J.M. (1998) Unsupervised Texture Segmentation in a Deterministic Annealing Framework, *IEEE PAMI*, 20(8):803–818.

Jain, A. and Farrokhnia, F. (1991) Unsupervised Texture Segmentation using Gabor Filters, *Pattern Recognition*, 24(12):1167–1186.

Mao, J. and Jain, A. (1992) Texture classification and segmentation using multiresolution simultaneous autoregressive models, *Pattern Recognition*, 25:173–188.

Pereira, F., Tishby, N. and Lee, L. (1993) Distributional clustering of English words, *30th Annual Meeting of the Association for Computational Linguistics*, Columbus, Ohio, 183–190.

Puzicha, J., Hofmann, T. and Buhmann, J.M. (1999) Histogram Clustering for Unsupervised Segmentation and Image Retrieval, *Pattern Recognition Letters*, 20(9):899–909.

Puzicha, J. and Buhmann, J.M. (2000) Multiscale Annealing for Grouping and Unsupervised Texture Segmentation, *Computer Vision and Image Understanding*, in press.

Rose, K., Gurewitz, E. and Fox, G. (1990) A deterministic annealing approach to clustering, *Pattern Recognition Letters*, 11:589–594.

Shi, J. and Malik, J. (1997) Normalized Cuts and Image Segmentation, *Proceedings of the IEEE Conference on Computer Vision and Pattern Recognition (CVPR'97)*, 731–737.

van der Vaart, A.W. and Wellner, J.A. (1996) *Weak Convergence and Empirical Processes*, New York, Berlin, Heidelberg, Springer-Verlag.

Vapnik, V. and Chervonenkis, A. (1971) On the uniform convergence of relative Frequencies of Events to their Probabilities, *Theory of Probability and its Applications*, 16(2):264–280.

Vapnik, V. (1982) *Estimation of Dependencies based on Empirical Data*, Springer Series in Statistics, Springer.

Vapnik, V. (1995) *The Nature of Statistical Learning Theory*, Springer Verlag.

Wald, A. (1947) *Sequential Analysis*, John Wiley & Sons, New York, first edition.

CONFIDENCE OF GROUND CONTROL FOR VALIDATING STEREO TERRAIN RECONSTRUCTION

GEORGY GIMEL'FARB
Dept. of Computer Science
The University of Auckland
Tamaki Campus, Private Bag 92019
Auckland, New Zealand

1. Introduction

Validation of computational stereo has attracted a great deal of notice in recent years (Gülch, 1991; Faugeras *et al.*, 1992; Hsieh *et al.*, 1992; Krzystek and Wild, 1992; Bolles *et al.*, 1993; Förstner, 1996; Maimone and Shafer, 1996). Terrain reconstruction from stereopairs of space and aerial images falls within the domains of digital photogrammetry and computer vision. Hence, at first glance, reconstruction techniques should be validated in a similar manner. But there exists a notable difference between these domains.

Traditional photogrammetry is based mainly on human stereo perception. Digital photogrammetry (Ackermann, 1996; Schenk, 1996) uses computational stereo techniques but mostly to make easier the subsequent visual reconstruction by interactive editing of computed "rough" terrain models.

Today's computer binocular stereo pursues the much longer-term goal of accurate automatic terrain reconstruction by directly matching the images of a stereopair and finding pixels that correspond to each visible terrain point. Because such a search for the corresponding pixels is an ill-posed mathematical problem, the natural desire to compute complete and precise digital models that closely approximate true terrains goes far beyond the real possibilities of binocular stereo and, in most cases, even beyond practical needs. Photogrammetric reconstruction is quantitatively validated for specific ground control points (GCP) which are easily detected

R. Klette et al. (eds.), Performance Characterization in Computer Vision, 211–225.
© 2000 *Kluwer Academic Publishers.*

in stereopairs. The majority of other reconstructed points approximate only a visually perceived stereomodel of the terrain. If human stereo perception is hampered due to partial occlusions or specific optical patterns then these terrain parts are interpolated from the valid surrounding parts, and such interpolation falls outside the reconstruction itself.

Some aspects of the use of ground control to validate computational terrain reconstruction are discussed below. Image features provided for stereo matching allow the deduction of simple confidence measures for reconstructed terrains, and only sufficiently confident terrain points should be validated by the available control data.

2. Confidence of Reconstructed Terrains

Let $\mathbf{g}^l = [g_{x,y}^l : (x,y) \in \mathbf{R}_l; g_{x,y}^l \in \mathbf{Q}]$ and $\mathbf{g}^r = [g_{x,y}^r : (x,y) \in \mathbf{R}_r; g_{x,y}^r \in \mathbf{Q}]$ where $\mathbf{R}_l$ and $\mathbf{R}_r$ are 2D rectangular finite lattices and $\mathbf{Q}$ denotes a finite set of gray values be the left and the right image of a horizontal digital stereopair, respectively. The corresponding epipolar lines of the horizontal pair are parallel to the x-axis and have the same y-coordinate of the pixels.

A digital parallax map (DPM) represents the digital terrain in terms of x-parallaxes, or disparities, of the corresponding pixels in the stereopair. Let $\mathbf{p} = [p_{x,y} : (x,y) \in \mathbf{R}; p_{x,y} \in \mathbf{\Gamma}]$ denote a DPM reconstructed from a digital stereopair $(\mathbf{g}^l, \mathbf{g}^r)$. Here, $\mathbf{R}$ is a 2D rectangular finite lattice and $\mathbf{\Gamma}$ denotes a finite set of possible x-parallaxes.

Let $\mathbf{g} = [g_{x,y} : (x,y) \in \mathbf{R}; g_{x,y} \in \mathbf{Q}]$ be the orthoimage of the terrain $\mathbf{p}$ estimated from the left $\mathbf{g}_l$ and right $\mathbf{g}_r$ images of the stereopair as follows:

$$g(x,y) = 0.5 \left(g_{x+\frac{p_{x,y}}{2},y}^l + g_{x-\frac{p_{x,y}}{2},y}^r \right).$$

Let $\mathbf{c} = [c_{x,y} : (x,y) \in \mathbf{R}; c_{x,y} \in \mathbf{C}]$ denote a confidence map for the DPM $\mathbf{p}$ with a confidence range $\mathbf{C} = [0, \ldots, c_{\max}]$.

High-confidence terrain points are represented in both images of a stereopair by closely matched signal combinations that have no like matches in the near neighborhood. Low- or zero-confidence points are present only in one image, due to partial occlusions, or correspond to uniform, shaded, or textured image regions. The validation should refer to quantitative confidence estimates for the reconstructed points. Computational and visual confidences may not agree but in both cases there is little point in comparing the low-confidence terrain parts to the ground control, even if it exists.

From the confidence standpoint, it makes no sense to contrast the "sparse" DPMs obtained by a feature-based stereo and the "dense" ones of an intensity-based stereo. Feature-based reconstruction involves only the high-confidence terrain points represented by characteristic features detected in both images. Other terrain points are assumed to be zero-confidence and are not considered at all. Intensity-based reconstruction forms dense DPMs but the confidence of their points may vary over a wide range. Thus in both approaches only a portion of the reconstructed points is of sufficient confidence to be compared to the ground control.

In (Bolles $et\ al.$, 1993), two confidence measures for the correlation-based matching are compared: (i) the difference $c_{x,y} = p_{x,y} - p_{x,y}^{s}$ between the best-match disparity $p_{x,y} \in \mathbf{p}$ and the second-best-match disparity $p_{x,y}^{s}$ for the same position (x, y) in the lattice $\mathbf{R}$ and (ii) the ratio $c_{x,y} = \theta_{x,y}/\alpha_{x,y}$ of the best-match cross-correlation value $\theta_{x,y}$ to the autocorrelation threshold $\alpha_{x,y}$.

Dynamic programming matching in (Gimel'farb, 1991) allows for an admissible range of ratios between the corresponding gray level differences along the epipolar lines in the images. It suggests the following confidence measure:

$$c_{x,y} = |g_{x,y} - g_{x_{\mathrm{b}},y}| \tag{1}$$

where (x, y) and (x_{b}, y) denote the planar coordinates of the neighboring binocularly visible points of the DPM in the reconstructed epipolar profile. The DPM point $(x_{\mathrm{b}}, y, p_{x_{\mathrm{b}},y})$ precedes the binocularly visible point $(x, y, p_{x,y})$ along the reconstructed profile. The "vertical" gray level differences take no part in this confidence measure because of the independent line-by-line matching. The measure in Eq. (1) is more convenient than the above-mentioned ones because it is based only on the image signals and the reconstructed DPM and does not involve details of the matching itself. But it does not resolve the repetitive matches.

3.   Ground Control – Pros and Cons

Pro. To evaluate the actual photogrammetric accuracy of terrain reconstruction, there is no way other than GCPs. Thus, by different estimates, from 20 to 50 percent of the total photogrammetric mapping costs are consumed by field surveys creating a permanent and well-described ground control (Wolf, 1974). First, a basic reference network of special control monuments and bench marks is established in the area to be mapped. The network, called the *basic control*, serves as a reference framework for subsequently establishing object space positions of specific GCPs which are detected in stereo images and form the *image control*. This is done by field surveys originating from the basic control network. The image control contains the corresponding image points which are easily identified and lie in favourable locations in the images and their 3D positions in the terrain.

Contra. Traditional photogrammetry defines GCPs in fuzzy terms such as "easily identified" or "characteristic topographic features" (Wolf, 1974). Therefore a choice of the GCPs is more an art than a science and is hardly formalized. Photogrammetric field surveys are conducted after a careful stereoscopic view of all the points selected in the images, and the objects that cause difficulties for stereoscopic depth perception are ill advised to be used as the GCPs (Wolf, 1974; Hsieh *et al.*, 1992).

Pro. National map standards require that about 90 percent of the most characteristic terrain features have to be plotted with a precision corresponding to a map scale. But usually no more than a few dozen actual GCPs per stereopair serve as a sufficient basic control for validating the reconstruction. Errors in human identification of the corresponding points are considered as negligibly small, and the visually perceived stereomodel is supposed to represent the true terrain.

Contra. In those regions where difficulties in stereoscopic depth perception exist, the mapped terrain differs from the true one, the error depending on spatial positions of the points taking part in the surface interpolation. Also, today's photogrammetic digital terrain models (DTM) are created by excluding "non-characteristic" objects like buildings or forest canopy so that the true surface may differ in principle from the available DTM.

Pro. To validate computational terrain reconstruction, usually partial image control is sufficient. Partial image control contains only the corresponding pixels which can be obtained by simple photogrammetric hardware or software (Aschwagen and Guggenbühl, 1992; Faugeras *et al.*, 1992; Hsieh *et al.*, 1992; Krzystek and Wild, 1992). This allows the circumventing of difficulties in finding actual GCPs and orienting stereo images with respect to available reference DTMs. Photogrammetric reconstruction combines a few easily detectable GCPs with a great quantity of only "stereo perceived" terrain points. These latter yield stable human stereo perception and can be precisely measured by photogrammetric techniques, but cannot be individually localized in each image. For brevity, they are called "stereo control points" (SCP) below. Partial image control contains mostly the SCPs which have a sufficiently high confidence.

Contra. In spite of long-term attempts to create reliable stereo image databases for validating and comparing stereo algorithms (see, for instance, (Bolles *et al.*, 1993; Faugeras *et al.*, 1992; Gülch, 1991; Hsieh *et al.*, 1992; Maimone and Shafer, 1996)) this problem is still open, as concerning terrain reconstruction. Expensive photogrammetric processing of the images is still necessary because their basic and image control are usually unavailable. Thus, most known databases include only a few oriented stereopairs of the Earth's surface with sufficiently dense and complete control data.

Conclusions. Human and computational definitions result in different ground controls to validate the reconstruction. It is hard or impossible to measure correct SCPs for partially occluded terrain points (Hsieh *et al.*, 1992) as well as to expect that these disparities will be correctly computed. Also, to check the reconstruction quality, terrain areas with no characteristic photometric features (for instance, homogeneous, with repetitive texture, or shaded areas) must be detected and analysed separately (Hsieh *et al.*, 1992; Krzystek and Wild, 1992). Therefore, it makes no sense to compare point-by-point the reconstructed and the reference DPMs if the confidences of terrain points are not involved. In the limiting case, the low-confidence points are excluded from stereo matching and validation (Bolles *et al.*, 1993).

The weakness of validation based only on high-confidence terrain points is that the valid terrain may not comply with our expectations to closely approximate a true terrain. But this follows from the ill-posedness of the binocular stereo problem and can hardly be overcome by using one or another regularizing heuristics. The confidence estimates suggest that computational and human stereo may be brought closer together if most of the visually confident SCPs possess high confidences in terms of image features for stereo matching, too.

If most of the reconstructed terrain points both are high-confidence and closely approximate the available SCPs then the remaining low-confidence parts can be reconstructed, if possible, by more adequate non-binocular (say, photometric) stereo. In this case, the confidence maps can guide the integration of different stereo techniques.

4. Experiments in Stereo Validation

We consider the reconstruction of the well-known "Pentagon" scene shown in Figure 1 by the dynamic programming algorithm in (Gimel'farb, 1991) with simultaneous inter-line processing. The partial reference DPM covering about 34% of the total area (namely, 89348 from 262144 points) has been formed by visual choice of 140 characteristic points in both the images and interpolation of the intermediate points. The similar reference DPM for the total scene in (Hsieh *et al.*, 1992) uses about 200 characteristic points. Both these reference DPMs do not contain many small structural details of the building and environs; these were not included to save time but are characteristic for a complete description of the scene. Nonetheless, our partial DPM includes the principal areas presenting difficulties for reconstruction (such as partially occluded and shaded areas around the building) but excludes less difficult open terrains with no easily detected GCPs.

Figure 2a shows the range image of the reference DPM reduced to the

Figure 1.   Stereopair "Pentagon" 512 × 512.

lattice $\mathbf{R}_l$ (the brighter the pixel, the higher the disparity). Black areas in Figure 2a are excluded from the reference DPM. Figure 2b presents the thresholded confidence map based on the gray level differences of Eq. (1). The threshold is set to 4 % of the gray range $[0, 255]$ that corresponds to the average gray level difference resolution of human vision. Such a threshold separates about 20% of the lattice points as the high-confidence SCPs (they are represented by black points in Figure 2b).

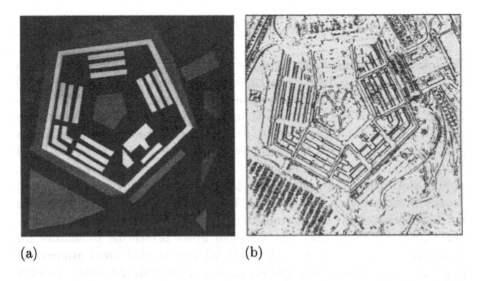

(a)   (b)

Figure 2.   Reference DPM (a) and the confidence map of 53274 points (b). The reference DPM contains 89348 points (34 % of the total area) and has the disparity range $[-8, 8]$.

Figure 3 shows the reconstructed DPM and reconstruction errors with respect to the reference DPM. A similar reconstructed DPM is obtained in (Hsieh *et al.*, 1992), too.

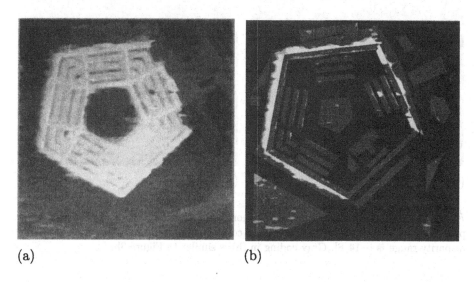

(a)   (b)

Figure 3.   Typical reconstructed DPM (a) and reconstruction errors (b). The disparity range is $[-13, 8]$. Gray coding in (b): black – the excluded areas, dark gray, light gray, and white – the reference areas with the absolute errors 0–1, 2–3, and ≥ 4, respectively.

The human and computational reconstruction differ in this case, mainly, in the shaded regions along the outer and inner walls of the building and along the right upper outer wall. Here, due to partial occlusion, the right image contains a bright narrow strip which is absent in the left image but quite similar to the binocularly visible roof details along the edge of this wall. As a result, the matching cannot discriminate between the present wrong signals and the absent true ones. Human vision avoids these ambiguities because it does not rely only on binocular stereo perception.

By a scrupulous selection of proper parameters, the dynamic programming algorithm results in DPMs which are somewhat closer to visual perception. Such a DPM and corresponding reconstruction errors are shown in Figure 4. But the DPM in Figure 3a is more typical in our experiments because the similar ones are obtained for the most part of the parameter combinations.

The error distributions in Figures 3 and 4 allow to conclude that the main "topographic landmarks" of Figure 2b result in correct matches. Errors of the reconstructed surface are caused mostly by homogeneous, shaded, or partially occluded areas. But, as Figures 2 and 3 show, the details in the right image, which have been matched – and quite plausibly

218 G. Gimel'farb

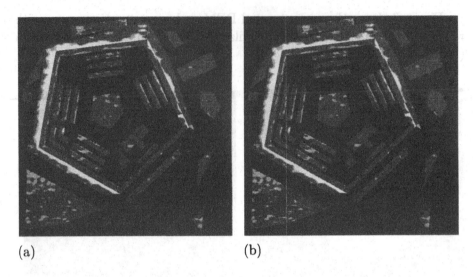

(a)　　　(b)

Figure 4. DPM obtained by selecting more appropriate parameters of the dynamic programming stereo reconstruction (a) and corresponding reconstruction errors (b). The disparity range is $[-14, 8]$. Gray coding in (b) is similar to Figure 3b.

– to the visible details in the left image instead of being treated as partially occluded ones, contain many high-confidence reconstructed points. Thus, without a prior geometric model showing the symmetries in the Pentagon building, it is hardly possible to avoid such deviations between the human and computational stereo. Most of the parts in this scene are closely approximated by the reconstructed DPM with absolute errors from 0 to 1.

It is worth noting that human visual perception simply eliminates many occluded details from stereo matching. This can be shown by artificial stereograms of this scene. Let $\mathbf{g}_A^l$ and $\mathbf{g}_A^r$ denote the artificial left and right image, respectively. The artificial left image is obtained by mapping the initial right image $\mathbf{g}^r$ onto the lattice $\mathbf{R}_l$ in accord with the reconstructed DPM in Figure 3a. The artificial right image is obtained by the similar mapping of the initial left image onto the lattice $\mathbf{R}_r$. Below, the following four stereograms are studied: $A_0 = (\mathbf{g}^l, \mathbf{g}_A^l)$, $A_1 = (\mathbf{g}^l, \mathbf{g}_A^r)$, $A_2 = (\mathbf{g}_A^l, \mathbf{g}_A^r)$, and A_3 – the random-dot stereogram obtained from a random-dot orthoimage with independent random gray levels in the pixels uniformly distributed over the range of $[0, 255]$.

As expected, the stereogram A_0 is visually perceived as the almost planar surface. Computational reconstruction results in a DPM with disparity range of $[-4, 4]$ (see Table I). The mean absolute error (m.a.e.) with respect to the zero-disparity plane is equal to 0.058 for the 53274 high-confidence SCPs in Figure 2b and 0.084 for all the scene of 262144 points.

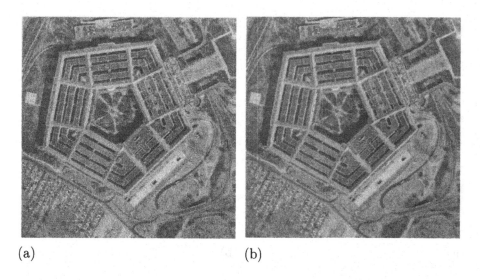

(a)   (b)

Figure 5.   Artificial stereogram A_0 "Pentagon" of the initial left image $\mathbf{g}^l$ (a) and the transformed initial right image $\mathbf{g}^l_A$ (b).

TABLE I.   Absolute reconstruction errors with respect to the zero-disparity plane for the artificial stereopair A_0.

Absolute error	0	1	2	3	4	m.a.e.
All 262144	242115	18233	1568	194	34	0.084
pixels (%)	(92.36)	(6.96)	(0.60)	(0.07)	(0.01)	
89348 reference	79690	8920	598	106	34	0.118
pixels (%)	(89.19)	(9.98)	(0.67)	(0.12)	(0.04)	
All 53274 SCPs	50322	2826	106	16	4	0.058
(%)	(94.46)	(5.30)	(0.20)	(0.03)	(0.01)	
High-confidence	17896	1251	53	9	4	0.073
19213 SCPs (%)	(93.15)	(6.50)	(0.28)	(0.05)	(0.02)	

Human stereo perception of the random-dot stereopair A_3 in Figure 8 agrees in general with the "true" DPM in Figure 3a although it is impossible to check local details for the random patterns. But the stereograms A_1 and A_2 (see Figures 6 and 7) result in visually perceived terrains which differ from the original scene only in minor details. Here, human stereo perception gives almost the same 3D appearance of the building and environs as the

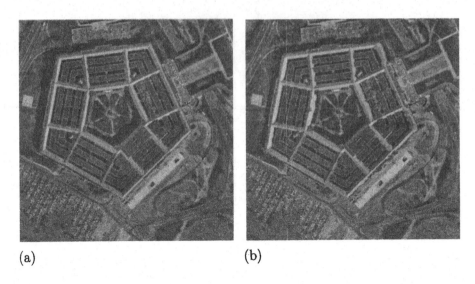

(a)   (b)

Figure 6. Artificial stereogram A_1 "Pentagon" of the initial left image $\mathbf{g}^l$ (a) and the transformed initial left image $\mathbf{g}_A^r$ (b).

initial pair in Figure 1. Therefore, at least in these cases human stereo is not purely binocular, and some visually found GCPs or SCPs may differ from the true control although most of the SCPs give the correct matching.

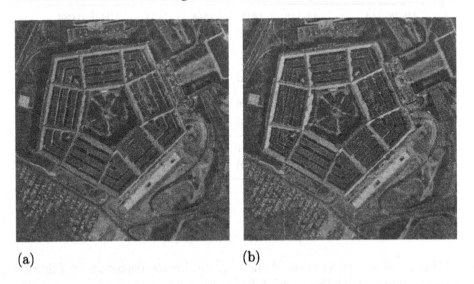

(a)   (b)

Figure 7. Artificial stereogram A_2 "Pentagon" of the transformed initial right image $\mathbf{g}_A^l$ (a) and the transformed initial left image $\mathbf{g}_A^r$ (b).

Figure 8.   Artificial random-dot stereogram A_3 "Pentagon".

TABLE II.   Absolute reconstruction errors with respect to the reference DPM for the initial stereopair in Figure 1.

Abs. error	0	1	2	3	4	5	6–10
Pixels	39997	34671	4563	1834	1559	1496	5228
(%)	(44.77)	(38.80)	(5.11)	(2.05)	(1.75)	(1.67)	(5.85)
SCPs	8509	7375	1046	292	234	198	1559
(%)	(44.29)	(38.39)	(5.44)	(1.52)	(1.22)	(1.03)	(8.11)

TABLE III.   Absolute reconstruction errors with respect to the reference DPM for the artificial stereogram A_1 in Figure 6.

Abs. error	0	1	2	3	4	5	6–9
Pixels	39944	35302	4029	1835	1567	1528	5143
(%)	(44.71)	(39.51)	(4.51)	(2.05)	(1.75)	(1.71)	(5.76)
SCPs	8514	7446	1021	280	244	181	1527
(%)	(44.31)	(38.76)	(5.31)	(1.46)	(1.27)	(0.94)	(7.85)

TABLE IV.   Absolute reconstruction errors with respect to the reference DPM for the artificial stereogram A_2 in Figure 7.

Abs. error	0	1	2	3	4	5	6–9
Pixels	35120	36381	6647	2680	2156	1356	5008
(%)	(39.31)	(40.72)	(7.44)	(3.00)	(2.41)	(1.52)	(5.60)
SCPs	7748	7550	1467	506	274	164	1504
(%)	(40.33)	(39.30)	(7.64)	(2.63)	(1.43)	(0.85)	(7.82)

TABLE V.   Absolute reconstruction errors with respect to the reference DPM for the artificial random-dot stereogram A_3 in Figure 8.

Abs. error	0	1	2	3	4	5	6–9
Pixels	35950	31930	11614	1769	1549	1500	5036
(%)	(40.24)	(35.74)	(13.00)	(1.98)	(1.73)	(1.68)	(5.63)
SCPs	7355	7011	2584	323	245	205	1490
(%)	(38.28)	(36.49)	(13.45)	(1.68)	(1.28)	(1.07)	(7.75)

TABLE VI.   Mean absolute reconstruction errors with respect to the total reference DPM (89348 points) and to the high-confidence SCPs in the reference area (19213 points).

Stereopair	Initial	A_1	A_2	A_3
Total reference DPM	1.138	1.124	1.216	1.243
High-confidence SCPs	1.249	1.202	1.293	1.342

Tables II – V show the distributions of the absolute errors of terrain reconstruction from the initial stereopair and three artificial stereograms $A_1 - A_3$ with respect to the reference DPM in Figure 2a. Table VI presents the corresponding mean absolute errors. The relatively high error rate is due to excluding from the reference DPM all the open areas which have no easily detected GCPs but yield stable stereo perception and possess many high-confidence SCPs. The DTM in Figure 4a gives almost the same mean absolute errors in spite of its better visual appearance: 1.129 with respect to the total reference DPM and 1.245 with respect to the high-confidence SCPs.

TABLE VII.   Absolute pixel-wise deviations between the DPMs reconstructed from the initial stereopair and artificial stereogram A_2.

Abs. deviation	0	1	2	3	4–11	m.a.d.
All 262144	183276	63904	11115	2504	1345	0.382
pixels (%)	(69.91)	(24.38)	(4.24)	(0.96)	(0.51)	
89348 reference	20858	27746	16726	7620	16398	1.917
pixels (%)	(23.35)	(31.05)	(18.72)	(8.53)	(18.35)	
All 53274 SCPs	39505	11924	1355	262	228	0.309
(%)	(74.15)	(22.38)	(2.54)	(0.49)	(0.44)	
High-confidence	13686	4799	490	119	119	0.349
19213 SCPs (%)	(71.23)	(24.98)	(2.55)	(0.62)	(0.62)	

To roughly estimate the overall reconstruction accuracy, the typical DTM reconstructed from the initial stereopair (see Figure 3a) is compared with the similar DPM but reconstructed from the artificial stereogram A_2 in Figure 7. Table VII presents the distributions of absolute deviations and mean absolute deviations (m.a.d.) between these DPMs. It follows that the chosen reference DPM really contains most places of the scene that are difficult for the stereo reconstruction. But one may expect that the mean absolute error over all the confident SCPs is about 0.35-0.4 of the disparity unit, or about 2.5 % of the disparity range $[-8, 8]$ for this scene.

5. Concluding remarks

Binocular stereo that searches for a terrain giving close matches between the images of a stereopair is an ill-posed computational problem in that

the same pair may be produced by many different terrains. Even if the
dense ground control be obtained by field surveys, the photogrammetric
terrain reconstruction hardly fits this control in regions with homogeneous
or repetitive visual patterns, without characteristic and easily detected
landmarks, or with objects, such as forest canopy and buildings, which are
removed from the control data. Therefore, even human photogrammetric
reconstruction approximates a true terrain mostly around the visually confident points. In the case of computational stereo, only the terrain points that
have sufficiently high confidences with respect to image matching should
be compared with the ground control.

An explicit usage of dense confidence maps for the terrain points both
in matching the images and in regularizing the desired solution may permit
bringing of human and computational stereo perception closer together.
The more "human-detected" GCPs or SCPs with high-confidence computed
values are present, the closer the validation is to our expectations. In other
words, stereo algorithms should be ranked not only relative to their performance in image matching for the terrain areas with a sufficiently high
confidence but also relative to the closeness of the human and computational definitions of the high-confidence terrain points. But because of the
ill-posedness of binocular stereo, there can always exist certain parts of a
reconstructed terrain that both are computationally high-confidence and
differ from the corresponding photogrammetric ground control.

Acknowledgements

This research was supported in part by the University of Auckland Research
Committee grant T01/XXXXX/62090/F3414076 and by the project UKR-
035-96 of the Deutsche Forschungsanstalt für Luft- und Raumfahrt e.V.
and the International Research and Training Centre of Information Technologies and Systems of the National Academy of Sciences and Ministry of
Education of Ukraine.

References

Ackermann, F. (1996) Techniques and strategies for DEM generation, *Digital Photogram-
metry: An Addendum to the Manual of Photogrammetry*, Greve, C. (ed.), ASPRS:
Bethesda, 135–141.
Aschwanden, P. and Guggenbühl, W. (1992) Experimental results from a comparative
study on correlation-type registration algorithms, *Robust Computer Vision: Quality of
Vision Algorithms*, Förstner, W. and Ruwiedel, S. (eds), Karlsruhe, Herbert Wichmann
Verlag, 268–289.
Bolles, R.C., Baker, H.H. and Hannah, M.J. (1993) The JISCT stereo evaluation,
Proc. DAPRA Image Understanding Workshop, Washington, DC, San Mateo, Morgan
Kaufmann, 263–274.

Faugeras, O., Fua, P., Hotz, B., Ma, R., Robert, L., Thonnat, M. and Zhang, Z. (1992) Quantitative and qualitative comparison of some area and feature-based stereo algorithms, *Robust Computer Vision: Quality of Vision Algorithms*, Förstner, W. and Ruwiedel, S. (eds), Karlsruhe, Herbert Wichmann Verlag, 1–26.

Förstner, W. (1996) 10 pros and cons against performance characterisation of vision algorithms, *Proc. Workshop on Performance Characteristics of Vision Algorithms*, Christensen, H.I., Förstner, W. and Madsen, C.B. (eds), Cambridge, UK, ECVNet, 13–29.

Gimel'farb, G.L. (1991) Intensity-based computer binocular stereo vision: signal models and algorithms, *Int. J. of Imaging Systems and Technology*, 3(3):189–200.

Gülch, E. (1991) Results of test on image matching of ISPRS WG III/4, *ISPRS Journal of Photogrammetry and Remote Sensing*, 46, 1–18.

Hsieh, Y.C., McKeown, D.M. and Perlant, F.P. (1992) Performance evaluation of scene registration and stereo matching for cartographic feature extraction, *IEEE PAMI*, 14(2):214–238.

Krzystek, P. and Wild, D. (1992) Experimental accuracy analysis of automatically measured digital terrain models, *Robust Computer Vision: Quality of Vision Algorithms*, Förstner, W. and Ruwiedel, S. (eds.), Karlsruhe, Herbert Wichmann Verlag, 372–390.

Maimone, M.W. and Shafer, S.A. (1996) A taxonomy for stereo computer vision experiments, *Proc. Workshop on Performance Characteristics of Vision Algorithms*, Christensen, H.I., Förstner, W. and Madsen, C.B. (eds), Cambridge, UK, ECVNet, 59–79.

Schenk, A.F. (1996) Automatic generation of DEM's, *Digital Photogrammetry: An Addendum to the Manual of Photogrammetry*, Greve, C. (ed.), Bethesda, ASPRS, 145–150.

Wolf, P.R. (1974) *Elements of Photogrammetry*, New York, McGraw-Hill.

PERFORMANCE ANALYSIS OF SHAPE RECOVERY
BY RANDOM SAMPLING AND VOTING

ATSUSHI IMIYA and KAZUHIKO KAWAMOTO
Dept. of Information and Image Sciences
Chiba University
1-33, Yayoi-cho, Inage-ku, 263-8522
Chiba, Japan

1. Introduction

In this chapter, we propose and evaluate a framework for recovering the
three-dimensional positions of points and edges of an object from a sequence
of images. For this image sequence, we assume that no point correspondences are *a priori* established. The usual point recovery from multifocal
images, which assumes predetermination of point correspondences among
image frames, achieves the detection of the three-dimensional points from
sequences of points. However, if we do not know point correspondences, we
must recover the three-dimensional points from a sequence of collections
of points which are sampled from each image. The purpose of the present
chapter thus is to develop a procedure for the grouping of points and the
extraction of a collection of curves in the spatio-temporal domain.

Attention has been given to shape recovery from a sequence of images as a data acquisition method for three-dimensional image database
systems and three-dimensional model generation for computer graphics
systems. The silhouette-based method (Laurentini, 1994) and the factorization method (Poelman and Kanade, 1987; Tomasi and Kanade, 1987)
are typical methods used for solving this type of shape recovery problem. The silhouette-based method enables the recovery of convex polyhedrons which encircle original objects without the need to assume the
predetermination of point correspondences for points in a sequence of images. Assuming the predetermination of point correspondences in an image
stream, the factorization method enables the recovery of nonconvex ob-

R. Klette et al. (eds.), Performance Characterization in Computer Vision, 227–240.

jects and the separation of objects in a three-dimensional space from an image stream (Kanatani, 1998a; Kanatani, 1998b). The recovered three-dimensional points are used as reference points for texture mapping or mosaic procedures for the generation of three-dimensional pictures. Therefore, point recovery in three-dimensional space from an image stream can be used as a basis for the generation of an artificial world.

A sequence of images defines a spatio-temporal image. In the spatio-temporal domain, each sequence of corresponding points among images defines a spatio-temporal curve. Therefore, an appropriate curve detection algorithm for spatio-temporal data enables the estimation of point correspondences of images. Since sample points in the spatio-temporal space are always noisy because of digitization and errors in the measurements, the curve detection algorithm must achieve an appropriate optimization. Furthermore, finding an analytical expression of these curves is usually impossible. Therefore, point correspondences are established by grouping noisy points in a discrete space.

For n two-dimensional images of an object, constraints exist for point correspondences for n equals 2, 3, or 4. For $n = 2$, the relation is called the epipolar geometry. For $n = 3$ and 4, these relations are described using n-focal tensors, which are called the tri-focal tensor and quad-focal tensor, respectively. For the estimation of point correspondences among images, it is possible to adopt any of these three constraints. The epipolar geometry is the simplest and computationally cheapest method, since the epipolar equation is a two-argument vector function whose arguments are two points from different images.

Even if a pair of points from a pair of images satisfies the epipolar condition, it does not necessarily mean that these points are the projections of one point. Therefore, for the estimation of point correspondences, we must solve an inverse problem. The sampling and voting procedure is the fundamental idea of the Hough transform. The Hough transform solves an inverse problem by collecting many pieces of evidence and evaluates these pieces of evidence by voting them to the accumulator space and detecting the peaks of voting scores. This procedure is capable of detecting curves from noisy data. Furthermore, the Hough transform realizes grouping of points by detecting the parameters of curves. This mathematical property implies that an extension of the Hough transform for curve detection in a higher dimensional space enables the detection of point correspondences to extract groups of points. Once point correspondences are established, it is possible to recover the three-dimensional positions of points.

The random sampling and voting method for line detection (Xu and Oja, 1993) and motion analysis (Imiya and Fermin, 1999) speeds up parameter detection and is low on memory requirements. Therefore, we also make our method for recovering of three-dimensional points from a sequence of images random. For the extraction of point correspondences between images, the correlation between two images is computed. For the peaks of correlation of images, the epipolar condition is applied to establish point correspondences. Our method directly checks the epipolar condition for the points on images and collects many pieces of evidence for inference.

2.   Recovery of Object from an Image Sequence

Given $\mathbf{R}^n$ to be n-dimensional Euclidean space, we denote by (x, y, z) an orthogonal coordinate system in $\mathbf{R}^3$. We call the system the world coordinate system. A vector $\boldsymbol{x}$ is denoted by $(x, y, z)^\top$, where $\top$ expresses the transpose of a vector. Setting $\boldsymbol{x}^\top \boldsymbol{y}$ to be the inner product of $\boldsymbol{x}$ and $\boldsymbol{y}$, we define the length of a vector as $|\boldsymbol{x}| = \sqrt{\boldsymbol{x}^\top \boldsymbol{x}}$. Thus, $|\boldsymbol{x} - \boldsymbol{y}|$ is the Euclidean distance between $\boldsymbol{x}$ and $\boldsymbol{y}$.

We assume that the camera motion and the camera center of each image are predetermined. Therefore, for a point $\tilde{\boldsymbol{x}}$ on an image I, setting $\boldsymbol{x}$ to be the expression of $\tilde{\boldsymbol{x}}$ in the world coordinate system, there exists a one-to-one mapping between $\boldsymbol{x}$ and $\tilde{\boldsymbol{x}}$, which is expressed as an affine transformation using the camera-motion parameters and the positions of the camera center. Let $\{I_i\}_{i=1}^n$ be a sequence of images whose camera centers are $\{e_i\}_{i=1}^n$ and $\{\boldsymbol{x}_{i\alpha}\}_{\alpha=1}^m$ for $i = 1, 2 \cdots$, and let n be sample points on each I_i. If we know point correspondences among the image sequence—that is, if we know that $\boldsymbol{x}_{i\alpha}$ and $\boldsymbol{x}_{j\beta}$ are the projections of the same point $\boldsymbol{p}$ in a three-dimensional space—we can recover the points $\boldsymbol{p}$ from a pair of points.

If $\boldsymbol{x}_{i\alpha}$ and $\boldsymbol{x}_{j\beta}$ are the projections of the same point $\boldsymbol{p}$, then $\boldsymbol{x}_{i\alpha}$ and $\boldsymbol{x}_{j\beta}$ satisfy the epipolar condition (Kanatani, 1993)

$$|\boldsymbol{x}_{i\alpha} - e_i \; \boldsymbol{x}_{j\beta} - e_j \; e_i - e_j| = 0. \tag{1}$$

Furthermore, setting $e_{ij} = (e_i - e_j)$, $n_{i\alpha} = (\boldsymbol{x}_{i\alpha} - e_i)$, and $m_{j\alpha} = n_{i\alpha}/|n_{i\alpha}|$, a point $\boldsymbol{p}$ on an object is recovered as

$$\boldsymbol{p} = e_i + \frac{e_{ij}^\top m_{i\alpha} - m_{i\alpha}^\top m_{j\beta} e_{ij}^\top m_{j\beta}}{1 - (m_{i\alpha}^\top m_{j\beta})^2} m_{i\alpha}, \tag{2}$$

since the point $\boldsymbol{p}$ is the common point of a pair of half lines

$$\boldsymbol{x} = e_i + s(\boldsymbol{x}_{i\alpha} - e_i), \quad \boldsymbol{x} = e_j + t(\boldsymbol{x}_{j\beta} - e_j), \; s, t \geq 0. \tag{3}$$

While projections of one point satisfy the epipolar condition, the reverse is not necessarily true. When the epipolar condition is satisfied by a pair of points, one may not conclude that these points are the projections of one point. In other words, these points are not necessarily corresponding points in a sequence of images. Furthermore, a pair of points which satisfy eq. (1) do not always define a point on an object. Therefore, if we do not know point correspondences, we require some additional information for the recovery of points on an object.

Even if point correspondences are not established, a half line

$$L_{i\alpha} = \{x | x = e_i + t(x_{i\alpha} - e_i),\ t \geq 0\} \tag{4}$$

passes through point p which yields point $x_{i\alpha}$ on image I_i as the projection. This mathematical property suggests the following primitive algorithm for the recovery of three-dimensional points from a collection of images.

1. Vote 1 for all points on $L_{i\alpha}$, for $i = 1, 2, \cdots, n$ and $\alpha = 1, 2, \cdots, m$ in $\mathbf{R}^3$.
2. Detect points whose voting scores are larger than the predetermined constant as points on an object.

This algorithm is based on the idea that a point computed as the common point of many lines which pass through the camera centers and points on images should be a point on an object. Points on the boundaries of images define the silhouettes of an object. Therefore, if we only adopt points on the boundaries of images, this algorithm is mathematically equivalent to the silhouette-based method. This algorithm is an extension of the classical Hough transform. In analogy with the Hough transform, we vote lines or curves in the voting stage. Furthermore, in the present algorithm, we treat the whole space in which an object exists as the accumulator space. Therefore, we should deal with many points on lines or curves which do not affect the peaks. The detected peaks determine the three-dimensional points.

Since the randomized Hough transform deals with points instead of lines or curves in the accumulator space (Xu and Oja, 1993), the randomized Hough transform is fast and requires a simple data structure in the accumulator space. Therefore, we propose a new voting method for the recovery of three-dimensional points without assuming point correspondences using the idea of the randomized Hough transform.

1. Randomly select a pair of points $x_{i\alpha}$ and $x_{j\beta}$.
2. Vote 1 to the point derived by eq. (2).
3. Detect points whose voting scores are larger than the predetermined constant as points on an object.

This algorithm is also based on the idea that if a point is computed as the common point of many lines which pass through the camera centers and the sample points on images, it should be a point on an object. However, this algorithm still selects pairs of points which do not solve eq. (3). If $(x_{i\alpha} - e_i)$

and $(\boldsymbol{x}_{j\beta} - \boldsymbol{e}_j)$ are linearly independent, then eq. (3) has a unique solution. Furthermore, if point pairs are the projections of one point, then they satisfy the epipolar condition. Therefore, we add steps which test correspondences of points.

1. Randomly select a pair of points $\boldsymbol{x}_{i\alpha}$ and $\boldsymbol{x}_{j\beta}$.
2. Check whether $(\boldsymbol{x}_{i\alpha} - \boldsymbol{e}_i)$ and $(\boldsymbol{x}_{j\beta} - \boldsymbol{e}_j)$ are linearly independent.
3. Check whether $\boldsymbol{x}_{i\alpha}$ and $\boldsymbol{x}_{j\beta}$ satisfy the epipolar condition.
4. If a pair of points satisfies two conditions, vote 1 to the point derived by eq. (2).
5. Detect points whose voting scores are larger than the predetermined constant as points on an object.

For the recovery of spatial points from a sequence of images, a pair of points observed from different directions is necessary. However, these points do not provide the sufficient condition for the recovery of spatial points. Therefore, in these algorithms, we detect the peaks in the accumulator space. This is an inference procedure from many pieces of evidence.

According to the data structure of the randomized Hough transform, we express the structure of cells in the accumulator in the manner of the binary tree, using the dictionary order of points in a three-dimensional Euclidean space. Furthermore, we dynamically maintain the cells which hold the voting scores, that is, starting from the null tree, we successively add a cell which holds the voting score as a new leaf of this tree. Expressing accumulator space by this data structure, we can reduce memory requirements for the voting procedure and quickly search for the peaks of voting scores. The following is the pseudo-PASCAL expression of the main algorithm.

```
 1 :   while  k ≠ N  do
 2 :     begin
 3 :       select randomly x_iα and x_jβ
 4 :       if  |n_iα n_jβ e_ij| ≤ ε for n_iα ≠ λn_jβ   then
 5 :         compute p
 6 :         vote 1 to p
 7 :       if there are peaks higher than γ   then
 8 :         output peaks
 9 :       k := k + 1
10 :     end
```

Here γ and N are parameters which define the height of peaks and the maximum number of iterations, respectively. Furthermore, ε is an appropriately small positive number which defines the accuracy of the epipolar condition. In line 5, we adopt the following dynamic voting procedure for an appropriately small positive number δ which defines the resolution of the point distribution in the world coordinate system.

```
1 :   for  q and a new point p   do
2 :     begin
3 :       if  there exists  q s.t. |p − q| ≤ δ   then
4 :         vote 1 to q
5 :       else
6 :         vote 1 to p
7 :     end
```

Setting $x_{i\alpha}$ and $x_{j\beta}$ to be the projections of the same point onto images I_i and I_j, respectively, we express this relation by $x_{i\alpha} \sim x_{j\beta}$. This is a binary relation which defines a collection of points. A sequence which is derived by this binary relation defines a curve in the spatio-temporal space. Furthermore, this relation realizes grouping of points. The Hough transform also realizes the grouping of points by estimating parameters of lines and curves. Therefore, our algorithm can be considered as an extension of the Hough transform. In our case, the parameters are three-dimensional points on an object, since these points are detected as the peaks in the accumulator space.

Since our images are sampled and digitized, their boundaries are polygons. Furthermore, in an artificial environment, many objects consist of planes and polyhedrons. The projections of these objects have edges which connect vertices. Here, a vertex is the common point of at least two lines or line segments on images or objects. Therefore, the detection of the edges of an object from a sequence of images is essential for the reconstruction of polyhedral objects. Next, we derive an algorithm for the recovery of edges of polyhedral objects from the edges on images.

Setting $x_{i\alpha}$ and $x_{i\beta}$ to be projections of points p_α and p_β, respectively, if p_α and p_β are connected by an edge $\overline{p_\alpha p_\beta}$, then $x_{i\alpha}$ and $x_{i\beta}$ are connected by an edge $\overline{x_{i\alpha} x_{i\beta}}$. However, if a pair of points on an image is connected by an edge, this does not necessarily conclude that three-dimensional recovered points are connected by an edge. Therefore, the edge detection from an image sequence is achieved by solving an inverse problem. It is also possible to solve this problem using the random sampling and voting procedure. We can estimate the spatial edge connecting a pair of spatial points whose projections are connected by an edge. For this procedure, we need labels which indicate the pairs of spatial points and their projections on images. This leads to the following edge detection algorithm described in pseudo-PASCAL manner. In this algorithm $(p, x_{i\alpha})$ expresses the relation that $x_{i\alpha}$ is the projection of point p onto image I_i.

```
 1 :   while   k ≠ N   do
 2 :   begin
 3 :      randomly select x_{iα} and x_{iβ}
 4 :      if |n_{iα} n_{jβ} e_{ij}| ≤ ε for n_{iα} ≠ λn_{jβ}   then
 5 :         compute p
 6 :         vote 1 to (p, x_{iα}) and (p, x_{jβ})
 7 :      if  there are peaks higher than gamma   then
 8 :         output peaks
 9 :      for   a pair (p_α, x_{iα}) and (p_β, x_{iβ})   do
10 :         begin
11 :            if  x_{iα} and x_{iβ} are connected by an edge   then
12 :               vote 1 to the edge \overline{p_α p_β}
13 :         end
14 :      k := k + 1
15 :   end
```

3. Parameter Bounds

The positive number ε in the procedure for point detection mainly depends on quantization errors on imaging planes. For a positive real number Δ, we set $|a_k| \leq \Delta$ for $k = i, j$, and

$$n'_{i\alpha} = n_{i\alpha} + a_i, \ n'_{j\beta} = n_{j\beta} + a_j. \tag{5}$$

These perturbations of vectors derive the relation

$$|n'_{i\alpha} n'_{j\beta} e_{ij}| \cong |n_{i\alpha} n_{j\beta} e_{ij}| + |a_i n_{j\beta} e_{ij}| + |n_{i\alpha} a_j e_{ij}|$$
$$\leq (|n_{i\alpha}| + |n_{j\beta}|)|e_{ij}|\Delta$$
$$\cong 2fR\Delta. \tag{6}$$

Furthermore, since

$$m'^{\mathsf{T}}_{i\alpha} m'_{j\beta} \cong m^{\mathsf{T}}_{i\alpha} m_{i\beta} + m^{\mathsf{T}}_{i\alpha} a_j + m^{\mathsf{T}}_{j\beta} a_i \tag{7}$$

and

$$\frac{1}{1 - (m'^{\mathsf{T}}_{i\alpha} m'_{j\beta})^2} \cong \frac{1}{1 - (m^{\mathsf{T}}_{i\alpha} m_{j\beta})^2} \left(1 + 2\frac{m^{\mathsf{T}}_{i\alpha} a_j + m^{\mathsf{T}}_{j\beta} a_i}{1 - (m^{\mathsf{T}}_{i\beta} m_{j\beta})^2} \right) \tag{8}$$

we obtain

$$|x' - x| \leq 4\frac{R}{f}\Delta \tag{9}$$

for

$$x' = e_i + \frac{e_{ij}^\top m'_{i\alpha} - m'^\top_{i\alpha} m'_{j\beta} e_{ij}^\top m'_{j\beta}}{1 - (m'^\top_{i\alpha} m'_{j\beta})^2} m'_{i\beta}. \qquad (10)$$

If we assume there is no error in the positions of the camera centers, these relations derive the following theorems, setting $R = \max_{ij} |e_{ij}|$. For the parameter of point detection, we have the relation $\varepsilon \leq 2fR\Delta$.

THEOREM 18.1. *For the parameter of the voting procedure, we have the relation $\delta \leq 4\frac{R}{f}\Delta$.*

These two theorems imply that it is possible to detect an accurate solution by increasing the image resolution. Furthermore, the resolution of accumulator space δ depends on the resolution of imaging planes.

4. Numerical Examples

Using synthetic data, we evaluated the performance of our algorithms. First, we recovered points on the edges of a three-dimensional object shown in Figure 1 from a sequence of images $\{(a), (b), (c), (d), (e), (f)\}$ shown in Figure 2. In Figure 2, each image is expressed in pixel form. Therefore, points on each image are digitized. In this example, we assume that our camera is calibrated. The recovered points indicates that qualitatively, our algorithm for the point recovery performs well.

Second, we show the edge-recovery algorithm. In this example, we recovered the vertices and edges of random convex polyhedrons. According to the algorithm, we recovered the spatial positions of points and edges as pairs of vertices.

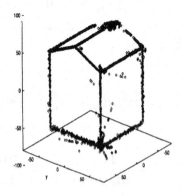

Figure 1. Recovered points in a three-dimensional space.

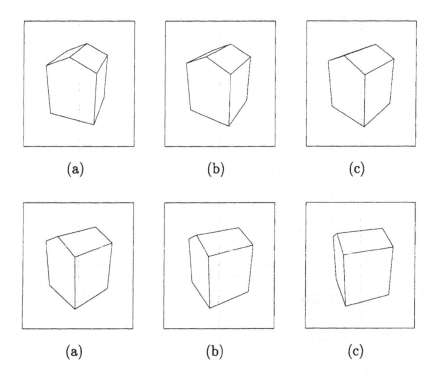

(a)   (b)   (c)

(a)   (b)   (c)

Figure 2.   An image sequence for recovering points in Figure 1.

We generated random convex polyhedrons according to the following algorithm.

1. Generate 3 random variables A, B, and C, such that $-1 < A, B, C < 1$.
2. Normalize the length of vector $(A, B, C)^{\top}$ using the relations

$$ a = \frac{A}{\sqrt{A^2 + B^2 + C^2}}, \ b = \frac{B}{\sqrt{A^2 + B^2 + C^2}}, \ c = \frac{C}{\sqrt{A^2 + B^2 + C^2}}. $$

3. Map the vector $\boldsymbol{a} = (a, b, c)^{\top}$ on to the unit sphere.
4. After generating an appropriate number of points on the unit sphere, construct the convex hull of these points.

Since vertices of polyhedrons lie on the unit sphere, the edges of the convex hull connect three neighboring points and all faces of the convex hull are triangles. In the numerical examples, we set the number of random points on the unit sphere from 4 to 12. Therefore, we generated the random n-hedrons for $n = 4, 5, \cdots, 12$. In Figure 3, we illustrate some images of these polyhedrons, where CH_n expresses the generated random n-hedron.

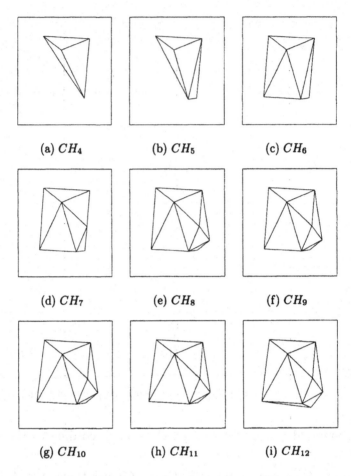

(a) CH_4 (b) CH_5 (c) CH_6

(d) CH_7 (e) CH_8 (f) CH_9

(g) CH_{10} (h) CH_{11} (i) CH_{12}

Figure 3.   Some images of random convex polyhedrons.

Figure 4 illustrates the spatial distribution of the camera centers. The camera centers lie on two parallel circles. There are 12 points on each circle, so we have, at most, 24 views for each polyhedron. The distribution of the camera centers determines the density of data in the spatio-temporal domain. Therefore, the distribution of the camera centers affects the accuracy of the recovered points. For the analysis of the stability of the algorithm against the distribution of data in the spatio-temporal domain, we prepared three cases of camera-center distributions.

(a) We used all 24 views.
(b) We used uniformly distributed $2n$ views for n-hedra.
(c) We used nonuniformly distributed $2n$ views for n-hedra.

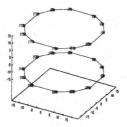

Figure 4. The positions of the camera centers.

The positions of camera centers for (b) and (c) are listed in Table I. Figures 5a, 5b, and 5c show the error curves for the various numbers of vertices. From these curves, we conclude that the uniformly distributed camera centers are necessary for accurate recovery. Furthermore, a collection of a large number of images accurately recovers three-dimensional points. In the figures, the errors are of the order of 10^{-6}. The results show that for the synthetic data, our algorithm works well up to digitization errors.

We evaluated the error using

$$\epsilon = \frac{1}{m} \sum_{k=1}^{m} \frac{|v_k - w_k|}{|v_k|}, \tag{11}$$

where w_k is the recovered vertex of v_k. It is possible to compute this error while checking the correspondences among original vertices and reconstructed vertices. Point correspondences between the original vertices

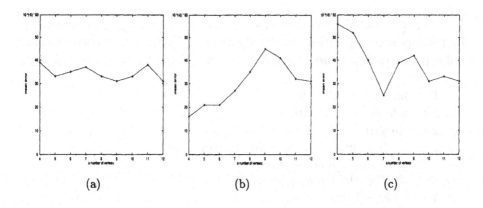

Figure 5. Error analysis, numerical errors vs the number of vertices of polyhedrons.

TABLE I.   The distributions of camera centers for the recovery of shapes.

CH_4		CH_5		CH_6		CH_7		CH_8		CH_9		CH_{10}		CH_{11}		CH_{12}	
(b)	(c)	(b)	(c)	(b)	(c)	(b)	(c)	(b)	(c)	(b)	(c)	(b)	(c)	(b)	(c)	(b)	(c)
(9)	(3)	(5)	(3)	(1)	(3)	(1)	(3)	(1)	(3)	(1)	(3)	(1)	(3)	(1)	(2)	(1)	(1)
(11)	(4)	(7)	(4)	(3)	(4)	(3)	(4)	(3)	(4)	(3)	(4)	(3)	(4)	(3)	(3)	(2)	(2)
(13)	(9)	(9)	(9)	(5)	(9)	(5)	(6)	(5)	(5)	(5)	(5)	(5)	(5)	(5)	(4)	(3)	(3)
(15)	(10)	(11)	(10)	(7)	(10)	(7)	(9)	(7)	(6)	(7)	(6)	(7)	(6)	(6)	(5)	(4)	(4)
(17)	(15)	(13)	(12)	(9)	(11)	(9)	(10)	(9)	(9)	(9)	(8)	(9)	(7)	(7)	(6)	(5)	(5)
(19)	(16)	(15)	(15)	(11)	(12)	(11)	(11)	(11)	(10)	(11)	(9)	(10)	(8)	(8)	(7)	(6)	(6)
(21)	(21)	(17)	(16)	(13)	(15)	(13)	(12)	(13)	(11)	(13)	(10)	(11)	(9)	(9)	(8)	(7)	(7)
(23)	(22)	(19)	(21)	(15)	(16)	(15)	(15)	(15)	(12)	(14)	(11)	(12)	(10)	(10)	(9)	(8)	(8)
		(21)	(22)	(17)	(21)	(17)	(16)	(17)	(15)	(15)	(12)	(13)	(11)	(11)	(10)	(9)	(9)
		(23)	(23)	(19)	(22)	(19)	(17)	(18)	(16)	(16)	(15)	(14)	(12)	(12)	(11)	(10)	(10)
				(21)	(23)	(21)	(21)	(19)	(17)	(17)	(16)	(15)	(15)	(13)	(12)	(11)	(11)
				(23)	(24)	(22)	(22)	(20)	(18)	(18)	(17)	(16)	(16)	(14)	(13)	(12)	(12)
						(23)	(23)	(21)	(21)	(19)	(18)	(17)	(17)	(15)	(15)	(13)	(13)
						(24)	(24)	(22)	(22)	(20)	(19)	(18)	(18)	(16)	(16)	(14)	(14)
								(23)	(23)	(21)	(21)	(19)	(19)	(17)	(17)	(15)	(15)
								(24)	(24)	(22)	(22)	(20)	(20)	(18)	(18)	(16)	(16)
										(23)	(23)	(21)	(21)	(19)	(19)	(17)	(17)
										(23)	(24)	(22)	(22)	(20)	(20)	(18)	(18)
												(23)	(23)	(21)	(21)	(19)	(19)
												(24)	(24)	(22)	(22)	(20)	(20)
														(23)	(23)	(21)	(21)
														(24)	(24)	(22)	(22)
																(23)	(23)
																(24)	(24)

$V = \{\boldsymbol{v}_k\}_{k=1}^m$ and the reconstructed vertices $V' = \{\boldsymbol{w}_{k'}\}_{k'=1}^m$ are computed by the following algorithm. In the algorithm, C is the set of corresponding point pairs, and $\boldsymbol{v}_k \leftrightarrow \boldsymbol{w}_{k'}$ indicates that $\boldsymbol{w}_{k'}$ is the recovered vertex of $\boldsymbol{v}_k$.

```
1 :   set k := 1, C := ∅
2 :   while  V ≠ ∅  do
3 :   begin
4 :       find w_k' which minimizes |v_k − w_k'|
5 :       C := C ∪ {v_k ↔ w_k'}
6 :       V' := V' \ {w_k'}
7 :       k := k + 1
8 :   end
```

We assumed that the camera is calibrated. However, using an uncalibrated camera, we can likewise recover the correct topological relations of points (Kanatani, 1999). Then, using additional *a priori* information for objects, for instance that the angles between planes are right angles (Sugihara, 1986; Huffman, 1977a; Huffman, 1977b), we can completely recover the objects using an uncalibrated camera. This assumption is valid, if we deal with a world consisting of parallelepipeds and cubes on a plane.

5. Conclusions

In this chapter, we have proposed a randomized algorithm for object recovery from a sequence of images without predetermining the point correspondences among frames. We estimated errors which are mainly caused by quantization in the computer. This analysis clarified the bound of parameters in the algorithm and the size of cells for the voting process. Furthermore, we proposed a dynamic data structure in the accumulator space which enables to decrease the memory size for peak detection.

Experimental results with synthetic data show that our algorithms perform satisfactorily. Consequently, for a calibrated camera and little noise and measurement errors, our algorithm is expected to be applicable to practical data. Our method preserves the same mathematical expression regardless of the projection geometries, because we only use points on images and the camera centers for the recovery of spatial points. This is one distinct advantage of our method. Furthermore, our method only requires little memory for a large amount of spatio-temporal data.

Setting x to be the variable in n-dimensional Euclidean space, the Hough transform is used for the estimation of parameters $\{a_i\}_{i=1}^{k}$ for a collection of equations,

$$f_i(a_i, x) = 0, \ i = 1, 2, \cdots, k \tag{12}$$

from a large number of samples $\{x_j\}_{j=1}^{m}$ such that $m \gg k \geq 1$, using the voting procedure. The equation $f_i(x, a_i) = 0$ is called the model for the parameter estimation. The two-dimensional conventional models for the Hough transform are planar line and conic. The Euclidean motion equation such that $y = Rx + t$ is expressed in the form,

$$\begin{pmatrix} R & t & -I & o \\ o^\top & 1 & o^\top & -1 \end{pmatrix} \begin{pmatrix} x \\ 1 \\ y \\ 1 \end{pmatrix} = 0, \tag{13}$$

where I is the identity matrix and o is the null vector. This description implies that motion analysis from a collection of noisy corresponding points is a model-fitting problem (Kanatani, 1993). Random sampling and voting thus achieves the estimation of the motion parameters R and t of a Euclidean motion from a large number of samples (Imiya and Fermin, 1999).

The shape recovery dealt with in this study did not assume any models for objects which are recovered from a sequence of images. Therefore, our results show that the sampling and voting procedure is also effective for problems in machine vision that do not rely on an *a priori* model.

Acknowledgements

Part of this research was conducted while the first author was visiting the Department of Applied Mathematics, University of Hamburg. Thanks are due to Professor Dr. Ulrich Eckhardt for his hospitality. While staying in Germany the author was supported by the Program for Overseas Researchers of the Ministry of Education, Science, Sport, and Culture of Japan. Furthermore, the authors express their thanks to the editors for their useful comments to improve the final manuscript.

References

Huffman, D.A. (1977) A duality concept for the analysis of polyhedral sceans, Elcock, E.W. and Michie, D. (eds.), *Machine Inteligence 8*, Ellis Horwood Ltd., Sussex, England, 475–492.

Huffman, D.A. (1977) Realizable configurations of lines in pictures of polyhedra, Elcock, E.W. and Michie, D. (eds.), *Machine Inteligence 8*, Ellis Horwood Ltd., Sussex, England, 493–509.

Imiya, A. and Fermin, I. (1999) Motion analysis by random sampling and voting process, *Computer Vision and Image Understanding*, 73:309–328.

Kanatani, K. (1993) *Geometric Computation for Machine Vision*, Oxford University Press, Oxford.

Kanatani, K. (1998a) Factorization method without factorization: from orthographic to perspective, *Technical Report of IEICE Japan*, PRMU98-26.

Kanatani, K. (1998b) Factorization method without factorization: multibody segmentation, *Technical Report of IEICE Japan*, PRMU98-117.

Kanatani, K. (1999) personal communication.

Laurentini, A. (1994) The visual hull concept for silhouette-based image understanding, *IEEE PAMI*, 16:150–162.

Poelman, C.J. and Kanade, T. (1997) A perspective factorization method for shape and motion recovery, *IEEE PAMI*, 19:206–218.

Sugihara, K. (1986) *Machine Interpretation of Line Drawings*, MIT Press, Cambridge.

Tomasi, C. and Kanade, T. (1997) Shape and motion from image streams under orthography, a factorization method, *International Journal of Computer Vision*, 9:137–154.

Xu, L. and Oja, E. (1993) Randomized Hough transform (RHT): Basic mechanisms, algorithms, and computational complexites, *CVGIP, Image Understanding*, 57:131–154.

MULTIGRID CONVERGENCE BASED EVALUATION
OF SURFACE APPROXIMATIONS

REINHARD KLETTE, FENG WU and SHAO-ZHENG ZHOU
Dept. of Computer Science
The University of Auckland
Tamaki Campus, Private Bag 92019
Auckland, New Zealand

1. Introduction

This chapter reports on multigrid convergence based evaluation of surface approximations, and this approach is suggested to be one option for model-based evaluations of computer vision algorithms in general. This criterion is in common use in numerical mathematics. In general, algorithms may be judged according to criteria, such as methodological complexity of underlying theory, expected time for implementation, or run-time behaviour and storage requirements of the implemented algorithm. Accuracy is an important criterion as well, and this can be modeled as convergence towards the true value for grid based calculations.

Multigrid convergence is discussed in this chapter for two different tasks. Both tasks are related to 3D surface approximation or 3D surface recovery. The existence of convergent algorithms is discussed for

(i) the problems of volume and surface area measurement for Jordan sets or 3D objects based on *regular, orthogonal grids*: convergent volume measurement is known since the end of the 19th century, see, e.g. (Scherer, 1922), a provable convergent surface area measurement is a recent result in the theory of geometric approximations (Sloboda, 1997), and

(ii) the problem of (incremental) 3D reconstructions of Jordan faces based on *irregular grids*: many techniques in computer vision are directed on reconstructing 3D surfaces; assuming that these techniques have successfully reconstructed a surface, then the next step is to represent

R. Klette et al. (eds.), Performance Characterization in Computer Vision, 241–253.
© 2000 *Kluwer Academic Publishers.*

this surface under special (e.g. incremental transmission) conditions (Zhou and Klette, 1997).

Jordan faces, surfaces and sets are proper models for discussing surface approximations. In this chapter, a *3D object* in three-dimensional Euclidean space is a simply-connected compact set bounded by a (measurable) Jordan surface (Mangoldt and Knopp, 1965; Klette, 1998). A Jordan surface is a finite union of Jordan faces.

3D objects are studied based on given digitizations in computer vision, image analysis, or object visualisation. Regular grids are of common use in computer vision or image analysis. Let $\mathbf{Z}_r = \{m \cdot 2^{-r} : m \in \mathbf{Z}\}$, where $\mathbf{Z}$ is the set of integers and $r = 0, 1, 2, \dots$ specifies the grid constant 2^{-r}. The set $\mathbf{Z}_r^n$ is the set of all *r-grid points* in n-dimensional Euclidean space. Each r-grid point $(x_1, \dots, x_n)$ defines a topological unit (a *grid cube*)

$$\mathbf{C}_r(x_1, \dots, x_n) = \{(y_1, \dots, y_n) : (x_i - .5)2^{-r} \le y_i \le (x_i + .5)2^{-r}, i = 1, \dots, n\}.$$

Irregular grids, as Voronoi or Delaunay diagrams, are favoured for object visualisations. However, the vertices of these irregular grids are often restricted to be points in $\mathbf{Z}_r^n$.

In evaluations we have to compare truth against obtained results. A *true entity* is normally well-defined within mathematical studies, however in general not in image analysis applications. In this chapter we propose and study a *mathematical problem*: A multigrid digitization model for 3D objects, either regular (Klette, 1985) or irregular (Zhou and Klette, 1997), assumes an ideal mapping of a given set (the "true 3D object" having the "true surface area", the "true samples of a terrain map", etc.) into a finite digital data set. The problem consists in analyzing the behavior of a given technique or algorithm assuming finer and finer grid resolution. For regular grids we reduce the grid constant 2^{-r} (= side length of grid cubes). It converges towards zero for $r = 0, 1, 2, \dots$ For irregular grids we increase the number of vertices until we reach a given maximum of sample points. Assume that a Jordan face is given by values at these n vertices, and a specification of their neighbourhoods. The task consists in finding a series of approximation surfaces with m vertices ($m \in (i, i + 1, \dots, n); i > 0$) with approximation error ε_m and $\varepsilon_1 \ge \varepsilon_2 \ge \dots \ge \varepsilon_m \ge 0$, for $m \le n$. Convergence studies are directed on cases $n \to \infty$.

The convergence issue addressed in this chapter corresponds not only to the continued progress in imaging technology. It is of special value also for understanding the *soundness of a chosen approach*. The convergence problem may be studied based on experimental evaluations of approaches, algorithms or implementations, using, e.g., synthetic 3D objects and a selected digitization model. We provide a few examples for this evaluation strategy in the following two sections. These examples may highlight the importance of convergence studies. Produced data sheets as the provided ones may be of value for practical situations. However a theoretical analysis leads (hopefully) to the complete answers as illustrated in the next section. Irregular approximations may be based on the suggested minimum Jordan surface constructions as well if the correct surface area of the reconstructed surface is desirable.

2. Regular Grids: Volume and Surface Area

Algorithms for measuring surface area and volume should be consistent for different data sets of the same object taken at different spatial resolutions. In our image analysis applications we do expect that measured surface areas and volume values converge towards proper values assuming an increase in spatial resolution. For example, volume or surface area measurement should not be influenced by the rotation angle of the given 3D object. Feature convergence is of fundamental importance in 3D object analysis.

2.1. DIGITIZATION

Grid cube inclusion (with respect to the topological interior of the given 3D object) and *grid cube intersection* digitizations are assumed for 3D objects having interior points. Grid cube inclusion digitization defines the *inner interior* $I_r^-(\Theta)$ of a given 3D object Θ, and grid cube intersection digitization defines the *outer interior* $I_r^+(\Theta)$. The resulting digital objects can be described as being grid continua, see, e.g., (Sloboda *et al.*, 1998).

We consider synthetic objects. Assume, e.g., a cube Θ as a given three-dimensional set and a digitization of this cube with respect to a chosen grid constant. The resulting isothetic polyhedron $I_r^-(\Theta)$ contains all grid cubes C_r which are completely inside of the given cube. An *isothetic polyhedral Jordan surface* is a polyhedral Jordan surface whose faces are coplanar either with the XY-, XZ-, or YZ-plane. An *isothetic polyhedron* is a polyhedron whose boundary is an isothetic polyhedral Jordan surface.

2.2. VOLUME AND SURFACE AREA OF CELLULAR COMPLEXES

Classical results can be cited for grid based volume area measurement, see, e.g. (Scherer, 1922). The convergence of these measurements towards the true value is illustrated in Figure 1. For different rotational positions we have digitized a cube, for $r \to \infty$. For each grid constant 2^{-r} we calculate the volume of the resulting cellular complex as number of 3D cells contained in the cellular complex times the volume 2^{-3r} of a single 3D cell.

Now we consider the total surface area of all the two-dimensional surface cells of the resulting cellular complexes $I_r^-(\Theta)$ (Figure 2) using the

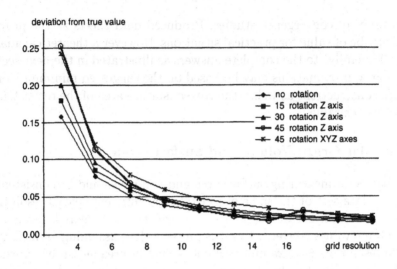

Figure 1. Measured convergence of volume values $(1+d)s$ of cellular complexes towards the true value s, the volume of the given cube, where d is the deviation

algorithm published in (Artzy *et al.*, 1981) for visiting all 2D surface cells exactly once. The figure shows that there is "obvious convergence" in all cases. However, the measured surface area values depend upon the given rotation of the cube, and the deviation d can be equal to 0 if the cube was in isothetic position, and about 0.90 (i.e. 90% error!) if it was rotated

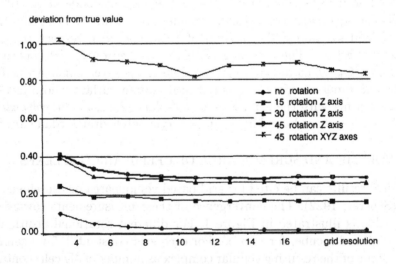

Figure 2. Each curve points out that there is "obvious convergence" of the measured surface area of all the two-dimensional surface faces of the cellular complex for a given rotational position of the cube towards a value $(1+d)s$

about 45° with respect to X, Y, and Z axes. These values are inappropriate for estimating a surface area of a cube if the rotation angle is unknown. A surface area measurement based on counts of 2D surface cells of 3D cellular complexes is *not related* to the true surface area value. Since the length of a staircase function remains constant and does not converge towards the length of a diagonal straight line segment, similar statements can be said for using counts of two-dimensional faces on the surface of three-dimensional cellular complexes with respect of estimates of the surface area of the three-dimensional set represented by this cellular complex.

2.3. USE OF LOCAL APPROXIMATIONS

The inclusion of diagonal elements into a simple local approximation approach as "8-neighborhood contours" in 2D, or local triangulations in 3D does not resolve this inconsistency. The use of a marching cubes algorithm (Lorensen and Cline, 1987) is one of the options of local approximations. Each elementary grid cube, defined by eight grid points, is treated according to a look-up table for defining triangular or planar surface patches within this elementary grid cube. A marching cubes algorithm determines the surface by deciding how the surface intersects a local configuration of eight voxels. A surface is assumed to intersect such a local configuration in 2^8 different ways (i.e. no multiple intersections of grid edges), and these can be represented as fourteen major cases with respect to rotational symmetry. Alternatively a method developed by Wyvill *et al.* (1986) calculates the contour chains immediately without using a look-up table of all 2^8 different cases. The fourteen basic configurations originally suggested by Lorensen and Cline (1987) are incomplete. Occasionally they generate surfaces with holes.

Ambiguities of the marching cube look-up tables are discussed in (Wilhelms and Gelder, 1994). See (Sloboda *et al.*, 1998) for local situations of marching cubes configurations where at least two different topological interpretations are possible. More important, the calculated values do not converge towards the true value as illustrated in Figure 3. The surface area and the volume is calculated based on values for the different look-up table situations.

A marching tetrahedra algorithm was suggested in (Roberts, 1993). It generates more triangles than the marching cubes algorithm in general. Trilinear interpolation functions were used in (Cheng, 1997) for the different basic cases of the marching cubes algorithm. In comparison to the linear marching cube algorithm (Heiden *et al.*, 1991) the accuracy of the calculated surface area was slightly improved by using this trilinear marching cubes algorithm, which was confirmed for a few synthetic Jordan faces.

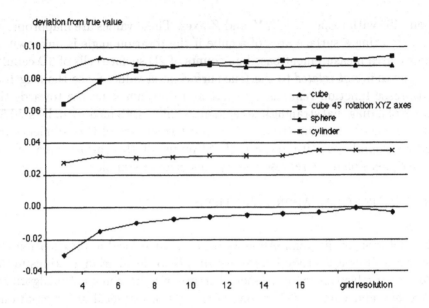

Figure 3. These curves show "obvious convergence" of the measured surface area towards values $(1 + d)s$ where a marching cubes algorithm was applied to two cubes in different rotational positions, a sphere and a cylinder

These local approximation techniques, such as marching cubes algorithms, also generate very large numbers of triangles what restricts their practical use for high resolution data, such as, e.g., in computer assisted radiology.

2.4. MINIMUM JORDAN SURFACES

The surface area measurement approach introduced in (Sloboda, 1997), is basically different from the concepts in digital geometry, or from local surface approximation approaches. It is a special approach towards global surface approximations. Assume that both the inner interior $I_r^-(\Theta)$ and the outer interior $I_r^+(\Theta)$ of a given 3D object Θ are simply connected sets with respect to the given grid constant 2^{-r}. Assume $I_r^-(\Theta) \neq \emptyset$. Let $S_r^-(\Theta)$ be the surface of the isothetic polyhedron $I_r^-(\Theta)$, and let $S_r^+(\Theta)$ be the surface of the isothetic polyhedron $I_r^+(\Theta)$. Then it holds that

$$\emptyset \subset I_r^-(\Theta) \subset I(I_r^+(\Theta)) \quad \text{and} \quad S_r^-(\Theta) \cap S_r^+(\Theta) = \emptyset,$$

and $I_r^+(\Theta) \setminus I(I_r^-(\Theta))$ is an isothetic polyhedron homomorphic with the torus.

Furthermore, let d_∞ be the Hausdorff-Chebyshev metric for sets of points A, B of points which originated from the point metric d_∞ as introduced in (Hausdorff, 1927),

$$d_\infty(A, B) = \max\left\{\max_{p \in A} \min_{q \in B} d_\infty(p, q), \max_{p \in B} \min_{q \in A} d_\infty(p, q)\right\},$$

where $d_\infty(p, q) = \max\{|x_1 - y_1|, |x_2 - y_2|\}$, for $p = (x_1, x_2)$ and $q = (y_1, y_2)$. It follows that

$$d_\infty(S_r^-(\Theta), S_r^+(\Theta)) \geq 2^{-r}.$$

Under the given assumptions the constraint $d_\infty(S_r^-(\Theta), S_r(\Theta)) = 2^{-r}$ leads to a uniquely defined isothetic polyhedron $I_r(\Theta)$, with $I_r^-(\Theta) \subset I_r(\Theta) \subseteq I_r^+(\Theta)$. Let $S_r(\Theta)$ be the surface of $I_r(\Theta)$. The difference set (*r-boundary* of Θ)

$$B_r(\Theta) = I_r(\Theta) \setminus I(I_r^-(\Theta))$$

is a *simple closed two-dimensional grid continuum* as defined in (Sloboda *et al.*, 1998). We denote it by $B_r(\Theta) = [S_1, S_2]$, where $\partial B_r(\Theta) = S_1 \cup S_2$ with $S_1 = S_r^-(\Theta)$ as inner simple closed polyhedral surface, and $S_2 = S_r(\Theta)$ as outer closed polyhedral surface. Note the proper inclusion $\emptyset \subset I_r^-(\Theta)$.

The *surface area of a simple closed two-dimensional grid continuum* $[S_1, S_2]$ in R^3 is defined to be the surface area of a minimum area polyhedral simple closed Jordan surface in $[S_1, S_2]$ containing S_1. The following two theorems were proved in (Sloboda, 1997):

THEOREM 19.1. *Assume a simple closed two-dimensional grid continuum* $[S_1, S_2]$. *Then there exists a uniquely defined polyhedral simple closed Jordan surface with minimum area in* $[S_1, S_2]$ *containing* S_1.

We call this the *minimum Jordan surface* of $B_r(\Theta) = [S_1, S_2]$. Thus a Jordan set Θ and a grid resolution $r \geq r_0$ (such that both the inner interior $I_r^-(\Theta)$ and the outer interior $I_r^+(\Theta)$ are simply connected sets) uniquely define a minimum Jordan surface $MJS_r(\Theta)$ having a surface area of $J_{area}(MJS_r(\Theta))$.

THEOREM 19.2. *For any smooth Jordan set* $\Theta \subset \mathbf{R}^3$ *it holds that*

$$J_{area}(\partial\Theta) = \lim_{r \to \infty} J_{area}(MJS_r(\Theta))$$

where $MJS_r(\Theta)$ *is the minimum Jordan surface for resolution* $r \geq r_0$.

The theorem is also valid for Jordan surfaces which possess a finite number of edges. A polyhedron has its surface area well defined. Altogether this specifies a sound (i.e. convergence and convergence towards the proper value) procedure for calculating the surface area of a digitized Jordan set.

3. Reconstruction of Multiresolution Terrain Surfaces

Multiresolution terrain surfaces are especially useful for fast rendering, real-time display, and progressive transmission. The general problem of reconstructing surfaces of 3D objects is restricted to a situation where only Jordan faces (terrain surfaces or height maps) have to be reconstructed. However, accuracy may be modeled by convergence considerations as well. We herein propose and discuss a greedy refinement approach for the reconstruction of multiresolution terrain surfaces or the progressive reconstruction of terrain surfaces.

3.1. BRIEF REVIEW OF TECHNIQUES

The problem of triangulating a set of points to produce a surface is a well researched topic in computer graphics and computational geometry. We mainly explore ways of triangulating a set of points to represent, visualize and transmit terrain surfaces in multiresolutions. A terrain surface can be modelled in much simpler ways comparing with a generic $3D$ surface. A terrain surface can be represented by a single-valued bivariate function over the domain of the model. The reconstruction of terrain surface is referred to as a $2\frac{1}{2}D$ modelling problem. A terrain is mathematically described by a height function: $\Phi : \mathbf{D} \subseteq \mathbf{R}^2 \to \mathbf{R}$. In practical applications, the function Φ is sampled at a finite set of points $P = \{p_1, ..., p_n\} \subset \mathbf{D}$. In this case the function Φ can be defined piecewise over a subdivision Σ of $\mathbf{D}$ with vertices in P. The main goal is to reconstruct terrain surfaces at high speed, from an initial coarse resolution to full resolution. In the context of this chapter we are interested in evaluating the quality increase during this process of approaching full resolution, and in convergence properties assuming that the number n of sample points goes to infinity.

There are various algorithms for terrain simplification or polygonal simplification. They can be categorized as

(i) *simple uniform grid methods* as cellular complexes or marching cubes (see section above): They are simple for representation but impossible for real-time display or fast rendering. Downsampling can be used to represent simplified models, but the quality is not desirable.

(ii) *hierarchical subdivision methods*: They include quad-tree, k-d tree, and hierarchical triangulation data structures. However, it seems difficult for them to maintain the continuity of the surface where patches of surfaces with different resolutions meet.

(iii) *feature methods*: Using local features for simplification like curvatures does not produce results with globally desirable quality. See also the integration problem as stated in (Klette, 1998).

(iv) *decimation methods* (Ciampalini *et al.*, 1997): Those algorithms simply remove the point whose absence adds the smallest error to the appoximation. The main advantage for decimation methods is that they can remove several points in one step. However, their retriangulation seems complicated and not efficient enough.

(v) *refinement techniques* (Garland and Heckbert, 1995; Cignoni *et al.*, 1997): They start with a minimal approximation, then progressively refine it by adding the point which will introduce the minimal sum of approximation errors to the approximation, and executing Delaunay retriangulation. Delaunay retriangulations are necessary because they are essential for the future numerical interpolation or retrieval of elevation values and for minimizing the aliazing problems in terrain surfaces' visualization or display.

Refinement techniques are especially suitable for the reconstruction of surfaces with continuous resolutions.

3.2. GREEDY REFINEMENT

We designed a refinement algorithm following the general greedy refinement approach with Delaunay retriangulation. Let P be a finite set of points in $\mathbf{R}^2$. The main idea of the greedy refinement algorithm can be described as follows. An initial triangulation T is constructed first, whose vertex set is composed of all extreme points of the convex hull of P. The triangulation or mesh is then refined through the iterative insertion of new vertices, one at a time (at each iteration, select the point p which will introduce the minimal sum of all approximation errors). The triangulation or mesh is updated accordingly by Delaunay retriangulation. This refinement process continues until the specified goal (e.g. error threshold) is met.

For measuring the approximation error we take the absolute value of the difference between the interpolated elevation value $S(x, y)$ and the actual elevation value $\Phi(x, y)$ at vertex $\mathbf{p} = (x, y)$ as the approximation error $\varepsilon(x, y) = |\Phi(x, y) - S(x, y)|$. For every grid cell Δ containing a certain set of points, say $\{p_0, ..., p_k\}$, we select that point p_i, with $0 \le i \le k$, whose selection as a new triangulation point will introduce the minimal sum σ of approximation errors of the remaining vertices inside of cell Δ. Then the new error measure value of cell Δ is $\sigma = \varepsilon_0 + ... + \varepsilon_{i-1} + \varepsilon_{i+1} + ... + \varepsilon_k$.

Every cell has three vertices, three possible neighbors, points which are included inside, its error measure value, and the sum of error measure values of all the other cells. The mesh is composed of cells. The mesh's array stores all pointers of cells (dead and living). A heap data structure makes the greedy refinement more efficient. The heap includes pairs of (ErrorMeasure e, long p), where p points to to a cell's position in the Array of Cells.

Figure 4 shows an original terrain model which is created by the bivariate function $\Phi(x, y) = \frac{1}{2}(sin(3x)^4 + cos(2y)^4 + sin(x+4y)^3 - cos(xy)^5) + 1.0$, where $x \in [0, 1]$, and $y \in [0, 1]$.

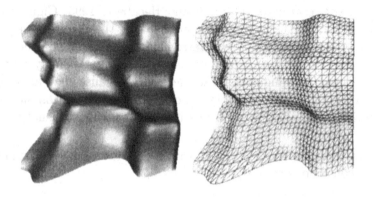

Figure 4.   Original terrain surface with 32x32 = 1024 vertices

Figure 5 indicates the refinement result refined with 15% percent of the vertices of the original model. It is evident that Figure 5 keeps the important features like peaks and valleys in Figure 4.

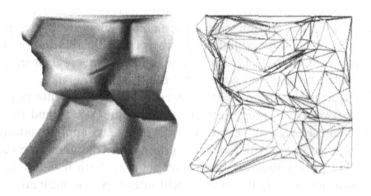

Figure 5.   Approximation using 15% percent of the original model's vertices

From the Figure 6, it is clear that the approximation errors are initially reduced drastically when the vertex number increases, but slowly after 30 percent of vertices has been added. However, this behavior depends on the chosen global approximation error measure. This figure also illustrates that the median error measure is of interest only for less than 50 percent of vertices because it is always zero afterwards.

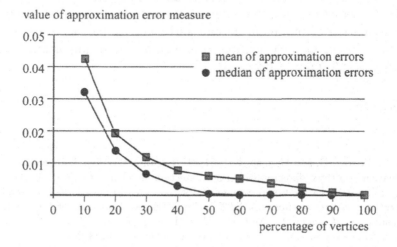

Figure 6. Approximation errors vs percentage of original model's vertices

A more general study would require to analyse such algorithms for classes of surface functions Φ, and for increases in the number n of sampling points with $n \to \infty$.

4. Conclusion

Surface measurement for 3D objects Θ can be based on calculating minimum Jordan surfaces as shown in (Sloboda, 1997). Marching cubes algorithms do not lead to convergent approximations of minimum Jordan surfaces, and surfaces of isothetic polyhedrons $I_r^-(\Theta)$ or $I_r^+(\Theta)$ are unrelated to the true surface area value.

Surface reconstructions of Jordan faces (e.g. terrain models), given by just a finite number n of surface points, can be obtained by incremental reconstructions based on irregular grids where the selection procedure of points, and the surface approximation strategy decides about the error vs percentage of vertices ratio. We proposed a revised greedy refinement approach to progressively reconstruct terrain surfaces. We employed a very straightforward data structure. Based on greedy refinement and our data structure, we can reconstruct a family of terrain surfaces with continuous resolutions, which are necessary for fast-rendering and real-time display. This will support more detailed studies of convergence behaviour (i.e. convergence with respect to an increase in the number of given sample points) in the future.

Assuming that the original n sample points form a regular $N \times N$ grid and that the given surface (terrain) is non-convex, a local triangulation is not convergent towards the true surface area value if $N \to \infty$. This follows by similar experiments as illustrated for the marching cubes algorithm. The calculation of minimum Jordan surfaces may be suggested instead. Accurate surface area calculations are, e.g., of crucial importance in GIS (geographic information systems).

References

Artzy, E., Frieder, G. and Herman, G.T. (1981) The theory, design, implementation and evaluation of a three-dimensional surface detection algorithm, *CGIP*, 15:1–24.

Cheng, S.L. (1997) Estimation of volume and surface area from isosurface, *Postgraduate project in computer science*, 415.780 FC, CITR Tamaki, University of Auckland.

Ciampalini, A., Cignoni, P., Montani, C. and Scopigno, R. (1997) Multiresolution decimation based on global error, *The Visual Computer*, 13:228–246.

Cignoni, P., Puppo, E. and Scopigno, R. (1997) Representation and Visualization of Terrain Surfaces at Variable Resolution, *The Visual Computer*, 13:199–217.

Garland, M. and Heckbert, P.S. (1995) Fast polygonal approximations of terrains and height fields, Carnegie Mellon University, School of Computer Science, TR CMU-CS-95-181.

Hausdorff, F. (1927) *Mengenlehre*, Walter de Gruyter & Co., Berlin, page 100.

Heiden, W., Goetze, T. and Brickmann, J. (1991) 'Marching cube' Algorithmen zur schnellen Generierung von Isoflächen auf der Basis dreidimensionaler Datenfelder, *Visualisierung von Volumendaten*, Springer, Berlin, 112–117.

Klette, R. (1985) The m-dimensional grid point space, *CVGIP*, 30:1–12.

Klette, R. (1998) Approximation and representation of 3D objects, *Advances in Digital and Computational Geometry*, Klette, R., Rosenfeld, A. and Sloboda, F. (eds.), Springer, Singapore, 161–194.

Lorensen, W.E. and Cline, H.E. (1987) Marching cubes: a high resolution 3D surface construction algorithm, *Computer Graphics*, 21:163–169.

Mangoldt, H.v. and Knopp, K. (1965) *Einführung in die höhere Mathematik*, III. Band, 12. Auflage, Leipzig, S. Hirzel Verlag.

Roberts, J.C. (1993) An overview of rendering from volume data including surface and volume rendering, TR, University of Kent at Canterbury.

Scherer, W. (1922) Ein Satz über Gitter und Volumen, *Mathematische Annalen*, 86:99–107.

Sloboda, F. (1997) On Approximation of Jordan Surfaces; a Topological Approach, Int. Memo, CITR group, Tamaki, The University of Auckland.

Sloboda, F., Zaťko, B.B. and Klette, R. (1998) On the topology of grid continua, *Proc. Vision Geometry VII*, SPIE Volume 3454, San Diego, 20-22 July, 52–63.

Wilhelms, J. and Gelder, A.V. (1994) Topological considerations in isosurface generation, Baskin Center for Computer Engineering and Information Sciences, University of California, Santa Cruz, UCSC-CRL-94-31.

Wyvill, G., McPheeters, C. and Wyvill, B. (1986) Data structures for soft objects, *The Visual Computer*, 2:227–234.

Zhou, S.-Z. and Klette, R. (1997) Multiresolution surface reconstruction: edge collapsing + simplification envelopes, Keynote paper, DICTA/IVCNZ'97 conference, Albany/Auckland, December, Massey University, Dep. of Production Technology, 397–402.

SENSITIVITY ANALYSIS OF PROJECTIVE GEOMETRY 3D RECONSTRUCTION

MARIA PETROU, NIKOLAOS GEORGIS and
JOSEF KITTLER
School of Electronic Engineering
Information Technology and Mathematics
University of Surrey
Guildford GU2 5XH, UK

1. Introduction

One of the most powerful methods for 3D scene reconstruction without camera calibration is based on Projective Geometry (Coxeter, 1994; Faugeras, 1992; Mohr and Arbogast, 1991) This method is very elegant and relies on the solution of a series of non-linear equations that allow the determination of the 3D coordinates of a point given the identity and 3D position of at least 6 reference points relying on two intersecting planes. The method is an ideal testbed for application of the variance propagation methodology for performance evaluation proposed by Haralick (1994).

As it relies on the solution of non-linear equations, it is possible that a small error in the input data may be damped for certain parameter settings, or significantly amplified for others. Our whole approach is based on the simple idea that if $y = f(x)$, then an error Δx in x will give rise to an error $\Delta y = \frac{df}{dx} \Delta x$. If $f(x)$ is a nonlinear equation, $\frac{df}{dx}$ is a function of x and our aim is to identify ranges of values of x for which $\frac{df}{dx}$ is significantly larger than 1, and therefore acts as an error amplifier.

In this chapter we follow this process step by step so that we can draw useful conclusions and guidelines for the practical applications of the method of projective geometry-based 3D reconstruction. We shall start by giving a brief overview of the approach and then we shall proceed in the stage of error analysis.

R. Klette et al. (eds.), Performance Characterization in Computer Vision, 255–264.

2. An overview of Projective Geometry

If A, B, C and D are four co-linear points on a line l, then their *cross-ratio* is defined as:

$$[A, B, C, D] = \frac{\overline{CA}}{\overline{CB}} \cdot \frac{\overline{DB}}{\overline{DA}} \qquad (1)$$

where $\overline{AB}$ is the *directed Euclidean distance* of the two points A and B. This means that $\overline{AB} = -\overline{BA}$.

If the barycentric representation of the line is used, i.e.: $\vec{b} + \mu\vec{d} = \vec{r}$, where $\vec{r}$ is the position vector of any point along the line, μ is a parameter taking real values and $\vec{b}$ and $\vec{d}$ are the (known) base and directional vectors of the line respectively, then the cross-ratio can be expressed in terms of the μ value of every point in the line l, that is:

$$[A, B, C, D] = \frac{\mu_C - \mu_A}{\mu_C - \mu_B} \cdot \frac{\mu_D - \mu_B}{\mu_D - \mu_A} \qquad (2)$$

where μ_A is the value of parameter μ in the equation of the line for which point A is defined and μ_B, μ_C and μ_D have similar interpretation.

The cross-ratio of a pencil of four coplanar lines l_1, l_2, l_3 and l_4 going through O, is defined as the cross-ratio $[A, B, C, D]$ of the points of intersection of the four lines with any line l not going through O. This is independent of the choice of line l.

Let A, B, C and D be four coplanar points, no three of them co-linear. These points are said to define a projective coordinate system in the plane, $\mathcal{P}$, they belong to. The projective coordinates (k_1, k_2, k_3) of any point P of $\mathcal{P}$ are the three real numbers defined as:

$$k_1 = [CA, CB, CD, CP]$$
$$k_2 = [AB, AC, AD, AP]$$
$$k_3 = [BC, BA, BD, BP] \qquad (3)$$

Any point on $\mathcal{P}$ is uniquely referenced by any two of its projective coordinates with respect to the $\{A, B, C, D\}$ projective coordinate system.

The cross-ratio of a pencil of four planes $\mathcal{P}_1$, $\mathcal{P}_2$, $\mathcal{P}_3$ and $\mathcal{P}_4$, is defined as the cross-ratio of their four lines of intersection with any plane not passing through the common line of the pencil. This is independent of the crossing plane.

A pencil of planes is formed when we view a scene under perspective projection. For simplicity we adopt the pinhole camera model with a frontal image plane (Figure 1).

We assume that we are viewing down the negative z axis with the centre of projection being the origin of the coordinate system O. The coordinate

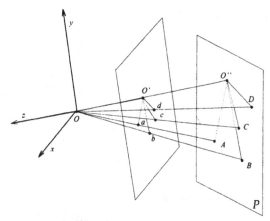

Figure 1.   The cross-ratio is preserved by perspective projection.

axes Ox and Oy are parallel to the image plane which is based at a distance f (the focal length of the camera) away from the origin and in the direction of viewing. The implication is that the cross ratio is preserved under perspective projection.

We shall describe next how projective geometry techniques can be used to reconstruct a point P in the world coordinate system, given its left and right image coordinates as well as the exact position and correspondences of a set of eight reference points $\{A, B, C, D, E, F, G, H\}$, consisting of two sets of 4 coplanar points, $\{A, B, C, D\}$ and $\{E, F, G, H\}$.

First, the equation of the viewing line OP (Figure 2) has to be determined. Consider the first set of reference points $\{A, B, C, D\}$ and their projections to the left image plane $\{a, b, c, d\}$. The projective coordinates k_1, k_2 and k_3 of image point p with respect to the $\{a, b, c, d\}$ projective coordinate system can be determined according to equation (3). If P_1 is the intersection of the viewing line OP with the $ABCD$ plane, the coordinates of P_1 can be determined. The projective coordinates of p in the image plane with respect to $\{a, b, c, d\}$ are the same as the projective coordinates of P_1 in the $ABCD$ plane with respect to $\{A, B, C, D\}$ because of the cross-ratio invariance under perspective projection (Georgis *et al.*, 1998). Therefore, since the exact positions of A, B, C and D are known, so are the world coordinates of P_1.

In a similar way the coordinates of point P_2 can be calculated. The two points P_1 and P_2 are enough to define uniquely the equation of the viewing line OP.

This way, the viewing line for the left image can be obtained. Working in exactly the same manner the right viewing line can also be determined. Then, it is trivial to find P as it is the point of intersection of the two viewing lines.

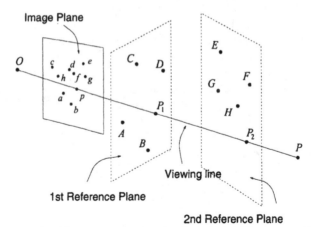

Figure 2. Each of the reference planes contains four reference points.

3. Error Analysis

Using the analytical formulae of the approach, one can compute the way the error propagates at each stage of the reconstruction process, starting from the estimation of the error in the calculation of the projective coordinates on the image plane, and finishing with the estimation of the error in the calculation of the 3D position of point P (Georgis *et al.*, 1998).

Let us now assume that each of the reference pairs of coordinates can be estimated with error normally distributed with zero mean and covariance matrix

$$\Sigma = \begin{pmatrix} \sigma_{xx}^2 & 0 \\ 0 & \sigma_{yy}^2 \end{pmatrix}. \tag{4}$$

Then, we can calculate (to the linear approximation) the variance of the error distribution in the calculation of each one of the projective coordinates. The coefficients which multiply σ_{xx}^2 and σ_{yy}^2 in these expressions are the error amplification factors. As long as these factors are less or equal to 1 the error is damped but when these factors exceed 1, the error is amplified.

In Figures 3a, 3b and 3c we fixed the positions of the reference points and allowed the position of p to scan the whole plane. We mark with black the regions where amplification of the error is expected due to k_1, k_2 and k_3 respectively. Figure 3d is simply an overlap of the previous three figures showing in black the regions where at least one projective coordinate is very sensitive to noise. Finally, the most meaningful result is shown in 3e where the median of the first three figures is plotted, indicating the regions where 2 projective coordinates are unstable. Notice that apart from three small regions around points a, b and c where two projective coordinates are with

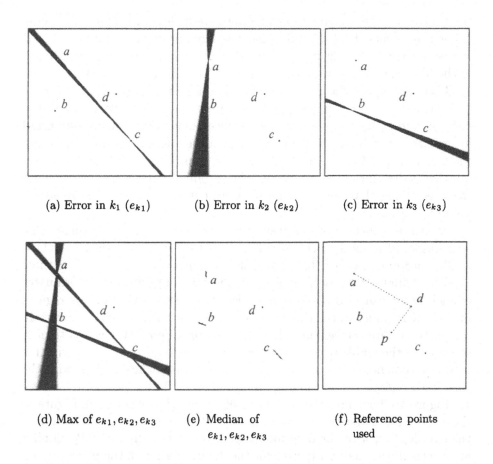

(a) Error in k_1 (e_{k1})   (b) Error in k_2 (e_{k2})   (c) Error in k_3 (e_{k3})

(d) Max of e_{k1}, e_{k2}, e_{k3} (e) Median of   (f) Reference points
                                   e_{k1}, e_{k2}, e_{k3} used

Figure 3.   Regions of instability for the determination of k.

amplified error, in all other places p has at least two projective coordinates which can be calculated reliably, and this is enough for the determination of the position of point P in the 3D space.

By permuting the reference points a, b, c and d (see Figure 3f) one can obtain $4! = 24$ distinct valued cross–ratios although only two of them are independent. For each configuration the k_i cross–ratio was obtained as well as the associated amplification factors. It was noticed that they could be divided into pairs with identical noise behaviour. That is because only the choice of the first line of the pencil of the four makes a difference as far as the expected error is concerned. That can also be seen in Figures 3a-c where the most unstable regions were across the first line of the pencil of lines used in the determination of k_1-k_3.

Let us say that of the three projective coordinates of p computed in the previous stage, k_1 and k_2 are the most reliable. Point P_1 on the plane defined by points A, B, C and D has the same projective coordinates and the next stage is to find its 3D Cartesian coordinates from the knowledge of the 3D Cartesian coordinates of A, B, C and D and k_1 and k_2.

Then, we repeat the process we followed for the construction of Figure 3: As point p scans the image plane we compute at each position the values of k_1, k_2 and k_3 for the given set of reference points. Since we are interested in the error introduced by the inaccuracy in the reference points, we ignore the fact that k_1, k_2 and k_3 are themselves computed with some error, we put their values into the formulae for the amplification factors and calculate them assuming that the error in all coordinate positions of the reference points is the same.

We define a local coordinate system (x', y') on the reference plane. The coordinates of a point in the world coordinate system are related to these local coordinates with a linear transformation. After the errors in these local coordinates have been computed, the errors in the world coordinates of each point can also be computed. Figure 4a shows the various regions in the image plane where the coefficient of σ_{xx}^2 for $P_{1x'}$ is within a certain range. White are the regions where the amplification factor is less than 1, so they are the stable regions. Each shade corresponds to the amplification factor incremented by 1 as we move away from the white region, with the very dark regions corresponding to error amplification factors more than 10. Figure 4b illustrates the coefficient of σ_{yy}^2 for $P_{1x'}$, whereas in Figure 4c the maximum of the two coefficients is plotted to give us an indication of the expected error in the determination of the x' coordinate of P_1. Similar analysis is illustrated in Figure 5 for the determination of the y' coordinate of P_1, and finally, in Figure 6 the regions where both x' and y' coordinates of P_1 are expected to have maximum robustness to noise are shown in white. Similar analysis can be performed to find the instability regions for P_2 but the only difference with the above analysis is the reference points used. After computing the 3D coordinates of P_1, the intersection of the left viewing line, l, with the first reference plane, we repeat the process and calculate the 3D coordinates of P_2, the intersection of the viewing line with the second reference plane. Similarly, the coordinates of P_1' and P_2', the intersection of the right viewing line, l', with the first and second reference plane respectively, can be found. Therefore, the equations of both the left and right viewing lines can be found:

$$\vec{L} = \vec{P_1} + \mu_L (\vec{P_2} - \vec{P_1}) \tag{5}$$

$$\vec{L'} = \vec{P_1'} + \mu_{L'} (\vec{P_2'} - \vec{P_1'}) \tag{6}$$

where $\vec{L}$ is any point on the left viewing line l and $\vec{L'}$ is any point on the right viewing line l'.

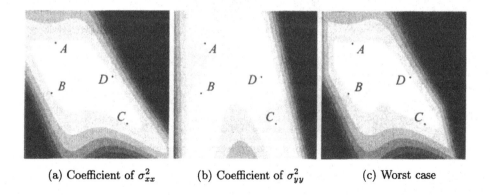

(a) Coefficient of σ_{xx}^2 (b) Coefficient of σ_{yy}^2 (c) Worst case

Figure 4.   Regions of instability for determination of $P_{1x'}$.

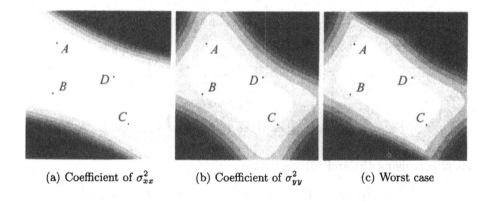

(a) Coefficient of σ_{xx}^2 (b) Coefficient of σ_{yy}^2 (c) Worst case

Figure 5.   Regions of instability for determination of $P_{1y'}$.

In theory, the two viewing lines l and l' must be coplanar because they intersect at point P. However, in general this is not true, mainly due to various errors introduced in the first two steps of the projective reconstruction process. In this case the coordinates of P can be estimated by finding the midpoint of the minimum-length line segment, LL', which has one of its endpoint on l and the other on l' (see Figure 7). The direction vector of the line segment LL', $\vec{d}$, is the cross product of the direction vectors of l and l'. Therefore,

$$\vec{d} = (\vec{P_2} - \vec{P_1}) \times (\vec{P_2'} - \vec{P_1'}) \qquad (7)$$

The vector difference $(\vec{L} - \vec{L'})$ should result in $\vec{d}$ scaled by a constant α.

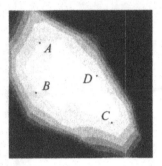

Figure 6. Worst case for reconstruction of P_1.

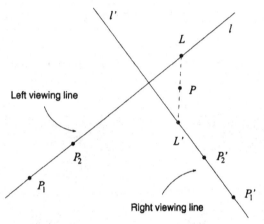

Figure 7. Determination of the 3D coordinates of point P.

Therefore, using (5) and (6) we obtain

$$\left[\vec{P_1} + \mu_L (\vec{P_2} - \vec{P_1})\right] - \left[\vec{P_1'} + \mu_{L'} (\vec{P_2'} - \vec{P_1'})\right] = \alpha \, \vec{d}$$

The constant factor α can easily be eliminated from the above set of equations by dividing the first two by the third one by parts. The resulting set of equations is linear in μ_L and $\mu_{L'}$ and it can be solved for them in terms of the coordinates of P_1, P_2, P_1' and P_2'. Having obtained the values for μ_L and $\mu_{L'}$, the coordinates of P can be found by:

$$\vec{P} = \frac{1}{2} \left[\vec{P_1} + \mu_L(\vec{P_2} - \vec{P_1}) + \vec{P_1'} + \mu_{L'}(\vec{P_2'} - \vec{P_1'})\right] \qquad (8)$$

Then, it is possible to find the variances of the distribution of the errors in the position of P in terms of $\sigma^2_{P_x P_x}$, $\sigma^2_{P_y P_y}$, $\sigma^2_{P_z P_z}$, $\sigma^2_{P_x P_y}$, $\sigma^2_{P_x P_z}$ and $\sigma^2_{P_y P_z}$. For example, the variance of the distribution of the error in the x component of P is given by:

$$\sigma^2_{P_x P_x} = \frac{1}{4} \left[(1 + \mu_L^2)\sigma^2_{P_{1x} P_{1x}} + \mu_L^2 \sigma^2_{P_{2x} P_{2x}} + (1 + \mu_{L'}^2)\sigma^2_{P_{1x}' P_{1x}'} + \mu_{L'}^2 \sigma^2_{P_{2x}' P_{2x}'}\right]$$

$$(9)$$

As parameters μ_L and $\mu_{L'}$ vary between 0 and 1 only for points that lie between points P_1 and P_2 and P_1' and P_2' respectively, it is obvious from the above expression that unless P lies in the space *between* the two reference planes, μ_L and $\mu_{L'}$ will be larger than 1 and we shall have error amplification factors significantly greater than 1.

4. Conclusions: Guidelines in choosing the reference points

In order to apply the method of Projective Geometry to 3D reconstruction we need to take the following cautionary steps to avoid the introduction of large errors:

1. It is best if the two reference planes are apart from each other and intersect along a line well away from the area of viewing. This is in order to maximise the volume over which parameters μ_L and μ_L' in equation 9 take values between 0 and 1. As the reference points have to be visible in the image, this requirement implies that a setting like the one shown in Figure (8) is appropriate. However, such an arrangement of reference points may not always be possible. Depending on the set up, one could use for example, two sets of reference planes; planes $ABCD$ and $ABGH$ (assuming that points A, B, G and H are co-planar) for the reconstruction of all those points that fall on the right half of the image, and planes $ABCD$ and $CDEF$ (assuming that points C, D, E and F are also co-planar) for the reconstruction of all those points which are on the left half of the image (as shown in Figure 8). Such a setting would reduce the source of error amplification described in section 3.

2. Provided the accuracy of the measurements of positions on the image plane is known, the error with which each of the projective coordinates of point p is computed can be estimated and the most reliable coordinates of point p may be used each time. There are only three small patches on the image plane where there is only one reliable projective coordinate.

3. Once the projective coordinates of a point have been found, and given the uncertainty in the measurement of the 3D position of the reference points, the error in the 3D position of point P can be estimated. This stage, however, is the most difficult to handle as it seems that unless the points are projected within a region more or less surrounded by the reference points, we are bound to have amplification of the error. The only thing we can do is to try to monitor it carefully. For example, one

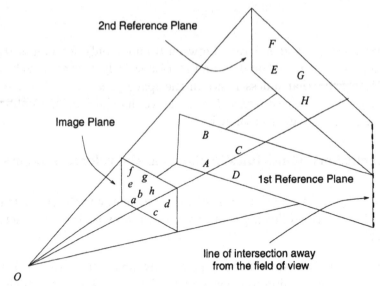

Figure 8. Setup of reference planes and points for minimum sensitivity to noise.

may try to reconstruct a flat surface using several points, of which only the most reliable are eventually used.

Alternatively, one may consider several sets of reference points and compute the position of each point under consideration using all of these sets and every time keep the most reliable set.

References

Coxeter, H.S.M. (1974) *Projective Geometry*, University of Toronto Press.

Faugeras, O.D. (1992) What can be seen in 3D with an uncalibrated stereo rig? *Second European Conference on Computer Vision*, Italy, 563–578.

Georgis, N., Petrou, M. and Kittler, J. (1998) Error guided design of a 3d vision system, *IEEE PAMI*, 20:366–379.

Haralick, R.M. (1994) Propagating covariance in computer vision, *Proc. 12th Int. Conf. on Pattern Recognition*, Jerusalem, 1:493–498.

Mohr, R. and Arbogast, E. (1991) It can be done without camera calibration, *Pattern Recognition Letters*, 12:39–43.

A SYSTEMATIC APPROACH TO ERROR SOURCES FOR THE EVALUATION AND VALIDATION OF A BINOCULAR VISION SYSTEM FOR ROBOT CONTROL

DETLEF RICHTER
Wiesbaden University of Applied Sciences
Department of Computer Science
D-65197 Wiesbaden, Germany

1. Introduction

The automatic control of production lines may be done in appropriate cases by robots controlled by digital image processing. CCD video cameras are used as optical sensors. When a two-dimensional image of a three-dimensional scene is generated the depth information is lost, however applications with a high degree of automation commonly require an exact recognition of three-dimensional objects and their positions. Therefore, binocular video cameras are used. For the application of image processing algorithms and subsequent robot control, a comprehensive calibrating procedure is required for the cameras and for the robot basis. An evaluation procedure of the corresponding software estimates only the reliability of the whole system, ignoring single effects of errors. In the paper presented, model dependent error sources are recorded systematically to find appropriate procedures for independent verification. It is presumed that no logical errors or errors due to computer internal process communications are present. This approach may be applied to similar complex model dependent software systems.

2. Description of the binocular vision system for robot control

The model of a binocular camera system is based on a proposal of Tsai (1986) and Lenz (1987) and was successfully used in previous applications (Posch, 1990). It is composed of two ideal pinhole cameras with

265

R. Klette et al. (eds.), Performance Characterization in Computer Vision, 265–272.
© 2000 *Kluwer Academic Publishers.*

parallel optical axes and with radial symmetrical distortions of the images
caused by non-ideal optical lenses. The model uses the following different
mathematical and physical quantities :

- the image width of the lenses,
- the distance and the orientation of the cameras with respect to the
  objects observed,
- the stereobasis, which means the lateral distance between the cameras,
- mathematical coefficients defining the radial symmetrical distortions,
- the positions of the intersections of the optical axes of the lenses with
  the surfaces of the sensor chips,
- distortions of the width and height ratio caused by subsequent digital
  to analog and analog to digital conversions of the video signals.

This chapter does not specify the mathematical relationships of these quantities. An overview is given in (Richter *et al.*, 1996).

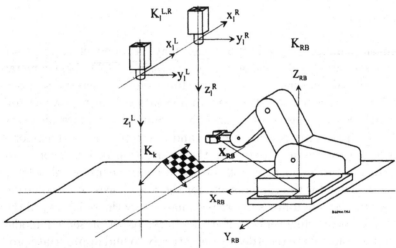

Figure 1.   Arrangement of the binocular camera system for calibration, object
recognition and robot control

The binocular camera system has a viewing direction perpendicular
to the scene to be analysed (Figure 1). After analysis of the images, the
positions and heights of objects are calculated by triangulation from their
differing positions in the stereoscopic images. When these values have been
calculated, the movement and application of the robot can be controlled.

3. Calibration of the vision system

The precise mathematical and physical parameters of the cameras used are necessary for the computation of the three-dimensional information of the production environment. These parameters are determined by a calibrating procedure. Some can be determined independently, such as the intersections of the optical axes of the lenses with the surfaces of the sensor chips and the distortion of the width and height ratio. The remaining parameters are mutually dependent and are determined by solving an equational system.

To determine the intersection of the optical axis with the surface of the sensor chip, the lens of the camera is removed and substituted by a precise arrangement of a tube with three diapragms in a row. The diaphragms, which are mounted at 30 cm intervals, have holes of 0.3 mm diameter along a single axis. Using digital image processing, the maximum light distribution caused by the apertures of the diaphragms is determined and taken as the position of the intersection.

Next, by a subpixel precise analysis of the horizontal and vertical dimensions of the image of a circular disk, the parameter describing the distortion of the width and height ratio is determined. Ideally the ratio of both dimensions should be equal to 1.

The remaining mutually dependent geometrical parameters are calculated by analysing a chessboard-like calibrating pattern of known dimensions. The calibrating pattern is inclined with a slope of 45 degrees against the optical axes of the cameras (Figure 1). Because of the inclination, the cross points of the pattern have different distances from the binocular camera system and give the necessary depth information. From the differing positions of the cross points in both images of the binocular camera system the remaining parameters are calculated by solving an overdefined equational system.

4. Calibration of the robot basis

To control the movement of the robot by image processing with the now calibrated binocular camera system, it is necessary to analyse the geometric transformation between the camera system and the robot basis by a subsequent calibration procedure.

Various methods are described to find this geometric transformation (Rembold, 1990). For this chapter we chose the simple and easily replicated procedure of tracking an infrared light emitting diode moved by the robot along a known path by the stereo camera system, which was equipped with infrared transmission filters to suppress light of visible wavelengths. The geometric transformation between the positions seen by the binocular camera system and the corresponding positions within the robot basis system specify the numerical values of the second set of parameters.

For applications with object positions varying over time, the video frame read-outs have to be synchronised.

5. A generalised model for validating complex vision systems

For the treatment of complex vision systems, the objects of a scene and the optical sensors themselves are described by mathematical or physical models to allow simplification of the image processing algorithms by use of a high degree of a-priori-knowledge. The models have to be transposed into mathematical equations and implemented as coded algorithms into a computer system. The conformity of the model to reality, the correctness of the transposed mathematical equations, the correctness of the implemented coding and its functional faultlessness regarding process communication, data types, range of definition and values have to be verified (Figure 2). When modelling complex procedures, various partial models may be repeated at different stages. Figure 2 shows the formalism used in the systematic validation process. To verify these basic models, it is necessary to prove the results of an algorithm by observable and physically measurable quantities and, in many cases, this cannot be carried out with reasonable effort.

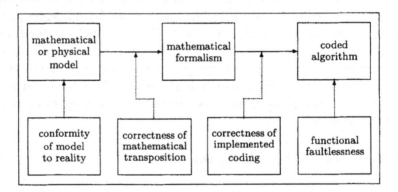

Figure 2.   Flow of a model based programming

6. Modelling of error sources of the environment

A rough analysis of the robot application is shown in Figure 3. The middle column represents the sequential operations of the software application and in the left column their relationship to the physical components used. The software application uses known image processing algorithms for the two-dimensional object recognition in both images of the stereo camera system.

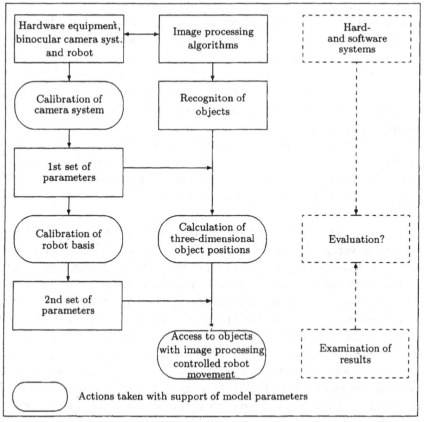

Figure 3.   Model based analysis of the robot control system

From this information, the three-dimensional positions of the recognised objects are calculated using a set of parameters describing the camera model. To control the robot's movement we use a second set of parameters describing the robot's position and orientation relative to the camera system. The first set of parameters is generated during the calibrating process of the cameras, and is used to solve the three-dimensional calculation of the application. It is also used for calibrating the robot basis and thus for generating the second set of parameters as well. Therefore, errors occurring while generating the first set of parameters will propagate into the second set of parameters. Those errors of the second set may eliminate the errors of the first set and remain undetected. The right hand column outlines the principle of merely evaluating the results of the software system for robot control for a given hardware configuration. This evaluation makes a statement about the reliability and precision of the system, but fails to define the causes and relevance of possible deviations.

To detect possible error sources we have to subdivide the whole system into partial model components, which, ideally, should all be verifyable by the measurement of observable quantities. But it is not always possible to find easily measurable model components. For example, the model of the ideal pinhole camera uses the physical quantity of image width of the camera objectives, which is only measurable with an extensive optical equipment in a time consuming procedure.

Figure 4 shows the basic model components for the robot control system presented. The left column defines the various actions taken, the middle column the model dependent quantities or the physical or electronical influences, and the right column the methods of testing these quantities or influences.

The necessary synchronisation of video cameras for time dependent operations was verified by an electronical measurement of the S-components of the BAS-video-signals. The deviation of the width and height ratio caused by subsequent digital to analog and analog to digital conversions of the video signals was calculated by a subpixel precise analysis of the horizontal and vertical dimensions of an image of a circular disk. A result of the computed ratio in the range of 1 was accepted without further proof. The linearity and the identity of the slopes of the D/A- and D/A-converters built in the cameras and frame grabbers could not be measured without extensive experimental work and therefore was assumed to be correct. The intersections of the optical axes with the sensor chips were defined by the analysis of the distribution of light caused by a narrow aligned light beam. As verification, similar results were reproduced after subsequent dismounting and mounting of the assembly. However, the possibility of systematic errors cannot be excluded. The coefficients describing the radial symmetrical distortions of the lenses could not be proved without extensive experimental work, which was not carried out. A description of the evaluation of different camera models is given in (Abraham and Foerstner, 1997). The image widths of the objectives were assumed to be correct according to the computed trustworthy range of the quantities. The remaining geometrical dimensions of this set of mutually dependent parameters were checked by measuring the resultant stereo basis of the cameras.

The calibration of the robot basis is carried out with the above described method of marker tracking, which gives the second set of parameters. This procedure uses the first set of parameters as shown in Figure 3 and 4 and assumes its correctness. The differences between the depth measurement produced by the image processing system and the predefined robot positions were taken as an evaluation of the correctness of the models chosen and of the accuracy of calibration.

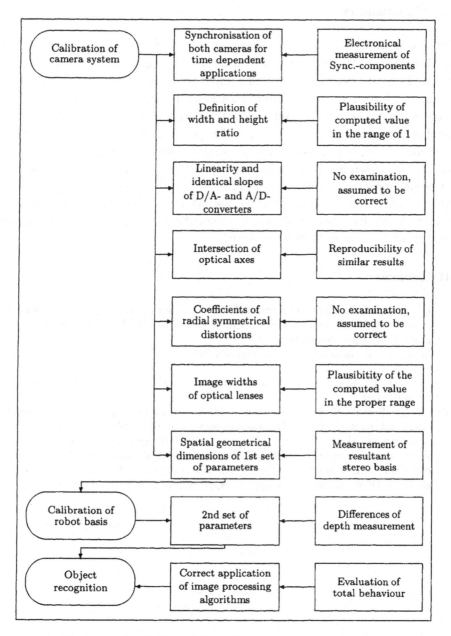

Figure 4. Subdivision of the entire model into partial models

7. Conclusions

The evaluation of model dependent complex software systems is insufficient with respect to the reliability and accuracy of programs. In addition to the normal tests to detect logical and computational errors or errors caused by computer internal process communications, it is necessary to verify important model dependent procedures for their conformity to reality. To do this, profound mathematical, physical and experimental knowledge is often required. Furthermore it is not always possible to find model based observable quantities which are measurable with reasonable effort. For these reasons, thorough program verification is often not carried out. The applicant of the software usually does not know the extent to which the programs were tested. Software systems should have certification stating to what degree and in what manner they were tested.

References

Tsai, R. (1986) An Efficient and Accurate Camera Calibration Technique for 3-D Machine Vision, *Proc. Computer Vision and Pattern Recognition*, IEEE, Miami Beach.

Lenz, R. (1987) Linsenfehlerkorrigierte Eichung von Halbleiterkameras mit Standardobjektiven fuer hochgenaue 3-D-Messungen in Echtzeit, *9. DAGM-Symposium*, Springer Verlag.

Posch, S. (1990) *Automatische Tiefenbestimmung aus Grauwertbildern*, Deutscher Universitaetsverlag.

Richter, D., Schick, W. and Vormbrock, S. (1996) Verifikation einer Roboterbasiskalibrierung mit einem Stereo-Bildverarbeitungssystem durch Evaluierung der Tiefenbestimmung innerhalb des Kalibriervolumens, *18. DAGM-Symposium*, Springer Verlag.

Abraham, S. and Foerstner, W. (1997) Zur automatischen Modellwahl bei der Kalibrierung von CCD-Kameras, *19. DAGM-Symposium*, Springer Verlag.

Rembold, U. (1990) *Robot Technology and Applications*, New York, Marcel Dekker.

Part VI

Domain-specific Evaluation: Medical Imaging

ERROR METRICS FOR QUANTITATIVE EVALUATION OF MEDICAL IMAGE SEGMENTATION

WIRO J. NIESSEN, CAROLIEN J. BOUMA,
KOEN L. VINCKEN and MAX A. VIERGEVER
Image Sciences Institute
University Medical Center Utrecht
room E01.334, Heidelberglaan 100
3584 CX Utrecht, The Netherlands

1. Introduction

There is a large effort to construct algorithms performing objective, reproducible segmentations of medical image data. However, the introduction of these techniques into clinical practice has been hampered by the lack of thorough evaluation of performance. If the gold standard is defined by human performance, a full validation study is costly, since it should comprise both a large number of datasets and a large number of trained medical experts to inspect these. In this case one should compare the weighted average of the observers with the result of the algorithm. An algorithm performs well enough if it is closer to the average than the variance of the medical experts. Three important steps in this procedure are selecting the parameter to be compared, determining a gold standard (the weighted average) and an error metric to define how much an individual result differs from the gold standard. The different steps of this procedure are illustrated by a clinical evaluation of different techniques for segmenting intravascular ultrasound images.

A promising tool to partially replace costly evaluation procedures is the use of simulations which model the main image degrading effects in acquisition, and the anatomical variability of individuals. We tested an algorithm for segmenting grey matter and white matter from simulated 3D MRI data, which were generated from a digital phantom. Since ground truth is available, we could compare results to other algorithms. Moreover, dependence on image degrading effects can be tested. This showed that in case of MRI segmentation, modeling of partial volume voxels (*i.e.* voxels

R. Klette et al. (eds.), Performance Characterization in Computer Vision, 275–284.
© *2000 Kluwer Academic Publishers.*

containing multiple tissue types) is one of the essential steps to improve accuracy. We believe that further sophistication of the simulation of image formation will improve the design of future algorithms, although extensive evaluation studies will eventually be required for new techniques to gain acceptance in clinical practice.

2. Task-based evaluation performance

2.1. INTRODUCTION

Performance analysis of a segmentation tool is impossible without specifying a task. In many applications the task will be to arrive at some quantitative measurements derived from the segmentations. In this case a perfect segmentation is not always necessary. Volumetric measurements can be performed with high accuracy without precisely outlining the contours of an object. Three-dimensional volume rendering techniques can yield high quality images without having to segment structures up to the last voxel by incorporating information from the original dataset. Therefore, for a specific application, a well-defined task has to be defined prior to an evaluation study. Moreover, a task-based approach will prove to be very helpful in designing the underlying algorithm of the segmentation tool.

If an algorithm should be widely applicable, it is more difficult to arrive at a parameter which should be used to compare performances. In this case the segmentation result itself should be evaluated. If a classification scheme is close to the true distributions, or if the segmented contours accurately follow the true boundaries, it is more likely that derived entities are estimated properly. However, concepts as "close to the true boundaries" already entail choices. To define what is close an error metric needs to be defined. Moreover, the definition of the true boundaries as reference contour or gold standard is not a trivial task in many applications.

For two main classes of segmentation we discuss the problems of defining a gold standard and an error metric. The first class assigns a class label to each voxel in a dataset. This is typically performed using classification techniques or using region-based segmentation procedures. The second class of techniques extracts boundaries of objects, *i.e.* contours from two-dimensional images, and surfaces from three-dimensional images.

2.2. OBTAINING THE GOLD STANDARD

The typical procedure to validate segmentation tools in medical imaging is to compare results of medical experts with those generated by the algorithm. Since manual results are subject to inter- and intra-observer variability, a single manual segmentation can not act as a standard. Therefore a gold standard reference image is calculated as the average shape of the manual segmentations. We first consider the case that a binary segmentation is present, *i.e.* pixels are labeled to belong to object or background. In this case a shape-based interpolation (Raya and Udupa, 1990; Herman *et al.*, 1992) can be used. This technique uses the shapes of the binary object in each manual segmentation to calculate so-called distance scenes. In a distance scene, each pixel is given the value that represents the distance to the nearest pixel of the object, *i.e.* the lumen contour. Pixels inside the object are assigned negative distance values. The average shape is subsequently calculated by adding the distance scenes of all manual segmentations; the transition from positive to negative values yields the average contour. Apart from the contour this approach yields a measure of the variability of the observers along the contour. This can be used in order to define an error metric which takes the uncertainty of manual observers into account.

If the result of a segmentation procedure is not a binary object, but a parameterized contour or surface, an iterative iterative closest point algorithm (Besl and McKay, 1992) can be used. This procedure only requires an algorithm to define the closest point from a pixel on one contour to (a pixel on) another contour. The algorithm starts on one of the manually traced contours and identifies all closest points on the other contours. A new point is defined by the average location of these points. This procedure is performed for all points of the manually traced contour, yielding a new contour. The algorithm is now iterated with this resulting contour as starting point, until the procedure converges.

2.3. DEFINING THE ERROR METRIC

If a gold standard is available, the distance between an individual contour and the gold standard has to be defined. Therefore, we have to define a metric space which determines distances between segmentations. Here the task dependence plays a crucial role. Let $\mathbf{X}$ and $\mathbf{Y}$ denote two segmentations. We will first establish the main properties that a distance measure $d(\mathbf{X}, \mathbf{Y})$ should have to be a metric:

$$
\begin{array}{lll}
\text{(a)} & d(\mathbf{X}, \mathbf{Y}) = 0 & \text{if and only if} \quad \mathbf{X} = \mathbf{Y} \\
\text{(b)} & d(\mathbf{X}, \mathbf{Y}) = d(\mathbf{Y}, \mathbf{X}) & \qquad\qquad (1) \\
\text{(c)} & d(\mathbf{X}, \mathbf{Z}) \leq d(\mathbf{X}, \mathbf{Y}) + d(\mathbf{Y}, \mathbf{Z}) &
\end{array}
$$

Several error metrics which can be used are:

- The percentage of misclassified voxels $MV(A_1, A_2)$. This measure is most commonly used for classification based segmentations that yield binary objects. It is important to note that contrary to volume differences between segmentations, in which over- and underestimates cancel, this measure constitutes a metric. It can also be quantified using a similarity measure $E(A_1, A_2)$ (Zijdenbos $et\ al.$, 1994) between two binary segmentations A_1 and A_2:

$$MV(A_1, A_2) = 1 - E(A_1, A_2) = 2\frac{\|A_1 \cap A_2\|}{\|A_1\| + \|A_2\|} \qquad (2)$$

The number of misclassified voxels gives a measure of the $global$ performance of the segmentation tool. Spatial information is not considered. No distinction is made between a small error along the entire object and a generally more accurate segmentation which misses a single larger subsegment of an object. For example, in case of segmentation as a preprocessing step for visualization the former error is not as significant as the latter. Therefore, a next step to extract the error source is to inspect the distribution of wrongly classified voxels. Another step to a more stringent validation is to convert the segmented object to a surface or contour model, and inspect the distances along the surface or contour, which is the subject of the other error metrics desribed in this section.

— The Hausdorff-Chebyshev metric. This metric defines the largest minimal distance between two contours ($\mathbf{X}$ and $\mathbf{Y}$ denote the boundary curve of the segmented object). First we determine for all points $\mathbf{x}_i$ of a curve $\mathbf{X}$ the minimal distance to a point $\mathbf{y}_i$ of $\mathbf{Y}$:

$$d(\mathbf{x}_i, \mathbf{Y}) = min_j(\mathbf{y}_j - \mathbf{x}_i) \qquad (3)$$

We subsequently perform the same procedure to determine the minimal distance between all points $\mathbf{y}_j$ of curve $\mathbf{Y}$ to a point $\mathbf{x}_i$ of X. The Hausdorff metric is now defined as the maximum minimal distance, $i.e.$:

$$d_{HD}(\mathbf{X}, \mathbf{Y}) = max(max_i(d(\mathbf{x}_i, \mathbf{Y})), max_j(d(\mathbf{y}_j, \mathbf{X}))) \qquad (4)$$

In this definition both the distance from $\mathbf{Y}$ to $\mathbf{X}$ and from $\mathbf{X}$ to $\mathbf{Y}$ are taken into account. This is required in order to satisfy criterion (b) in Eq. 1, which is illustrated by Figure 1.

— The squared distance metric. This metric defines the squared distance between curves $\mathbf{X}$ and $\mathbf{Y}$. We can either determine the maximum squared distance between two curves:

$$d_{SDmax}(\mathbf{X}, \mathbf{Y}) = max(\sum_i d(\mathbf{x}_i, \mathbf{Y})^2, \sum_j d(\mathbf{y}_j, \mathbf{X})^2) \qquad (5)$$

or the average squared distance between curves:

$$d_{SDmean}(\mathbf{X}, \mathbf{Y}) = \frac{1}{2}(\sum_i d(\mathbf{x}_i, \mathbf{Y})^2 + \sum_j d(\mathbf{y}_j, \mathbf{X})^2) \qquad (6)$$

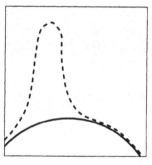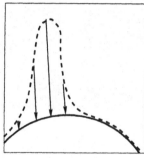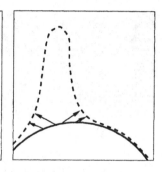

Figure 1. In order to satisfy the criteria for being a metric, both distances from the estimated contour to the reference contour and vice versa should be taken into account. Otherwise the distance from contour **X** to **Y** is not necessarily equal to the distance from contour **Y** to **X**.

– The Mahalanobis distance. The squared distance does not take observer variability into account. It is reasonable that at places where the observers have a good agreement the method has to perform well, while at places with disagreement between the different observers the method may also have larger variations. The squared Mahalanobis distance takes the variation at each point on the reference contour into account:

$$d_{Maha}(\mathbf{X}, \mathbf{Y}) = max(\frac{\sum_i d(\mathbf{x}_i, \mathbf{Y})^2}{\sigma^2 + \sigma_\epsilon^2}, \frac{\sum_j d(\mathbf{y}_j, \mathbf{X})^2}{\sigma^2 + \sigma_\epsilon^2}) \qquad (7)$$

in which $D_{Maha}(\mathbf{X}, \mathbf{Y})$ denotes the squared Mahalanobis distance, σ^2 denotes the variation of the manual observers, and $\sigma_\epsilon(x, y)^2$ is the variation due to discretization.

3. Intravascular ultrasound segmentation

The validation of segmentation methods is now illustrated by briefly describing a study which investigated whether it is possible to automatically determine the lumen boundary from intravascular ultrasound (IVUS) subtraction images, with a quality similar to manual segmentation (Bouma *et al.*, 1997). IVUS imaging is a modality which depicts detailed spatial information of the vessel wall and lumen (see Figure 2). In the validation study manual segmentations of 15 femoral artery images (7 images were obtained before balloon dilation, 8 images were obtained after balloon dilation) were obtained from four experienced observers. Each observer traced the contour of the lumen twice with a period of one week between the tracings.

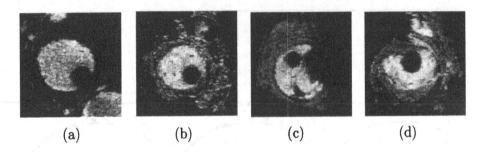

(a)	(b)	(c)	(d)

Figure 2.   Examples of IVUS images prior to (a,b) and post dilation (c,d).

Automated and semi-automated segmentations of the same dataset were obtained by combining various smoothing procedures (linear filtering, non-linear filtering and median filtering) with object definition methods (morphological segmentation procedures, region growing and deformable model approaches).

3.1. RESULTS

In all methods, pre-dilation and post-dilation images are treated separately, because variations found in the manual segmentations are much larger for post-dilation images than for pre-dilation images. These larger variations for post-dilation images can be caused by irregular lumina due to balloon dilation. To evaluate the manual segmentation we first find the average contour using the method described in section 2.2. The errors of the individual manual segmentations with respect to this gold standard are measured by squared distance values (Eq. 5) and the Mahalanobis distance values (Eq. 7), and are shown in the first four columns of Table I.

The manual segmentations show a large variability between different observers and occasionally also between the two traces of one observer. The distances of the post-dilation images measured by observer 1 are very high when compared to the other observers. By retrospectively inspecting the results it was found that this observer traced more dissections and indentations. To be able to assess the influence of this variation, all measurements on the post-dilation images were also performed while excluding this observer. These additional results for the manual traces are shown in the right column of Table I.

An automated segmentation method can now be considered a good alternative for manual segmentation if the distance of the estimated contour lies within the range of distances of the observers to the reference contour. This validation approach is similar to the Williams index (Williams76a,

TABLE I. Maximum Mean Square distance and Maximum Mahalanobis distances of
manual segmentations from different observers for the 7 pre-dilation images and the 8
post-dilation images. The figures are in squared pixel units for the squared distances,
and dimensionless for the Mahalanobis distances.

Observer	pre-dilation		post-dilation		post-dilation; excl.	
	MaxMean	MaxMaha	MaxMean	MaxMaha	MaxMean	MaxMaha
1a	1.34	1.07	36.3	2.24	–	–
1b	1.34	1.00	25.8	1.48	–	–
2a	0.56	0.61	1.83	0.74	1.88	0.76
2b	0.81	0.68	1.96	0.79	1.90	0.84
3a	1.57	1.08	10.2	1.57	11.0	1.69
3b	1.38	0.98	6.38	1.20	6.79	1.39
4a	1.08	0.89	3.03	1.01	3.17	1.22
4b	1.66	1.04	5.87	1.23	4.53	1.40
mean	1.22	0.92	11.4	1.28	4.88	1.22

1976; Chalana and Kim, 1997), in which the result of one method or observer is evaluated against multiple observer results by dividing the result of
the first by the latter. From the automated segmentation methods that are
considered in this study, combinations of a median filter with either region
growing, a semi-automated or a fully automated version of an active contour
model performed best (Bouma et al., 1997). Results of these procedures are
shown in Table II.

The results show that for all pre-dilation images the squared distances
and the Mahalanobis distances are smaller than the mean value of the manual traces. For the post-dilation images, the results depend on whether observer 1 is excluded. If excluded, the automated methods do not give better
results than the manual observers. However, all values of the Mahalanobis
distance are well within the $p = 0.05$ confidence interval.

From the study a number of conclusions can be drawn: A major hurdle
in this study has been the large inter-operator variations in the manually
segmented lumen contours, which in this study mainly occurred for the
post-dilation images. Therefore, no definitive conclusions can be drawn
for the post-dilation images. For the pre-dilation images it is shown that
a number of procedures are viable alternatives for manual segmentation.
In this respect, the purpose of the study to show that automated lumen
representation of IVUS images is possible, so as to pave the way for clinical
use of IVUS, has been accomplished for pre-dilation images, whereas a
further evaluation for post-dilation images is required.

TABLE II.   Distances of three segmentation methods to reference contour (reggr, M; region growing preceded by median filtering, hdcm, M; active contour model with manual initialization preceded by median filtering, adcm, M; active contour model with automatic initialization by thresholding and median filtering as preprocessing).

Method	pre-dilation		post-dilation		post-dilation; excl.	
	MaxMean	MaxMaha	MaxMean	MaxMaha	MaxMean	MaxMaha
reggr, M	1.09	0.72	6.52	1.25	6.50	1.38
hdcm, M	1.06	0.66	8.21	1.37	7.95	1.48
adcm, M	1.10	0.70	5.67	1.13	6.16	1.27

4. Evaluation by simulation: MRI brain segmentation

Since clinical evaluation studies as presented in the previous section are costly, simulation is an alternative which can at least partially replace steps in the validation procedure. In this section we illustrate the possibilities of simulation by evaluating the performance of MRI brain segmentation on simulated MR datasets of a digital brain phantom[1]. The brain phantom models typical artefacts of MRI acquisition such as field inhomogeneity and noise, and also takes the partial volume effect into account. The voxel size of the brain phantom is $1 \times 1 \times 1$ mm. Examples of the object distribution of grey and white matter are shown in Figure 3.

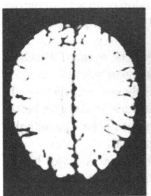

Figure 3.   Montreal brain dataset. From left to right the fuzzy object distribution of total brain, white matter and grey matter.

---

[1] The simulated MRI volumes were provided by the McConnell Brain Imaging Centre at the Montreal Neurological Institute at the Web site http://bic.mni.mcgill.ca.

TABLE III.   Errors in segmentation. Column 1: Tissue type, *viz.* white matter (WM), grey matter (GM), and total brain (TB) Column 2 and 3: Errors introduced in segmentation owing to binarization. Column 4 and 5: Errors in binary segmentation tool. Column 6 and 7: Errors in probabilistic segmentation tool.

	binarization error		binary segmentation		prob. segmentation	
Type	Vol. err.	Classif. err.	Vol. err.	Class. err.	Vol. err.	Class err.
WM	+1.72%	15.3%	0.08%	17.4%	2.99%	10.1%
GM	−1.30%	20.2%	−1.40%	24.7%	1.47%	21.1%
TB	−0.02%	5.4%	−0.77%	6.4%	2.12%	4.7%

We first determined the magnitude of error which can be expected if a segmentation scheme does not allow voxels to contain multiple tissue types (*i.e.* a binary segmentation is produced). In the first two columns of Table III we list the errors of the best possible binary segmentation. The binary segmentations are obtained by setting a voxel to a certain tissue type if more than half of the voxel contains this tissue. Errors are calculated between the binarized version and the probabilistic version. Note that this leads to the concept of partially misclassified voxels, *i.e.* if in the segmentation a voxel containing 40% white tissue is not present in the binary segmentation, this contributes a volume error of 0.4 voxel.

The errors in the estimated volume are in the range of 0-4%. These errors are relatively small, owing to cancelation of misclassifications, and therefore inappropriate determinants for segmentation procedure performance. The volume of misclassified voxels is considerably larger. For the total brain (white matter plus grey matter) the volume of wrongly classified voxels is in the order of 5% for the total brain, and in the order of 20 % for grey and white matter (all numbers are normalized with respect to the volume of the tissue itself). Since we compare the probabilistic model with the best possible binary segmentation, this implies that any binary segmentation result for the latter regions will at least have approximately 20 volume percent segmented into the wrong tissue type. For any quantitative application relying on a binary segmentation the figures reported in Table III are important. If effects are to be measured which are smaller than the errors which are introduced owing to binarization, special care is required. If exactly the same protocol is utilized, (part of) the error may be systematic and cancel. Another possibility is to introduce segmentation tools with sub pixel accuracy, *e.g.* using interpolation or by having a probabilistic segmentation. In a recent article (Niessen *et al.*, 1999) we have shown that for the brain phantom a smaller volume of misclassified voxels for total brain and white matter segmentation using a probabilistic approach is obtained than would ever be possible using a binary segmentation (last row Table III).

5. Discussion

Validating medical image segmentation algorithms requires the choice of a parameter to be compared, the definition of a gold standard, and the definition of an error metric. All three steps reveal its strong task dependence; it is impossible to establish objective criteria for the quality of a segmentation. If the goal is to directly compare segmentation results, the most common approach is to define a reference contour, surface or volume, and measure the distance of an obtained result to this reference object. A main problem is that the reference contour is not so easily defined. There is large inter and intra-observer variability in tracing contours for example; it requires considerable effort to arrive at statistically significant results. A second challenge is establishing the most proper metric to measure distances between contours. Therefore, the influence of the segmentation result on further decision making should be understood.

A promising approach to improve algorithm design and perform first validations is the use of realistic simulations. Whereas they will most probably never totally replace a clinical validation, the main variations and sources of errors can be tested in a controlled environment.

References

Besl, P. and McKay, N.D. (1997) A method for registration of 3-D shapes, *IEEE Trans. on Pattern Recognition and Machine Intelligence*, 14:239–256.

Bouma, C.J., Niessen, W.J., Zuiderveld, K.J., Gussenhoven, E.J. and Viergever, M.A. (1997) Automated lumen definition from 30 MHz intravascular ultrasound images, *Medical Image Analysis*, 1:363–377.

Chalana, V. and Kim, Y. (1996) A methodology for evaluation of boundary detection algorithms on medical images, *IEEE Transactions on Medical Imaging*, 16:642–652.

Herman, G.T., Zheng, J. and Bucholtz, C.A. (1992) Shape-based interpolation, *IEEE Computer Graphics and Applications*, 12:69–79.

Niessen, W.J., Vincken, K.L. Weickert, J., ter Haar Romeny, B.M. and Viergever, M.A. (1999) Multiscale segmentation of three-dimensional MR brain images, *International Journal of Computer Vision*, 31:185–202.

Raya, S.P. and Udupa, J.K. (1990) Shape-based interpolation of multidimensional objects, *IEEE Transactions on Medical Imaging*, 9:32–42.

Williams, G.W. (1976) Comparing the joint agreement of several raters with another rater, *Biometrics*, 32:619–627.

Zijdenbos, A. and Dawant, B.M. and Margolin, R.A. and Palmer, A.C. (1994) Morphometric analysis of white matter lesions in MR images, *IEEE Transactions on Medical Imaging*, 14:716–724.

PERFORMANCE CHARACTERIZATION OF LANDMARK OPERATORS

KARL ROHR, H. SIEGFRIED STIEHL, SÖNKE FRANTZ
and THOMAS HARTKENS
Universität Hamburg
FB Informatik
AB Kognitive Systeme
Vogt-Kölln-Str. 30
D-22527 Hamburg, Germany

1. Introduction

Prominent points in multi-dimensional digital images of different modalities are key features for a variety of computer vision tasks. As point landmarks we define, e.g., corners in 2D projection images or tips of anatomical structures in 3D spatial images, both of which are represented by geometric properties of the underlying intensity function. Note that, in the case of 3D spatial images, the geometry of the intensity function in general directly reflects the geometry of the depicted anatomical structures, which is generally not the case for 2D projection images.

In this chapter, we describe our studies on the performance characterization of operators for the detection and localization of point landmarks. First, we discuss the general problem as well as our approach to the validation and evaluation of landmark operators. Then, we detail our investigations for the case of 2D as well as 3D landmark operators.

2. General Approach to the Evaluation of Landmark Operators

As a methodical basis we adopt a general approach to the validation and evaluation of landmark operators. This approach consists of three principal steps as depicted in Figure 1. Central to this scheme is the formalization of the signal structure which in our opinion is of paramount importance and is

285

R. Klette et al. (eds.), Performance Characterization in Computer Vision, 285–297.
© 2000 *Kluwer Academic Publishers.*

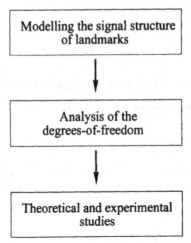

Figure 1. General approach to the evaluation of landmark operators.

a key issue in the development of algorithms with predictable performance. Examples are the modelling of the systematic intensity variations in 2D projection images (see section 3) or the modelling of structures in 3D tomographic images of the human brain (see section 4). A prerequisite in the latter case is a careful analysis of brain anatomy. In either case, we have to find a mathematical description of geometric properties, e.g., in terms of differential geometry.

A second main step is a detailed analysis of the degrees-of-freedom. Here, a fundamental problem is that the number of the degrees-of-freedom are often very large. Particularly, this is true in the case of 3D landmark operators, where we can classify the degrees-of-freedom w.r.t. (i) anatomy (e.g., landmark type, scale, anatomical variability), (ii) imaging (e.g., contrast, noise, resolution, modality), as well as (iii) the algorithm (e.g., operator type, filter widths, thresholds). In experimental studies it is often possible to analyze the performance w.r.t. only a subset of the degrees-of-freedom. Priorities may be set on the basis of application scenaria, requirement analyses, and criteria catalogues comprising criteria such as accuracy, robustness, and reproducibility.

Third, theoretical as well as experimental studies should be performed. A theoretical assessment of operator performance should be strived for to a maximum extent, provided a mathematical treatment is possible at all. In addition, experimental studies are indispensable for performance prediction in real applications. To this end, we advocate an incremental approach building upon a hierarchy of test data (e.g., (Neumann and Stiehl, 1987)). By this, we mean an experimental strategy that starts out from synthetic ideal signal structures of landmark prototypes and incrementally

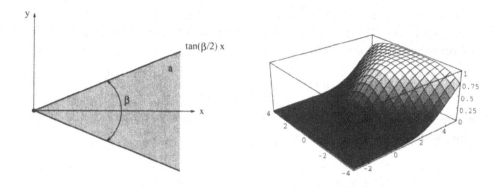

Figure 2.   Model of an L-corner.

increases the complexity of the test data by incorporating, e.g., image blur, noise, different sampling schemes, and further degradations. The usage of synthetic images at first in comparison to real images has the advantage that 'ground truth' is available.

3. 2D Landmark Operators

In this section, we describe an analytic study to characterize the performance of operators for extracting 2D point landmarks. We consider corners of polyhedral objects and analyze the localization properties of ten well-known differential corner detectors. Note, that this study is not only relevant for 2D projection images but also for 2D slices of 3D tomographic images exhibiting similar tip-like structures. Our study is based on an analytic model of the intensities of an L-corner in (Rohr 1990; 1992). We have analyzed the dependence of the localization accuracy on all model parameters given the full range of the parameter values (Rohr, 1994). Another analytic study of corner operators by Deriche and Giraudon (1993) only considered specific aperture angles of an L-corner (45° and 90°) to compare three different operators. In alternative studies, the performance of corner operators has been investigated experimentally, either by visual judgment of the results (e.g., (Kitchen and Rosenfeld, 1982)), by applying statistical measures (e.g., (Zuniga and Haralick, 1983)), by using projective invariants (e.g., (Coelho *et al.*, 1992; Heyden and Rohr, 1996)), or by computing the number of corresponding points under elastic transformations (e.g., (Hartkens *et al.*, 1996)) and projective transformations of planar scenes (e.g., (Schmid *et al.*, 1998)).

An L-corner can be modelled by Gaussian convolution of a wedge-shaped structure (see Figure 2). Taking advantage of the symmetry of this structure, we can derive an analytic model which can be written as the superposition of two functions representing the upper and lower part of the L-corner, resp. (Rohr, 1992):

$$g_{ML}(x, y, \beta, a, \sigma) = a \left(M(\frac{x}{\sigma}, \frac{y}{\sigma}, \beta) + M(\frac{x}{\sigma}, -\frac{y}{\sigma}, \beta) \right), \tag{1}$$

where β is the aperture angle, a the contrast, and σ quantifies the image blur, while

$$M(x, y, \beta) = \phi(x, y) - \int\limits_{-\infty}^{x} G(\xi) \, \phi(t\xi - \zeta_2) d\xi, \tag{2}$$

with

$$\phi(x, y) = \phi(x)\phi(y), \quad \phi(x) = \int\limits_{-\infty}^{x} G(\xi) d\xi, \quad G(x) = \frac{1}{\sqrt{2\pi}} e^{-\frac{x^2}{2}}, \tag{3}$$

and $t = \tan(\beta/2)$, $\zeta_2 = tx - y$.

For this model we have analyzed the localization accuracy of ten differential operators (Rohr, 1994). It turned out that some of the operators are either equivalent or do not yield any point. For the remaining six operators, the localized corner points are independent of the contrast, i.e. $x(a) = const.$, but there is a linear dependence on the image blur, i.e. $x(\sigma) = x \cdot \sigma$. Note, that since we have a symmetric structure the localized points lie on the x-axis (cf. Figure 2) and therefore we only have to compute the positions along this axis. The dependence on the aperture angle, $x(\beta)$, is nonlinear and is depicted in Figure 3 for the whole range of $0^o \leq \beta \leq 180^o$ while choosing $\sigma = 1$. From this figure we see that the operator of Beaudet (1978) yields two positions for the corner model (denoted by x_{Bp} and x_{Bn} and represented by the solid curves). The other operators yield only one position and are abbreviated and depicted as follows: Dreschler and Nagel (1981) by x_{DN} and the solid curve, Kitchen and Rosenfeld (1982) by x_{KR} and the boldfaced dashed curve, Förstner (1986) by x_F and the dashed curve, Rohr (1987) by x_R and the dotted curve, and Blom (1992) by x_{BRK} and the dashed dotted curve. It can be seen that the localization accuracy strongly depends on β. For $\beta = 90^o$ most operators have a localization error to the tip of the unblurred structure of about $1pix$, where pix denotes spatial unity. For smaller values of β we have significantly larger errors.

As additional reference position we have also computed the positions of the (exact) curvature extremum along the Canny edge line (denoted by x_L and represented by the bold-faced curve). Although the differential operator corresponding to this definition is rather extensive, we can derive

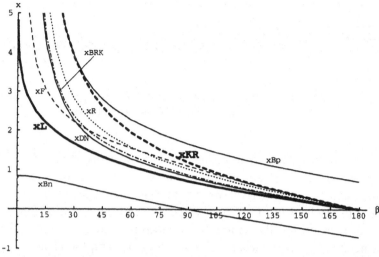

Figure 3. Localization of different 2D corner operators as a function of the aperture angle β of an L-corner with an image blur of $\sigma = 1$.

a relatively simple equation which determines its positions. With $x' = x/q$, $q = \sqrt{1 + t^2}$ and $t = \tan(\beta/2)$, this equation can be stated as (Rohr, 1992):

$$G(x') - t^2 x' \phi(x') = 0, \qquad (4)$$

which is an implicit equation involving the aperture angle β. Also in this case the positions are independent of the contrast a and there is a linear dependence on the image blur σ. From Figure 3 it can be seen that the dependence on β qualitatively agrees with that for the corner operators discussed above.

Recently, we have shown analytically that the localization errors of differential corner operators can significantly be reduced by applying multi-step approaches (Frantz *et al.*, 1998a). Note also, that a model-based approach to the localization of corners (Rohr 1990; 1992) allows to determine the correct position independently of all three parameters β, a, and σ.

4. 3D Landmark Operators

In the case of 3D landmark operators, we consider the extraction of anatomical point landmarks in tomographic images of the human brain. Generally, these landmarks serve as features for the registration of 3D multi-modality image data (e.g., MR and CT images as well as digital atlases). Thirion (1996), for example, has introduced 3D differential operators to detect extremal points on ridge lines. These operators employ partial derivatives of an image up to the third order. However, the computation of high order

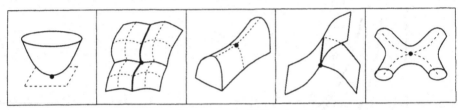

Figure 4.   Different types of 3D point landmarks.

partial derivatives generally is rather sensitive to noise. Related ridge-line based operators as well as operators based on the mean and Gaussian curvature using partial derivatives up to the second order have been investigated in (Beil *et al.*, 1997) (see also, e.g., (Florack *et al.*, 1994)). Rohr (1997) has introduced 3D differential operators which are generalizations of existing 2D corner detectors. These operators employ either only first order partial derivatives or first and second order partial derivatives of an image. Therefore, these operators are computationally efficient and they do not suffer from instabilities of computing high order partial derivatives. All operators mentioned above have only been designed for landmark detection and yield voxel positions. Recently, we have also proposed multi-step differential approaches for refined localization of 3D landmarks which yield subvoxel positions (Frantz *et al.*, 1998a).

To assess the performance of the different 3D operators we have carried out several studies. These studies include investigations of the localization accuracy as a function of image blur and noise, as well as the application of statistical measures to quantify the detection performance. The studies are based on 3D synthetic data (e.g., tetrahedra and ellipsoids), where ground truth is available, as well as on 3D tomographic images of the human brain (MR and CT images). The basis of our evaluation studies is a detailed analysis of brain anatomy resulting in a geometric characterization of point landmarks (Rohr and Stiehl, 1997). Examples of different classes of point landmarks are shown in Figure 4. It appears that many point landmarks can be classified as either tips or saddle points (e.g., the tips of the ventricular horns or the saddle point at the zygomatic bone). In the following, we focus on these types of landmarks. Other types of landmarks are, for example, surface-surface and line-surface intersections (e.g., junctions of sulci) or center points of cylinder crossings (e.g., optic chiasm).

4.1. EVALUATION OF 3D DETECTION OPERATORS

We have investigated nine different 3D differential operators for detecting anatomical point landmarks in 3D images $g(x, y, z)$. Since most of these operators are 3D extensions of 2D corner operators we denote them by the names of the corresponding authors who introduced the 2D operators. Three of the nine operators are based on the mean curvature H of isocontours, two operators are based on the Gaussian curvature K, and one exploits the Hessian matrix $\mathbf{H}_g$. Another three operators are based on the matrix $\mathbf{C}_g = \overline{\nabla g\,(\nabla g)^T}$, which is the averaged dyadic product of the image gradient $\nabla g = (g_x, g_y, g_z)^T$. In summary, we have the following nine 3D operators: H, $Kitchen\&Rosenfeld3D = H \cdot 2|\nabla g|$, $Blom3D = H \cdot 2|\nabla g|^3$, K, $K^* = K \cdot |\nabla g|^4$, $Beaudet3D = det\mathbf{H}_g$, $Op3 = det\mathbf{C}_g/trace\mathbf{C}_g$, $Rohr3D = det\mathbf{C}_g$, $Förstner3D = 1/trace\mathbf{C}_g^{-1}$ (see also (Rohr, 1997; Hartkens et al., 1999)).

The detection performance of these operators has been assessed on the basis of statistical measures using 3D synthetic data as well as 3D MR and CT images (Hartkens et al., 1999). Alternative studies are based on the number of matched points in rigid (Thirion, 1996) or elastic (Hartkens et al., 1999) registration, or determine the rigid or affine registration accuracy (e.g., (Thirion, 1996; Beil et al., 1997)). In a previous study, we compared the performance of the operators based on the mean and Gaussian curvature with ridge-line based operators (Beil et al., 1997). Analyzing the localization accuracy as a function of blur and noise, the number of false detections as a function of the size of the region-of-interest (ROI), and the affine registration accuracy, we found that the operator K^* from above yielded the best result together with the ridge-line based operators (which are computationally more expensive). Therefore, we did not consider ridge-line based operators in the present study.

To compute statistical measures for the detection performance, we consider around each landmark a ROI ($25 \times 25 \times 25$ voxels) as well as a detection region ($7 \times 7 \times 7$ voxels). The usage of a detection region has the advantage that small localization errors of the operators (cf. (Rohr, 1994; Frantz et al., 1998a)) do not falsify the detection performance. The measures used in our study are based on the following quantities: n_d as the overall number of detections, $n_{d,in}$ as the number of correct detections (detections inside the detection region), n_l as the overall number of landmarks, and $n_{l,detect}$ as the number of landmarks with at least one detection inside the detection region. Based on these quantities we compute the following measures for the detection performance:

$$P_{in} = \frac{n_{d,in}}{n_d}, \qquad P_{detect} = \frac{n_{l,detect}}{n_l}, \qquad P_{multiple} = \frac{n_{d,in}}{n_l}, \qquad (5)$$

which quantify the fraction of correct detections, the fraction of detected landmarks, and the average number of multiple detections per landmark, resp. Previously, statistical measures have been applied in the case of 2D corner operators (e.g., (Zuniga and Haralick, 1983)). However, only two measures have been employed there and detection regions around corners

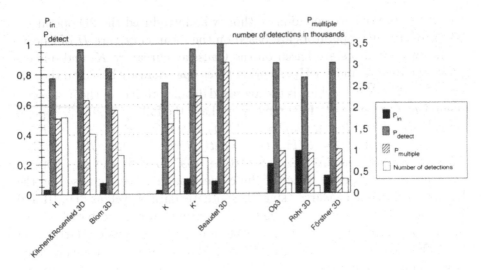

Figure 5. Detection performance of the nine investigated 3D operators for MR images.

have not been considered. Thus, the resulting detection performance in that work depends more strongly on the localization accuracy.

In the case of 3D synthetic images (tetrahedra, ellipsoids, hyperbolic paraboloids), we have analyzed the measures in (5) as a function of the parameters of the modelled landmarks as well as the noise level. In the case of 3D MR and CT images, we have computed the mean values of the measures for all considered landmarks (see Figure 5 for the case of MR images). In total, we have analyzed 242 synthetic and 43 real images, where image here means image volumes around the considered landmarks. From these studies it turns out, that the operators based on only first order partial derivatives of an image (*Op3, Rohr3D, Förstner3D*) yield the best results. Although the fraction of detected landmarks P_{detect} in Figure 5, for example, is comparable for all operators, the fraction of correct detections P_{in} is significantly higher for the mentioned three operators. Additionally, the average number of multiple detections is $P_{multiple} \approx 1$ for these operators which is much better in comparison to the other operators (note the different units on the left and right side of the diagram). Out of the mentioned three operators, the operators *Op3* and *Rohr3D* show superior performance.

4.2. EVALUATION OF 3D MULTI-STEP PROCEDURES

Recently, we introduced multi-step differential approaches for 3D landmark extraction, combining landmark detection with additional steps for refined localization (Frantz *et al.*, 1998a; 1998b). As detection operators we utilize one of the operators *Op3*, *Rohr3D*, or *Förstner3D*. Subvoxel positions of the landmarks can be determined by applying a 3D extension of the 2D differential edge intersection approach of Förstner and Gülch (1987). With this extended approach, the 3D position estimate $\hat{x}$ is determined by

$$\overline{\nabla g \, (\nabla g)^T} \, \hat{x} = \overline{\nabla g \, (\nabla g)^T \, x}, \tag{6}$$

where ∇g is the 3D image gradient and 'overline' means average. In summary, we have the following three multi-step procedures:

i) *Two-step procedure*: Application of a 3D detection operator of large and small scales for robust detection as well as refined localization.

ii) *Two-step procedure*: After landmark detection, the 3D differential edge intersection approach is applied. This procedure yields subvoxel positions and is the direct 3D extension of the two-step procedure in (Förstner and Gülch, 1987).

iii) *Three-step procedure*: Combination of the procedures i) and ii).

The multi-step procedures have been evaluated using 3D synthetic data and 3D MR images of the human head. In the latter case, we have considered as landmarks the tips of the frontal, occipital, and temporal horns of the ventricular system in three different MR data sets (see Figure 6). The localization accuracy has been plotted in Figure 7 separately for each landmark and for each MR image. We have computed the mean values $\bar{e}$ of the Euclidean distances from the localized positions to the manually specified positions, which we consider as 'ground truth' (although we know that manual localization of 3D landmarks generally is difficult and may be prone to error). It can be seen that the multi-step procedures significantly improve the localization accuracy in comparison to applying a detection operator alone (DET). As detection operator we here applied the operator *Op3*. In the mean, the approaches i), ii) and iii) yield an improvement of $0.93 vox$, $1.14 vox$, and $1.52 vox$ w.r.t. DET, resp., where *vox* denotes spatial unity. As an example, the localized positions for the tip of the left occipital horn have been visualized in Figure 8 by three orthogonal sections of the 3D data.

5. Conclusions

We have described our studies on the validation and evaluation of 2D and 3D landmark operators. Our general approach consists of three main steps, (i) modelling the signal structure of landmarks, (ii) analysis of the degrees-of-freedom, and (iii) theoretical and experimental performance analysis. The formalization of the signal structure in our opinion is of paramount importance and is a key issue in the development of algorithms with predictable performance. In the broader context of computer vision technology,

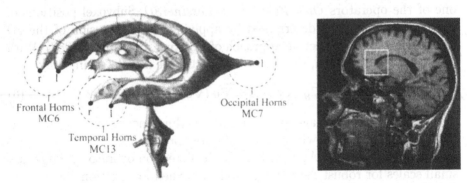

Figure 6. Ventricular system of the human brain adapted from (Sobotta, 1988) with marked landmarks (left), and frontal horn of the ventricular system in a 3D MR image (right).

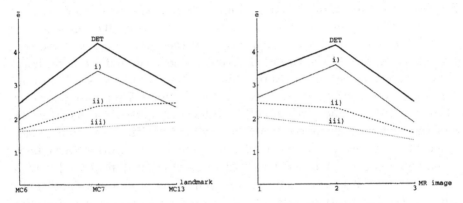

Figure 7. Mean localization accuracy $\bar{e}$ (mean of the Euclidean distances in voxel units to the manual positions) of the detection operator alone (DET) and the multi-step procedures i), ii), and iii) separately for each landmark (left) and for each MR image (right).

our work is also relevant in the sense of shaping a methodology which allows to bridge the gaps between application problems, computational theories, and algorithms.

Acknowledgements

Support of Philips Research Hamburg, project IMAGINE (IMage- and Atlas-Guided Interventions in NEurosurgery), is gratefully acknowledged. The tomographic image data have kindly been provided by Philips Research Hamburg, the AIM project COVIRA of the EU, the IMDM of the University Hospital Eppendorf (UKE) as well as W.P.Th.M. Mali, L. Ramos, and

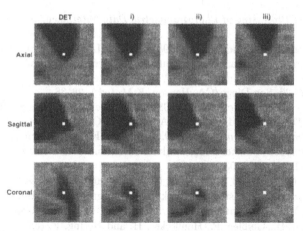

Figure 8.   Localized positions for the tip of the left occipital horn of the ventricular system in a 3D MR image using the detection operator alone (DET) and the multi-step procedures i), ii), and iii) in axial, sagittal, and coronal views.

C.W.M. van Veelen (Utrecht University Hospital) via ICS-AD of Philips Medical Systems Best.

References

Beaudet, P.R. (1978) Rotationally invariant image operators, *Proc. Intern. Joint Conf. on Pattern Recognition*, Kyoto/Japan, Nov. 7-10, 579–583.

Beil, W., Rohr, K. and Stiehl, H.S. (1997) Investigation of Approaches for the Localization of Anatomical Landmarks in 3D Medical Images, *Proc. Computer Assisted Radiology and Surgery (CAR'97)*, Berlin, Germany, June 25-28, Lemke, H.U., Vannier, M.W. and Inamura, K. (eds.), Elsevier Amsterdam Lausanne, 265–270.

Blom, J. (1992) Topological and Geometrical Aspects of Image Structure, PhD Thesis, University of Utrecht.

Coelho, C., Heller, A., Mundy, J.L., Forsyth, D.A. and Zisserman, A. (1992) An Experimental Evaluation of Projective Invariants, *Geometric Invariance in Computer Vision*, Mundy, J.L. and Zisserman, A. (eds.), The MIT Press, Cambridge, MA, 87–104.

Deriche, R. and Giraudon, G. (1993) A Computational Approach for Corner and Vertex Detection, *Internat. J. of Computer Vision*, 10(2):101–124.

Dreschler, L. and Nagel, H.-H. (1981) Volumetric Model and 3D-Trajectory of a Moving Car Derived from Monocular TV-Frame Sequences of a Street Scene, *Proc. IJCAI'81*, Vancouver, BC, 692–697, see also: *Computer Graphics and Image Processing* 20 (1982) 199–228.

Florack, L.M.J., ter Haar Romeny, B.M., Koenderink, J.J. and Viergever, M.A. (1994) General Intensity Transformations and Differential Invariants, *J. of Mathematical Imaging and Vision*, 4:171–187.

Förstner, W. (1986) A Feature Based Correspondence Algorithm for Image Matching, *Intern. Arch. of Photogrammetry and Remote Sensing* 26-3/3, 150–166.

Förstner, W. and Gülch, E. (1987) A Fast Operator for Detection and Precise Location of Distinct Points, Corners and Centres of Circular Features, *Proc. ISPRS Intercomission*

Conf. on Fast Processing of Photogrammetric Data, Interlaken/Switzerland, June 2-4, 281-305.

Frantz, S., Rohr, K. and Stiehl, H.S. (1998a) Refined Localization of Three-Dimensional Anatomical Point Landmarks Using Multi-Step Differential Approaches, *Medical Imaging 1998 - Image Processing (MI'98)*, Proc. SPIE Internat. Symposium, Vol. 3338, Part One, Febr. 23-26, San Diego/CA, Hanson, K.M. (ed.), 28-38.

Frantz, S., Rohr, K. and Stiehl, H.S. (1998b) Multi-Step Procedures for the Localization of 2D and 3D Point Landmarks and Automatic ROI Size Selection, *Proc. European Conf. on Computer Vision (ECCV'98)*, June 1998, Freiburg, Germany, Vol. I, *Lecture Notes in Computer Science* 1406, Burkhardt, H. and Neumann, B. (eds.), Springer, Berlin, Heidelberg, 687-703.

Hartkens, T., Rohr, K. and Stiehl, H.S. (1996) Evaluierung von Differentialoperatoren zur Detektion charakteristischer Punkte in tomographischen Bildern, *18. DAGM-Symposium Mustererkennung*, 11.-13. Sept. 1996, Heidelberg/Germany, *Informatik aktuell*, Jähne, B., Geißler, P., Haußecker, H. and Hering, F. (eds.), Springer-Verlag, Berlin, Heidelberg, 637-644.

Hartkens, T., Rohr, K. and Stiehl, H.S. (1999) Performance of 3D differential operators for the detection of anatomical point landmarks in MR and CT images, *Medical Imaging 1999 - Image Processing (MI'99)*, Proc. SPIE Internat. Symposium, Febr. 20-26, San Diego/CA, to appear.

Heyden, A. and Rohr, K. (1996) Evaluation of Corner Extraction Schemes Using Invariance Methods, *Proc. 13th Internat. Conf. on Pattern Recognition (ICPR'96)*, Vienna, Austria, Aug. 25-29, Vol. I, IEEE Computer Society Press, 895-899.

Kitchen, L. and Rosenfeld, A. (1982) Gray-level corner detection, *Pattern Recognition Letters* 1:95-102.

Neumann, H. and Stiehl, H.S. (1987) Towards a Testbed for Evaluation of Early Vision Processes, *Proc. Internat. Conf. on Computer Analysis of Images and Patterns (CAIP'87)*, Wismar, GDR, Sept. 2-4, Yaroslavskii, L.P., Rosenfeld, A. and Wilhelmi, W. (eds.), Akademie-Verlag, Berlin, 202-208.

Rohr, K. (1987) Untersuchung von grauwertabhängigen Transformationen zur Ermittlung des optischen Flusses in Bildfolgen, Diplomarbeit, Institut für Nachrichtensysteme, Universität Karlsruhe.

Rohr, K. (1990) Über die Modellierung und Identifikation charakteristischer Grauwertverläufe in Realweltbildern, *12. DAGM - Symposium Mustererkennung*, 24.-26. Sept. 1990, Oberkochen-Aalen, Germany, *Informatik-Fachberichte* 254, Großkopf, R.E. (ed.), Springer-Verlag, Berlin, Heidelberg, 217-224.

Rohr, K. (1992) Recognizing Corners by Fitting Parametric Models, *Internat. J. of Computer Vision* 9(3):213-230.

Rohr, K. (1994) Localization Properties of Direct Corner Detectors, *J. of Mathematical Imaging and Vision* 4(2):139-150.

Rohr, K. (1997) On 3D Differential Operators for Detecting Point Landmarks, *Image and Vision Computing* 15(3):219-233.

Rohr, K. and Stiehl, H.S. (1997) Characterization and Localization of Anatomical Landmarks in Medical Images, *Proc. 1st Aachen Conf. on Neuropsychology in Neurosurgery, Psychiatry, and Neurology*, Dec. 12-14, Aachen/Germany, Hütter, B.O. and Gilsbach, J.M. (eds.), Verlag der Augustinus Buchhandlung, 9-12.

Schmid, C., Mohr, R. and Bauckhage, C. (1998) Comparing and Evaluating Interest Points, *Proc. Int. Conf. on Computer Vision (ICCV'98)*, Bombay, India, Jan. 4-7, Narosa Publishing House, New Delhi Madras, 230-235.

Sobotta, J. (1988) *Atlas der Anatomie des Menschen, 1. Band,* Ferner, H. and Staubesand, J. (eds.), Urban und Schwarzenberg, München, Wien, Baltimore.

Thirion, J.-P. (1996) New Feature Points based on Geometric Invariants for 3D Image Registration, *Internat. J. of Computer Vision* 18(2):121–137.

Zuniga, O.A. and Haralick, R.M. (1983) Corner detection using the facet model, *Proc. IEEE Conf. on Computer Vision and Pattern Recognition,* Washington/D.C., June 19-23, 30–37.

MODEL-BASED EVALUATION OF IMAGE SEGMENTATION METHODS

KOEN L. VINCKEN, ANDRÉ S.E. KOSTER,
CORNELIS N. DE GRAAF and MAX A. VIERGEVER
Image Sciences Institute
University Medical Center Utrecht
room E01.334, Heidelberglaan 100
3584 CX Utrecht, The Netherlands

1. Introduction

Image segmentation is the division of an image into (meaningful) parts. In spite of the numerous methods that have been presented over the years, it is surprising to see how little effort has been made to evaluate the results of the various segmentation methods. In the literature, we discovered three main approaches to handle the difficult problem of evaluation.

The first approach is to visually judge the automatic segmentations directly (Gerig *et al.*, 1989), or to compare them with manual segmentations of experts. An error measure can be defined to validate these results (Karssemeijer, 1990).

A second popular evaluation method is to show images and their segmentation (Ortendahl and Carlson, 1988; Raya, 1990; Snyder *et al.*, 1991) accompanied by validating comments like "good results (...) quite acceptable" (Horowitz and Pavlidis, 1976), "It can be seen that this (...) improves the segmentation considerably" (Griffin *et al.*, 1991), "Many correct image segmentations have been produced" (Lifshitz and Pizer, 1988).

A third way is to only express the difficulty of evaluation, without an explicit evaluation itself (Chen, 1991; Kennedy *et al.*, 1989).

A straightforward evaluation of segmentation results is possible only if the purpose of the segmentation process is well defined. In practical problems, however, the segmentation task is not known in advance, or may serve a variety of purposes (*e.g.,* texture classification, volumetric visual-

299

ization, quantitative analysis), which defies a simple evaluation. In order to evaluate segmentation methods even if the application is not properly specified, we propose an intermediate task: the transformation of an image to a *object distribution* (*i.e.*, the 'gold standard'). This object distribution can be derived from the mathematical description of an artificial image, from a hardware phantom, or from a manual segmentation of a real world image. The latter, however, introduces a human factor which precludes an objective evaluation.

The objective of this chapter is to present a new method for evaluating image segmentation methods, based on the costs needed to postprocess a segmented image by manual editing. until an objectively defined quality limit has been reached.

2. The evaluation concept

A method to evaluate image segmentation results should have a number of characteristics to ensure its general applicability. In particular, an evaluation method should be:

- independent of the purpose of segmentation (notice that this does not preclude that the segmentation itself is task-dependent);
- objective, *i.e.*, independent of human factors (which does not preclude that the object distribution itself is subjective);
- not restricted to images of a particular dimension or type (artificial, real world).

Furthermore, an evaluation method should provide a figure of merit how well the segmentation task has been performed. We assume that automatic segmentation methods will not provide satisfactory segmentations of complex images in the near future. This implies that in most cases, postprocessing editing (PPE) of the segmented image is needed. In reality, it is not necessary to segment an image correctly *up to the very last pixel.* In most cases, a less-than-perfect segmentation will suffice.

We propose that the performance of a segmentation method can be measured in terms of the post-processing editing effort needed to obtain a satisfactory segmentation.

This brings us to the three basic aspects of our evaluation method:

- a quality measure for segmentations;
- an editing scenario for post-processing;
- a tolerance area.

These aspects are discussed in the following sections (see also (Zander, 1995) for details).

3. The quality measure

The appreciation of a segmentation is generally task dependent. For instance, in the case of quantitative measurements of the areas or volumes of segments the spatial location of erroneous pixels or voxels within a segment is unimportant. On the other hand, if the segmented (3D) image is used for volumetric visualization, erroneous voxels near the rendered surfaces deteriorate the presentation, whereas errors far away from object edges are harmless. In the sequel, we will—for reasons of simplicity—assume that the spatial location of erroneous pixels is not relevant, since this does not affect the method itself.

Suppose we are given an image (containing N pixels) with an object distribution O containing N_o objects, and a segmentation S containing N_s segments. Objects and segments are non-overlapping, $i.e.$, each pixel is part of exactly one object (or segment). The *segment parts* P_i are determined by overlaying S and O. Segments of S are broken into segment parts by the edges of the objects in O. The segment parts are sorted in size, such that $|P_1| \geq |P_2| \geq \ldots \geq |P_n|$, with n the number of segment parts, and $|P_i|$ denoting the size of segment part P_i (see Figure 1).

We introduce a quality measure called *correctness*:

$$Q_S = \frac{1}{N} \sum_{k=1}^{n} \left| P_k \cap \overline{\bigcup_{m=1}^{k-1} S(P_m) \cup O(P_m)} \right| \qquad (1)$$

with $S(P_m)$ and $O(P_m)$ denoting the segment and object identified with segment part P_m. In words, the correctness tries to maximize the sum of the area of a number of segment parts, such that every segment part belongs to exactly one object and one segment (and vice versa).

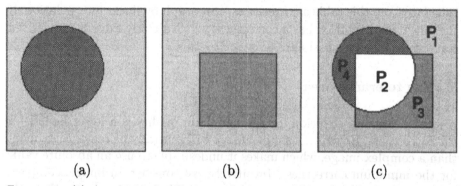

(a)	(b)	(c)

Figure 1.   (a) An object distribution, containing two objects; (b) A segmentation, containing two segments; (c) The resulting four segment parts in decreasing order.

The correctness gives a measure of quality of the segmentation. A perfectly segmented image will have $Q_S = 1$. The worst possible segmentation (*i.e.*, $N = N_s$, a 'segmentation' in which each single pixel constitutes a segment) will not have $Q_S = 0$, however, but $Q_S = N_o/N$. Our correction definition subsumes that the spatial locations of erroneous pixels within a segment are not taken into account. Otherwise, the correctness definition should be modified accordingly.

4. The editing scenario

The post-processing of segmented images can be divided into two basic actions: *splitting* and *merging* of segments. The costs of these actions can either be measured by observing how much time people need to perform these actions, or be modeled, *e.g.*, by the number of mouse clicks needed for each action. We have chosen the latter option. Logically, a merge amounts to two mouse clicks, since two segments have to be identified. A split consists of two consecutive actions: (*i*) identification of the segment to be split (one mouse click), and (*ii*) the drawing of a contour. Since most contour pixels are linked, they need not be identified individually. Hence, it is reasonable to allow a 'discount' for contour pixels (typically 0.5 for the cost of a contour pixel).

The editing costs for split and merge actions (expressed in mouse clicks) have been implemented as variables in our algorithm, and can thus be changed instantly.

After the initial correctness of the segmentation S has been determined, we transform it into the object distribution O by repeatedly merging and splitting segment parts. After each step, one more segment part will correspond to the object distribution. The segment parts are chosen in order of smallest cost/quality-gain ratio to optimize the performance of the editing scenario. This yields a table of discrete correctness and cost values. We calculate from this table a correctness/cost graph by linear interpolation. If the initial segmentation has a correctness which already exceeds the desired correctness, the PPE costs are 0.

5. The tolerance area

A straightforward criterion for the minimum quality is a lower bound for the correctness. However, a simple image will generally be easier to segment than a complex image, which makes it undesirable to use an absolute value for the minimum correctness. Intuitively, we consider an image 'complex' if it contains multiple objects or objects with a complex shape. Hence, a simple measure of image complexity is the number of edge pixels of all the objects. The number of tolerated erroneously segmented pixels can then be related to the number of edge pixels, *e.g.*, allowing a fifth of the number of edge pixels being segmented incorrectly.

For mathematically generated artificial images the number of pixels containing an object edge are known exactly. In the case of real world images, the contours of the manually segmented object distribution can be used. It is generally extremely difficult to create a perfect segmentation by hand—if at all possible. By allowing a tolerance area around object borders this problem can be alleviated *and* a quality criterion is defined at the same time: all pixels outside the tolerance area must be segmented correctly. A typical tolerance area is a band of one pixel around object borders.

Different segmentation methods can now be compared objectively by calculating the PPE costs and the editing costs for a full manual segmentation (using the same quality criterion).

The tolerance area is defined by a *tolerance distance t* which is taken to be constant for the entire image. The tolerance area hence contains all pixels at a distance smaller than t from the object border. All segment borders lying within the tolerance area are regarded correct.

The split and merge operations in itself are unaltered when using tolerance areas. However, the procedure to define where segments have to be split, has become more complex. The issues involved will now be discussed.

5.1. SPLITTING SEGMENTS

Editing the segmentation to transform it into the object distribution is an easy task when the object distribution is crisp. When segments cross object edges, we just split along that border-line. The fuzzy object distribution that occurs because of the tolerance areas requires a different approach. There are now many ways to split a segment and still have the segment border lie within the tolerance area. The two most obvious methods are:

1. Split along the actual object border just as before.
2. Split along one of the two tolerance area borders.

The first method does not require a modification of the implementation, and so is attractive from this point of view. It has, however, a major drawback that the split-line will often be unnecessary long (see Figure 2). Hence, the shortest of the two tolerance area borders is chosen to split.

5.2. UNDEFINED AREAS AND CORRECTNESS

Enlarging the object borders by providing a tolerance area will cause small objects to consist of just the tolerance area. The same applies for details of

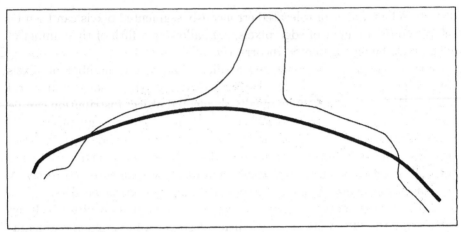

Figure 2. Thick line: object border, thin line: segment border, gray area: object border tolerance area. Splitting along the upper tolerance area border will result in a much shorter split-line than cutting along the actual object border. Note: We could also think of a segment where cutting along the actual object border is advantageous. In practical situations, however, when segment borders are close to object borders, the above case will be the most likely.

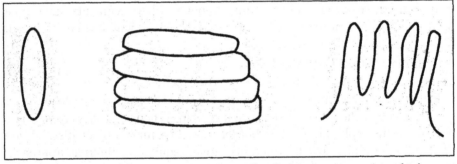

Figure 3. Three examples of undefined areas. Small objects may consists of tolerance area only (left and center). Larger objects may contain details that are not taken into consideration (right).

larger objects, as illustrated by Figure 3. We call such parts of the image *undefined areas*.

We require each segment part to contain at least one pixel outside the tolerance areas. Segment parts that do not meet this requirement are not taken into account. Hence, calculations of the correctness of the segmentation is done by considering pixels outside the tolerance areas only. In keeping with this, the correctness is calculated relative to the size of the image minus the tolerance areas (*i.e.*, a correction of N).

When using tolerance areas, one allows the segmentation to be different from the object distribution as long as they are sufficiently close. Admitting a correctness of less than 1 has a similar effect. In order not to mix the effects of relaxing the segmentation requirements, we have always used a correctness threshold of 1 when working with tolerance areas.

6. Results

In this section we will illustrate the use of the postprocessing editing scenario by evaluating segmentations of a number of example images. As a quality measure, both the correctness threshold and a tolerance area will be used. Furthermore, the sensitivity of the evaluation method for parameter changes is investigated.

6.1. A SIMPLE ARTIFICIAL 2D IMAGE

The first example is shown in Figure 4. The original image (4a) is an ellipse with a grey value of 2000 and a background grey value of 1000. The image features Gaussian noise with a standard deviation of 400 as well as partial volume effects (Vincken and Appelman, 1991). The latter manifests itself as more than one object represented by one and the same pixel (which frequently occurs at object edges). The result are pixels with grey values between those of the pixels of either object. The object distribution of the ellipse is shown in Figure 4b, and a segmentation into three segments in Figure 4c. According to the definition of correctness (equation (1)), the white segment is identified with the ellipse object. Table I lists the output of our PPE emulation algorithm; the segmentation of Figure 4c has a correctness of 0.914. The first action would be a merge of the grey and the white segment. The result is Figure 4d; the correctness increases to 0.993 at a cost of 2 units. Now, the only errors are 29 border pixels shown in Figure 4e. These should be split off the background segment and merged with the ellipse segment. Note that this is not done in two separate split and merge steps, but in one step. The one-to-one relation between objects and segments implies that the correctness is not increased unless the split is combined with a merge. The cost of the split is $29 \cdot 0.5 + 1 = 15.5$ cost units, the following merge accounts for 2 cost units. The grand total of all editing actions than accumulates to 19.5, and this is the cost to transform the given segmentation into the object distribution.

The order of the editing steps is determined by the gain in correctness they yield per cost unit. The merge of the grey and white segments produces a correctness gain of 0.04 per cost unit. The splitting of border pixels and merging them with the ellipse gives a correctness gain of 0.0004 per cost unit. The latter is much less efficient, and hence, merging the grey and white segments is done first.

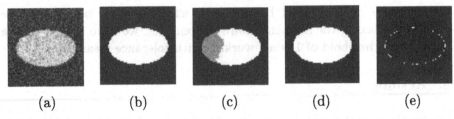

Figure 4.   First validation example: (a) the original image; (b) the object distribution; (c) a segmentation of a) with a correctness of 0.914; (d) result of an emulated merge, the correctness has risen to 0.993; (e) the border pixels who are split off the background segment and merged with the ellipse segment.

TABLE I.   Output of the PPE emulation algorithm with the object distribution of Figure 4b and the segmentation of Figure 4c.

Cost	Correctness
0.0	0.914
2.0	0.993
19.5	1.000

6.2. TWO REAL WORLD (MEDICAL) 2D IMAGES

The next example demonstrates the effect of the correctness threshold. Figure 5a shows a coronal Magnetic Resonance (MR) brain image. An expert produced a manual delineation of the cortex, which produces the object distribution (Figure 5b). Note that the task for which the image is segmented is implicitly contained in this object distribution: only brain tissue needs to be defined. The segmentation method used is simply intensity thresholding. (We are aware that this is not the optimal method to segment MR brain images, but it is suited for the evaluation of our PPE emulation.) It is interesting to know which threshold needs the least editing to obtain a satisfying segmentation. By performing numerous intensity thresholdings, each with a slightly different threshold, the PPE costs can be plotted against the intensity threshold. In Figure 6 this is done for various correctness thresholds.

The graph of Figure 6 shows that the intensity threshold resulting in the least PPE costs shifts as the correctness threshold is lowered. In Table II the output of the PPE emulation algorithm for both intensity thresholds is listed. This show sthat when high correctness of segmentation is desired, a lower intensity threshold is needed. If a less correct segmentation suffices, a higher intensity threshold is more favorable. Hence, the the choice of the intensity threshold depends on the application for which the segmentation will be used.

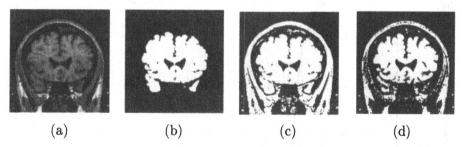

(a)   (b)   (c)   (d)

Figure 5.   Second validation example: (a) the original image (a coronal slice of a 3D brain MRI) with an intensity range of 0–4095; (b) the object distribution; (c) a segmentation by intensity thresholding at 1100 (correctness of 0.792); (d) idem at 1450 (correctness of 0.846).

TABLE II.   *Output of the* PPE *emulation algorithm for the segmentation of Figure 5c (left, intensity threshold 1100), and of Figure 5d (right, intensity threshold of 1450).*

Cost	Correctness		Cost	Correctness
0.0	0.792		0.0	0.846
12.0	0.999		2.0	0.956
33.0	1.000		419.5	1.000

Another example of validating the segmentation of a real world image is shown in Figure 7. The original image (a transversal slice of an MR brain image) is depicted in Figure 7a, and a manual segmentation serving as the object distribution in Figure 7b. The object distribution now is significantly more complicated than in the previous example. The segmentation method used, the *hyperstack* (Koster *et al.*, 1997; Vincken *et al.*, 1997), has a parameter to control the number of segments created. More precisely, the parameter defines the number of *roots* that are identified in the segmentation process. A root is a node in the tree of linkages created by the hyperstack, where the leaves of the tree are the pixels of the input image. All pixels in the original image connected to the one root constitute a segment. Roots can be at any level of the hyperstack tree, but roots at lower levels have priority over root at higher levels. Hence, some roots are blocked by other roots at lower levels. This makes the number of roots an upper limit to the number of segments created.

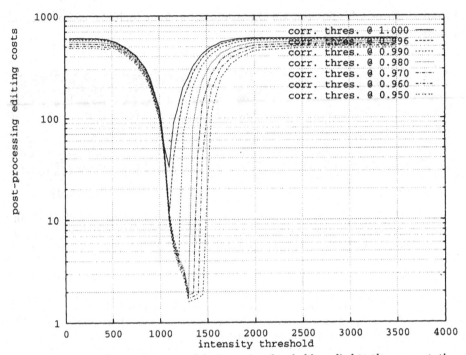

Figure 6. PPE costs as a function of the intensity threshold applied to the segmentation of the coronal MR image of Figure 5a. The editing costs for seven different correctness thresholds are displayed.

To find the best possible segmentation with the hyperstack, a range of segmentations should be made with an increasing number of roots. Our evaluation method can then be used to automatically select the best segmentation according to the PPE costs criterion.

Figure 8 shows the graph of the number of roots set out against the PPE costs. This is done for five different correctness thresholds. As an alternative to using a correctness threshold, a tolerance area of one pixel is used. The tolerance area has one clear advantage over a correctness threshold. The erroneously segmented pixels are only allowed in a small part of the image, instead of anywhere in the image. The downside is that even a tolerance area of just one pixel means that a large number of pixels are allowed to be incorrectly segmented. The percentage depends on the complexity of the object distribution; for Figure 7 it turns out to be 15% of the pixels. Tolerance areas larger than 1 pixel generally allow to many incorrectly segmented pixels.

The PPE costs graph of Figure 8 shows that the quality of the segmentation depends on the number of roots in a seemingly capricious fashion. Two parts of the graphs where a major improvement takes place are considered

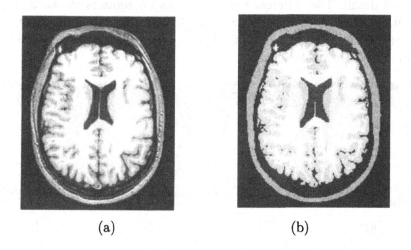

(a)   (b)

Figure 7. Segmentation: (a) the original image (a transversal slice of a 3D brain MRI); (b) the object distribution distinguishing the ventricles, white brain matter, grey brain matter, liquor & bone, skin & connective tissue, and the background.

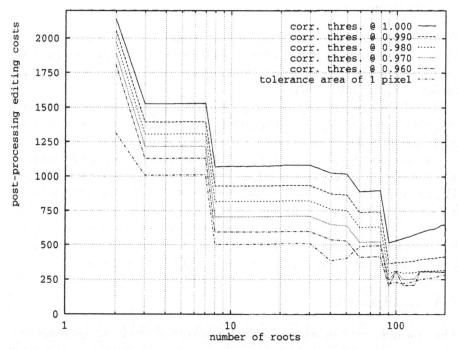

Figure 8. PPE *costs of hyperstack segmentations of Figure 7a with an increasing number of roots, for different correctness thresholds and for a tolerance area of 1 pixel.*

in more detail. The difference between 7 and 8 roots is shown in Figure 9. With 8 roots (6 segments), the liquor & bone tissue becomes a separate segment. Between 80 and 90 roots (34 and 40 segments), the grey and white brain matter segments separate.

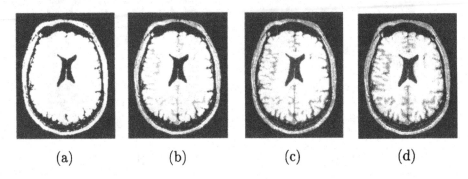

(a)   (b)   (c)   (d)

Figure 9. Hyperstack segmentations of Figure 7a made with: (a) 7 roots; (b) 8 roots, the liquor & bone tissue emerges as a segment; (c) 80 roots; (d) 90 roots, the grey brain matter emerges as a segment.

7. Conclusions

We have introduced and validated a new method for evaluation of image segmentation methods, based on the costs needed to postprocess by manual editing an automatically segmented image until an objectively defined quality limit has been reached.

The desired quality of the segmentation can be expressed by a correctness threshold or a tolerance area around object edges, where segmentation errors are not taken into account.

The method allows evaluation of large numbers of segmented images, which is a very laborious—and subjective–affair if done by visual inspection. The sensitivity of the results to parameter changes of the editing scenario is low.

We conclude that emulation of postprocessing editing costs is a useful tool to evaluate segmented images. It allows an objective assessment of segmentations, and hence, of the value of segmentation methods.

Acknowledgements

This research was carried out in the framework of the Imaging Science research program, supported by the Netherlands Computer Science Research Foundation (SION) with financial support from the Netherlands Organization for Scientific Research (NWO), and the industrial companies Philips

Medical Systems, KEMA, Shell International Exploration and Production, and ADAC.

Furthermore, we thank Wim Baaré of the Psychiatric Department of University Hospital Utrecht for providing the coronal brain MR image and its manual segmentation, and Wiro Niessen (University Medical Center Utrecht) for his contributions to the discussions.

References

Chen, Q. (1991) Medical Image Segmentation by a Constraint Satisfaction Neural Network, *IEEE Transactions on Nuclear Science*, 38(2):678–686.

Gerig, G., Kuoni, W., Kikinis, R. and Kubler, O. (1989) Medical imaging and computer vision: an integrated approach for diagnosis and planning, ' *11. DAGM-Symposium Mustererkennung, Informatik Fachberichte IFB 219*, Berlin, Springer-Verlag, 425–432.

Griffin, L.D., Colchester, A.C.F. and Robinson, G.P. (1991) Scale and segmentation of gray-level images using maximum gradient paths, Colchester, A.C.F. and Hawkes, D.J. (eds.), *IPMI, Proc. of the 12th conference*, Berlin, 256–272.

Horowitz, S.L. and Pavlidis, T. (1976) Picture segmentation by a direct split-and-merge procedure, *Journal of the ACM*, 17:368–388.

Karssemeijer, N. (1990) A relaxation method for image segmentation using a spatially dependent stochastic model, *Pattern Recognition Letters*, 11:13–23.

Kennedy, D.N., Filipek, P.A. and Cavines jr., V.S. (1989) Anatomic segmentation and volumetric calculations in nuclear magnetic resonance imaging, *IEEE Transactions on Medical Imaging*, 8(1):1–7.

Koster, A.S.E., Vincken, K.L., De Graaf, C.N., Zander, O.C. and Viergever, M.A. (1997) Heuristic linking models in multiscale image segmentation, *Computer Vision and Image Understanding*, 65(3):382–402.

Lifshitz, L.M. and Pizer, S.M. (1988) A multiresolution hierarchical approach to image segmentation based on intensity extrema, *IPMI, Proc. of the 10th conference*, New York, 107–130.

Ortendahl, D.A. and Carlson, J.W. (1988) Segmentation of magnetic resonance images using fuzzy clustering, de Graaf, C.N. and Viergever, M.A. (eds.), *IPMI, Proc. of the 10th conference*, New York, Plenum Press, 91–106.

Raya, S.P. (1990) Low-level segmentation of 3-D magnetic resonance brain images–a rule-based system, *IEEE Transactions on Medical Imaging*, 9(3):327–337.

Snyder, W., Logenthiran, A., Santago, P., Link, K., Bilbro, G. and Rajala, S. (1991) Segmentation of magnetic resonance using mean field annealing, Colchester, A.C.F. and Hawkes, D.J. (eds.), *IPMI, Proc. of the 12th conference*, Berlin, 218–226.

Vincken, K.L. and Appelman, F.J.R. (1991) Accurate conversion of geometrical objects to voxel-based images, Report 3DCV 91-20, Utrecht University.

Vincken, K.L., Koster, A.S.E. and Viergever, M.A. (1997) Probabilistic multiscale image segmentation, *IEEE PAMI*, 19(2):109–120.

Zander, O.C. (1995) CostQ: Evaluating segmentations of two- and three dimensional medical images, Master's thesis, Delft, University of Technology, The Netherlands, Report 3DCV 91-27, Utrecht University.

Index

Computational Imaging and Vision

1. B.M. ter Haar Romeny (ed.): *Geometry-Driven Diffusion in Computer Vision*. 1994
ISBN 0-7923-3087-0
2. J. Serra and P. Soille (eds.): *Mathematical Morphology and Its Applications to Image Processing*. 1994
ISBN 0-7923-3093-5
3. Y. Bizais, C. Barillot, and R. Di Paola (eds.): *Information Processing in Medical Imaging*. 1995
ISBN 0-7923-3593-7
4. P. Grangeat and J.-L. Amans (eds.): *Three-Dimensional Image Reconstruction in Radiology and Nuclear Medicine*. 1996
ISBN 0-7923-4129-5
5. P. Maragos, R.W. Schafer and M.A. Butt (eds.): *Mathematical Morphology and Its Applications to Image and Signal Processing*. 1996
ISBN 0-7923-9733-9
6. G. Xu and Z. Zhang: *Epipolar Geometry in Stereo, Motion and Object Recognition. A Unified Approach*. 1996
ISBN 0-7923-4199-6
7. D. Eberly: *Ridges in Image and Data Analysis*. 1996
ISBN 0-7923-4268-2
8. J. Sporring, M. Nielsen, L. Florack and P. Johansen (eds.): *Gaussian Scale-Space Theory*. 1997
ISBN 0-7923-4561-4
9. M. Shah and R. Jain (eds.): *Motion-Based Recognition*. 1997   ISBN 0-7923-4618-1
10. L. Florack: *Image Structure*. 1997
ISBN 0-7923-4808-7
11. L.J. Latecki: *Discrete Representation of Spatial Objects in Computer Vision*. 1998
ISBN 0-7923-4912-1
12. H.J.A.M. Heijmans and J.B.T.M. Roerdink: *Mathematical Morphology and its Applications to Image and Signal Processing*. 1998
ISBN 0-7923-5133-9
13. N. Karssemeijer, M. Thijssen, J. Hendriks and L. van Erning (eds.): *Digital Mammography*. 1998
ISBN 0-7923-5274-2
14. R. Highnam and M. Brady: *Mammographic Image Analysis*. 1999
ISBN 0-7923-5620-9
15. I. Amidror: *The Theory of the Moiré Phenomenon*. 2000
ISBN 0-7923-5949-6;
Pb: ISBN 0-7923-5950-x
16. G.L. Gimelffarb: *Image Textures and Gibbs Random Fields*. 1999 ISBN 0-7923-5961
17. R. Klette, H.S. Stiehl, M.A. Viergever and K.L. Vincken (eds.): *Performance Characterization in Computer Vision*. 2000
ISBN 0-7923-6374-4
18. Z.C. Li: *Numerical Algorithms for Digital Images and Patterns Under Geometric Transformations*. 2000
ISBN 0-7923-6476-7

Kluwer Academic Publishers – Dordrecht / Boston / London